Gender and Citizenship in the Middle East

Contemporary Issues in the Middle East

Gender and Citizenship in the Middle East

Edited by

SUAD JOSEPH

With a Foreword by

DENIZ KANDIYOTI

SYRACUSE UNIVERSITY PRESS

First Edition 2000
00 01 02 03 04 05   6 5 4 3 2 1

The paper used in this publication meets the minimum requirements of
American National Standard for Information Sciences—Permanence of
Paper for Printed Library Materials, ANSI Z39.48–1984.

Library of Congress Cataloging-in-Publication Data

Gender and citizenship in the Middle East / edited by Suad Joseph ; with a foreword by
Deniz Kandiyoti. — 1st ed.
p. cm. — (Contemporary issues in the Middle East)
Includes bibliographical references and index.
ISBN 0-8156-2864-1 (cloth : alk. paper) — ISBN 0-8156-2865-X (paperback : alk. paper)
1. Citizenship—Middle East. 2. Sex role—Middle East. I. Joseph, Suad. II. Series.
JQ1758.A92 G45 2000
323.6'0956—dc21   00-037015

Manufactured in the United States of America

To Mama Rose, Sara Rose,
and all our mothers and daughters

Contents

Tables

Foreword

DENIZ KANDIYOTI

THE FIELD of Middle East women's studies has undergone a series of remarkable transformations over the last two decades of the twentieth century. Starting with an almost exclusive focus on the role of Islam in shaping women's life options, it progressively moved toward analyses of complex historical and political processes that have resulted in diverse trajectories for the different countries in the region. Varying histories of colonialism and postcolonial state formation, different attempts at nation building, and modes of insertion into global capitalism and international governance have been shown to have had a decisive bearing on the types and levels of social and political participation of their citizenry. Analyses of women's movements and feminism in the Middle East have also achieved remarkable levels of sophistication through both a better historical contextualization of their origins and evolution and a critical reexamination of the various projects of modernity enacted through local attempts at modernization and social reform. Finally, writings on gender in the Middle East have increasingly engaged in dialogues with mainstream social theory, and feminist theory in particular, both using and contesting some of their central insights.

This volume represents an important milestone on the road traversed by scholarship on gender in the Middle East. By addressing the issue of citizenship it inscribes itself into broader debates concerning the gender-specific ways in which women are incorporated in modern polities, adding an important regional dimension to these debates. The chapters within it illustrate the various ways in which women fall short of being vested with the rights and privileges that would define them as fully enfranchised citizens. Many offer an exhaustive examination of national legislation (on nationality, personal status, penal law, labor law, and social security law); others also include indicators such as female education and employment, and most comment on the types of mobilization and activism engaged in by women themselves to press for an expansion of their citizenship rights. The volume raises a number of important and controversial issues that merit serious consideration.

The concepts of citizenship and civil society, as meaningful analytic categories, have been the subject of heated controversies in the context of the Middle East. Processes of postdynastic and postcolonial state formation have reshaped societies into new national entities, redefining former subjects as citizens of modern states. The continuing debate over the compatibility of the nation-state with some of the sociocultural formations in the region, however, has acted to problematize the notions of modern citizenship and political participation. This debate has divided "neo-orientalists," who argue for the specificity of Middle Eastern polities and their intrinsic differences from the West, from commentators and scholars who interpret the development of new associational spheres in the region as avenues for the articulation of popular demands and democratization. Because most concepts of citizenship are based upon nationally defined political communities that establish the normative framework for rights and social membership, an analysis of the nature of the polities in question remains a relevant issue.

The reader cannot help being struck by the heterogeneity of the entities described as "states" in this volume. These range from dynastic formations and rentier states, in the case of the Gulf countries, to a protostate in the case of Palestine, to countries like Turkey, Egypt, and Iran with a long history of centralized, bureaucratic-administrative state apparatuses. The various forms of governance, from monarchic or dynastic rule to multiparty democracy, that characterize these countries necessarily shape and constrain the avenues of political and civic participation for both men and women. It is also evident that new pressures and international events may occasion a contestation of existing arrangements as in Saudi Arabia and Kuwait in the aftermath of the Gulf War. Nonetheless, women everywhere appear to suffer from a "double jeopardy," sharing in the limitations set to full civic and political participation in each context and at the same time being denied full juridical status by being defined as wards of their male relatives with respect to some of the most fundamental rights in their persons—to marry, to work, to travel, or to be able to retain custody of their children upon divorce. The unwritten rules governing violence against women, as in honor killings and domestic abuse, further reinforce their status as second-class citizens. Admittedly, there are important variations in this respect across different countries, as the cases reviewed in this volume clearly demonstrate. Taken in their entirety, however, all the country cases suggest that women's rights reveal the most serious fault lines in modern concepts of citizenship for the region.

Does this constitute the *differencia specifica* of the Middle East? And, if so, from where does it originate? On this question all contributors appear to concur that patriarchy, defined as a system of social relations privileging male seniors over juniors and women, both in the private and public spheres plays a determining role. It is not Islam per se, although *shari' a*-derived codes are often based on the most conservative interpretations of texts, that accounts for the main difference because women are equally subject to the strictures of Christian and Jewish religious laws in what are essentially non-secular polities (such as Israel and Lebanon). The ways in which Middle Eastern patriarchies might differ from the "masculinist" states that have been the target of feminist critiques reside in the continuing role of kin-based, communal entities and their particular forms of incorporation into different systems of governance either as recognized parts of the political system or as the source of various forms of nepotism and clientelism. These distinctions raise the issue of the extent to which concepts of citizenship articulated in Western political theory find resonance in Middle Eastern societies. The latter, Joseph argues, do not fit the central premises of liberal bourgeois political theory particularly well. We should call for a more pluralistic approach, one that acknowledges cultural specificities without "pathologizing" states in the Middle East. This leaves, however, the question of how and on what basis women could mobilize to expand their rights unanswered. Indeed, this is an issue that appears to divide rather than unite contributors to this volume. Whereas some argue forcefully for the expansion of women's rights as individuals and condemn the stranglehold that communal and religious forces exercise over them, others argue for working through kinship and communal structures that may act to empower and to disempower women simultaneously. The tension between these positions mirrors broader debates among feminists in the West over the implications for women of libertarian versus communitarian models of citizenship. Although these issues remain unresolved and will undoubtedly continue to generate controversy, this volume offers provocative suggestions about how they can be put on the agenda and addressed in Middle Eastern societies.

Preface

AS A FIELD OF STUDY, citizenship has gained much attention over the last few years, not the least in Europe, where the viability of existing nation-states has been questioned in view of the challenge emerging from the sub-national level (e.g., in ethnic and religious mobilization) and from processes of regional integration and globalization. Where do these processes leave citizens—their rights and obligations vis-à-vis the state and their role in shaping the political future? Can the traditional ideas of democratic citizenship survive these challenges?

The challenges faced by contemporary Middle Eastern states are no less acute than in Europe, but the nature of these challenges may be different. There is a growing literature on the nature of the state in the Middle East, but the question of citizenship in this context has not been systematically addressed in the same way.

Citizenship refers to a legal relationship between the legitimate members of the political community and the state. It can be viewed from a number of angles but is inseparably related to the nature of political authority of the state. It further designates the legal and institutional foundations of the rights of citizens besides obligations toward state authorities. Citizenship is a certificate of membership in a political community and, thus, represents political identities and loyalties. It regulates the access of the citizen to the civil, political, social, and material resources of the state and can be seen as a core concept in the analysis of political and social relations in any state.

This volume, *Gender and Citizenship in the Middle East,* and its sister volume, *Citizenship and the State in the Middle East: Approaches and Applications,* edited by Nils Butenschon, Uri Davis, and Manuel Hassassian, represents a pioneering attempt to approach the Middle East from a citizenship perspective. It is the first systematic undertaking of its kind, bringing together contributions by experts from many fields of study with the purpose of effecting a deeper insight into the complex nature of Middle Eastern states and politics.

Both volumes include theoretical chapters and case studies. The *Citizenship and State in the Middle East* volume has two main sections. In the first part the citizenship approach is introduced from the perspective of both social sciences and international human rights law. The applicability of the approach in a Middle Eastern context is discussed both in general terms and with references to individual countries. This part also includes a chapter on Lebanon and Kuwait. The second part focuses specifically on Israel and Palestine. In the *Gender and Citizenship in the Middle East* volume the gendering of citizenship in Middle Eastern politics is investigated. After the editor's theoretical introduction, this volume is divided into four regional areas of the Middle East to offer fifteen country case studies. Taken together we believe the reader of these two volumes is offered the first comprehensive overview of the subject.

Needless to say, it was essential for a four-member Editorial Committee, residing in three different continents and traveling internationally, one of whom (Manuel Hassassian) is living under Israeli occupation, to agree to a division of labor and to support each other when circumstances beyond their control intervened with the work.

Suad Joseph introduced the project to the publisher. She assumed sole responsibility for the editorial work of the volume *Gender and Citizenship in the Middle East*. Because the international conference had few papers on gender and citizenship, she solicited entirely new contributions for the volume. None of the chapters in this volume were presented at the conference.

Nils Butenschon, Uri Davis, and Manuel Hassassian were responsible for the editorial work of the *Citizenship and the State in the Middle East* volume. Butenschon and Davis did the better part of the editorial work for that volume in consultation with Hassassian. Butenschon assumed the main responsibility for the organization of the international conference and the funding for the project; negotiated the contract with the publisher; and coordinated the editorial work and international correspondence with the contributors. Davis brought to the project the international networking and driving force that made the project possible; assumed responsibility for coordination of correspondence and administration in geographical Palestine; and organized several of the Editorial Committee meetings. Hassassian provided the anchor for the project at Bethlehem University; coordinated among Palestinian contributors; and hosted two Editorial Committee meetings and two delegations from the University of Oslo.

The publication of these two volumes completes the sustained five-year individual and collective efforts of the four editors. In 1992 Tim Niblock and Uri Davis, both still at the Department of Politics, University of Exeter (U.K.), and Nils Butenschon and Rania Maktabi at the Department of Political Science, University of Oslo, started to discuss the possibility of cooperation based on a shared academic interest in questions of citizenship and democratization in the Middle East.

The project took off when Niblock and Davis received funding from the Economic and Social and Research Council (ESRC) of the United Kingdom in 1993 for their research proposal "Creating the Basis for Democracy in the Middle East: Conceptions of Citizenship in the Levant" (award ref. no. R0023446201). Shortly after the award of the ESRC grant, Niblock and Davis moved to the Centre for Middle Eastern and Islamic Studies (CMEIS), University of Durham, where the bulk of the research project was administered and carried out (1993–95).

On a parallel track in Oslo, Butenschon and Maktabi received funding from the Norwegian Research Council for their project "The Politics of Citizenship in the Middle East." In the academic year 1993–94, Butenschon joined Niblock and Davis at CMEIS for his sabbatical year, at which time the conceptual and administrative guidelines were established for an international conference in Oslo, "Citizenship and the State in the Middle East." In 1994 also, Butenschon and Manuel Hassassian of the Faculty of Arts, Bethlehem University, established a working relationship, and Hassassian was invited to join the convening committee of this international conference.

On an independent track Suad Joseph had applied and was funded by the American Council of Learned Societies/Social Science Research Council, in 1994, to carry out field work on how children in a village in Lebanon learn their concepts of citizenship, nationality, and rights. She had also begun guest editing a special issue of *Middle East Reports* on gender and citizenship in the Middle East that appeared in 1996 (vol. 26, no. 1). In 1996 she proposed to Omar Traboulsi of Oxfam, U.K., to fund two conferences: one on citizenship in Lebanon and one on gender and citizenship in Lebanon. Both conferences were funded and held in 1997. The first was co-organized with Walid Moubarak and Antoine Messarra, co-funded by the Fredrik Ebert Foundation, and published in 1999 in Arabic as *Building Citizenship in Lebanon* (Beirut: Lebanese American University Press). The second was co-organized with Najla Hamadeh and Jean Said Makdisi, co-funded by Ford Foundation, Cairo, and published in 1999 in Arabic as *Gender and Citizenship in Lebanon* (Beirut: Dar al-Jadid Press).

The conference on citizenship and the state in the Middle East was organized as a separate project within the framework of the University of Oslo's Programme of Cooperation with Palestine universities. The Palestinian

Council of Higher Education (now part of the Palestinian Ministry of Higher Education) directed and coordinated the program on the Palestinian side. Through 1994 and 1995 the Programme of Cooperation was developed by the two sides in the form of thirteen project proposals and was presented to the Norwegian Agency for Development and Cooperation (NORAD) for funding. In 1996 four projects were accepted for funding, among them the international conference "Citizenship and the State in the Middle East." (In 1997 the administration of the funding was taken over by the National Programme for University Cooperation in Norway, NUFU.) Nils Butenschon was program coordinator on the Norwegian side, Manuel Hassassian on the Palestinian side; Uri Davis represented Durham University as the third convening partner.

The Department of Political Science, University of Oslo, organized the conference with encouragement and support from the Faculty of Social Science and the university leadership. On 22–24 November 1996 more than one hundred participants from five continents met in Oslo. The conference was videotaped and excerpts shown on channel 2 of the Norwegian Broadcasting Corporation on two consecutive weekends in May 1997. The project was also awarded the University of Oslo 1997 prize for distinguished educational achievement.

Subsequent to the conference, Suad Joseph (who presented a plenary on gender and citizenship in the Middle East) agreed to join the members of the convening committee to form the editorial committee for the two volumes, and the editorial committee was co-opted by the new international journal, *Citizenship Studies*, as the Middle East regional committee. The editorial committee held its first meeting in Oslo immediately after the conference and benefited greatly from the advice of Bryan Turner, founding editor of *Citizenship Studies* and director of the Citizenship Center at Deakin University at the time. Meeting in Oslo, Bethlehem, Jerusalem, Sakhnin, and Syracuse, the editorial committee used the conference papers as the groundwork for the two-volume project.

The members of the editorial committee extend their special thanks to the funding institutions that have made this research and publication project possible: the ESRC, the Norwegian Research Council, and the Norwegian Agency for Development and Cooperation (NORAD). We also thank our own institutions, which have contributed extra finances, infrastructure, and moral support—particularly the universities of Bethlehem, Durham, and Oslo, and their relevant academic and administrative departments, but also the Department of Politics, University of Exeter; University of California at Davis; *Citizenship Studies*, Cambridge University; MIFTAH (Consultancy Office), Kefar Shemayahu, Arab Institute for Vocational Completion, Sakhnin. Special thanks go to the Royal Norwegian Ministry for Foreign Affairs, which assisted us whenever necessary.

All this said, the final product presented here is inescapably our own responsibility.

Nils Butenschon, Oslo
Uri Davis, Sakhnin
Manuel Hassassian, Bethlehem
Suad Joseph, Cairo

Acknowledgments

THIS VOLUME EMERGED from discussions at the "Citizenship and the State in the Middle East" organized by Nils Butenschon, Uri Davis, and Manuel Hassassian in Oslo, Norway, in November 1997. The conference organizers had invited me to present the opening plenary on gender and citizenship in the Middle East. During the conference they invited me to meet with their Convening Committee for the Editorial Committee, which was to publish the proceedings of the conference. Because there were very few papers on gender at the conference, and none appropriate for this project, the conference organizers invited me to join the Editorial Committee and to organize a companion volume, based on entirely new solicitations, on gender and citizenship in the Middle East to be published in tandem with selected papers from the conference. Throughout the solicitations and editing work for this volume, my fellow Editorial Committee members have been unstinting in their support and collegiality. I must express particular thanks to Uri Davis, who kindly extended help and hospitality at and between our various Editorial Committee meetings.

I extend special thanks to the funding institutions (noted in the preface) that made the conference possible and the support staffs at related institutions. I am particularly indebted to the University of California, Davis, and to the University of California Humanities Research Institute (UCHRI) for support on work related to this project on gender and citizenship. UC Davis offices of Dean Cristina Gonzalez of Graduate Studies, Dean Barbara Metcalf of Social Sciences, Dean JoAnn Cannon of Humanities, Arts and Cultural Studies, Directors Alan Olmstead and Steve Sheffrine of the Institute for Government Affairs, Director Kim Longworth of the Consortium for Women and Research and the Office for Diversity, in conjunction with UCHRI funded two related conferences in Davis, California: "Gender and Citizenship in Muslim Communities" in May 1997 and "Women and Human Rights in Muslim Communities" in May 1998. Both conferences gave me an opportunity to work through some of the ideas in this volume. Some of the contributors to this volume participated in these conferences. The first conference appeared in 1999 as a special issue of *Citizenship Studies* (vol. 3., no. 3), and the second is in preparation as a separate edited volume. I am also indebted to the UCHRI, which funded me as convener of a six-month scholar-in-residency seminar on "Gender and Citizenship in Muslim Communities" at the University of California, Irvine. The director of UCHRI, Pat O'Brien, and the staff gave kindly and generously of their time beyond my ability to thank them. Some of the contributors to this volume participated in that residency as well, further building our community of knowledge. The work from that seminar is also in preparation as a separate edited volume.

The Department of Anthropology, UC Davis, handled all the administrative work related to these conferences and publications. My thanks especially to Gayle Bacon, Nancy McLaughlin, Jane Foster, Royce McClelland, and Peggy Slaven for years and years of selfless giving. My students have been invaluable in their assistance on this project. Linda Nutile worked on the volume tirelessly for a year. Grace Kim picked up the project in the second year and worked with a great sense of responsibility and care. Carrie Andrews, Jen Hoover, Javan Howard, and Heather Nelson joined in the final editing of the volume. My particular gratitude goes to Mimi Saunders, who worked closely with me on the final copyediting. It has been a joy to work with them, learn from them, and, I hope, teach them.

Syracuse University Press, from the director, Robert Mandel, to all levels of the staff, have been wonderfully supportive—including doing a shopping run for clothes with me when my suitcases did not arrive with my flight for our Editorial Committee meeting with SUP. When I introduced the two-volume project to SUP, the editors responded enthusiastically. The efficiency of their response saved us time and funds. Most particularly, I would like to thank Mary Selden Evans, chief acquisitions editor, who, in every respect, is an author's ideal editor. She was always upbeat, ready with a good word on a bad day, and responding to every inquiry (even the nuisance ones) in a timely fashion and with good humor. I could not have asked for a more collegial editor.

Of course, I thank the contributors who responded to my requests and worked under a disciplined time frame and put up with my numerous "ASAP" e-mails. The value of the volume is largely the result of their challenging research and scholarship.

My deepest gratitude to my mother, Rose Haddad Joseph, the visionary in my life, and my daughter, Sara Rose Joseph, who will shape her own vision to which I bear witness each day.

The final responsibility for this volume, however, rests with me.

Suad Joseph
Cairo, December 1999

Contributors

Soraya Altorki is a professor in the Anthropology Department at the American University in Cairo. She is the author of *Women in Saudi Arabia: Ideology and Practice among the Elite* (1986); coauthor of *Arabian Oasis City: The Transformation of Unayzah* (1989); and of *Bedouin, Settlers and Holiday-Makers; Egypt's Changing Northwest Coast* (1998); and coeditor of *Arab Women in the Field: Studying Your Own Society* (1988). She has received numerous postdoctoral research awards and appointments as a research scholar at such institutions as Harvard University, Georgetown University, University of Pennsylvania, University of Texas, and University of California, Los Angeles. She specializes in the anthropology of gender, the anthropology of religion, and the sociology of development.

Abla Amawi is an assistant resident representative, United Nations Development Program (UNDP) in Sudan. Previously a visiting assistant professor at the Center for Contemporary Arab Studies at Georgetown University and visiting assistant professor at Randolph-Macon College, she has published "Democracy Dilemmas in Jordan," in *Middle East Report* (1992), and "The Consolidation of the Merchant Class in Transjordan During the Second World War," in *Village, Steppe, and State: The Social Origins of Jordan* (1994).

Yeşim Arat is a professor in the Department of Political Science and International Relations in Istanbul, Turkey. She has written extensively on women's political participation in Turkey. Presently, she is studying Islamist women activists in Turkey.

Sheila Carapico is currently associate professor and chairperson of the Department of Political Science at the University of Richmond. She also chairs

the Editorial Committee of the *Middle East Report*. She is the author of
Civil Society in Yemen: A Political Economy of Activism in Modern Arabia
(1998) and several articles and book chapters on Yemen. She also occasionally serves as a consultant to international organizations, most recently
Human Rights Watch.

Mounira M. Charrad is an assistant professor of sociology and Middle East
studies at the University of Texas at Austin. She received her undergraduate
education at the Sorbonne in Paris and her Ph.D. from Harvard University.
Her publications in French and in English concern issues of state formation,
culture, women's rights, and law. She is the author of a comparative-histori-
cal study of the Maghrib, *Origins of Women's Rights: State and Tribe in
Tunisia, Algeria, and Morocco* (in press). She has coedited and contributed
to the book *Femmes, culture et societe au Maghreb* (2 vols., 1996). Her other
publications include: "Cultural Diversity Within Islam: Veils and Laws in
Tunisia," in *Women in Muslim Societies: Diversity Within Unity* (1998);
"Policy Shifts: State, Islam, and Gender in Tunisia, 1930s–1990s," in *Social
Politics* (1997); "Repudiation Versus Divorce: Responses to State Policy in
Tunisia," in *Women, the Family, and Policy: A Global Pespective* (1994); and
"State and Gender in the Maghrib," in *Middle East Report* (1990). She has
held faculty appointments at Harvard, Brown, and the University of Califor-
nia, San Diego.

Rita Giacaman is a member of the faculty and director of the Institute of
Community and Public Health at Birzeit University. She teaches and does
research in the areas of health policy and women's health with a particular
interest in fertility and population issues related to women's rights. She has
published in both health and women's areas.

Sondra Hale is adjunct professor of anthropology and women's studies,
University of California, Los Angeles. Hale is the author of *Gender Politics
in Sudan: Islamism, Socialism, and the State* (1996) and of numerous arti-
cles, among which are "International Gender Discourses . . . The Middle
East and the United States," in *Cairo Papers in Social Science* (1997);
"Women of Sudan's National Islamic Front," in *Political Islam* (1997)
"Ideology and Identity," in *Mixed Blessings: Gender and Religious Funda-
mentalism* (1997); " 'The New Muslim Woman,' " in *Muslim World* (1996);
"Gender and Economics; Islam and Polygamy—A Question of Causality,"
in *Feminist Economics* (1995); "Gender Politics and Islamization in Sudan,"
in *South Asia Bulletin* (1994); "Gender, Religious Identity, and Political
Mobilization in Sudan," in *Identity Politics and Women* (1994); "Trans-

forming Culture or Fostering Second-Hand Consciousness?" in *Arab Women* (1993); and "The Politics of Gender in the Middle East," in *Gender and Anthropology* (1989). She is a past-president of the Association for Middle East Women's Studies.

Mervat F. Hatem is a professor of political science at Howard University in Washington, D.C. Her research interests include gender and politics in Egypt and the Middle East. Her latest publications include: "Secularist and Islamist Discourses on Modernity in Egypt and the Evolution of the Postcolonial Nation-State," in *Islam, Gender and Social Change* (1998), and "'A'icha Tymur's Tears and the Critique of the Modernist and Feminist Discourses in Nineteenth Century Egypt," in *Remaking Women, Feminism and Modernity in the Middle East* (1998).

Homa Hoodfar is an associate professor in the Department of Sociology and Anthropology at Concordia University in Montreal. She has conducted extensive field work in Cairo, Tehran, and Montreal. Her areas of interests are household economy, Islam, gender ideology, and women and law. Her most recent publications are *Between Marriage and the Market: Intimate Politics and Survival in Cairo* (1996), *Development, Change and Gender in Cairo*, coedited with Diane Singerman (1996), and *The Woman's Movement in Iran* (1999).

Jacqueline S. Ismael is professor of social work at the University of Calgary (Canada) and adjunct professor of international relations at Eastern Mediterranean University. Her recent publications include *Kuwait: Dependency and Class in a Rentier State* (1993), *Social Policy in the Arab World* (1995), *International Social Welfare in a Changing World* (1997), *Social Welfare and Social Development: Asian Experiences* (1998).

Shereen T. Ismael is an assistant professor of social work at the University of Northern British Columbia. She is currently doing research in the areas of population health, participatory action research, and women and development.

Islah Jad is a lecturer at Birzeit University in cultural studies and women's studies. Her work focuses on the Palestinian women's movement and Palestinian women's political participation. She was a member of a team of researchers convened by Suad Joseph to work on "Gender and Citizenship in Muslim Communities." She is one of the founders of the Women's Studies Center at Birzeit University. She is also one of the founders of the

Women's Affairs Committee (an umbrella organization grouping all Palestinian women's committees and centers).

Penny Johnson is a member of the Women's Studies Center at Birzeit University and chairs the university's Human Rights Committee. She was a staff writer for the Palestinian delegation to the Israeli-Palestinian bilateral negotiations and served on the delegation's Human Rights Committee. She is an associate editor of *Middle East Report*.

Suad Joseph is a professor of anthropology and women's studies at the University of California, Davis. Her research on her native Lebanon has focused on ethnic/religious conflicts, women's networks, family systems and the state, the socialization of children in notions of selfhood, rights, citizenship, and nationhood. Her books include *Muslim Christian Conflicts: Economic, Political and Social Origins*, co-edited with Barbara Pillsbury (1978); *Intimate Selving in Arab Families: Gender, Self, and Identity*, editor (1999); *Gender and Citizenship in Lebanon*, coedited with Najla Hamadeh and Jean Said Makdisi (1999); *Citizenship in Lebanon*, coedited with Walid Moubarak and Antoine Messarra (1999), and *Gender and Power in the Middle East*, coedited with Susan Slyomovics (in press). She is the founder and past-president of the Association for Middle East Women's Studies. In 1999 she convened a faculty seminar, "Gender and Citizenship in Muslim Communities," at the University of California Humanities Research Institute.

Marnia Lazreg is a professor of sociology and women's studies at the Graduate School and University Center and Hunter College of the City University of New York. She is a former fellow of the Bunting Institute at Radcliffe-Harvard, and the Pembroke Center for Teaching and Research on Women at Brown University. She has published in the areas of social theory, social class, human rights, cultural movements, development, and gender. Her latest book is *The Eloquence of Silence: Algerian Women in Question* (1994).

Haya al-Mughni is an independent scholar who lives and works in Kuwait. She studied sociology at the University of Geneva, Switzerland, and received her Ph.D. in 1990 from the University of Exeter, Great Britain. Her research interests, focusing on Kuwait, include gender politics, citizenship, and women's movements. She has published numerous articles and contributed to a number of books on these subjects.

Barbara Swirski is a founder and director of the Adva Center for the Study of Israeli Society, an action-oriented policy analysis institute that focuses on budget analysis and social justice issues (www.adva.org). She was a cofounder of the first shelter for battered women in Israel (1977) and has written and edited several books and articles on women in Israel, among them "Calling the Equality Bluff: Women in Israel," with Marilyn Safir (1993).

Mary Ann Tétreault is the Una Chapman Cox Distinguished Professor of International Affairs at Trinity University in San Antonio. She has written four books, including *The Kuwait Petroleum Corporation and the Economics of the New World Order* (1995) and *Stories of Democracy: Politics and Society in Contemporary Kuwait* (2000); and edited five others, among them *Women and Revolution in Africa, Asia, and the New World* (1994).

Anna Wuerth wrote her dissertation at the Free University of Berlin on the development of the legal and judicial system in Yemen and the application of family law in a court in Sanaa ("As-Sari'a fi Bab al-Yaman: Judges, the Law, and Its Application in the South-Sanaa Court [Republic of Yemen] 1983–1995," in German, 2000). Apart from extensive research in Yemeni courts, she has done research and consulting in Greece, Egypt, and Yemen on minority and gender issues. She is currently a fellow with the Middle East Division of Human Rights Watch.

PART ONE

THEORETICAL INTRODUCTION

1

Gendering Citizenship
in the Middle East

SUAD JOSEPH

Constituting the Legal Subject in the Middle East

CITIZENSHIP, IN THE FIRST INSTANCE, entails the juridical processes by which legal subjects of a state are constituted. Juridical processes define the criteria for citizenship in a state and the rights and obligations of citizens in relation to the state. As such, juridical citizenship, to use Collier, Maurer, and Suarez-Navaz's (1995, 5) phrase "constructs the subject of law," delimits, through law, the nature of the legal subject of a state. Citizenship, however, as Bryan Turner (1993b, 2) has noted, is also a set of practices—juridical, political, economic, and cultural. The practices of citizenship, although constrained by the laws of citizenship, differ from juridical citizenship. Constitutions and laws of states, usually written in terms of the abstract citizen, may appear, on paper, equitable. Scrutiny of legal texts and empirical investigation of citizenship practices has exposed systematic means by which citizenship, in most countries, has been a highly gendered enterprise—juridically, politically, economically, and culturally (Pateman 1988; Phillips 1991, 1993; Yuval-Davis 1991, 1993, 1997; Lister 1997a; Voet 1998).

Citizenship is not only a legal process but also what Aihwa Ong (1996, 737) has called a "cultural process of subjectification," of subject-making (Foucault 1983). Classical political thinkers usually have discussed the citizen in terms of an abstract personhood—the citizen as an "individual" with undifferentiated, uniform, and universal properties, entitlements, and duties. Through such homogenizing abstractions, prominent scholars theorizing

3

citizenship (Marshall 1950; Bendix 1964; Keane 1988a; Barbalet 1988; Culpitt 1992; Turner 1993a, 1993b, 1993c; Twine 1994) appear to have rendered the citizen neutral in gender and/or cultural terms and in terms of race, class, ethnicity, and sexuality. In this volume we investigate the impact of culture and gender in the production of the differing relationships of Middle Eastern women and men to the laws and practices of citizenship in their states. The contributors analyze key laws and practices by which the construction of the legal subject in Middle Eastern states has privileged a masculine citizen, exposing what Rogers M. Smith (1997) has called the "civic myths" that underlie notions of citizenship in these states. If citizenship is mandatory in the modern "nation-state," as Sami Zubaida (1988) has argued, then the modern nation-state has mandated a masculine citizen. The masculinization of citizenship in Middle Eastern states has disempowered and empowered women and men differently in some ways and similarly in others to women in other regions of the world.

Proceeding through country-specific studies, in the volume we outline the history of the idea of citizenship and detail the twentieth-century transformations in citizenship laws and practices in Middle Eastern states. The initial solicitation included chapters for all the countries usually considered "Middle Eastern." Given the timeliness of the material included, it became important to move toward publication, although several chapters did not materialize. Fifteen countries are studied in this volume, organized by regional proximity. The authors were given a guideline of questions to address to facilitate comparative analysis. Although they did not have the benefit of hearing each other's papers at a conference or of reading each other's papers, the contributors have offered rich sources for theorizing similarities and differences in the gendering of citizenship in Middle Eastern countries. Many of the issues the contributors unravel appear to bear the prints of regional specificity. Some appear in a number of the Middle Eastern countries studied, but not in others. Others are not unique to the Middle East. Yet others seem to concern historical/global transformations that take on different forms in articulation with local structures and processes. Through detailed country-specific case studies, the volume offers the possibility for cross-cultural comparisons and for gleaning Middle Eastern specificities. The case studies lay the ground for both challenging the misplaced assumptions of cultural homogeneity and for more sharply identifying the arenas for productive pursuit of continuities in the gendering of citizenship in the Middle East.

The Imagined Middle East

The Middle East, as a construct, emerged historically as an imagined region designed by European states and scholars for their state and nation-building projects. That it has taken on local and international meanings and has come to have a life of its own is attributable to the enduring legacies of colonialism, to the active local forces of absorption and resistance, and to globalization projects that regionalize as they globalize. The term usually includes at least the Arabic-speaking countries of North Africa and the Eastern Mediterranean and Iran, Turkey, and Israel. Because these contemporary states do not share a common culture, language, or political boundary, the diversity of the findings in this volume cautions us against essentializing the Middle East or stabilizing any aspect of these continually changing societies (Kandiyoti 1998). Most of the states are twentieth-century creations. Most have changed boundaries and exchanged peoples repeatedly over time. Although the region is predominately Islamic, nevertheless, Christian, Jewish, and a multitude of smaller religious cultures and institutions have been critical to the gendering of laws and practices historically and currently. Furthermore, Islam, like all the many religions, is not only composed of many different and competing sects, its various sects have and continue to transform their laws and practices in response to internal and external forces. The assumption of regional coherence is, therefore, empirically unfounded and theoretically problematical. Yet the region offers useful analytical and empirical points of departure for comparisons. The historical traffic of people and ideas within the region has left its overlapping footprints economically, politically, and culturally throughout the region. Parts of this region have been unified under the same state at different points in time, giving some of them some shared elements of political history. All of the states of this region were molded, mostly in the late twentieth century, out of ashes of empires that joined various parts of the region. The Ottoman and European (particularly British and French) empires have left institutional traces in juridical, political, and social patterns. Various nationalists, pan-nationalists, religious, ethnic, and social movements have and do link people across political boundaries. Regional trade, tourism, and media continue the traffic in people and products. The web of historical and contemporary threads linking these crossroads of civilizations offers rich analytical and empirical points of departure for theorizing similarities and differences in the gendering of citizenship.

Departures: Nations

The nation, as an imagined community (Anderson 1983), has written women large in national imaginaries. The bodies and behaviors of women have become critical frames for weaving together unified national tapestries for peoples who are highly diverse—explosively divided by "national," religious, ethnic, tribal, linguistic, regional, and class differences (Parker, Russo, Sommer, and Yaeger 1992; Kaplan, Alarcon, and Moallem 1999; Sharoni

1995). The multiplicity of groupings within the nation more often than not has led to conflicting identities and loyalties that do not correspond to the boundaries of the national community. The imaginary of "woman," authenticating a place of "belonging," a community of kin, a safe haven for family, a "home," has animated the most powerful rhetoric of nation (Layoun 1992; Peteet 1991).

Nineteenth- and twentieth-century Middle Eastern nationalist reformers and leaders have often used women to imagine their communities as modern. Ataturk in Turkey (Tekeli 1981; Kandiyoti 1991), the Baathist of Iraq (Joseph 1991), the shah in Iran (Najmabadi 1991), Qasim Amin in Egypt (Ahmed 1992) argued that it was in the interests of the "nation" to educate women, to recruit them into the labor market, to transform their dress-wear and symbolically to integrate them into the political process as emblems of modernity. Often, however, as Deniz Kandiyoti (1998, 271) observed, these reformers salvaged modernity "by asserting its indigenous pedigree." Indeed, Kandiyoti noted, "What, if anything, singles out Middle Eastern reformers is the relentless search for local roots for their reformist ideals and the references they make to a 'tradition' that better approximates their modernist vision than do the current arrangements in their societies" (1998, 271). Resistance movements, particularly political Islamic movements, also have used women's bodies and behavior for imagining their political community in opposition to dominant national visions.

Nationalist and liberationist movements have activated each other throughout the region. In their struggles for national identity, these movements animated women as actors and as symbols (Sayigh 1993; Badran 1995; Afkhami and Friedl 1997). In each of the nation-building projects, the contributors to this volume contend, the symbolic connection between the idea of woman and nation has been critical to the gendering of women's membership in the national community (see chaps. 2, 4, 8, 13, 14). Despite the diversity of identities and loyalties emerging from citizens' experience of themselves as parts of multiple groupings, the ideal of "woman" has often fueled the ideals of "authentic" national cultures, "indigenous" religions, "traditional" family forms (see chaps. 3, 11). The iconic category of "woman" as a stand-in for "nation," throughout the region, has been deployed oppositionally to mark "national" boundaries (see chaps. 6, 7). Across the area, such usage of "woman" has meant the imposition of forms of bodily discipline and behavioral control on "women," in the name of the nation, in the name of liberation and progress, and in the name of God (Donzelot 1997; chaps. 5, 9, 10, 12, 15, this vol.).

The written and unwritten text of the domesticated woman upholding the sacred family as the authentic core of the nation has been reproduced in political treatises, manuals, and advice literature from the earliest nineteenth and twentieth century nation-building projects of the region (Metcalf 1990; Katz 1996; Najmabadi 1998; Shakry 1998). Embedded in these Middle Eastern constructs of nationhood, modernist and antimodernist, are articulated and unarticulated constructs of patriarchy (Kandiyoti 1991; Hatem 1986). As Hanna Papaneck (1994) has noted for India, when women are used as icons of the nation, they become captive to the structures and ideologies of patriarchy. The iconic scripting of woman as "mother of the nation" (see chap. 2) may come with many different forms of patriarchy.

Lynn Hunt (1992) found the idea of woman as mother of the nation was central to the romance literature of the French Revolution and, she contended, signaled the shift from paternal to fraternal patriarchy (Pateman 1988). In Turkey, Carol Delaney (1995) argued, as Katz (1996) has argued for Israel, the state has been seen as father, whereas the land has been seen as mother, even as forms of patriarchy have differed. Delaney's (1995) argument implied that the gendered scripting of "father state" and "mother land" prescribed a compulsory heterosexual union to found the Turkish nation-state. Howard Eilberg-Schwartz (1996, 37), in a fascinating parallel analysis of nation building and patrilineality, has argued that the veiling of God's sex in Ancient Judaism was necessary to gloss over the contradictions between the mandate for heterosexuality and procreation, on the one hand, and the expectation that males were made in the image of a God who could neither procreate nor have sexual relations, on the other hand.

Necessary and self-confirming though such notions of distinctive "fatherhood" (and distinctive "motherhood") may have seemed to the founding of states and nations, Sara Ruddick has suggested that such fantasies have been dangerous, bringing in "the worst of fatherhood: a right, often conjoined with real power, to intrude, humiliate, exploit, and assault" (1997, 213). The ideas of both fatherhood and motherhood, she argued, have been deployed to judge and to exclude (1997, 217). Although the forms of patriarchy have differed and changed, the discursive linkage of woman/mother to nation (and man/father to state) has reinforced the reproduction of gendered hierarchy, facilitating the institutionalization of gendered citizenship in state-building projects. Nation-building projects and state-building projects, although often conjoined in the past century, have not necessarily had the same or compatible outcomes for women. Women, at times, have been caught between the conflicting demands of nation-building and state-building projects (Joseph 1999b).

Departures: States

No actor is more critical to the gendering of citizenship than the state. In addition to the rights and responsibilities of citizens, state legislation regulates the rules by which one becomes a citizen, by which citizens pass citizenship on to their children and spouses, and by which citizens can lose citizenship. As Kandiyoti observed in the foreword (this vol.), the diversity of states represented in this book suggest both the diversity of rules and multiplicity of means by which rules come to be codified and practiced in the region. The possibilities and avenues for mobilization on behalf of citizenship issues and the venues for redress, necessarily, will vary considerably.

The rules that govern the practices of citizenship are detailed in the chapters in this volume as are the practices that govern the lived lives of citizens. Throughout their analyses, the scholars in this volume argue that the tensions between passing citizenship on through land versus blood are critical to the gendering of citizenship. Most states deploy both land and blood criteria. In almost all the countries covered, however, the privileging of blood in citizenship rules has gone hand in hand with the masculinization of descent and the hyper-valorization of patrilineality (Joseph 1999a). That most of the states of the region (except Turkey, Israel, and, to a degree, Tunisia) have permitted fathers, but not mothers to pass citizenship on to their children and husbands, but not wives, to pass citizenship on to their spouses is further testimony to the privileging of masculine blood in citizenship rules.

The fascinating exception is Israel, where matrilineality has been, in the past, the defining criteria of Jewry (see chap. 15). The companion compelling case is that of the Palestinians. What has the struggle for citizenship meant for Palestinian women when there has been no state? What can the citizenship through relationship to the land mean when the Palestinian Authority has no control over its own boundaries and where the question of what is Palestinian land is contested daily and the contests more often than not are lost?

It is clear throughout the case studies in this volume that rules for acquiring citizenship have changed over time and that what it means to be a "citizen" of any particular country is, in all cases, a modern invention. Yet the elision between "citizen" and "national" has acted to imbue the idea of "being a citizen" with a historicity that has appeared to precede the modern state. The efforts to give a genealogy to citizens (especially the linkage to "blood"), have appeared to "naturalize" being a citizen. In the process of "naturalizing" who is and is not a citizen, states have asserted a continuity to their existence that elevates both the idea of membership and the being of statehood into the realm of the sacred.

Rogers M. Smith (1997) has located this process of "naturalizing" the boundaries of belonging in the realm of "civic myth." Such civic myths regulate forms of inclusion and exclusion that inevitably transport all manner of inequalities—gender, racial, ethnic, class. It has been the "naturalization" of these myths, these genealogies, these boundaries of belonging, these notions of who is and is not entitled to citizenship, that has empowered them with a sacred aura (Yanagisako and Delaney 1995, 3). Perhaps no institution has had more resources available to naturalize its sense of membership than has the state. The concomitant inequalities have become encoded in the regulations concerning the rights and responsibilities of citizenship.

Women, personally and in collective efforts, have actively worked to define the rights and responsibilities of citizenship. Nevertheless, throughout the region, these rights and responsibilities have been defined mainly top down (see chaps. 8–11). Not only has the initiative been top down but the defining of rights and responsibilities of citizenship, including women citizens, has been primarily a masculine enterprise (see chaps. 3, 5, 14). The struggles, by women, to reread the ideas of citizenship (whether by focusing on *shari'a* or state legislation) from women-centered perspectives inject a disruptive force into the masculinist discourses of citizenship, giving many women of the region hope, as Homa Hoodfar documents (chap. 14).

Defining the rights and responsibilities of citizens as citizens has been the task of the state. Through legislation, through regulation of courts, through its practices, and through what it has not been willing to do, the state has carved out the arenas of the state, civil society, and the domestic or what might be called the arenas of government, nongovernment, and kinship (Yuval-Davis 1997; Joseph 1997). The nongovernmental, "civil society," has been as invented a domain (Joseph in press a) as has been the "social" that has been the milieu of the family (Deleuze 1997, x).

The idea of citizenship in Europe emerged in conjunction with emerging bourgeois classes intent on carving out domains of authority and activity relatively autonomously from the state (hence the arenas of civil society and the domestic/kinship). In the Middle East the enterprise of state building emerged less as an expression of specific local class formations and more in conjunction with the demise of empires, resulting in top-down citizenship. Parallel to these processes has been the on-going enmeshment of state and civil society (see chap. 7), state and kinship (see chaps. 3–6, 8, 10, 11), kinship and civil society (Joseph in press c; chap. 10, this vol.; al-Mughni 1996). The fluidity of boundaries between the governmental, nongovernmental, and kinship has often resulted in continuities in patriarchal practices in a multitude of domains (Joseph in press a).

The contributions to this volume are particularly rich in complicating the relationships of women to the state. In oppositional politics, feminists, viewing the state as external to society, have often regarded the state as a single-

minded actor with a unified set of interests. These contributions demonstrate that the state has been composed of different, conflicting, and changing sets of interests (see chaps. 3, 5, 9, 12). Political leaders are shown to be
embedded in local, national, and global communities (chaps. 4, 6, 7, 15).
The state emerges, in these studies, as a contested terrain, its actions reflecting local, national, and global conflicts and contradiction (see chaps. 2, 3, 5,
7, 13–15). Women are documented to have acted directly to shape state
legislation and policy, to have actively resisted state interventions or complicity, and to have participated in state programs (see chaps. 2, 3, 5, 7, 13,
14). Women in some societies have looked to the state (often unsuccessfully) to protect them from the tyrannies of their families (see chaps. 4,
8, 15, this vol.; Joseph 1982b), whereas in other states they have sought
their families (often unsuccessfully) as a haven from the tyrannies of the
state (see chaps. 9, 10, 15). At times, women both sought out and resisted
the state (see chaps. 2, 3, 14, 15) as the tyrannies of states and families have
readily woven into each other (Hunt 1992, 17; Donzelot 1997).

Nowhere has the necessity to de-essentialize the category of women appeared more dramatically than in their relationship to the programs and
institutions of the state. The political initiatives of the state often have required concerted responses that delineate, at least situationally, the boundaries of common interests. Although interests have shifted and allegiances
and identities have been fluid, rarely have the authors found large numbers
of women acting categorically on behalf of their shared interests as women
across the lines of class, ethnicity, race, religion, tribe, family, or nation. The
pro-women actions of numerous women's groups are documented in these
chapters. That they are women working for women, however, has not guaranteed that other women of their societies will accept them as their representatives. The chapters by Swirski and Jad, Johnson, and Giacaman are
particularly revealing for their analysis of complex efforts made by Israeli and
Palestinian women to work across national and religious boundaries on behalf of mutual gendered interests (also, Sharoni 1995).

Women, these scholars reveal, although sharing some interests and circumstances, have not been a homogeneous category or "class" (Spelman
1988; Kandiyoti 1998). Their differing identities and commitments more
often have aligned them with men of their class, religion, ethnicity, tribe, or
family than with other women across these social boundaries despite the
multiplicity and fluidity of boundaries. Thus, women need to be differentiated not only from men but also from other women in relationship to their
class, race, ethnicity, religion, tribe, and other memberships and statuses
(such as age and marital status) (Yuval-Davis 1997). Class, race, religion, or
related variables have been, at times, more salient than gender in affording

or curtailing women's rights and responsibilities as citizens (although rarely have any social forces worked independently of other social forces). Women have experienced citizenship differently from men not only because they are women but also because they are women *and* members of particular classes, races, ethnicities, religions—all of which gender them in complex and contradictory ways. Women's experiences of citizenship has been refracted through the lens of these multiple subject positionalities. Of the multiple identities negotiated by women, religion has received most attention as a fault line of difference.

Departures: Religion

Religion has been a central force in politics in the Middle East, directly marking the gendering of citizenship (Keddie 1999). In most Middle Eastern states the citizen as legal subject has been constituted through membership in religious communities, institutionalizing religious identity as political identity. In some states, such as Lebanon, religious membership has been specified on citizens' identity cards. Representation in government or access to governmental goods and services has been organized on the basis of the distribution of religious sects in the population. Citizens, in such states, have experienced their relationship to the state as mediated through religious communities. The implication of the elevation of religious identity to civil status has been that the nation has come to be constituted and imagined as a series of subcommunities. Such Middle Eastern states have become nations of fragments (Chatterjee 1993).

The Middle Eastern citizen, in all of the cases explored in this volume, has not been imagined as the homogenized, undifferentiated, detached, separable, bounded, individual imagined in Western liberal and contractarian theory. The mediation of citizenship through subnational communities appears to be an alternative to the allocation of citizenship and rights to individualized citizens. Although Middle Eastern states have often envisioned their citizens as members of subnational collectivities (kin, ethnic, tribal, religious), scholars must be careful to recognize the fluidity of such communal identifications. Much of the research on the Middle East has a tendency to essentialize communities, particularly religious and ethnic communities. Some states have indeed invested in the naturalization of subnational national communities by giving legal authority to institutions that "represent" "the community," such as religious courts (see chaps. 2, 6, 15). Other states have attempted to destabilize subnational communities with varying degrees of success (see chaps. 4, 5, 9). Communities, however, are not coherent, bounded, or fixed entities with shared mutual interests. They are differentiated internally by class, status, region, religion, nationality, ethnicity, race, and gender. Membership in communities has historically shifted as peoples and boundaries have moved and transported ideas and identities with them or absorbed new ideas and identities. People change religions, ethnic identities, nationalities, regional affiliations, and class memberships. The meanings, structures, and boundaries of religions, ethnicities, nationalities, regions, classes, and races also change. Perhaps with no other subnational category than religion, however, has there been a greater tendency to link the essentialization of community with the gendering of the boundary of "community."

Middle Eastern states have imagined their citizens to be differentiated by religious attachments and primordial identities and loyalties preceding the state. This "civic myth" has fostered a series of state-sanctioned religious intermediaries between the state and citizens (Joseph 1999a). Membership in a religious sect has been, in practice, a requirement of citizenship in most Middle Eastern states. When Middle Eastern states have mandated compliance with the rules of religion, they have constituted the legal subject in terms of religion. Middle Eastern states have not only legalized a social reality but have actively constructed it by requiring and making membership in religious communities strategically necessary for citizens.

That religion has been seen as the domain of the sacred, the moral, the domain of truth and absolutes has meant that religion has not been a discourse of contract and negotiation. It has been, in some sense, the opposite of what contractarians and democracy theorists argued that civil society should be. Civil society has been conceptualized as a contractual arena of negotiations and compromise. But the only salient contract for religious communities has been their contract with God (Arat 1996, 30). As Zubaida (1988, 132) observed, "In the world of Islam, the political sphere, in so far as it is distinct from the religious, is not subject to challenges in terms of systematic discourses of legitimacy other than that which would abolish it. The regular political process of contest and opposition is, therefore, ruled out."

Despite religious activists' claims of continuities, interpretations of Islamic positions on gender, on the citizen-subject, and especially on gender and citizenship have changed (as with all religions) significantly over time (Ahmed 1992; Lazreg 1994; Mernissi 1996; Messick 1998). Barbara F. Stowasser (1996) argued that Islam has been contested from within by traditionalists, modernists, and Islamists. These three scriptualist paradigms on women's citizenship, she contended, have coexisted for some time. Every theological interpretation of Islam's position on women's citizenship,

Stowasser concluded, has become ascendant or powerful only as long as its advocates have been situated in positions of power. The sacred authority of religion has underwritten the gendering of citizenship also by its subsidization of patriarchy. That clerics in all churches in the Middle East have been exclusively male and that they themselves have been mostly hierarchically organized has invested most religious institutions in systems of male authority. Clerics have supported patriarchy through their support of hierarchical family relations. Religious institutions have tried to integrate persons in their families by teaching respect of family elders and have celebrated sacrifice of self for family love. The ongoing use of kin idioms ("father," "mother," "son," "daughter," "brother," "sister") by most religions similarly has reinforced kin patriarchy.

In addition, Muslim and Christian religious institutions have supported patriarchy through their support of patrilineality. Although patriarchy (privileging of males and seniors, legitimated by kin idioms and morality) and patrilineality (reckoning descent through male lines) should not be conflated analytically (Joseph 1999a), in practice, they have reinforced each other. Muslim and Christian religions have assumed that children belonged to their fathers and their fathers' lineages. The patrilineal acquisition of religious status has underwritten the patrilineal acquisition of many rights and privileges. The historic matrilineal descent of Jewish identity has not prevented Jewish families from being patriarchal (see chap. 15), however. It is significant that the Israeli state now deems Jewish identity to descend through both father and mother (see chap. 15).

Laws differ from sect to sect, yet, in general, religious institutions have assumed that children become members of their father's lineages and support the claims of the father's lineage over a mother's claim to children. In divorces Muslim women eventually have lost possession and control over children. Many women have avoided divorce for fear of losing their children. Such is the strength of the patrilineality supported by Muslim religious institutions that a Muslim man's parents and siblings have had rights over his children at his death, superseding those of the children's mother. Although Christians vary in their laws concerning custody, they, too, have shared the assumption that children belong to their fathers and their father's lineages.

Muslim and some Christian religious institutions have supported patrilineality by privileging kin endogamy. The preferred marriage pattern among Muslims has been for marriage between paternal parallel cousins. In some regions of the Middle East, Muslim religious institutions have supported a man's right of first refusal in marrying certain paternal kinswomen. Although the ideal marriage (between the children of brothers) has accounted for less than 10 percent of Middle Eastern marriages typically, other forms of kin endogamy have been significant. Even when matrilineal kin endogamy has been practiced, the outcome has been to privilege patriarchy.

The absence of civil marriage and divorce laws (see section on family law below) in many Middle Eastern states has left citizens subject to the regulations of their churches in terms of whom and how they can marry. Most religious institutions have preferred religious endogamy. Muslim clerics have encouraged Muslims to marry other Muslims; Arab Christian churches have encouraged Arab Christians to marry other Arab Christians; Jewish clerics have encouraged Jews to marry other Jews. At times, clergy have even discouraged marriages across religious sects within the same religious rubric (e.g., Roman Catholic and Greek Orthodox). A person wanting to marry outside his or her religious sect or rubric, in some countries, has been able to do so only with the permission of either the husband or wife's religious institution or by leaving the country.

Such religious constraints have disproportionately impacted women. Because it has been assumed that women will change their religion to that of their husbands and that children will follow the religion of their fathers, religious communities have policed the marriages of their women more than those of men. Muslim women have not been allowed to marry non-Muslims in most Middle Eastern countries, giving Muslim men more marriage choices than Muslim women. This practice has made the consequences of intermarriage negligible for men but often profound for women. Muslim and Christian women, but not men, usually have lost their religious identities in intersectarian marriages.

The contentious interpretations of Islam's role in the gendering of citizenship practices and laws can be vividly seen in Muslim feminists' rereading the Qur'an. Hoodfar (chap. 14) argues that Islamic *shari'a* has been a masculine discipline. Women-centered rereadings of holy Islamic texts in Iran, however, have attempted to advance the position of women from within Islam. The intense debates between masculinist and feminists groups revolving around women's roles in the family, women as mothers, family as the basic unit of society, and women's responsibilities to build the nation in the aftermath of the Islamic revolution in Iran highlight the volatility and fluidity of the meanings of Islam.

The regionally specific engendering of citizenship in Middle Eastern states, then, has been closely linked with elevation of religious status to civil status by most Middle Eastern states. The sanctification of the patriarchal family by most religious communities—Muslim, Christian, and Jewish—has come to have legal force. The organization of citizenship through subnationalities, therefore, has had a far greater discriminatory impact on women than it has had on men.

Departures: Family

Lynn Hunt suggested, "If kinship is the basis of most if not all organized social relations, then it is also an essential category for understanding political power" (1992, 196). During the French Revolution, Hunt contended, "the most obvious material at hand for thinking politically was the family, not the family as some kind of model social experience, but the family as an imaginative construct of power relations" (1992, 196). Family, both as a model of social experience and as an imaginative construct, has been the most obvious material for thinking politically in the Middle East. As Peter Gran has succinctly argued, "The family ought to be studied as a part of politics, if for no other reason than the fact that the state invests a great deal of its resources in upholding its conceptions of an ideal family" (1996, 77). State investments in family structure invariably have led to transformations and subsidization of specific relationships within the family, particularly in relationship to women.

For all the countries discussed in this volume, the contributors describe the family as the core social institution. Almost all the constitutions of the states in this region define family as the basic unit of society. All the contributors to this volume label family structures as patriarchal although the meanings and dynamics vary. In each of the states discussed, the state has reinforced patriarchal family structures and, to varying degrees, family processes have been woven into state dynamics. Although Middle Eastern states have varied in the degree to which they have challenged or assimilated family systems (see chap. 4), the false dichotomy of state intervention versus nonintervention in the family (Olsen 1985) has been a nonissue here. Contemporary Middle Eastern states have always had relatively explicit policies of subsidizing family structures.

Afsaneh Najmabadi (1998) offered a striking analysis of the discursive debates about the nature of the family, the relationship of family to the nation, and the state and the role of women in the family in late nineteenth and early twentieth-century Iran. Najmabadi argued that as the family was reenvisaged as the foundation of the nation, the notion of woman and wife had to be reconfigured from that of "house" to that of "manager of the house," a role that required undermining female homosociality in the household, educating and scientifically training women to be mothers (of the nation), and transforming the house into a "social space of citizenship."

Through this scientific discipline (Donzelot 1997) the family became "relo-
cated in relation to the national community, rather than in relation to other
kin groups and families" (Najmabadi 1998, 102). Within the enterprise of
nation building, the family became a central political project for political
thinkers and for state leaders.

In a parallel argument Omnia Shakry (1998) has detailed the culturally
specific discourses of childrearing, mothering, and family formation in the
nineteenth- through twentieth-century Egyptian nation-building project.
Although developed in tandem with European discourses, the Egyptian social and political leaders, male and female, situated their notions of modernity within reformist Islamic contexts, as opposed to the co-contemporary
European secular discourses. The relocation of general responsibility for
childrearing from "private to "public" spaces, the shift from fathers to
mothers as the key actors responsible for the development of children and
the articulation of rational-economic and scientific-hygienic childrearing
practices required the creation of those spaces, those roles, those identities,
those new notions of selfhood, and those practices to construct the "effi-
cient citizens of the nation" (Shakry 1998, 143).

The centrality of family to Middle Eastern society and politics has been
widely recognized and documented. But what has been meant by family has
varied tremendously among states, social classes, rural/urban/pastoral communities, religious/ethnic communities. The "extended" family has been
important in Lebanon (see chap. 6), Jordan (see chap. 8), Saudi Arabia (see
chap. 10), Kuwait (see chap. 11). Variations of the nuclear family are found
in all the Middle Eastern countries although most especially in Israel (see
chap. 15), Tunisia (see chap. 4), Turkey (see chap. 13).

Although the concept of patriarchy is important to most of the analyses
in this volume, there are numerous uses of the term at play. Given the
diversity of social structures and cultural settings, such variable applications
has enriched theorization of the complex dynamics of gendering hierarchy.
Nevertheless, the threads of commonalities in the Middle Eastern usages of
patriarchy are worth noting. For most of the case studies, patriarchy entails
the privileging of male and elder rights. In most of the case studies, patriarchal dynamics mobilize kinship structures, morality, and idioms to legitimate male and elder privilege. That is, through most of the Middle East,
patriarchy has been and largely remains nested in kinship, distinguishing it
from the notions of patriarchy common among Western feminist scholars
who often disarticulate patriarchy and kinship. This difference is crucial for
understanding some of the specificities of the gendering of citizenship in the
Middle East.

Men, as primary citizens, have been constituted as citizen through their roles as heads of patriarchal families. Middle Eastern states predominately have located women within patriarchal structures as subordinate mothers, wives, children, siblings (Giacaman, Jad, and Johnson 1996; al-Mughni 1996; Berkovitch 1996; Arat 1996). As Giacaman, Jad, and Johnson (1996) pointed out, in social legislation entertained by the Palestinian Authority, women's rights have been defined primarily as wives and mothers. Attempts to revitalize clans as the basis of representation in the emerging Palestinian state will likely reinforce patriarchies to the detriment of women (Giacaman, Jad, and Johnson this volume). Women, as citizens, have been conflated with children (Giacaman, Jad, and Johnson 1996); valorized primarily in terms of their familial roles (Berkovitch 1996; al-Mughni 1996) have been expected to continue to prioritize their subordinate familial roles even when they achieve powerful public positions (Arat 1996; Joseph 1982b). Regarding women as less than adequate citizens (Cheriat 1996), most Middle Eastern states have seen women as needing control and care. The infantilization of women has been expressed in a number of countries in state/family law regulations that require women to obtain the permissions of their fathers/ brothers or other male guardians to marry. A number of states have required women to have permissions of fathers/brothers/husbands to travel or to open businesses (see chaps. 3, 8, 10, 11, 14).

That Middle Eastern family systems are predominately patriarchal has been well established. The connections between the patriarchal family systems and the organization of politics, economy, and society have been addressed by a few political theorists (Sharabi 1988; Barakat 1993). But the implications of Middle Eastern patriarchal family systems, their legal and sanctified status in Middle Eastern states, the implications of family systems for the constitution of the legal subject as citizen, and the critical differences of this legal subject from the imagined Western legal subject has been undertheorized (Joseph 1993b, 1996b).

Perhaps the most complex and insightful theorization of Western political patriarchy has come from the work of Carole Pateman (1988). Pateman argued the development of the philosophical work of the Western classical social contract theorists represented a shift from paternal to fraternal patriarchy, from rule of the "fathers" to rule of the "brothers." For Pateman, political liberalism has been characterized by the privileging of men as men, rather then of men as kinsmen. The distinction between fraternal patriarchy and kin-based patriarchy is crucial for understanding the specificities of the gendering of citizenship in many Middle Eastern states.

Middle Eastern patriarchy has been forceful, in part, because of its rooting in kinship. The impact of patriarchy on the gendering of citizenship has been profound because kinship has permeated all domains, all spheres of

life: private/public, state/civil society/kinship, governmental/nongovern-
mental/domestic. Kin-based patriarchy has been transported into political,
economic, social, and religious dynamics. That kin-based patriarchy has
woven threads through all domains and levels of Middle Eastern societies
has produced not "seamless" societies but integrally connective social tis-
sues. Boundaries are not so much walls as they are windows that can be
closed as needed and opened with the appropriate pulls and tugs.

Family structures, morality, and idioms have been necessary to survival in
these societies (see chaps. 4, 6, 8, 10, 11). Political leaders have brought
their own family members into governance and mobilized some of the population through family units (see chaps. 6, 7, 9, 10). They have dispensed
goods and services through family-based networks (see chaps. 6–10). They
have used family idioms to rationalize their political roles and their relationships to citizens, not only valorizing the family as a political unit of society
but making membership in it politically strategic for citizens (see chaps. 4,
8, 14).

Family has also been central to citizens' political identities in most Middle Eastern countries. National identity in most Middle Eastern countries
has been patrilineally ascribed. Political identity has come through a male
genealogy. The nation has been constructed as descending through a series
of patrilineal lineages, male descent lines that are kin based. A citizen has
had to belong to a male-defined kin group to belong to a religious sect, to
belong to the nation, to acquire the rights and responsibilities of citizenship.
The alliance between many Middle Eastern states and religious institutions
to funnel citizenship through religious sects has meant that the state and
religious institutions have reinforced children's political identification with
their fathers. Children have been assigned the religious identity of their fathers by both religious institutions and the state, absorbing them into the
father's political identity. By not allowing women to pass citizenship on to
their children (or their spouses), most Middle Eastern states (except Turkey,
Israel and Tunisia) have cemented the linkage between religious identity,
political identity, patrilineality, and patriarchy—that is, between religion, nation, state, and kinship.

Middle Eastern states engaged in a variety of state and nation-building
projects during the twentieth century. Family has been central to all of
them. In states such as Lebanon (see chap. 6), Jordan (chap. 8), Saudi
Arabia (chap. 10), Tunisia and Morocco (chap. 4), the issues of family and
kinship have often underpinned or overshadowed the issues of religion in
state building. The state has attempted to challenge family in Tunisia and
Turkey (chaps. 4, 13), has attempted to co-opt family in Iraq (Joseph
1982b), has built on existing family and tribal structures in Saudi Arabia

(see chap. 10), Lebanon (chap. 6), Jordan (chap. 8), Morocco (chap. 4) and has revived family and clan structures as a base of state rule in Palestine (chap. 7).

In the escalating contests for authenticity, the family as a backbone of "tradition" often emerges symbolically, if not juridically and socially, as a site where women's "authentic" place in society is shaped. But as Linda Nicholson (1997) has pointed out, for the United States, the idea of a "traditional" family has been a myth shaped out of contemporary debates and institutional forces. In the Middle East, it qualifies as a component of "civic myths" of citizenship. Regardless of the evident variability and change-ability in family structures, family dynamics, and family cultures within and throughout each of these states, the idea of family and kin as the bedrock of society and as a linchpin of local "civic myths" appears unshaken. Although no institution has more resources available to "naturalize" itself than the state, one might claim that no institution has achieved "naturalization" in the gen-eral culture more than the "family" (Yanagisako and Delaney 1995). As David M. Schneider (1984) drew attention to the constructedness of kinship, so he argued that the power of kinship has been to draw attention away from its constructedness through discourses of naturalness.

The success of the "family" in naturalizing itself has been underwritten by the two most powerful institutions in society invested in naturalizing the family—state and religion. The family has occupied almost a sacred space in Middle Eastern societies. Not only have states privileged family above the individual legally (see chaps. 4, 6, 8, 10), but they have engaged in dis-courses that represent the family as something a priori, "prepolitical," a do-main so beyond current time and conditions that it is best apprehended in the domain of the divine.

The absorption of family moralities into religious moralities has been further enhanced by the religious control over family regulations. This has been most directly observed in the widespread delegation, throughout the Middle East, of family law or laws of personal status to religious courts. Middle Eastern states have privileged the family unit over the individual as the basic unit of the political community. It has been the sanctification of the family domain through locating family law in religious law, however, that has enshrined the family and codified its patriarchal rules. In elevating religious law to civil status, Middle Eastern states have given senior men and not women and juniors the right to own property in their persons. That women and juniors have not had property in their persons has re-sulted partly from the intertwining of patriarchal family structures, moral-ity, and idioms with religious law that have been state-certified as public law.

Departures: Family Law

Family law, a critical feature of citizenship laws and practices, has been anchored in religious law in most Middle Eastern countries. In the states studied in this volume, family law, a benchmark of feminist struggle, has been a site of contestation in the making of state and nation. Family law has been among the highest agenda items of liberal reformist movements, political Islamic movements, Islamic and secular women's movements—a testimony to the centrality of women's bodies and behavior to scripts of nationhood and statehood and a testimony to the centrality of "family" to social and political projects in the region. Usually covering the regulation of marriage, divorce, child custody, and inheritance, family law (also called personal status code) has been a crucial site for the gendering of citizenship in Middle Eastern countries.

Family law may rightfully be said to be the most critical site in which membership in religious communities has been a venue for constituting the Middle Eastern legal subject. Most Middle Eastern states either have deferred family law directly to the different legally recognized religious sects in their countries and have offered no civil alternatives or have incorporated the family codes of the dominant religious sect into the civil code. Only Turkey (which early on adopted the Swiss Civil Code), Tunisia, and Yemen have legislated civil family law, but even these civil codes have been based upon, challenged by, revised by, and in varying degrees shaped by religious codes. Because all Middle Eastern countries have multiple religious communities, the recognition of a plurality of family codes by most of the states has left women without a common legal framework for experiencing or contesting this arena of citizenship.

In the extreme case of Lebanon, eighteen different formally recognized religious sects adjudicate matters of personal status. Those not legally recognized (such as Jehovah's Witnesses and Bahiis) must marry abroad. Although such foreign marriages have been legally recognized, they have created a legal nightmare in cases of divorce. Civil courts established to adjudicate foreign marriages must follow the personal status codes of the country in which the marriage was performed.

Middle Eastern women in different religious communities have often experienced different legal realities from which they have had no civil recourse, for which there is no shared legal culture as a common referent. As Yolla Sharara argued (1978), women in Lebanon have not felt the impact of the state in their lives so much as they have felt the impact of the men of their religious communities. Yeşim Arat (1996, 31) contended that, in Turkey, a secular concept of citizenship was irrelevant for women "whose rights and responsibilities are communally defined."

Whether such legal pluralism operates to the detriment of women's citizenship rights has become a contested issue. In a highly provocative historical study, Judith Tucker (1998) has shown that Islamic *muftis* and *qadis* (legal scholars and jurists) of seventeenth- and eighteenth-century Syria and Palestine often navigated between and among the four Islamic schools of law to protect women's rights. Though masculinist and patriarchal in their mentalities and decisions, the three *muftis* that she studied tempered patriarchy by veering from their Hanafi *madhhab* (legal school) and drawing on precedents and codes from Shafi'i and other schools. The existence of multiple legal schools allowed these learned men to arrive at situationally specific rulings that often advantaged women. By documenting the ongoing legal activism of Islamic jurists in interpreting family law, Tucker's careful analysis challenges the Orientalist notion that Islamic law became "fixed." Although few Middle Eastern feminists argue on behalf of legal pluralism in the current political context, Tucker's work raises the interesting question of the possible beneficial "side effects" of legal pluralism, at least historically.

In practice in most Middle Eastern states, family law has upheld men's property in their children. To paraphrase Pateman (1988, 44), political right has emerged in fatherhood, as a paternal right, in the Middle East. Children have been born subjects of their fathers. That in almost all Islamic law, upon divorce, control of children eventually has reverted to the father and that the father's family has had priority over the mother when the father is dead or not available is evidence of men's property in their children. Men's ownership of women's bodies has been upheld by religious laws that have given men rights of access to wives' bodies that their wives cannot refuse. Marital rape has not been recognized in practice and, in many cases, by law in most Middle Eastern states. Some Middle Eastern states have permitted, either in law or practice (or given lenient sentences for), honor crimes in which male relatives have taken the lives of female relatives if they believed that they had "dishonored" their families. In so doing, these states have reinforced the notion that women and children are properties of males of their paternal kin—a privilege not only of fathers and husbands but of extended paternal male relatives. Pateman (1988, 13–14) argued that wives and children were viewed by the classical contractarians as the property of their fathers/ husbands. In the Middle East, family law has often codified the ownership of wives and children by fathers/husbands.

The Middle Eastern states that have deferred to religious institutions' control over matters of marriage, divorce, child custody, and inheritance and that have provided no civil alternatives have forced persons to submit to the control of religious authorities on these matters. In locating family law in the hands of religious authorities, these Middle Eastern states have sanctified the family in terms of rules perceived as absolute and nonnegotiable. If for Pateman (1988, 2) the "contract is the means through which modern patriarchy is constituted," one can argue that the moral, the sacred, the nonnegotiable sanctified arena of the family has been the means by which Middle Eastern paternal patriarchy has been constituted.

Departures: Self and Citizenship

The constitutions of most Western states define the basic unit of society as the individualized citizen. Most constitutions of Middle Eastern states identify the basic unit of society as the family and assert the state as the protector of the family. This position suggests some key issues concerning the regionally specific masculinization of the legal subject in Middle Eastern states. Particularly, it suggests that the masculine legal subject is privileged on the basis of his status as patriarch. The head of a patriarchal family, legally constituted as the basic unit of the political community, would accrue rights and responsibilities concomitant with that legal status. Bryan Turner (1993b, 5), reviewing the works of Parsons, Weber, Durkheim, Toennies, argued that the emergence of modernity, embodied in the concept of citizenship, is a transition from status to contract. Citizenship, in this sense, he added, opposes the particularistic ties of family, village, or tribe. C. B. MacPherson (1962, 262) argued that the social assumptions of seventeenth-century political theorists (Hobbes, the Levellers, Locke) who laid the foundation of Western citizenship theory constituted the subject-citizen as a possessive individual. According to MacPherson, Locke derived the natural individual right to property from his belief in the natural right to one's life and labor (MacPherson 1962, 199). The right to property was based on the right to appropriate, and the right to appropriate Locke derived from his postulate that "every Man has a Property in his own Person" (1962, 200).

Pateman (1988, 9–10), drawing on the work of Sir Henry Maine, linked the transition from status to contract to the "replacement of family by the 'individual' as the fundamental 'unit' of society." She contended that contractarianist theorists presumed the path to the individual's freedom was through contractual relations. But, as they believed only men were capable of contractual relations they, in effect, excluded women from the status of individual, from the ability to own property in themselves as persons, and from citizenship. Father right was displaced only to be replaced by the rights and privileges of men as men (fraternal patriarchy) and by the masculinization of citizenship. Jennifer Nedelsky (1990) has similarly argued that the idea of bounded property and the right to ownership of property was central to American constitutional history. She contended that the very notion of citizen rights was built on the metaphor of bounded private property. Rights of citizens were seen as boundaries or limits to the authority of the state (Nedelsky 1993). Seeing rights as boundaries between citizens and state implied also a notion of the citizen self based on an autonomy linked to ownership—ownership, by the citizen-self, of the self as property (Nedelsky 1989).

Contractarian and liberal bourgeois political theory constituted the legal subject of the Western nation-state as a free, autonomous, separative (masculine) self with boundaries clearly delineating one subject from another and the subject from the state. The bounded, autonomous, free, separate, individualized citizen was seen as having one kind of relationship with others in the political community—voluntary and contractual. These postulates and their derivatives set up the main parameters for Western discourses on citizenship. Boundedness of body, property ownership, and rights as properties have been essential for Western discourses of citizenship. The boundedness of citizen and property have been underwritten in the boundaries between state and citizen; between the state and civil society; between the state and family.

The concept of citizenship as a set of contractual relationships between "the individual" and the state exists on paper in most Middle East countries. According to Arat (see chap. 13) and Swirski (see chap. 15), the notion of contract is socially powerful in Turkey and Israel. For Arat, though, the citizenship "contract" in Turkey, secular and liberal though it may be, is the elite's strategy to promote forms of integration that subsidize their rule. As Altorki observed (see chap. 10), the idea of social contract may exist on paper in the form of constitutions and legislation but often is less prevalent in either public rhetoric or political practices. The individual as an "autonomous" subject, endowed with inalienable rights and responsibilities that accrue to her or him as a person, apart from social identities and networks, although juridically and (often) socially salient, has more often than not been overridden by the notion of the person as nestled in relationships of kinship and community (see chaps. 4, 6, 8, 10, 11).

As a result, women have not been seen as part of "the people" (see chap. 2), or have lacked "political personhood" in their countries (chaps. 3, 7, 11, 15). Women have become the dependents of men, who to a greater degree may have been seen as "individuals" or to have had relations with the state (chaps. 3, 7, 11). In many instances, women have seen the men of their families as their "safe haven" (Botman 1999, 107; chap. 10, this vol.). In some countries, authors argue, men also have not been treated as "individuals" but have had their relationships to the state mediated through kin and community (chaps. 6, 10).

Western notions of the citizen-self as "individual" have been supported to some degree formally, legally, and socially in most Middle Eastern societies. Other notions of the citizen-self, however, have also been supported. At times these differing notions of the citizen-self compete and contradict each other; at times they co-reside and mutually constitute each other. Notions of a relational or a connective self are particularly common in many Middle Eastern countries. I have, elsewhere (Joseph 1993a), characterized connectivity as a notion of self in which a person's boundaries are relatively fluid so that persons feel they are a part of significant others. Connective persons do not experience boundary, autonomy, separateness as their primary defining features. Rather, they focus on relatedness. Maturity is signaled in part by the successful enactment of a myriad of relationships. In Middle Eastern countries in which the family has been valued over and above the person (Barakat 1993, 98), identity has been defined in familial terms, and kin idioms and relationships have woven through society, connective relationships have become not only functional but necessary for successful social existence (Joseph 1999d).

In Lebanon connectivity and patriarchy have been linked to create a system that I have called patriarchal connectivity (Joseph 1993a). Patriarchal connectivity means the production of selves with fluid boundaries organized for gendered and aged domination in a culture valorizing kin structures, morality, and idioms. Patriarchy entails cultural constructs and structural relations that privilege the initiative of males and elders in directing the lives of others. Connectivity entails cultural constructs and structural relations in which persons invite, require, and initiate involvement with others in shaping the self. In patriarchal societies connectivity can support patriarchal power by crafting selves responding to, requiring, and socialized to initiate involvement with others in shaping the self. Patriarchy can help reproduce connectivity by crafting males and seniors prepared to direct the lives of females and juniors and females and juniors prepared to respond to the direction of males and seniors.

The fact that most Middle Eastern state constitutions claim the family as the basic unit of membership in the political community implies that it is persons' *status* as members of families that qualifies them for citizenship. Given the centrality of patriarchal connective idioms in many Middle Eastern political, economic, religious, and social cultures, this implies the transportation of patriarchal connectivity into the practices and discourses of citizenship, including what has been understood as citizens' rights in these countries. Connective or relational notions of selfhood can underpin relational, rather than contractual, notions of rights (Joseph 1994b). Relational rights are neither communal (based on an assumption of a coherent corporate-like group) nor individualist. Relational rights imply that a person's sense of rights flows out of relationships that he or she has. It is by being invested in relationships that one comes to have rights. As a basis for citizenship practices, relational rights further require that citizens embed themselves in family and other subnational communities such as religious sects, ethnic, and tribal groups to gain access to the rights and privileges of citizenship.

The differing notions of self and rights pose a dilemma, theoretically and politically, for feminists committed to activist agendas on behalf of women's citizenship rights. How one conceptualizes and/or organizes movements on behalf of rights will be impacted greatly by whether the operant notion of self and rights is individualist, relational, or communal (a notion not as consistently addressed in this volume but taken up by many scholars/activists of the region). Whether women claim rights as individuals, through person-specific sets of relationships, or as members of communities (defined by religion, ethnicity, tribe, or other salient variables) will necessarily lead to different outcomes. The multiplicity of notions of rights, self, and family that co-reside in the Middle East complicates and cautions our attempts to search for continuities in the gendering of citizenship. The arenas of continuities and discontinuities are particularly exposed in the search for coherent categories and clearly articulated boundaries.

Departures: Boundaries

Repeated throughout the volume are the themes of the intertwining of family and state, the meshing of "public" and "private," and the embeddedness of religion in politics—all of which have fed into the gendering of citizenship. The historical recency, cultural specificity, and empirical fluidity of social categories is documented repeatedly by the authors. The assumptions of separations of public and private, kinship and state, civil society and state, religion and state are readily challenged in the contributions to this volume. Swirski (chap. 15) notes that the private sphere may not be a refuge from the state in Israel. Jad, Johnson, and Giacaman (chap. 7) contend that the "state" controls civil society in Palestine. As much can be said for Arab and non-Arab nations such as Iraq (chap. 9), Saudi Arabi (chap. 10), Kuwait (chap. 11), Sudan (chap. 5), Iran (chap. 14).

Civil society theorists have assumed democratic impulses are generated in the private sphere or in the tension between the private and public sphere (Pateman 1988; Nedelsky 1989; Young 1990). Arguing for the relative autonomy of public and private arenas, civil society theorists have blamed the weakness of that division, and particularly the minimal autonomy of the private sphere, for the absence or weakness of nationhood and democracy in Third World societies (Sadowski 1993). The premise of autonomy between civil society and state, as Pateman argued, assumed the irrelevance of kinship, family, and marriage to politics and civil life. The assumption of their irrelevance made possible the "perception of civil society as a post-patriarchal social order" (Pateman 1988, 10). The overprivileging of the public sphere as a source of democracy and the exclusive focus on the public/private binary have been made possible by glossing over gendered antidemocratic forces and the multiple sites in which they are constructed. Patriarchy, in particular, is a primary antidemocratic force neglected by most civil society theorists. To the degree that civil society theorists require the creation of autonomous spheres of social activity for democracy, then they must address the role of systemic patriarchy in undermining such autonomy.

The assumption of a public/private binary in civil society theory has its parallels in feminist theorizing. Early structuralist feminist theory, in the 1970s and 1980s, argued there was a universal division of social orders into public and private domains and that women's association with the devalued private domain explained women's (purported) universal subordination to men (Ortner 1974; Chodorow 1974; Rosaldo 1974). The public sphere was argued to be a sphere of rational discourse, abstract principles, the rule of contract law, and objective and impersonal judgments and relationships. The private sphere was argued to be the sphere of emotionalities, subjectivities, specificities, and the rule of natural law (Jagger 1983; Hartsock 1983). Later feminist theorists—Marxist, poststructuralist, critical theorists, and others—challenged the usefulness of the public/private in understanding gendered domination, even in the West (Eisenstein 1994; Williams 1991; Young 1990; Spelman 1988; Pateman 1988). Scholars argued the historical recency and cultural specificity of public and private sphere binaries (Nedelsky 1989; Minh-ha 1989). Some analyzed the porousness of the boundaries or the impact of boundedness on the visibility of women's activities (Kondo 1990; Nedelsky 1990; Young 1990; Joseph 1997). Others have analyzed the multiple subject positions of race, class, gender, and ethnicity, which are often glossed over by simplistic binaries (Williams and Chrisman 1994; Kymlicka 1995; Lavie and Swedenburg 1996; Razack 1998). Despite the controversies in feminist theory concerning the meaning and uses of the public and private paradigm, there has been widespread agreement among feminists that the gendering of public and private spheres has led to the gendering of discourses and practices predicated on this binary, such as civil society (Pateman 1988; Nedelsky 1989; Young 1990; Joseph 1993b, 1997).

The cases in this volume demonstrate that the binary between public and private assumed in the civil society model conflates multiple domains of social activity in such a way as to gloss over gender issues, particularly by ignoring the impact of patriarchy across political, economic, social, and religious fields (see chap. 7). In the Middle East the public/private binary can be reconceptualized into multiple spheres including the governmental (public), the nongovernmental (civil society), and domestic (kinship). Distinctions between governmental, nongovernmental, and domestic spheres are made in the Middle East. Social life is not seamless. The distinctions, however, are not premised on the notion that the spheres of social life are bounded, autonomous, utterly differentiated entities. The boundaries between and among spheres of social activity in the Middle East have been porous, elastic, and shifting. Antidemocratic forces have multiple sites of construction when gender is taken into account.

The patriarchal impetus to gendered and aged domination, found in the domestic sphere, is also found in governmental and nongovernmental spheres (Sharabi 1988). In many Middle Eastern countries incorporations of patriarchal kinship modes of operation, moralities, and idioms in other arenas are not perceived as disruptions to state or family boundaries but as continuous with them. Political leaders have recruited their relatives into public offices. Lay people have expected their relatives in public offices to act as kin to them rather than as public officials. The fluidity of kinship has provided a lubricant for social relationships outside domestic spheres. The distribution of resources on the basis of highly personalistic, face-to-face relationships grounded in kinship has reinforced patriarchy in multiple spheres. Political leaders have privileged the rights of males and elders over familial females and juniors in the distribution of resources or in the adjudication of legal matters. They often have deferred to family heads in matters related to members of their families. They have been often more willing to give services to women and juniors if they were represented by their men and elders. This has encouraged the expectation that citizenship and civic rights are conditional on the particular set of relationships one can muster—what I have called relational rights (Joseph 1990, 1994b). The continuities of patriarchal structures, modes of operation, and idioms of discourse in different social spheres are expressions of the power of patriarchy in Middle Eastern states.

Zubaida (1988, 163), following B. Badie, has called this the neopatrimonial state (personal or clique rule and use of patronage and clientism). Zubaida has argued that identification of the state with a particular leader is widespread in the Middle East (Saudi Arabia, Morocco, Iraq, Egypt, Syria, Libya). And the use of patronage to build and control support and supporters, Zubaida (1988, 165) has contended, has meant that those who benefit from the state do so "as individuals, families, particular communities, villages or regions." Central to these processes, I would add, has been patriarchal kinship.

Patriarchal relationships, morality, modes of operation, and idioms have been socially acceptable, expected, and ascendant in all arenas of social life in the Middle East. These continuities between governmental, nongovernmental, and domestic structures, modes of operation, and idioms, which have been constitutive of patriarchy, have been central to the culturally specific gendering of citizenship in Middle Eastern states. The boundaries of states, the parameters of nations, the memberships and meanings of ethnic/ religious communities, the contents of "public" and "private," the structures of families, the dynamics of patriarchies, and the identities of women and men have continually shifted in the Middle East. The constructedness and the contestedness of categories, however, has not diminished the passions with which they are embraced nor the power of their political and social consequences. As Sylvia Yanagisako and Carol Delaney (1995, 5) have insightfully argued, the power of social categories comes in their capacity to naturalize themselves. Rogers M. Smith (1997, 10) adds, this has been precisely the power of citizenship myths—they have been naturalized.

Points of Departure

Although Bryan Turner (1993b, 11) aptly argued against a unitary theory of citizenship even for Europe, political theorists who question the cultural applicability of Western constructs of citizenship to the Middle East, have done so often for the purpose of dysfunctionalizing Middle Eastern political culture. Some political scholars, refining the notion of culture for political analysis, have offered suggestive insights into state/society relations in the Middle East (Zubaida 1988; Sharabi 1988). Although a few political theorists have focused specifically on the question of citizen (Davis 1995, 1996), fewer have specifically concerned themselves with culturally specific gendered analyses of citizenship.

Western feminist scholars (Dietz 1985, 1987; Hernes 1987; Young 1990; Phillips 1991, 1993; Jones 1993; Eisenstein 1994; Yuval-Davis 1997; Lister 1997a; Voet 1998) have critiqued the masculinization of the Western legal subject. In this volume we document the need also to analyze its cultural specificity. Emerging during the Enlightenment and shaped during the rise of capitalism, global market economies, and Protestantism, the legal citizen-subject was constituted as a homogeneous, undifferentiated, interchangeable, detached, mobile and movable part of a rationally bureaucratized political system. This construction has been found problematical by some

Western feminists. Nedelsky has argued that the boundary is a destructive central metaphor for dealing with rights and human autonomy (Nedelsky 1990). Catherine Keller (1986) argued against the limitations of the separative self and for a relational construct of selfhood. Elizabeth Fox-Genovese (1991) has offered a provocative critique of feminist uses of individualism. And Carole Pateman cautioned feminists against building their arguments for women's rights on the basis of the construct of the individual (Pateman 1988, 14).

Western feminist theorists have profoundly challenged the masculinist assumptions embedded in laws and practices of citizenship in Western nation-states. In Western feminist discourse the centrality of women and gender to nation and state making has been extensively theorized (Pateman 1988; Phillips 1993; Young 1990; Williams 1991; McElroy 1991; MacKinnon 1989; Smith 1993; Eisenstein 1994; Lister 1997a, 1997b; Voet 1998). Such critiques of Western discourse of citizenship from within the West remind one of the ideological and cultural heterogeneity of the West. The West is no more monolithic and homogenous than is the Middle East. Competing and mutually constitutive discourses and practices have been engaging each other inside, outside, and between the Middle East and the West. Middle Eastern discourses, laws, and practices of citizenship have been influenced by Western legacies, colonial and postcolonial. Middle Eastern women's mobilizations around citizenship issues have also dialogued with Western women's movements (see chaps. 2, 13, 14, this vol.; Kandiyoti 1998). Women's movements in the West also have played off of Middle Eastern women's movements and subjectivities (Ahmed 1992; Grewal 1996). Globalization, the ongoing movement of peoples and ideas, and the emergence of several generations of human rights conventions through the United Nations and other international organizations (governmental and nongovernmental) have continued the active exchange between the Middle East and the West on issues related to the gendering of citizenship (see, especially, chap. 12).

A generation of feminist theorists have been investigating Middle Eastern state structures (Tekeli 1981; Kandiyoti 1991, 1998; Joseph 1991, 1993b, 1997, 1999a, b; Hatem 1986, 1994c, 1995; Charrad 1990; Najmabadi 1991, 1998; Molyneux 1991; Lazreg 1994; Badran 1995; Brand 1998; Botman 1999). Few studies, however, have established a systematic basis for a comparative analysis of the rules and practices of citizenship throughout the Middle East (Brand 1998). The contributions of this volume offer the possibility of identifying the specifically Middle Eastern aspects of the gendering of citizenship (Yuval-Davis 1997). While working towards de-essentializing the analytical categories of the Middle East, the state, the nation, religion, kinship, women, the citizen, and the self, the authors also facilitate the work of locating patterned similarities (Joseph 1996b). Clarifying what is specifically Islamic, Christian, or Jewish and what is common to these major religions of the region is also crucial. A critical reading of the contributions also sheds light on the broad categories of Arab, Turkish, Iranian, and Israeli. The country case studies offer material to clarify the gender patterns that are attributable to specific or to general processes of patriarchy (Arat 1996), to the privileging of family and of religion (Berkovitch 1996; Giacaman, Jad, and Johnson 1996), to the location of gender issues in family and in religion (Cheriat 1996; al-Mughni 1996), or other dynamics such as class, tribe, ethnicity, nationalism, and colonialism (Peteet 1991; Lazreg 1994; Badran 1995; Hale 1996a; Botman 1999).

The conversations engaged in this volume speak to the histories and dynamics of the gendering of citizenship in each country, one by one, to each other and to the gendering of citizenship elsewhere. Given that citizenship is mandatory in the modern nation-state, as Zubaida (1988) has argued, the complex intersections of citizenship and gender (besides class, race, ethnicity, religion) are fundamental to the lived realities of women in the region. As the Middle East enters the twenty-first century, the struggles and precedents of the twentieth century loom not only as a legacy but also as an agenda of unfinished business that is carried forward and lived, issue by issue. The issues covered in this volume are those lived on the ground in their separate and intertwined realities.

PART TWO

NORTH AFRICA

2

The Pitfalls of the Nationalist Discourses on Citizenship in Egypt

MERVAT F. HATEM

FRANTZ FANON'S "the pitfalls of national consciousness" (Fanon 1963, 148–205) has shaped the thought of many students of nationalism in what used to be described as the Third World. It offered a political-economic critique of the capabilities of the middle class that led the national liberation struggles, produced national ideologies, and formed postcolonial states. Fanon was also critical of the ethnic, but not the gendered, "pitfalls" of nationalist thought. In contrast, Benedict Anderson underlined the gendered character of the national "imagined communities" by identifying them as horizontal fraternities (Anderson 1983, 16). Anderson did not elaborate on the impact that the nation, as a fraternal entity, had on women as members of the new communities. The goal in this chapter is to examine the fraternal character of the Egyptian nationalist discourses on citizenship and how they were segmented by gender, ethnicity, and class.

I begin by suggesting that the Egyptian nationalist discourses on citizenship have had a relatively old history. The 1919 national revolution and its 1923 Constitution produced the earliest nationalist discourse on citizenship. The Constitution discussed the relationship that men and women had to the "nation" (*al-umma*) as the source of power/authority (*masdr al-sulutat*). It gave the monarchy powers and rights that clashed with those of the nation, revealing the existence of deep class and ethnic divisions.

The abolition of the Egyptian monarchy and the creation of a republican system of government produced new nationalist discourses and realities. It replaced the category of the nation with the more homogeneous "the Egyp-

33

tian people." The republican constitutions came close to creating a horizontal fraternity that minimized class and ethnic conflicts among men and conflicts between them and women. Finally, the nationalist discourses of the second and third republics have used religion to reconceptualize the constitutional definition of the national community, reintroducing serious ethnic divisions among men and divisions between men and women.

The 1923 Constitution and Its Definitions
of the Nation and Citizenship

The 1919 revolution represented a major turning point in Egypt's national history. The revolutionary quest for national independence and the right of Egyptians to representative government instituted a new discourse on citizenship. The 1923 Constitution offered new legal and political views of gender, class, ethnicity, and religion as internal characteristics of the nation and a definition of its external boundaries.

The trigger for the revolution was the British colonial government's rejection of the attempt by a delegation (*wafd*) of prominent Egyptians to negotiate the national independence of the country after the end of the First World War. In its meetings with the British high commissioner of Egypt, the delegation demanded political independence in recognition of Egyptian support of the allied military effort during the war. British arrest of the members of the *wafd* and their exile led to the outbreak of a mass rebellion that lasted three years. During this period the *wafd* was transformed into a mass political movement that appealed to, and mobilized, different segments of the population. The participation of men and women of different classes and religious groups, Muslims and Copts (members of the Orthodox Christian Church in Egypt), in lower and upper Egypt gave the revolution a genuine national character. It established the broad social and ethnic character of the new national community.

When the repeated efforts of Egyptian and British representatives to reach an agreement on the issue of national independence failed, the British government issued a unilateral declaration on 28 February 1923 that announced the end of the British protectorate in Egypt. It also declared Egypt to be an independent, sovereign state, but the British government retained—until Egyptian-British relations were formally negotiated in a treaty—the absolute right to control policy in the following areas: (1) the security of imperial British transportation in Egypt, (2) the defense of Egypt against outside aggression, (3) the protection of foreign interests in Egypt, including the rights of minorities, and (4) the Sudan (Ramadan n.d., 363).

The above gave Egypt a very ambiguous political status. It emerged as a semi-independent state that extended its national control over some policy areas and groups but which was unable to make important decisions in the critical areas of defense, foreign affairs, and the representation of some of its residents. In response to the acquisition of a new level of self-government, a cabinet was appointed to discuss and draft a constitution that defined the relationships of power in the new Egyptian nation. The 1923 Constitution established the masculine character of the nation by only recognizing adult male citizens as members. It gave them the right to vote in general elections and in this way participate in self-government. In theory, the new nation emerged as a horizontal fraternity of adult men. The members of this new "imagined national community" shared the experience of active struggle in the 1919 revolution against British colonial rule and the quest for self-government (Ramadan n.d., 375). Male citizenship was also based on the obligation of all adult males (twenty-one and older) to participate in the defense of the nation should it come under attack (Ramadan n.d.). In exchange, a liberal discourse on national politics recognized them as equal legal individuals who were entitled to suffrage. Article no. 32 of the Constitution also declared this fraternity of men to be the source of all legal and political power (*masdhar al-sultat*) in a new bicameral parliamentary system.

Religion did not make a difference in the exercise of the new rights of citizenship enjoyed by all male members of the nation. Among the preparatory committees that discussed the new Constitution was a minorities committee that included Muslims and Copts. When Muslim members proposed the use of proportional representation to secure fair legislative rights of the Copts and their agendas, the Coptic members rejected the proposal because it would have emphasized religious distinctions that could have undermined "national unity" (*al-wihda al-wataniya*). Instead, they supported the liberal political process and the Constitution, which generally outlined the rights of citizens in universal terms as institutional bases of their representation (Haykel 1983, 328).

The large and early participation of the Copts in the 1919 revolution and the visible role they played in the Wafd Party, which emerged as the party of the majority, provided the political backdrop for the above definition of ethnic membership in the nation. The political literature of the party described the new Egyptian nation as representing "the unity of the crescent and the cross" (Haykel 1983, 327). When Sa'd Zaghlul, the popular leader of the revolution, was asked by a group of prominent Copts what role he expected the Copts to play in the national/political movement, he answered: "The Copts are like the Muslims. They have the same rights and duties. All Egyptians are the same" (al-Fiqi 1991, 73). Sameness, not difference, was to be a central concept in the discussion of the unity of the na-

tion. It was echoed by another popular secular slogan adopted by the Wafd
Party, which declared that religion was for God, but the homeland (*al-watan*) was for all. This suggested that religious matters were to be treated
as spiritual matters that had no impact on the definition of the political
rights in the homeland. In addition to the Muslims and the Copts, Egyptian
Jews were included in this discussion of the unity of the nation (al-Fiqi
1991, 76). At that historical moment, these different groups shared a desire
to strengthen the nation (*al-umma*) and the homeland (*al-watan*).

The Copts, in particular, publicly refused British claims to represent all
minorities in Egypt. They declined British protection and declared themselves to be an indivisible part of the fabric of the nation (al-Fiqi 1991, 71).
The wish to preserve and to defend national unity distinguished the attitudes of Egyptian Copts and Jews as national minorities from those held by
European minority groups in Egypt. The latter accepted the principle of
British protection and representation. More significantly, the members of
these resident minorities did not consider themselves as part of the Egyptian
nation even though many of their members were born and raised in Egypt.
They preferred to be governed by the laws of European governments whose
passports they carried.

If religion did not separate male members of the new nation, class contributed an operational basis for who had the right to run for public office.
Anyone wishing to run in elections was required to pay the large fee—at the
time—150 Egyptian pounds (Ramadan n.d., 393). This identified the right
to run for public office with the well-to-do, who could afford this financial
requirement. It underlined the existence of vertical relations among the
male members of the nation whose middle and upper classes enjoyed more
political advantages.

In addition to these class divisions, other ethnic divisions provided a basis
for access to political power. The social and political history of the modern
nation-state in Egypt was identified with the ascension of Muhammed 'Ali
and his dynasty to political power. Although the founder of the dynasty
traced his birth to Kavala in Macedonia (al-Sayyid Marsot 1984, 24), the
dynasty (1805–1952) contributed to the building of a modern state. Its
interest in modernization was often discussed as providing new social and
economic bases of the nation. The new nation-state was also premised on
the political and ethnic dominance of the Egyptian majority by a small
Turco-Circassian elite. In the nineteenth century the monarchy's absolutist
form of government (Tucker 1985, 138) and antinationalist policies (Issa
1982, 147–54) put it on a collision course with the political aspirations of
the Egyptian majority during the 'Arabi (1880–82) and the 1919 national
revolutions. Not only did the monarchy maintain its right to rule through

heredity but it sought to reinforce its ethnic privilege with new sources of political power in the new parliamentary system.

The 1923 Constitution gave the king the right to dissolve parliament (Issa 1982, 376). In this way the monarchy was able to circumvent the legitimate right of popularly elected governments to rule. The king was also to appoint one-third of the members of the Senate and as a result accumulated considerable legislative power. He was the commander in chief of the armed forces with the power to promote and fire army officers. He also had the power to confer titles and commendations. Finally, the king had bureaucratic and financial control of Muslim religious institutions (Issa 1982, 393–96). In short, the Constitution gave the monarchy considerable political power that clashed in many instances with the political rights and the legislative wishes of the majority of adult male members of the nation. It represented a formal recognition of the continued ethnic (Turco-Circassian) privilege.

Because of the association between the monarchy and Muslim religious institutions, the former was often oblivious of its minority citizens. This was reflected in the ethnic makeup of the institutions it controlled. For example, the percentage of the Copts within the royal army was small (Hamrouch 1974, 215) and did not reflect their percentage within the general population. This provided a dramatic contrast to the visibility of the Copts in the ranks of the Wafd Party, which more accurately reflected the ethnic makeup of the nation.

The Wafdist secular discourse developed by both Muslim and Coptic members of the party was not without its problems. Although it formally ignored religious difference, it assumed the cultural legacy of Islam. It encouraged the Copts to accept this legacy as part of their national identity, but it did not incorporate Coptic history and cultural contributions as part of the new culture of the nation. This majority definition of national unity and its culture was actively accepted by Makram Ebeid, the popular general secretary of the Wafd and the minister of the treasury in many of its cabinets. His career as a celebrated lawyer and politician provided a prototype of the Wafdist definition of a nationalist Copt (al-Fiqi 1991, 73). Ebeid memorized the Qur'an and recited many of its verses in his political speeches and/or legal summations (al-Fiqi 1991). In this way he represented the strong belief in national unity. There was no Muslim equivalent of Ebeid. There was no Muslim public figure who was well versed in the Bible and could integrate Coptic history and culture in the discussion of national issues of the day (Shukri 1991, 7). As a result, the Wafd, as the representative of the "nation," failed to develop a national culture that equally recognized the contribution of the history and religion of the majority and the culture, history, and religion of the minority as well. Instead, Coptic acquiescence to the dominant cultural discourse of the majority (Shukri 1991, 6) was politically rewarded by the appointment of two Copts in visible and important cabinet positions such as minister of treasury (Hamrouch 1974, 215).

National unity aside, there was considerable political debate during this period about how to characterize the above constitutional arrangement and its definition of the relations between the nation, citizens, and the monarchy. The royalists supported a formalist interpretation of the Constitution that stressed the fact that it was issued in the form of a royal decree. This led them to describe the Constitution as a royal grant (*minha*) to the nation (Hamrouch 1974). As such, it could also be withdrawn or politically undermined by the king. The nationalists, represented by the Wafd Party, dismissed this view. They chose to emphasize article no. 32 of the Constitution, which stated that the nation was the source of all power/authority. According to this rule, the Constitution represented a contract (*'aqd*) among the members of the nation (Hamrouch 1974). It highlighted the consent of the nation as the basis of a representative form of government. Finally, a third view offered by a noted legal jurist, Abdel Aziz Fahmy, described the Constitution as a historic pledge (*'ahd*) made by the monarchy to the nation represented by its popularly elected governments (al-Sobki 1986, 18–19). Although the concept of a historic pledge served to stress the consensus of both the nation and the monarchy to operate within the parameters of a parliamentary political system, it was silent on the political competition, or the conflict between the two, which often pitted one against the other. If anything, the 1923 Constitution became the political expression of these opposing political views of whose interests representative governments were to serve.

The above political definitions of the Constitution were silent on women and their role as members of the nation and its political system. This was a puzzling omission given the fact that during the 1919 revolution women of different classes actively participated in such revolutionary activities as public and/or sexually segregated demonstrations (al-Sobki 1986, 35–36) and the boycott of British goods. Upper- and middle-class women also organized themselves into the Women's Central Committee of the Wafd Party. The committee issued press releases explaining their positions on different political issues and events of the day.

Despite this very public political engagement of women, the honorary title given to Safiya Zaghlul, the wife of Sa'd Zaghlul, the leader of the revolution, in recognition of her political contributions to the national cause, offered an early hint of how the leadership of the revolution discursively articulated women's relationship to the nation. After the exile of the national leadership of the revolution, which included her husband, Zaghlul, who had no children of her own, and until then was another upper-class housewife, emerged as a surrogate leader, ensuring the continuation of the national struggle. She encouraged the remaining leadership of the party to continue to meet at her house, as they had before, to plan for the different revolutionary activities. In response, she was given the title of *Um al-Masriyiin* (the mother of all Egyptians, or the mother of the nation). Her house was designated as *bayt al-umma*, the house of the nation.

The description of Zaghlul's role as that of a "mother" underlined a socially acceptable way of interpreting her actions. Instead of maintaining the political cohesion of the party and the national struggle, she was seen as nurturing the revolution. This characterization elevated the private and socially familiar role of caretaker, accepted by men and women of different classes, to new political heights. It also gave it a new public content. Mothering was now transposed to the public arena where women's caretaking skills were to service the nation.

The novelty of women's political participation and its characterization in familiar social terms did not reflect a throwback to traditional definitions of women's social roles. The Muslim personal status law of 1920 introduced *modern* formulations of gendered "personhood" within the family. The law was drafted by a committee made up of Shaykh al-Azhar, the *shaykh* of the Malki sect and his deputy, the head of the *shari'a* High Islamic Court, the *mufti* and other *ulema*. It was reviewed by the minister of justice and approved by the prime minister. In other words, the legal discourse on women's rights within the family was now considered to be the joint responsibility of Islamic jurists and the new national/secular state. The interpretations of Islamic law regarding the family lay in the domain of the Islamic jurists, but it required the legal and political approval of the minister of justice and the Council of Ministers.

On the surface, the law dealt with financial rights of a Muslim wife and how lack of support (*nafaqa*), abandonment, and irreversible illness (*'ayb mustahqam*) constituted grounds for her right to divorce. Chapter 1 of the law emphasized that she was entitled to the support of her husband even if she sued for a divorce. Financial support was treated as a debt that a husband was obligated to pay unless the wife chose to give it up (Jumhuriyat Misr 1956b). Chapter 2 was devoted to the discussion of how a husband's inability or unwillingness to support his wife entitled women to divorce. According to articles no. 4 and no. 5, a judge was immediately obligated to rule in favor of a wife getting a divorce if her husband was unable or unwilling to support her. For the same reasons, a wife was entitled to a divorce from an absent or an incarcerated husband. Finally, chapter 3 of the law explained that a wife had a right to file for a divorce if she discovered that her husband had an irreversible (medical) condition such as insanity or leprosy that caused her harm (*dharar*) regardless of whether this condition had existed before or after marriage or without her knowledge (al-Sobki 1986, 31–32).

The above represented some of the legal interpretations of Islamic law used in the nineteenth century to secure the rights of women in a marriage. Their codification into law and implementation by the modern legal system broke with the old Islamic legal system that had been practice oriented (Mitchell 1988, 82–83) and provided women with greater flexibility and freedom. The modern personal status law fixed the large array of rules and interpretations that were previously available to women as a basis for the discussion of their rights within the family. The 1920 law produced a new discourse that defined women as individuals (*Ashkhas*) whose status in the family was not autonomous. Not only were they financially dependent on men but they did not have an equal right to divorce. Only men enjoyed that legal right. These were modern assumptions that were absent in the premodern Islamic legal system and its practices. The court records of earlier centuries show that women of different classes creatively used the marriage contract to exercise their right to divorce (Sonbol 1998). All women were able to include in their marriage contract conditions under which they were entitled to divorce (Sonbol 1998).

The modern legal system put an end to this practice. In this way, it rigidly defined divorce as a male prerogative and specified what it considered to be new binding rules for women's rights to divorce. It thereby produced a dependent formal/legal status for women, as separate individuals, whose rights were to be protected. With this more homogenized and abstract definition of the marital relationship, the legal system began to produce a modern gendered consciousness that emphasized the autonomy of men and the dependence of women.

Amendments to the above law passed in 1929 attempted to rationalize a husband's exercise of the right to divorce. If a husband was drunk or coerced to divorce his wife, then the divorce was not valid. A husband could not use the threat of divorce to influence the actions of his wife. A husband could not divorce his wife more than once at a time. A divorce was to be explicitly stated or it was not valid. Every divorce is reversible unless it is the third one; then it is irreversible.

Marital discord (*shiqaq*) between husband and wife was considered an additional ground for divorce. A wife who claimed that her life with her husband was a source of harm that undermined her ability to live with him, like her other counterparts, could ask a judge to separate them. If she was able to show/prove harm, then the judge could grant her a divorce. If the judge turned down her claim, a woman could file again. At that point the judge could call on two men from their respective families to try and settle matters between them. If they failed, then the judge could divorce them.

Finally, women had custody of their sons until they were age seven and of their daughters until they were age nine. To protect the interest of the child, a judge could permit a woman to retain the custody of a son beyond seven years and until nine years. She could also retain the custody of her daughter beyond nine years and until eleven years (Sonbol 1998, 37).

A code organizing the personal status of the Copts was passed in 1938 that had the approval of Pope Yu'anis XIX and the Coptic Millet Council. It included ten grounds for granting divorce or separation of Christian spouses. In addition to adultery, which was explicitly mentioned in the Bible, conditions contributing to divorce included: insanity, irreversible and contagious diseases, illnesses that interfere with marital sexual relations, hurt/harm ('itha'), bad and unethical behavior, indulgence in vice, and the gross neglect of marital duties (Sh'ira 1995, 74).

With the exception of adultery, the grounds used to give Coptic women a divorce were not that much different from those outlined in the Muslim personal status laws. A variety of illnesses, not unlike those mentioned in the Muslim status laws, were treated as grounds for divorce. The gross neglect of marital duties was not specifically defined, but it could be interpreted as lack of financial support by a husband or the discord and/or harm highlighted in the Muslim law. Even though the different notion of 'itha' was used to signify harm or discord as grounds for divorce, the Coptic personal status laws embraced legal approaches and attitudes similar to what constituted a dysfunctional marriage. The emphasis on ethical behavior and avoidance of vice reflected a more puritanical Coptic view of the institution.

In both of the above laws, there was an attempt to nationalize the definition of the rights of a woman in the family and to identify her as a gendered individual with the less-autonomous status of wife and mother. These were the generally accepted social roles that entitled women to legal rights. Muslim and Coptic men were economically and legally responsible for their wives. When these Muslim and Coptic men became sick or lost their financial independence, they lost their privileged legal status as patriarchs. In these cases the state intervened to protect the rights of women by granting them divorces and/or separations. Given the emphasis on women's private roles in the family and their presumed economic and legal dependence on men, which the modern personal status law upheld, it was not surprising that the 1923 Constitution did not include them in its discussion of membership in the nation. As less-autonomous gendered actors, the Constitution denied them the rights of citizenship with the exception of article no. 19 of the Constitution, which recognized the right of young girls to education. It stated that "elementary education was obligatory for all Egyptians, including boys and girls. It was free at *al-Makateb al-'Amma*" (al-Sobki 1986, 110–12) (at the elementary level). Here, the right to education belonged only to young boys and girls. It was silent on whether education influenced the status of adult women in the nation.

Egyptian women's reaction to the 1923 Constitution, which formally excluded them from political membership in the nation, varied by class. Munira Thabit, a young middle-class member of the Wafd who was preparing to study law in France, emerged as the lone active voice that publicly protested the denial of Egyptian women's right to vote in the new political system (Sha'rawi 1981, 249–50). It was an issue that she often revisited in her Wafdist newspaper *Al-Amal* and her other public writings that defined the aspirations of the professional middle class and their belief in the legal ideal of political equality.

In contrast, the Egyptian Feminist Union, established by Hoda Sha'rawi in 1923, addressed the issue of women's political rights in vague terms. Rule no. 2 of the charter stated that its "goal was to raise the social and public level of women so that they could be worthy of participating with men in all rights and obligations" (Sha'rawi 1981, 249). Rule no. 3 declared the union's "commitment to use all legitimate means to give women their political and social rights" (Sha'rawi 1981, 330).

The above offered an indirect answer to the question of how upper-class women explained their denial of citizenship rights. Rule no. 2 of the charter suggested that the founders of the union agreed with the male framers of the Constitution that women were not yet worthy of political rights. The union vowed to remedy that by working to raise the social and public standard of women. Then, and only then, could women demand their social and political rights.

In 1924 the Egyptian Feminist Union and the Wafd's Central Committee for Women headed by Hoda Sha'rawi, issued a pamphlet with a statement that underlined the widespread acceptance of the above view among upper-class women. The pamphlet noted that Egyptian women represented half of the nation (*umma*) and that they were the caretakers of the next generation of men and women whether they were deputies in parliament or members of the general public (Sha'rawi 1981, 330). The denial of political rights to half of the Egyptian public, which did not participate in the drafting of the Constitution, could not vote in elections or occupy prosecutorial positions led the members of both organizations to focus attention on the need to reform (the conditions of) women and the reform of the nation

(Sha'rawi 1981, 331). Science and education were viewed as the best methods of reform. They prepared individuals for their role in the development of the community.

Toward that goal, the pamphlet emphasized the need to provide women with equal access to education and to public work, especially where they could service other women. This was, of course, the same view espoused by article no. 19 of the Constitution and one that supported women's education as a means of advancing the cause of women and the nation. After the success of these reforms, the electoral law could be amended so that women could participate along with men in the right to vote. The authors of the pamphlet were not opposed to the placement of some conditions on women's initial exercise of their voting rights, such as requiring a certain level of education and ownership of property (Sha'rawi 1981). Opposition to the participation of upper- and middle-class women was not anticipated because the electoral law allowed illiterate and propertyless men to elect and be elected. Under these future conditions, the political establishment would not deny (educated and propertied) women equality with these men. Women, who represented half of the population, could not be treated as objects of legislation without some form of representation (Sha'rawi 1981, 344).

By 1926 Hoda Sha'rawi could unequivocally state that women's involvement in politics was not the union's primary concern. Interest in politics could only develop after success in organizing women's affairs in the family and position in society. Women's past involvement in politics was dictated by the exceptional circumstances of the postwar period. With the present political stability, women could leave politics to men and concentrate on what concerned them as women (Mariscotti 1994, chap. 2).

The above position supported the findings of Cathlyn Mariscotti, who described the union as primarily preoccupied with cultural feminism as the basis for the articulation of a modern ideal of womanhood. As part of the development of this hegemonic construct of Egyptian womanhood (Mariscotti n.d., 53), their philanthropic activities emphasized teaching women how to read and write, the modern principles of hygiene, and the proper care of children. Their national goal was to enable working-class women to become better wives and mothers (Sha'rawi 1981, 53). These were the contributions that the union hoped women would make to the development of a modern nation. Toward that goal, the union supported raising the marriage age for women to sixteen years. In a memo to the minister of justice, Hoda Sha'rawi argued that before the age of sixteen, young women were not educated enough to perform their wifely duties to their husbands. She also suggested that at a young age women were not physically able to bear and care for children (Sha'rawi 1981, 264). For these reasons the state had a duty to change the law, to protect the rights of women, and to assist them to perform their modern roles as mothers and wives. In short, the union's entry into the public arena was identified with a commitment to transform the modern cult of domesticity from a private ideal into a national and a public one. It accepted the fraternal discourse of the 1919 nationalists who categorized Safiya Zaghlul as a mother and not as one of the surrogate leaders of the Wafd and the nation.

In conclusion, the fraternal character of the early nationalist discourse on citizenship contained the sources of serious class and ethnic divisions. In giving the Turco-Circassian monarchy the right to circumvent the rights of the Egyptian majority, the 1923 Constitution undermined the supposedly horizontal fraternal character of the nation. It also accepted class privilege within the Egyptian majority in the important arena of running for public office.

The exclusion of women from membership in the nation contributed to another serious political division. Active upper-class women accepted the claims and the terms of this early fraternal discourse that classified women as not yet worthy of membership in the nation. The Egyptian Feminist Union also embraced the discursive view that domesticity and education constituted the basis for women's future citizenship rights.

The Nationalist Discourse of the First Republic
(1952–1970)

The overthrow of the Egyptian monarchy in 1952 and the establishment of a republican political system had implications for the national discourse on citizenship. It eliminated the bases of social and political privilege of the Turco-Circassian elite and expanded the rights of "the Egyptian people" (*al-sha'b al-misri*). Republicanism enhanced the bases of fraternal solidarity. As part of the new populist category of "the people," women were given the rights of citizenship that established their subordinate status within the fraternal political arena.

The political overthrow of the last king of the Muhammad 'Ali dynasty went through two phases. Immediately after the military takeover of political power on 23 July 1952, King Farouk was forced to abdicate the throne in favor of his infant son on 26 July. Then, the monarchy was politically abolished on 18 June 1953 and replaced by a republic. These political developments had implications that were captured by the new national discourse used by the military to redefine Egypt as a nation.

In the ultimatum presented to the king by General Muhammed Naguib, the first leader of the 1952 revolution, the army referred to the "general chaos that resulted from the king's (personal) misbehavior, his lack of respect for the (1923) Constitution and his contempt for the will of the people (*'iradat al-sha'b*)" (Hamrouch 1974, 226). In the abdication document that the king was asked to sign, the army described his action as "serving the good of the nation and in response to the will of the people" (Hamrouch 1974, 228). Both of these documents represented an important transition from the old national discourse, emphasizing the nation but also accepting the (ethnic and political) privileges of the monarchy, to a new one in which the national army represented "the will of the people." Although the old national discourse accepted the existence of ethnic and class divisions within "the nation," the policy measures passed by the Revolutionary Command Council (RCC) of the army began the process of eliminating these dramatic distinctions to create a horizontal fraternity (a mass public who could be more appropriately described as "the people"). It abolished titles and civilian social ranks (Hamrouch 1974, 235). Soon thereafter, the council passed a land reform law that limited large land holdings and redistributed the land that was expropriated. This eliminated the major manifestations of ethnic and class privilege (Hamrouch 1974).

It paved the way for the establishment of a different type of society—one that could provide the material and social bases of a republic whose political discourse underlined the fact that the "Egyptian people" (*al-sha'b al-Misri*) were free from internal (social and political) and colonial forces that oppressed them. It also provided a basis for the RCC's powerful emotional claim that for the first time in their modern history, Egyptians were free to govern themselves. The monarchy, with its Turco-Circassian ethnic roots, had treated the majority of the relatively dark-skinned Egyptians with contempt. This attitude explained one of the early slogans of the revolution: "Raise your head up high my brother; the age of enslavement is over." This new republican slogan reaffirmed the fraternal character of the nation represented by the new category of the "Egyptian people." The change from a monarchial to a republican form of government promised to deepen the legal equality enjoyed by Egyptian men, who as members of the "people" and their political will, were to emerge as primary political actors. Most political speeches during this period began with the fraternal greeting *Akhi al-muwatin*, literally "brother citizen." It became one of the many republican/populist political concepts that underlined the position of men as a privileged national core group within the "Egyptian people."

How did the new national discourse deal with women as part of the "Egyptian people"? An early signal that the new republicanism did not include women in its definition of the "people" came when the Constituent Committee met to draft a new Constitution. The committee did not include any women among its members. This outraged a new generation of professional/middle-class feminists.

The death of Hoda Sha'rawi in 1947 dealt a major blow to the Egyptian Feminist Union, whose organizational cohesion was weakened further by feuding among its different factions on the approach to be used to push the agendas of their changing constituency. Leftist and liberal women formed competing organizations that appealed to middle-class women whose numbers within different professions had visibly increased.

In protest of the exclusion of women from the committee seeking to draft a new republican constitution for the country, women members of the Reporters' syndicate led by Duriya Shafiq launched a hunger strike in March 1954.[1] The action captured the public's imagination and that of the RCC. After eight days, the mayor of Cairo conveyed the following political promise to the women engaged in the strike: "President Naguib commissioned me to inform you that he received your demands (for women's constitutional rights and representation in the Constituent Committee) and that they were referred to the relevant committee that will consider them" (*Bint al-Nil* 1954, 7).

This vague commitment to consider the demands of women reflected the ambivalent attitude the new military leadership had regarding women's rights. They associated women's rights with the aristocratic activities of the Feminist Union and the social agendas of the *ancien regime*. They were suspicious of both. More seriously, they were concerned about how the support of women's political rights would undermine the support of the middle class for the revolution.

The dilemma of what to do regarding women's political rights continued from 1954 to a few days before the Constitution was announced (*Bint al-Nil* 1954). Rumors that the new Constitution would ignore the political rights of women threatened to bring about a new round of women's activism. It provoked Amina al-Said, the editor of *Hawa'* (Eve)—the first women's magazine published by a major publishing company, *Dar al-Hilal*—and an elected member to the council of the Reporters' Syndicate, to give a lecture at the syndicate in which she declared her support of women's right to vote. Until then, al-Said, a pioneering middle-class professional, had been one of Duriya Shafiq's critics, a supporter of the new regime, and one of its shining role models.[2] Diverse women's organizations publicly announced their plans to coordinate their public activities and efforts in the future (Hatem 1994b, 234).

---

1. For a detailed discussion of that event see Nelson 1996, chap. 11.
2. Interview with Amina al-Said, Dec. 1989, Cairo.

Women's activism aside, the potential exclusion of women from the new category of "the Egyptian people" threatened to weaken the revolutionary claims made by the new republic regarding its commitment to the expansion of the rights of the "Egyptian people" of which women were a part. It also provided a potential basis for an oppositional agenda that could be used by women of the professional middle class (lawyers, university professors, reporters, and teachers) against the state (Hatem 1994b).

In response to all of the above, the 1956 Constitution recognized women's political rights. It extended to women the right to vote and to run for public office that men had acquired in 1923. The emphasis on the "Egyptian people" that the preamble to the 1956 Constitution repeatedly used to describe the new egalitarian basis of the society became universal. The following is a quote from that preamble:

We, the Egyptian people, who wrested the right to liberty and life in a continuous battle against aggressive control from the outside and exploitative control from the inside; . . . we, the Egyptian people, who learned from our past, drew determination from the present and created the landposts to a future free from fear, need and humiliation, want to build . . . a society of affluence that puts an end to colonialism, feudalism, capitalist control of government, builds a strong army, social justice and an unblemished democratic life. We, the Egyptian people, who hold dignity, justice and equality to be sacred and genuine roots to liberty and peace . . . want to use all these principles in laying the bases of a constitution that organizes and protects our struggle. (Jumhuriyat Misr 1956a, 1–5)

The emphasis on the right to liberty, freedom from fear, need, and humiliation, the quest for dignity, justice, and equality stressed the inclusive character of the republican national discourse. The goal was to extend these rights to all groups without exception.

Next, the different chapters of the Constitution provided a detailed description of the new republican state and society. Chapter 1 focused its discussion on the ethnic, religious, and linguistic characteristics of the Egyptian state. Article no. 1 declared Egypt to be an Arab, independent, and a sovereign state. The Egyptian people were part of the Arab nation. Article no. 3 declared Islam to be the religion of the state (*din al-dawla*) and Arabic to be the official language (Jumhuriyat Misr 1956a, 7).

In the attempt to establish the ethnic distinctness of the citizens of the new republic, the Constitution emphasized Arabness as a key feature. The Egyptian people were part of the Arab nation. This gave them a clear ethnic and linguistic identity. The constitutional emphasis on the Arabness of the

Egyptians was new. It was partly designed to stress the homogeneity of the new nation. The old Egyptian nation had a ruling class whose Turkic ethnic and linguistic loyalties set them apart from the rest of the population. The new nation, both rulers and ruled, and Muslims and Copts spoke Arabic. In this discussion of Arabness, Islam was the religion of the majority and, therefore, the religion of the state.

The Constitution's formal emphasis on Islam as the religion of the state did not seek to subordinate the Copts to Muslims in the new national society. In the discussion of the rights and duties of Egyptian citizens, article no. 31 stated "Egyptians were the same (*sawa'*) in the eyes of the law. They were equal in rights and public duties. There was no discrimination among them on the basis of sex, ethnic origin ('*asl*), language, religion or creed" (Jumhuriyat Misr 1956a, 15). Article no. 43 stipulated that freedom of belief was absolute. The state protected the freedom to conduct religious rituals of different religions according to the practiced customs in Egypt and provided that these did not violate public order or morality (Jumhuriyat Misr 1956a, 18).

The above articles fostered a legal belief in the horizontal comradeship between Muslims and Copts and men and women. It purposely forbade the formal use of religion or gender differences as bases for discrimination. In this way it hoped to secure equal citizenship rights to all.

Chapter two of the Constitution discussed the basic constituents (*al-muqawimat al-'assassiya*) of Egyptian society. Article no. 4 stated that social solidarity was the basis of Egyptian society. Article no. 5 declared the family was at the base of the society and that it was constituted by religion, ethics, and patriotism. Article no. 6 stated the state's commitment to secure liberty, order, and security and equality of opportunity for all Egyptians (Jumhuriyat Misr 1956a, 8).

Article no. 18 declared that the state was to secure, in accordance with the law, the support of the family and the protection of mothering (*al-umuma*) and childrearing (*al-tufula*). Article no. 19 stated that the state will facilitate women's reconciliation of their work in the society and their obligations within the family (Jumhuriyat Misr 1956a, 11).

The above offered a discussion of the key social features of the new society. Some of these features were old and some were new. For example, social solidarity was seen as a key feature of society and that the family was the institution that provided this social function. Religion and social morality were to continue to shape that institution. Patriotism represented a new addition to this discussion. This hinted that the family was going to embrace the new national concerns.

In addition to the state's responsibility for liberty, security, and order, it also promised to deliver equality of opportunity for all. Article no. 49 declared education to be the right of all Egyptians. The state secured it through the building of different types of schools (Jumhuriyat Misr 1956a, 20). Article no. 52 stated that all Egyptians had the right to work and the state was committed to providing work to its citizens (Jumhuriyat Misr 1956a, 21). Article no. 56 declared health care to be another right available to all Egyptians (Jumhuriyat Misr 1956a, 22). All the above provided varied expressions of the new republicanism and underplayed the continued existence of class differences among the people.

The state also declared its commitment to support the family and the protection of mothering and childrearing activities. It viewed these activities as the basis of the gender specific roles of women. In many ways this reflected the continued belief that the primary roles of women were in the family. What was novel was the state's commitment to help working women reconcile their public work and their private occupations in the family. The need for state intervention to secure women's rights to work in the public arena suggested its fraternal nature. Not only did women's right to work need protection but the state was aware of the fact that their private/domestic roles as mothers and wives also needed its social support. By themselves, the legal rights given to women were not enough to secure their equality in the fraternal public space. The state believed that its political commitment was needed to create a space for them in these inhospitable arenas.

Article no. 58 addressed the gender specific roles of men within "the Egyptian people." It discussed the defense of the homeland as a sacred duty. Military service was defined as an honor to all Egyptians [men]. Military conscription was obligatory. Finally, article no. 61 declared voting to be a right for all Egyptians [that was to be exercised] as outlined by the law. The participation of Egyptians in public life was considered to be a patriotic duty (Jumhuriyat Misr 1956a, 22). The two articles combined old and new obligations as a basis for the privileged status of men within "the Egyptian people." The defense of the homeland provided the original basis for giving men early citizenship rights. With the elimination of financial requirements for political participation and the extension of political rights to women, men were to demonstrate through their political participation their right to dominate national politics.

Although the Constitution recognized universal suffrage for men and women, the procedural laws that organized the practice of this right established gender-specific procedures for the registration of the voters. It stated "all the men, who exercise their political rights must be registered to vote. It is also necessary to register those women who *request* [that right]"

(Muhammed 1979, 73). The memorandum accompanying the law explained that "the law observed the principle of equality between men and women in registering to vote as part of its recognition of the important role played by women in public life. . . . In view of the prevailing Egyptian customs, however, the registration of women to vote is left as a *choice* to be decided by each individual woman" (Majmu'at al-Muhtamat bi Shu'un al-Mar'at al-Misriyat 1988, 30).

To be registered, women had to petition the state to include them in the lists of registered voters. In contrast, men were automatically registered as voters at the police stations where they lived. The submission of a petition as a requirement to being registered disadvantaged illiterate rural and urban women. They had to find a literate person who would write the petition. It also required visiting police stations where they needed to deal with generally uncooperative bureaucrats to complete their registrations. To some extent, this explained the small number of women who registered to vote in 1956 when women exercised that right for the first time. It allowed the state to claim that the right to suffrage was the concern of a small minority of privileged women whose political concerns were not those of the illiterate and depoliticized majority. It allowed the state to preserve the fraternal character of national politics, which, in turn, provided another justification for trivializing women's citizenship rights.

Labor law no. 91, passed in 1959, gave working women other important citizenship rights. It supported women's right to work by giving them fifty days of paid maternity leave, providing them with day care services where there were more than one hundred workers, and protecting women from unfair termination during or after pregnancy (Markaz al-Abhath wa al-Dirasat al-Sukaniyya 1972, 77). Although these were important gains, most private employers and even some public ones avoided hiring more than ninety-nine women to avoid the costs of providing child care to working mothers. In short, fraternal public resistance continued even within public institutions, undermining the greater representation of working mothers in the labor force.

The passage of a provisional constitution in 1964 introduced new enframing national concepts that were to guide the socialist transformation of society. It did not radically redefine existing definitions of citizenship rights. For example, article no. 1 declared "the United Arab Republic [the name Egypt adopted after its unity with Syria in 1958 and which was retained after the Syrian secession (1961) until 1971] was a democratic and socialist state based on the alliance of the "peoples' working forces" (*quwa al-sha'b al-'amila*). The Egyptian people were a part of the Arab nation" (al-Jumhuriya al-'Arabiy al-Mutahida 1964, 3). Article no. 3 stated that national unity was forged out of the alliance of the peoples' forces representing the working population: the peasants, workers, soldiers, intellectuals, and the nonexploitative national capitalists. It formed the basis of the Arab Socialist Union that represented the authority of the people that pushes the capabilities of the revolution and protects true democratic values" (al-Jumhuriya al-'Arabiy al-Mutahida 1964, 3–4). Article no. 5 stated that Islam was the state religion and Arabic was the official language.

In privileging the new category of the "peoples' working forces" the Constitution hoped to identify the social agents of change in the new socialist democracy. The old definition of national unity that referred to the unity between Muslims and Copts gave way to a national alliance among working people and classes. It included peasants, workers, soldiers, intellectuals, and national capitalists. In theory, women were represented within most of these groups, but they were not identified as a "distinct working force" in this alliance. This distinction meant that the new socialist society was not going to introduce any change in its definition of women's roles. Like the 1956 Constitution, the new one promised in article no. 19 state support of the family and the protection of mothering and caretaking activities (al-Jumhuriya al-'Arabiya al-Mutahida 1964, 7).

Given the far-reaching economic and political changes that the state introduced in the organization of society during the 1950s and the 1960s, it was significant that the state's initiative in the legal arena did not result in the change of the gender-specific rights that men and women had in the family. In 1955, the state had passed law no. 462, which abolished the parallel *shari'a* (Islamic) and millet (representing other religious laws including Christian and Jewish ones) court systems, which addressed themselves to personal status. This resulted in the referral of the personal status cases to a national court system. As a result, the domain of the national (secular) court system was expanded. It nationalized the legal procedures and integrated the legal personnel who offered legal representation within that system. Graduates of the modern law faculties and the graduates of Al-Azhar's College of Principles of the *Shari'a* (*'Asul al-Shari'a*) could now both offer representation to those wishing to pursue personal status litigation. In fact, the graduates of the modern faculties of law who already knew the procedures in the nonreligious courts gained an edge over their Azharite counterparts.

The litigation of personal status cases continued to be governed, however, by the old personal status laws passed in the 1920s and the 1930s. The only change introduced into Muslim personal status law during this period was a cosmetic one. In February 1967 the minister of justice passed a ministerial decree that discontinued the practice of using the police to implement judgments by the courts requiring a wife to obey her husband and to return to the family home. In explaining his decision the minister declared that the previous practice was an insult to Islamic *shari' a* (law) and a humiliating blow to the dignity of any woman and of all male citizens (Hassouna 1990, 147). The minister claimed that more ambitious changes of the law were planned but that, according to him, the defeat suffered in the 1967 war had changed the political climate and agendas (Hassouna 1990, 148–49).

The 1938 code that organized personal status among the Copts continued to operate as before. Non-Muslims were to be governed by their own *shari' a* (religious laws) unless there was no clear statement (*nass*) on an issue, then the rule of Islamic *shari' a* was to be applied.[3] When the courts ruled in favor of the divorce, the parties involved usually submitted requests to the church, asking for permission to remarry. The church during this period usually granted its permission (Sh'ira 1995, 74). This liberal position changed, however, with the election of a new pope in 1970.

Overall, there were many reasons why the Constitutions of the first republic produced a national discourse on citizenship that delivered more egalitarian rights to men and women. The lobbying and pressure by professional middle-class women forced the hand of the state, bridging the political gap between men and women. This change, coupled with the populist claims of the new republicanism, represented by the 1956 socialist Constitution and maintained by the 1964 Constitution, led to the deemphasis of class and ethnic divisions within "the Egyptian people." Universal citizenship rights did not change the largely fraternal character of the public arenas where women worked, voted, and ran for public office. The state recognized this constraint and promised to protect women's new rights. Unfortunately, however, the new republicanism tolerated new and old forms of gender inequality in the registration of eligible voters and within the personal status laws.

The National Discourse of the Second and Third Republics

The attempt to distinguish the regimes of presidents Anwar al-Sadat (1970–81) and Hosni Mubarak (1981–present) from that of the founder of the republic, Gamal Abdel Nasser, led to the highlighting of the role of religion in its description of the Egyptian nation-state in the permanent constitution proclaimed in 1971. It led to alliances and then confrontations

---

3. Interview with Afaf Mahfuz, an Egyptian lawyer, on 16 Mar. 1998, Washington, D.C.

between the state and organized religious actors and organizations. The result was a recreation of ethnic and gendered divisions in Egyptian society. In the speech during which he asked the National Assembly to draft a permanent constitution for the republic, president Sadat suggested that the new constitution "express the true Egyptian way of life and tradition" (Saleh 1988, 310). This suggested the end of Egypt's revolutionary phase (Saleh 1988). It represented a return to more conservative cultural definitions and assumptions. The changes in the first two chapters of the 1971 Constitution supported this view. The most significant of these changes was represented by article no. 2, which discussed the relationship between religion and the state. It stipulated that "Islam is the religion of the state. Arabic is the official language and the principles of Islamic jurisprudence (*shari'a*) are a principal source of legislation" (Saleh 1988, 325). The description of Islam as the religion of the state was not new. The stipulation that Islamic law was a principal source of legislation gave religion a new visible and divisive public role. The advocates of this change suggested that without it the statement that Islam was the religion of the state was a mere formality. Islam was both a religion and a system of government (Saleh 1988, 325).

Chapter 2, in which the basic constituents of society were discussed, reiterated state support of equality of opportunity, the family, and the protection of mothering and childrearing activities. It also added the *shari'a* as a reference point for women's role in society. Article no. 11, in which the state's support of women in their effort to reconcile their obligations within the family and their public engagement in society was previously stipulated, now stated that "the state supports the reconciliation of women's obligations towards the family and her work in society. [It also supports] equating women with men in the political, social, cultural and economic arenas provided that this did not violate the judgments of Islamic *shari'a*" (Muhammed 1979, 75).

This represented a marked change in the way religion was defined by the first republic and its relation to women. The national charter, the blueprint of the planned socialist society passed in 1962, viewed religion as a liberating force in the development of society (Wizarat al-Tarbiya wa al-Ta'lim 1968, 161–62). It defined "proper religious beliefs as opposed to fanaticism and dogma. . . . It rejected any attempt to view world religions as [anything but] humanist revolutions whose goal was the honor, progress, and happiness of the human being" (Wizarat al-Tarbiya wa al-Ta'lim 1968, 163). Article no. 11 in the 1971 Constitution offered a marked contrast to these views. It employed Islamic *shari'a* in a restrictive way. Women's equality with men in the major public arenas was now limited by a more conservative reading of Islamic law that identified difference with public inequality. In 1980 the state introduced another amendment of article no. 2 of the Constitution. Instead of Islamic jurisprudence being a principal source of legislation, it was now described as *the* principal source of legislation.

The other group of citizens that felt threatened by the above amendments were the Copts. The previous political formula that restricted the role of religious law to the personal/familial arena was giving way to one that used the religion of the majority as a source for public policy/legislation. To ease the fears of the Copts, the drafting committee highlighted the fact that article no. 40 of the Constitution continued to maintain that "all citizens are equal before the law. They have equal public rights and duties without discrimination due to sex, ethnic origin, language, religion or creed" (Saleh 1988, 326). The Constitution also provided that the "state shall guarantee the freedom of belief and the freedom of practicing religious rites" (Saleh 1988). Finally, the observance of Islamic jurisprudence was said not to pose a threat to the rights of the minority because it recognized that non-Muslims were subject in their personal affairs to the rulings of their own religion (Saleh 1988).

Although the above amendments did not contribute to the change of any existing civil/public laws or the passage of new ones that challenged the previous exercise of citizenship rights, it was identified with the introduction of a new set of political actors, issues, and discourses into the political process. It contributed to the politicization of religious institutions and groups. For example, the Coptic Church under the leadership of Pope Shenouda felt compelled to respond to these political changes, using a variety of tactics including appeasement, civil disobedience, and confrontation. The church did not immediately react to the above constitutional amendments. It chose to wait and assess the consequences of change. When the government of Mamdouh Salem announced in 1977 that it would apply Islamic *shari'a* to punish Muslims who convert to Christianity, the pope called for a general fast by the Copts in protest of the new policy. The wide observance of the fast all over the country led the government to withdraw its legislation (Shukri 1991, 92). The church also began to mobilize expatriate Coptic communities, particularly in the United States, to pressure the Egyptian government to redress actual and perceived grievances of the Coptic minority (Shukri 1991).

The above climate of political crisis strengthened the conservative hand of the church in the arena of personal status. Under Pope Shenouda, the church no longer abided by court rulings that recommended divorce for Coptic couples. The newly elected pope put an end to these legal practices. He upheld the biblical verse that stated that divorce could only be permitted in cases of adultery. As a result, the church refused to recognize the divorce rulings by the court system that went beyond the biblical injunction regarding adultery. It denied these couples its permission to remarry (Shukri 1991).

Muslim personal status laws did not escape the political manipulations of the state and its Islamist opponents. The state's initial support of Islamist groups allowed the latter to begin the successful mobilization of a large segment of middle-class women. The widespread embrace of the Islamic mode of dress and the Islamist ideal of domesticity by middle-class women in the 1970s led the state to use the reform of the personal status law to mobilize its national and international sources of support. In 1979 President Anwar Sadat issued a presidential decree that introduced the following changes in the law: (1) It defined the husband's decision to take a second wife to be a source of harm to the first wife and, therefore, offered her a choice between staying married to her husband or getting a divorce. (2) It entitled the divorced mother to keep the family home until her custody of children ended.

Although the above amendments were described as significant, even their defenders admitted their modest character. Polygyny was not a serious social problem. Its incidence in Egypt did not exceed 6.8 percent of all marriages (Muhammed 1979, 122). Securing the right to divorce to women in polygynous marriage did not serve the rights of the majority. In contrast, securing housing for a divorced mother and her children was an important gain that protected them from displacement and homelessness.

The Islamist opponents of the law claimed that it contradicted *shari'a* by restricting the male unilateral right to divorce and to take more than one wife (Zulficar n.d., 17). The secularists condemned it as an antidemocratic tactic by an unpopular state. After the assassination of President Sadat, Islamist groups contested the legality of the law. The High Constitutional Court struck it down in 1985 on procedural grounds. The law was issued by a presidential decree and was not discussed by the Peoples' Assembly (Zulficar n.d., 18–19). In response, the Mubarak government introduced a new law to the Assembly that was passed in 1985. The new law made concessions to the Islamist critics. Women were now expected to prove material and nonmaterial harm to get a divorce after the decision of a husband to take a second wife. As for the rights of a divorced mother to the family home, the judge offered the husband the opportunity to provide alternative housing to his wife and children. The judge was also to determine the acceptability of that housing alternative.

The High Court also struck down law no. 30 of 1979, which was passed with the revised personal status law and which guaranteed women thirty seats in parliament as a basis of adequate representation. The court argued that it privileged women and ran counter to the constitutional principle of the legal equality of men and women (Zulficar n.d., 3–4). In an attempt to temper these serious reversals, the Mubarak regime passed law no. 41 that eliminated the procedural differences required of male and female voters. The state also appoints women to the Peoples' Assembly to ensure a minimum representation of women in that legislative body.

Although the second and third republics have not reversed any of the citizenship rights of women or the Copts, their constitutional manipulation of Islam for political purposes contributed to the development of new ethnic and gendered divisions in a new national entity. The Islamists consider Egypt to be part of the "Islamic *umma*" (the Islamic nation). Although this concept has not been incorporated into the Constitution, the state's opportunistic attempt to give the *shari'a* legislative teeth has undermined the secular basis of fraternal solidarity between Muslims and Copts. Paradoxically, the new prominent role played by religion in both the Coptic and Muslim communities contributed to the resurgence of conservative patriarchal attitudes and forces as bases for solidarity among men regarding the social roles that women should play in society. Some of these patriarchal attitudes and rules have been accepted by Islamist middle-class women. The division of middle-class women along ideological lines made women's citizenship rights an easy target in the polemical exchanges between the state and the Islamists (Hatem 1994b, 661–76).

Although the rights of citizenship enshrined in the Constitution have not changed, the development into market economies has made the promise of these rights hollow. Class differences have widened between the upper, middle, and working classes, between the countryside and the cities, and the northern and southern regions of the country. Some of the citizenship rights that promised equality of opportunity to men and women have been frozen. For example, the state used to guarantee access to relatively cheap public education and to work in the state and public sectors. The dismantling of the public sector and the state's withdrawal from the provision of social services such as education made equality of opportunity subject to the whims of the market (Hatem 1994c, 40–60).

◆   ◆   ◆

The discursive "pitfalls" of nationalist thought were an expression of the paradoxical use of the language of community to characterize fraternal political/social orders. At the same time, language of a horizontal national community based on legal equality of citizens veiled the privileged status of the dominant/majoritarian culture at the expense of those of the minority.

Viewed in this light, the national discourses on citizenship demonstrate the operation of the modern dynamics of power. They contribute to power not through repression or oppression but through the ability to produce the (subordinate) consciousness of their citizens. In the above presentation I show that the national discourses on citizenship sought the consent of women and minorities to unequal cultural, political, and class practices in the name of national, republican, social, or cultural revolution. The universal and/or particularistic claims of these discourses on citizenship served as sites of complicity, struggle, and resistance. The changing national discourses on citizenship that I discuss offer a dynamic view of the changes in the definition of the national community and who should legitimately control the power of representation and the production of consciousness. For students of gender, the critique of the assumed horizontal and fraternal nature of these national communities offers a first strategic step toward the reversal of the "pitfalls of national consciousness" and the influence it casts on citizenship rights.

3

Citizenship and Gender in Algeria

MARNIA LAZREG

IN THIS AGE of economic globalization and greater unequal cultural encounters, citizenship is emerging as the focal point of resistance to the cen-
tralizing tendencies of states in the developing world and to protests against
social exclusion in industrialized countries. In North Africa and the Middle
East, the developmentalist model that emphasized historical unity and social
solidarity has been severely eroded by a generally poor economic performance and a less than perfect implementation of citizenship rights. Increased poverty has gone hand in hand with a demand for greater political
participation. The incipient democratization of the political systems in many
countries of the region, especially Algeria, has brought to the fore a new
model of social organization based on citizenship instead of an abstract notion of development. Its reliance on rights rather than community makes
this model far more difficult to implement than the previous one because of
the demands for inclusion of conflicting interests that it places on the state.
This is exemplified by the social upheaval and chaos that have engulfed
Algeria since its experimentation with democracy in 1989. The "discovery"
of citizenship is a powerful tool of protest in the hands of political opposition groups and social groups such as women, traditionally excluded from
the full enjoyment of their political rights. It opens up a new area of inquiry
into the many dimensions of citizenship and their culturally specific expressions as well. Given its history of struggle to give its people access to
citizenship, Algeria provides an unusually interesting example of the social,
political, and legal paradoxes that the citizenship model faces, especially
with regard to women.

Theoretical Concerns

The rise of the citizenship model in Algeria resulted from a combination of external and internal demands. Internally, the youth revolt of 5 October 1988 signaled a crisis of confidence in the state's ability to include all of its citizens in its socioeconomic program of development. Externally, the structural adjustment program that the state agreed to in the aftermath of the oil crisis required political liberalization as a prerequisite for the establishment of a market economy. In 1989 the government passed laws enabling the creation of a multiparty system and guaranteeing citizens freedom of speech and the right to form associations. Apart from the decision to establish a multiparty system, these changes essentially amounted to a reassertion of rights that were already contained in the 1969, 1976, and 1989 constitutions. Implicitly, the state was compelled to recognize that there was more to citizenship than the formal right to vote that Algerians had already received in the last years of the colonial occupation and had reaffirmed in 1962. It is precisely this "supplement of meaning" that gives significance to the contemporary debate over citizenship.

T. H. Marshall's definition of citizenship as referring not only to political but also to civil and social rights adequately captures the scope and the complexity of this concept:

> The civil element is composed of the rights necessary for individual freedom— liberty of the person, freedom of speech, thought and faith, the right to own property and to conclude valid contracts, and the right to defend and assert all one's rights on terms of equality with others, and by due process of law. . . . By the political element I mean the right to participate in the exercise of political power, as a member of a body invested with political authority or as an elector of the members of such a body. . . . By the social element I mean the whole range from the right of a modicum of economic welfare and security to the right to share to the full in the social heritage and to live the life of a civilized being according to the standards prevailing in the society. (T. H. Marshall 1950 quoted in Ruth Lister 1997a, 15–6)

Implicit in this definition is the recognition that political citizenship may not be effective if social and civil rights are not exercised. While debates about the primacy of one type of rights over another or whether social rights are a legitimate part of citizenship continue to rage, some critics argue that the focus on social rights evokes notions such as autonomy and agency that are crucial to conducting one's life without constraints. In addition, proponents of social citizenship point out that it enables excluded groups, such as women, to claim their right to resources that would otherwise make the exercise of their political rights moot (Lister 1997a, 15–18). Feminists have argued that states need to facilitate women's agency and create the conditions necessary for the expansion of their autonomy. Thus, citizenship as "status" is different from citizenship as "practice" (Lister 1997a, 41). In other words, to have rights as a citizen is insufficient for the exercise of individual agency; what is needed is the practical exercise of and *participation* in the concretization of the status of being a citizen with a bundle of rights (Lister 1997a). Where the status of being a female citizen, as in Algeria, is divorced from the practice of being a citizen, citizenship remains abstract and carries *no obligation for the state to protect it or for women to exercise it.* This disjuncture between political and civil/social citizenship has prevented women in Algeria from fully participating in public life and from achieving autonomy in the conduct of their private lives. In this sense, formal citizenship precludes the emergence of substantive citizenship, which includes the protection of civil and social rights.

My thesis here is that all governments in Algeria since 1962 have emphasized a formal concept of citizenship that is eminently suitable to a paradoxical view of women's legal status. The extension of formal citizenship to women enabled the state to disregard the antinomy between the assertion of equality before the law, a secular requirement of (substantive) citizenship, and inequality between men and women as prescribed by the *shari'a*. This concept of citizenship simply masked the notion, operative in most official legal/political texts, that women are essentially subjects, lacking agency, who must be in the custody of males acting in the name of God. Within the Algerian context, women's rights evoke a threat to cultural authenticity and integrity because of the ideological centrality of the woman question in the cultural clash that took place in the nineteenth century between colonizers and colonized.

Citizenship Before Citizenship Rights

Debates concerning citizenship rights assume that individuals whose rights are discussed have already been defined as citizens of a given country unproblematically. Such definitions may be fraught with constraints, if not contradictions, that may spill over individuals' exercise of their political, civil, and social rights. In Algeria nationality law squarely discriminates against women because it privileges men. Thus, article no. 6 states that a citizen is a person whose father is Algerian. The mother confers citizenship on her child only if her husband has no nationality or is unknown (Code de la Nationalité 1970). Article no. 7, however, stipulates that children born in

Algeria to an Algerian mother and a foreign father are citizens unless they give up their nationality one year before reaching majority. In this case it is birth rather than parentage that determines citizenship status. Indeed, a child born in Algeria but whose parents are unknown is also considered a citizen. The Nationality Code does not subject fatherhood, as a vehicle through which citizenship is conferred, to any restriction. Article no. 32 specifies that having two Muslim paternal forebears born in Algeria consti- tutes proof of natural citizenship.

The gender differential in the condition of being a citizen may partially account for the legal difficulties encountered by children born to unwed mothers. Although an unwed mother may give her name to her child, social pressure militates against her doing so (Zidani 1992). At the same time, proving paternity is an arduous task. It is possible that had fatherhood not been so central to citizenship rights, unwed mothers who wished to keep their babies would have had an easier time of it.

It must be noted that the secondary role played by the mother in the conferral of nationality finds its functional equivalent in the category "na- tive" used by the colonial legal system. From 1830 to 1958 Algerians were French nationals who could travel on French passports. But they were not French citizens endowed with the same political and civic rights as the colo- nists. The Senatus Consultum of 14 July 1865 referred to Algerians as "Muslim natives" (or "*indigenes musulmans*") and declared them "French subjects" who could become citizens upon their request in order to enjoy the benefits of civil and political rights. A law passed on 4 February 1919 permitted natives to become naturalized under some very specific conditions such as having served in the armed forces, owning property, and holding public office. In becoming naturalized natives lost their "personal status," meaning they were no longer considered Muslims and the *shari' a* could not be applied to them. Thus, being a Muslim was an obstacle to acquiring political, civil, and social rights equal to those of the colonists, just as being a woman today is an obstacle to enjoying the same rights as men. It was not until 1946 that natives theoretically could become French citizens without relinquishing their "personal status."

Women in Political Texts

The foundational texts of postcolonial Algeria illustrate the severance of civil and social rights from political citizenship. The resulting deficit in rights is best exemplified by the ambiguous and indeterminate space occu- pied by the category women. Although individual men may have felt that they did not fare any better than women under the one-party system that held sway in 1962–1995, as a group they were able to use the social advantage they derived from being born to the male gender to overcome the citizenship deficit.

La Charte d'Alger

The first political text issued by the first government, La Charte d'Alger (1964), defines the socialist orientation of the country. It also lists Algeria's sociopolitical and economic problems and recommends how to solve them. It points out that during the transition from capitalism to socialism, the party of the Front of National Liberation (FLN) would "abolish the exploitation of man by man" and initiate the "beginning of an era of freedom" (La Charte d'Alger 1964, 63). Following the tradition established by the then socialist states, it identifies the people as the "masses" (61). This undifferentiated concept elides differences between women and men, rich and poor, rural and urban, thereby obscuring the issue of civil and social rights. The new socialist society created the mass-citizen, an essentially male construct as is connoted by the use of generic man, which occludes gender inequality. The drafters of the charter do address women's social position, however. Taking a historical perspective, they argue that "for centuries the Algerian woman was maintained in an inferior condition justified by retrograde concepts and erroneous interpretations of Islam. Colonialism aggravated this situation by triggering among women a natural reaction of self-defense that isolated women from the rest of society. The war of liberation enabled the Algerian woman to assert herself by carrying out responsibilities side by side with man and taking part in the struggle" (81–82, emphasis added). Women are thus perceived as having existed for the war, which effectively gave them birth. In this sense the charter reveals its unwillingness discursively to allow women's participation in the war to be the product of their chosen activity. Women's historical action is legitimized by their proximity to men ("side by side with men"), not by their agency.

Although the charter points out that equality between men and women must become real, it makes only general recommendations about how it might be achieved: "The Algerian woman should be able to participate effectively in politics and the building of socialism by joining the ranks of the party and national organizations and acceding to positions of responsibility. She should be able to put her energy in the service of the country by taking part in its economic life, thereby genuinely promoting herself through work" (82). There is no mention of women as citizens whose rights must be guaranteed by the state. In fact, the process of getting positions of responsibility within the ranks of the party expressed as it is in the conditional tense is seen as necessarily long, given the present level of development of Algerian society (82). The charter is silent about how the state might address the "social prejudices and retrograde concepts and erroneous interpretations of Islam" (81–82). Although cultural retrogression is adequately defined as a source of women's unequal status, its resolution is not specified. In the end the issue of women's political and legal position and rights is left in abeyance. The charter makes a feeble effort on behalf of war widows in advocating that they be given better pensions, job training, free medical care, and housing.

Constitutions

The constitutions formulated in 1976 and 1989 did not transcend the problematique of sex/gender and citizenship rights. The second president of Algeria, Houari Boumediene, redefined socialism as "Islamic." Boumediene's socialism was an economic mode of production operating within a cultural milieu based on Islamic values. The juxtaposition of socialist secular principles and a religious value system aggravated women's citizenship rights deficit. God, rather than rights upheld by a temporal authority, was not perceived as a problem. It prefigured women's contradictory position as citizens under socialism and subjects under the *shari' a*. Perhaps aware of this contradiction, however, Boumediene emphasized the rule of law and until his death in 1978 postponed the passage of a family code based on the *shari' a* of which several drafts had been prepared.

A new charter issued in 1976, after a heated public debate, denounced "mental attitudes and legal structures that sometimes prejudice her [woman's] acknowledged rights as wife and mother and her material and moral security" (Algérie: Naissance d'une Société Nouvelle 1976, 163). It also denounced "exorbitant and ruinous dowries, unscrupulous fathers who abandon their children to destitute mothers or unjustifiably wrench their children from their mothers' affection; unmotivated divorces that leave women without alimony or health care; violence against women perpetrated with impunity; and the exploitation of women by antisocial individuals [meaning pimps]" (163). Although some of these ills are clearly due to the unequal status of women under family law, the new charter suggests that their solution resides in women themselves: "It is woman herself who must ultimately remain the best defender of her own rights and dignity through her deportment and qualities as well as a relentless struggle against prejudice, injustice, and humiliation. . . . As for the state, it has already recognized woman's political rights and is committed to her education and inevitable social advancement" (163). These political rights were later identified in the 1976 Constitution as the freedom to work for both men and women (art. no. 32); the prohibition against discrimination on the basis of sex (art. no. 39); and the protection of "political, economic, social, and cultural rights" (art. no. 42). Women's exercise of these rights, however, was on occasion infringed upon. For example, in 1981, a temporary restriction on women's ability to travel abroad was put into effect without warning. In addition, although no government ordinance had been made public, passports were no longer issued to unemployed women during the same year. Clearly, citizenship in this case was perceived as a privilege that the state could withdraw at any time.

The Constitution of 1989 marks a significant change in the role that the category "women" plays in Algeria's political discourse. Gone are references to women as a special group of people in need of help. In a shift from socialism to political liberalism, the Constitution refers to women and men as *citoyens* (citizens), using the masculine gender. The word *Algériennes* is mentioned in article no. 31, which points out that the "fundamental rights of Man and the Citizen are guaranteed. These constitute the common patrimony of all Algerian men and women." Article no. 30 uses the concept of citizen in the feminine and masculine, but article no. 52 affirms the right to work to "les citoyens" without mentioning women, thereby creating the impression that only men have the right to work. In this Constitution women are subsumed under generic man. In other words, women have become invisible.

The Family Code

It is instructive to note that the 1989 Constitution was issued five years after the passage of a family code, inspired from the *shari' a*, which legalized inequality between women and men (in violation of the 1976 Constitution) in marriage, divorce, child custody, and inheritance. In an early draft form circulated in 1982, the code had made women's ability to work contingent upon their husbands' approval. Thus, just like natives during the colonial era, women do not enjoy equal rights. They are nationals, but not citizens. Thus, article no. 11 of the code obligates a woman to have a guardian to contract marriage and makes the dowry a condition of its legality; article no. 48 gives the husband an unqualified right to divorce, whereas a wife can divorce only under some specified conditions. Article no. 51 institutionalizes, although ambiguously, divorce by repudiation (a concept that the French-language version of the code does not mention specifically) by spelling out the penalty for a man "who has divorced his wife three consecutive times," one of the modalities of repudiation as prescribed by the *shari' a*.

Nevertheless, an attempt at reconciliation is prescribed before divorce is pronounced. Article no. 37 enjoins a polygamous man to treat his wives equitably, but he is not obligated, as he was under a draft of the code, to provide them with separate housing. The code makes a concession to women by enabling a mother to become the guardian of her children at her husband's death. It further enables a woman to have custody of a son until he becomes sixteen and of a daughter until she reaches the age of marriage, or eighteen. In matters of inheritance the code upholds the basic principles of the *shari' a*. In so doing, it negates women's political besides civil, citizenship rights. The code is, thus, the single most important text that demonstrates the precariousness of the notion of citizenship in societies with dual legal systems: one secular, the other inspired from religion. It is a reminder that citizenship is not merely a bundle of rights that a state grants the people; it presumes an understanding not only of the individual-qua-citizen who expects to have rights but also a distinction between civil rights and religious obligation. Where the latter is defined as the protection of gender asymmetry, citizenship can only be seen as a formal political requirement of the state that does not allow for citizens' participation in its implementation. Consequently, women appear as citizens (who can exercise the right to vote) in one sphere and *subjects* in another. Caught between the constitution and the code, women are not political persons endowed with rights that are guaranteed by the state. Rather, they are entities having primarily obligations toward state and family. It is this lack of political personhood with its concomitant lack of agency that paves the way for the violence that has targeted women since 1992 and the redefinition of women's roles in the Islamist discourse since 1989.

Citizenship and Nationality

Perhaps the lack of personhood that characterizes women's legal status is best exemplified by the Nationality Code of 27 March 1963. Individuals are considered citizens when they have at least two paternal ancestors that were born in Algeria and were/are Muslim. Religion is, thus, intertwined with citizenship. Women could not be vehicles for citizenship because they do not possess political personhood under the state and do not have agency under family law. The 1970 nationality code, however, enables the child of an Algerian mother and a foreign father to apply for citizenship after residing for eighteen months in Algeria. The child born in Algeria to an Algerian mother and a foreign father may apply for citizenship within twelve months of the child's eighteenth birthday. This male-centered view of citizenship is in direct contradiction to the view upheld in the popular culture that women are essential to the preservation of the family. Denying children of an Algerian mother and a foreigner the right to immediate citizenship dramatizes women's status of legal indeterminacy.

The Consequences of Formal Citizenship

Since 1989, the Islamist movement in Algeria, especially as represented by the banned Front of Islamic Salvation (FIS), has consistently portrayed women as needing protection from acculturation into Western values. This notion of protection is not only embedded in the controversial *Qur'anic sura* "empowering" men over women but also in the FIS rewriting of Algerian history. For the FIS, Algeria is still a colony. According to this view, the war of decolonization was only the French phase of the struggle against colonialism. The second phase centers on getting rid of the Algerian government, perceived as the native relay of French colonialism. The postindependence state is deemed illegitimate because it does not rule according to the "Qur'an, the Sunna, and the Calife's tradition" (Touati 1995). According to the Front of Islamic Salvation, "Colonialism denatured Algerian culture," and its "offspring" (the Algerian government) has caused women to neglect their religious duties, which center on their husbands and children (Amine Touati 1995, 257). Books written in Arabic have appeared in bookstores to explain to women their religious obligations to husband and family and how to lead a virtuous life (Lazreg 1994, 221).

The co-leader of the FIS, Ali Benhaj, recommended that women stay home and produce "lions" (sons) who will fight for the cause of Islam. During the 1991 strike called by the FIS, the government was told to compel women to retire early to make room for unemployed men. "Moderate" Islamists such as Abdallah Jaballah, head of the Nahda (Renaissance) Association, were willing to let women work but pointed out that they could not hold positions of judge or president (Lazreg 1994, 217). The Islamist discourse purports to protect women from the world of work, which brings them into contact with men, and to resocialize them away from the "colonial" culture allegedly supported by the state. Dissatisfied with the 1984 Family Code because it did not reproduce the *shari'a* in its entirety, the FIS sympathizers, who include a number of women, rejected it as the product of misguided men tampering with divine law. The code was likened to the French attempt to introduce changes in marriage and divorce during the colonial era, especiallly between 1956 and 1957. The Islamist intervention in women's political rights was dramatized during the 1990 municipal and 1991 parliamentary elections when it became known that Islamists had pressed men to vote for their wives because voting by proxy was not prohibited then.

Perhaps, the most telling consequence of women's lack of personhood as formal citizens under the Constitution and subjects under the Family Code is the violence that has affected women since 1992. In 1999 there was doubt whether some of the massacres of villagers, women, men, and children were committed by the various Islamist factions that have taken up arms to overthrow the government. The state secret police and the military were accused by the FIS and some of the Western media of having committed or abetted acts of violence against civilians. This controversy missed the point because it overlooked the environment that facilitates the commission of acts of violence. Women's lack of political personhood, an act of symbolic violence in its own right, created the conditions for possible attacks on women as women. By focusing on women and making them into the linchpins of the future Islamist society, the various speeches pronounced by leaders of the Islamist movement, whether moderate or radical, crystallized the notion that women are at once the weakest members of society in need of salvation and the embodiments of what is wrong with a state that does not live by the *shari'a*. In addition, the Islamist discourse on political matters was fiery, marked as it was with calls to civil disobedience that empowered men to act not only according to their beliefs but also according to their anger (Touati 1995, 257). Finally, the dissemination of definitions of women based on various texts of the *Hadith* (Traditions), some less reliable than others, helped to foster a climate of deprecation and denigration of femininity and exaltation of masculinity. Within this context acts that infringed on women's right to live, choose a husband, work, dress, and think acquire moral legitimacy. The progression from lacking political personhood to being a subject in family law and, finally, to losing one's life for the establishment of the kingdom of God is both logical and inescapable. Women have become one of the wrongs to be righted as a matter of duty to God.

The press, especially the daily *El Watan*, in Algeria and abroad has documented womens' accounts of rape, kidnaping, torture, humiliation, and mutilation. Whether it is the Armed Islamic Group, one of the most radical factions of the Islamist movement, or the Islamic Army of Salvation that committed these acts is less important than their occurrence. Where expedient, foreign customs have been introduced to legitimize violence against women. Thus, the *Shi'a* (mostly Iranian) practice of *mut'a*, temporary marriage, has been practiced by some Islamists to force women into sexual relations with them. Sexual slavery has been used routinely in the past year by men who, in the course of attacking a village, select the women they find the most attractive to take with them to their hideouts. The climate of violence has enabled new groups such as Men Angry with God, who purport to punish God for not leading them to victory in their struggle against the government, to exact further damage on women's, children's, and men's bodies.[1]

Perhaps women are not the only casualties of the formalistic concept of citizenship. Young men may be unable to continue their education beyond the elementary level. Needy elderly, whose fate is placed in their children's hands (if they have any) by the Family Code that requires children to support their parents in their old age, may suffer. The most important group is youth, however, because it constitutes a significant proportion of the population and has provided the Islamist factions with its rank and file. Their civil and social rights are just as unrecognized as women's. But, unlike women, they experiment with different ways of channeling their anger or dealing with unemployment by either joining an Islamist group or a government militia. I interviewed a twenty-two year-old high school dropout in November 1997, in Algiers, who had joined government security forces because he was tired and ashamed of hearing his mother waking him up in the morning to the cry, "Get up, you good for nothing, and find yourself a job like people your age do!" This mother was wrong in thinking that people her son's age were all employed. Nevertheless, it is the lack of jobs and a worsening economic situation that have compelled young men to swell the ranks of the violence machine, Islamist or state-sponsored.

Social Citizenship Rights

Formal citizenship thrives on political authoritarianism. Substantive citizenship begins to be a reality where and when individuals can exercise a number of freedoms, including the freedom of expression and association. Since 1989 Algeria has initiated a process of political liberalization with farreaching results despite the continued unrest. The generally free press and the creation of a multiparty system have provided the opportunity for women and men to demand civil and social rights as necessary complements to the right to vote. There is a gender difference in the ways in which individuals have taken advantage of this new opportunity. Men have tended to form parties or to start newspapers; women have created associations to address gender issues traditionally neglected by the state. Men's parties are

---

1. This section is based on reports from the Algerian, French, and U.S. presses such as *Le Monde* and *El Watan*.

better funded and have easier access to the media than do women's associations, which are often run on the personal budgets of their founders. Women's associations give women a platform from which to demand the implementation of civil and social rights. The lack of experience with participatory citizenship, however, jeopardizes women's quest for the enlargement of their rights by making them vulnerable to cooptation by male politicians. Many women's associations are affiliated with one political party or another, thus acting as their mouthpieces on social or civil rights. This tendency deprives women's associations of the independence necessary to address the multiplicity of socioeconomic problems that struggling women encounter in their daily lives. In addition, it compels women to confine their demands to what is politically convenient for the party with which they happen to be affiliated. For example, the most vocal associations have lumped together what is perceived as a demand for recognition of one of the Kabyle-Berber dialects as an official language of Algeria and the abolition of the Family Code. Yet the code concerns all women, whereas the language question is of interest to some women; it is also already the focus of two parties, the Rassemblement pour la Culture et la Démocratie (RCD) and the Front des Forces Socialistes (FFS). Few female leaders have focused on the economy and its impact on the poor, social security for the elderly, or the water and housing shortages that affect women principally.

The evolution of Algerian women's experience with formal citizenship specifies existing debates on the relationship between political, civil, and social rights, and their gender implications. The lesson to be drawn from the Algerian case is not so much that one-party rule and state socialism prevented the emergence of political freedoms that would have helped women to claim their rights although this is an important fact that has been noted in countries such as the former Soviet Union. Rather, citizenship cannot be but formal (reduced to the act of voting) under conditions of a dual legal system, one secular, the other inspired by religious texts. The ensuing loss of personhood and the subjectivization of women may lead to violence against them. For women to gain substantive citizenship that allows for the expansion of their civil and social rights requires basic political freedoms in addition to women's *active* and independent participation in public life.

4

Becoming a Citizen

Lineage Versus Individual in Tunisia and Morocco

MOUNIRA M. CHARRAD

CITIZENSHIP INVOLVES at its heart the mode of incorporation of individuals within the framework of a social and political community.[1] As such, it is a historical concept, and the form it takes varies widely from one society to another. The concept of citizenship as understood today took shape with the formation of formally autonomous nation-states. The starting point of contemporary debates in most of the world remains the liberal view of citizenship that involves a concept of the ideal society as a partnership of free and equal citizens within a political community.[2] In principle, citizenship applies to individuals who all have the same individual rights as defined by law within a nation-state. In actuality, access to individual rights within any particular nation-state is often differentiated by many dimensions, such as gender, level of education, socioeconomic status, religious affiliation, ethnicity, or language (Joseph 1996b, chap. 1, this volume; Orloff 1993; Soysal 1994; Young 1989; Shafir 1998; Walby 1994; Tilly 1996).

In this chapter I compare citizenship and its relation to gender in two countries: Tunisia and Morocco. Even though these two countries share many similarities in culture, language, and religion, citizenship rights for women have taken different paths: women as citizens have more individual

1. I thank Mary Freifeld and John Markoff for valuable comments on earlier drafts.

2. Rawls (1971) presents a contemporary formulation of the liberal view of citizenship. This view has been criticized from a variety of perspectives, several of which are discussed in Shafir 1998.

rights before the law in Tunisia than in Morocco. A key feature of social organization that has affected citizenship rights in Morocco and Tunisia has been the place of kin-based formations in the social structure and politics. The history of Morocco and Tunisia has been characterized by the centrality of the extended patrilineal family and its extension referred to as lineages, clans, kin groupings, or tribes. The relative role of kin-based formations in the political history of each country has been critical to developments in citizenship.

Although the Middle East is often seen as unique because of Islam, I suggest that treating Maghribi countries (and other parts of the Middle East) historically as *kin-based societies* sheds much light on the development of the state and the course taken by citizenship. Issues of citizenship have received much scholarly attention in the context of predominantly class-based Western societies where social class has historically been considered the major divide (Marshall 1964; Lipset 1963; Bendix 1964; Tilly 1996; Shafir 1998; Sommers 1993). Much remains to be understood, however, about citizenship in those societies where kinship has served as a fundamental mechanism of social integration and a basis for social conflict. If one is to develop a "culturally specific gendered analysis of citizenship in Middle Eastern states," (see chap. 1) one must pay close attention to the fact that Middle Eastern societies have been kin-based during most of their history.

Kin-based formations extending from the patrilineage have influenced the historical development of the nation-state in Morocco and Tunisia and the formulation of its laws and policies (Charrad in press, 1997, 1996, 1990). Lineages continue to occupy a central place in social relationships today. Kin-based patriarchy, by which I mean specifically the primacy of the kin group coupled with the power of male kin over women, has pervaded the history of the Maghrib and the Middle East. The extent to which it is codified in the law is a major determinant of the status of women as citizens.

I argue that citizenship took on different forms and became gendered in different ways in part as a result of the different place of kin-based formations in the development of the sovereign nation-state in Tunisia and Morocco. The theory proposed is that, in societies where lineages and kin-based social formations have remained central elements of the social structure and anchors for political power, the individual citizenship rights of women have suffered. They have been subordinated to the continuing privileges of men and of patrilineages.

Whereas in Morocco the legal discourse tends to enshrine kin privileges, in Tunisia the law provides considerably more space to a construct of self as an individual and, consequently, more rights to women. In Morocco, tribes and lineages have retained more prominence in politics than in Tunisia where they have become weaker. Morocco offers an example of how women's citizenship rights have been curtailed in favor of the power of male-dominated patrilineages. By contrast, in Tunisia, where kin-based formations have exerted much less social and political influence in the modern period, women have gained significant individual rights, even though many aspects of gender inequality persist. As kin-based formations have lost power in Tunisia and remained strong in Morocco, the legal discourse has offered a different balance between the universalism of individual rights and the particularism of male or lineage privileges.

Durkheim (1964), Weber (1978), Collins (1986), Toennies (1957), and Parsons (1971) have conceptualized the emergence of modern states as a social process that threatens and sometimes eradicates particularistic ties of village, local community, lineage, kin grouping, or tribe.[3] When discussing the development of the ideal of citizenship, Pocock (1998) underscores the transcending of tribal loyalties as a central dimension. The development of a modern state certainly entails the integration of the particularistic ties of village as in Western Europe (Tilly 1975) or tribe as in the Maghrib within a broader political entity. It does not, however, inevitably cause such particularistic ties to lose their political relevance within the nation-state.

There are many paths to state formation with different kinds of relationships between the central state and particularistic communities. Tunisia, Algeria, and Morocco alone have exhibited several paths and several relationships between state and tribe in the development of sovereign nation-states (Charrad in press, 1996, 1990). One path involves the persistence of particularistic communities such as tribal kin groupings under the umbrella authority of the state as in Morocco. Another path entails opposition between state and tribe as in Tunisia. The particular mode of integration of particularistic ties within the broader political community of the nation-state shapes the degree to which particularism remains central to the relationship between state and society and, therefore, to the forms taken by citizenship.

The greater weight of particularism in Morocco reflects the relationship between society and state as it emerged in the era of national sovereignty at the end of French colonial rule in the 1950s. In Morocco the sovereign state headed by the monarchy developed as the supra-authority under which particularistic allegiances were permitted and sometimes encouraged whether anchored in lineages or religion. In contrast, the Tunisian state developed in autonomy from such allegiances and once in power engaged in policies that

---

3. Although they have converged about the nature of the process, social theorists have disagreed on whether its consequences for social life were positive or negative.

minimized or eradicated them. Accordingly, many policies in Tunisia aimed at transferring loyalties from particularistic communities to the entity of the sovereign nation-state. These key differences in the relationship of state to society shaped the overall policy orientations as they were set in each country after the emergence of the sovereign state in the mid-1950s. They molded the framework for how issues of women's citizenship rights would be settled in Morocco and Tunisia.

Citizenship is best conceptualized as involving several related yet analytically separate arenas. T. H. Marshall (1964) advanced the discussion on citizenship in the West by distinguishing among what I call "arenas of rights," such as civil, political, and social rights.[4] Contrary to Marshall's expectation, the different arenas of individual rights do not necessarily evolve together and rights in every arena are reversible. The distinction is analytically useful nevertheless. In the same vein as Marshall's distinctions, citizenship rights in relation to gender in Tunisia and Morocco are best examined as part of related but distinct arenas.

One arena concerns the citizenship rights that make a person formally the citizen of a country as symbolized, for example, in the possession of a passport. I refer to that arena specifically as "nationality rights" to distinguish it from other arenas. A central issue concerns the respective ability of men and women to transmit citizenship rights to their children or foreign spouses. Another critical arena is that of basic personal rights as defined in family and personal status laws. This is one of the most contested arenas of citizenship rights for women in the Maghrib and the Middle East. It covers laws regulating issues such as marriage, divorce, and guardianship of children. A third arena concerns some of the rights enumerated in the constitutions of Morocco and Tunisia as applying universally to all citizens. These include among others the right of individuals to vote and to be eligible to hold public office.

A key question to examine is the extent to which the laws of Tunisia and Morocco give women individual rights and responsibilities or, on the contrary, protect the privileges of patrilineages as collectivities. At issue is kin-based patriarchy and the privileges of men as members of the patrilineage versus individual rights for all citizens including women. This chapter is organized in three parts: In the first part I examine nationality rights. In the second part I focus on basic personal rights in family and personal status

---

4. Civil rights include free speech, protection from the state, and equal access to the legal system. Political rights refer to the right to vote, to run for election, and, more generally, to participate in the exercise of political power. Social rights concern entitlements such as minimum income, Social Security, unemployment benefits, and health benefits.

laws. In the third part I consider universalistically stated rights enumerated in the constitution with respect to voting and holding office.

Nationality: Right of Blood and Right of Soil

A consideration of nationality rights raises the question of the conditions for membership in the community of citizens. At stake in particular in the Maghrib is the primacy of patrilineality, or paternal descent, in the transmission of nationality from one generation to another. Whether nationality by descent or right of blood devolves only from fathers or also from mothers is a central issue. For women to become equal citizens in the nation-state, "blood" should no longer mean only the blood of the paternal lineage but should include the blood of the mother. Gender differentiation enters into the formulation of nationality in both Morocco and Tunisia, but it is greater in Morocco than in Tunisia where mother's blood counts for more.

The concept of nationality as discussed in this section historically was absent in the Islamic tradition. What came closest to it was defined in religious terms and took a highly unequal form for men and women. Religion was a determining factor.[5] A Muslim man could marry a non-Muslim woman while retaining his membership in the community of Muslims. A woman, however, would automatically lose her status as part of the Muslim community if she married a non-Muslim.

In Morocco and Tunisia a *Code de Nationalité* delineates the conditions for membership in the community of citizens within the nation-state. Both countries combine elements of *jus sanguinis*, the right of blood, and elements of *jus soli*, the right of soil, in the attribution of nationality rights. *Jus sanguinis* confers nationality through blood descendance, whereas *jus soli* means that people born on the national territory are nationals. In both countries *jus sanguinis* through fathers is unconditional and automatic. By contrast, the transmission of nationality through mothers occurs only under limited and restricted conditions, carefully enumerated in each code.

In Morocco, the *Code de Nationalité* was promulgated in 1958 and has remained unchanged since. In Tunisia, the *Code de Nationalité* was first promulgated in 1957, revised in 1963, and revised again in 1993 when the conditions for *jus sanguinis* through mothers were expanded. In both countries, women as a source of nationality rights are at a disadvantage compared to men, but Tunisian mothers have greater rights than do Moroccan

---

5. All Muslims were represented by the imperial state or its representative in Tunisia (which was part of the Ottoman empire before French colonization) and by the sultan in Morocco.

mothers. In both countries, the patrilineage has primacy as a determinant of nationality in that membership in the political community of the nation-state flows directly from male descent or patrilineality. The Moroccan code states: "Is Moroccan the child born to a Moroccan father" (Kingdom of Morocco 1958, art. no. 6). The Tunisian code makes the equivalent statement: "Is Tunisian the child born to a Tunisian father" (République Tunisienne 1998a, art. no. 6).

In Morocco, *jus sanguinis* through mothers operates only when combined with *jus soli*, except when the father is unknown. A Moroccan mother may pass nationality to her child under the following specific circumstances: the child of a Moroccan mother and unknown father is Moroccan (art. no. 6, para 2) as is a child born in Morocco to a Moroccan mother and a stateless father (art. no. 7, para. 1). A child born in Morocco to a foreign father may obtain the Moroccan nationality under the following conditions: the child must reside permanently in Morocco and declare the intention to become Moroccan two years before reaching majority. Based on *jus soli*, the provision applies only to children born in Morocco. Moroccan women married to non-Moroccans and giving birth abroad, therefore, are unable to pass nationality to their children. As Moulay Rchid (1991, 76) remarks, a mother may pass Moroccan nationality to her child only under restricted circumstances.

In Tunisia the gendering of citizenship rights also permeates the provisions for the passing of nationality to children although women have gained an important right in the reforms of 1993. Because paternal filiation serves in all cases as a source of nationality rights, fathers have a definite advantage. A Tunisian father automatically passes nationality to his children regardless of whether the children were born on Tunisian national territory or abroad (art. no. 6). A child whose father and grandfather were born in Tunisia also is Tunisian (art. no. 7).

Before the reforms of 1993, *jus sanguinis* through mothers operated in Tunisia only in combination with *jus soli* or under restricted conditions similar to those in effect in Morocco: if her child was born on the Tunisian territory from a foreign father, if her child's father was unknown, if the father had no nationality or if his nationality was unknown (art. no. 6). Before 1993, *jus sanguinis* through mothers alone thus was not sufficient to confer nationality to a child born abroad to a Tunisian mother and a foreign father. Such a child could obtain Tunisian nationality only if the child made the request one year before majority, if no one raised opposition for a period of two years, and by special decree from the president of the Republic. These restrictions were in contrast to the automatic effect of *jus sanguinis* through fathers.

Tunisia took time to change the nationality provisions for children born abroad to a Tunisian mother and a foreign father. The Convention of Copenhagen of 1979, the Elimination of All Forms of Discrimination Against Women, stated: "States will grant women and men equal rights with respect to the nationality of their children" (quoted in Chamari 1991, 118). This convention reiterated the New York Convention of 20 February 1957 on women's nationality rights. Although Tunisia signed the New York Convention of 1957, the Tunisian government criticized the Copenhagen Convention of 1979 in the following terms: "The government of the Republic of Tunisia expresses reservations with respect to the dispositions of paragraph 2 of article no. 9 of the present Convention, as they would go against the dispositions of article no. 6 of the Tunisian *Code de Nationalité*" (quoted in Chamari 1991, 118).

Despite the reservations expressed about the 1979 convention, the Tunisian government nevertheless revised the *Code de Nationalité* in 1993. The reforms of 1993 introduced a significant change toward greater gender equality in that they expanded women's rights in regard to the attribution of nationality to children. Examined elsewhere, the complex reasons for the change in the four-year period involved a changing political climate, a regime open to change, and the role of women's rights advocates who were active in Tunisia in the early 1990s (Charrad 1997, 1998).

The important reform of 1993 concerned mothers as the source of *jus sanguinis* irrespective of *jus soli*. Addressing the issue of children born outside the Tunisian territory, the reform allowed a Tunisian woman married to a foreign man to pass nationality to children born abroad. Article no. 12 of the revised code states: "Becomes Tunisian, if he or she makes the request within one year before reaching the age of majority, a child born abroad from a Tunisian mother and a foreign father" (République Tunisienne 1998a, art. no. 12). This is a major innovation. The provision in effect introduced a new dimension in nationality rights: mothers are now a source of nationality rights in and by themselves. They become a source of *jus sanguinis* as much as fathers and independently of *jus soli*. The reform is also a major step when seen in the context of the cultural taboo against Muslim women marrying non-Muslims (such women often became outcasts in the Islamic tradition). For the first time, a Tunisian mother living abroad and married to a non-Tunisian man, even a non-Muslim, may pass the Tunisian nationality to her children born abroad.

Although the two countries differ in regard to the transmission of nationality to children, they are fairly similar with respect to the transmission of nationality to a foreign spouse. In both countries the procedure for a man to pass nationality to his foreign wife is not automatic as it is with children, but it is simple and straightforward. The Moroccan code only requires that the married couple should have established a permanent and regular residence in Morocco for at least two years. Article no. 10 (Kingdom of Morocco 1958), entitled "Acquisition of the Moroccan Nationality Through Marriage," reads as follows: "A foreign woman who has married a Moroccan man may, after the couple has established a permanent and regular residence in Morocco for at least two years, make a request to the Minister of Justice so as to obtain the Moroccan nationality." Foreign men married to Moroccan women cannot obtain nationality so easily. That issue is addressed in the sections of the code entitled "Exceptional Dispositions" and "Naturalization." The "Exceptional Dispositions" (art. no. 45) apply to anyone who is originally from a country where the language of the majority of the population is Arabic and its religion Islam. The dispositions concern only a person who belongs to that majority.

This means that a Moroccan woman may only transmit Moroccan nationality to her foreign husband if he comes from an Islamic and Arabic-speaking country. Article no. 45 reads as follows: "Every person who is originally from a country where the majority of the population consists in a community that has Arabic as its language and Islam as its religion and who belongs to that community may opt for the Moroccan nationality [in case of] . . . a marriage, never dissolved, with a Moroccan woman and a residence in Morocco for at least one year" (Kingdom of Morocco 1958, art. no. 45). The acquisition of nationality by a foreign man because of marriage to a Moroccan woman is treated as a case among others that fall under exceptional circumstances. The Moroccan code states that a man who is originally from a predominantly Muslim and Arabic-speaking country and who himself is Muslim and speaks Arabic may obtain the Moroccan nationality under any of the following conditions: (1) having had his permanent residence in Morocco for at least fifteen years; (2) having held a public office in the Moroccan civil service for at least ten years; and (3) because of a marriage, never dissolved, with a Moroccan woman in combination with a permanent residence in Morocco for at least one year (art. no. 45).

If they neither are Muslim nor speak Arabic, foreign husbands of Moroccan women can only become Moroccan by following the rules of "naturalization" that apply to foreigners in general (art. no. 11). The rules in this case are not much different from rules in many other countries in the world in that they involve such criteria as having resided in Morocco for at least five years, knowing the language, having adequate means of financial support, and so forth. In the case of naturalization of a foreign man from a non-Arabic speaking and non-Muslim country, marriage to a Moroccan woman is left out of the frame of reference. The Moroccan code deals with such a foreign man independently from his marriage to a Moroccan citizen. Marriage in and of itself thus serves as a basis for the spouse to acquire nationality in the case of a Moroccan man married with a foreign woman. Marriage also serves as a source of nationality rights among many other "exceptional" sources in the case of Muslim and Arabic-speaking husbands. It does not at all serve as such a basis for other categories of foreign husbands.

In Tunisia the implications of marriage for acquiring nationality have remained unequal for men and women. The provisions, promulgated in the code in 1957 and 1963 and still valid today, enable Tunisian men easily to pass nationality to their foreign wives, something that the law appears to encourage. If the wife of a Tunisian man has lost her nationality of origin because of her marriage, she automatically becomes Tunisian (art. no. 13 of the code). As in Morocco, a foreign wife who still has her nationality of origin may become Tunisian by making a request to the relevant authorities in the Ministry of Justice as long as the couple has resided in Tunisia for a minimum of two years (art. no. 14).

Like the Moroccan Code, the Tunisian Code also treats as "naturalization" the process by which a foreign man married to a Tunisian woman becomes Tunisian. In contrast to the Moroccan Code, however, the Tunisian code only requires that the husband know Arabic and the couple reside in Tunisia at the time of the request. Article no. 21 of the Tunisian code states: "May be naturalized the foreign man married to a Tunisian woman if the couple resides in Tunisia at the time the request is made" (République Tunisienne 1998a, 9). Requiring a knowledge of Arabic in all cases of naturalization, article no. 23 reads as follows: "No one may be naturalized . . . if he does not show a sufficient knowledge, appropriate to his condition, of the Arabic language" (République Tunisienne 1998a, 10).

In imposing the knowledge of Arabic and the general criteria of naturalization to foreign husbands but not to foreign wives, the *Code de Nationalité* treats male and female Tunisian citizens differently. In making no mention of religion or national origin, the Tunisian code is, nevertheless, more lenient than the Moroccan code. Presumably, anyone who can learn Arabic qualifies for naturalization.

Religion was introduced in an indirect way, however, by a government decree in 1973. The decree addressed the issue of a marriage between a Muslim woman and a non-Muslim man. It ordered public authorities to refrain from performing and registering such a marriage (Chamari 1991, 43). The objective stated by the government was the protection of Tunisian identity from Western cultural influences. The taboo about a Muslim woman marrying a non-Muslim man persists in Tunisia as it does in Morocco. The marriage contract of a Tunisian woman who marries a foreign non-Muslim man abroad, thus, is not recognized in Tunisia, and such a Tunisian woman cannot pass nationality to her foreign husband. One way this is usually handled in practice is through a conversion of the foreign husband to Islam before the marriage contract.

There are noteworthy differences between the two countries in regard to the marriage of a Muslim woman with a non-Muslim man, however. The taboo is expressed in one of the fundamental texts of the country in Morocco, whereas it appears only in a decree in Tunisia. In the official ranking of legislative texts, a decree has less weight and can more easily be revoked than an article in a *Code de Nationalité*. Second, a foreign husband's origin in an Arabic-speaking and Muslim country, which matters in Morocco, does not in Tunisia. Regardless of his origins, the non-Muslim foreign husband of a Tunisian woman always has the option of converting to Islam as a legal solution to the recognition of the marriage and the acquisition of Tunisian nationality. Nevertheless, the issue of a marriage between a Muslim woman and a non-Muslim man remains a highly contested point caught in contradictions between different legislative texts in Tunisia.

Although the two countries have fairly similar regulations on the transmission of nationality to foreign spouses, they differ considerably on the transmission of nationality to children. Moroccan women living abroad and married to a non-Muslim lack the legal capacity to pass Moroccan nationality to their children born abroad. In contrast, Tunisian women in the same situation can confer nationality to their children. The Tunisian provision of 1993 represents a major change with respect to women as a source of *jus sanguinis* in the attribution of nationality to children. Whereas in the past matrilineal descent could combine with *jus soli* to confer nationality rights to a child, it now stands in and of itself.

Widely applauded in Tunisia and elsewhere as a major gain for women, the 1993 provision has granted a critically important citizenship right to women. In introducing matrilineal descent as a legitimate and sufficient reason for *jus sanguinis* regardless of *jus soli*, the provision of 1993 challenges the special status of patrilineality as the source of membership in the political community. Calling into question the privileges of the patrilineage, the provision is an important step toward allowing women to become equal citizens in the nation-state.

Codes of Personal Status: Power of Kin or Basic Personal Rights

If one accepts Rawls's concept of citizenship as involving "equal basic rights and liberties" (quoted in Shafir 1998, 19), then one must include in these rights and liberties in today's world the right to choose one's spouse, the right to divorce, the right to have custody of one's children, and the right to inherit property from relatives. If women are to become equal citizens in the political community of the nation-state, as defined in the liberal tradition, then they are entitled to these rights as much as are men. The analysis that follows centers on marriage, divorce, and custody of children. In the context of this chapter, rights in these areas are referred to as basic personal rights and are treated as an essential arena of citizenship.

Family law as presented in texts called *Codes of Personal Status* in the Maghrib includes a construct of self. By construct of self in the context of the Middle East, I mean whether the person is defined primarily as an autonomous individual or as a member of a patrilineage. The codes regulate family relationships (Charrad in press, 1996, 1994). As the title suggests, they also define the status of persons in the social environment, which is the aspect emphasized here. The codes indicate how men and women are constituted as citizens: equal before the law or as two different classes of citizens with respect to family and personal life. They show whether women are recognized as equal citizens in the nation-state or are treated as subordinate to men in their roles as daughters, wives, mothers, siblings, nieces, or aunts.

Codes of Personal Status present a different dominant construct of self in Morocco and Tunisia. Called the *Mudawwana* (Chafi 1996), the Moroccan code offers a construct of self as rooted in lineages. It sanctions the extended patrilineal kin group, which it identifies as the major locus of social solidarity. By the same token, it differentiates personal rights by gender and gives power over women to men as husbands and to men as kin. Presenting a different dominant construct, the Tunisian Code of Personal Status, called the *Majalla* (République Tunisienne 1997), underplays the ties within the extended patrilineal kinship network. It defines the individual as the focus of rights and obligations. The Tunisian Code of Personal Status offers a construct of self as having greater autonomy from kin-based formations and grants women more basic personal rights than does its Moroccan counterpart. The different constructs apply to both men and women. The contrast between Tunisian and Moroccan law is sharper for women than for men, however, because women face more restrictions as a result of the form of kin-based patriarchy that permeates the social organization of patrilineages.

Family law has gone through phases in Morocco and Tunisia since both countries achieved sovereignty from French colonial rule in 1956. The first and most important phase, which occurred shortly after the formation of the newly sovereign state, set the stage for all developments since. Morocco promulgated the *Mudawwana* in several installments in 1957–58, and Tunisia enacted the *Majalla* on 13 August 1956. The next most significant phase occurred in 1993 when both countries reformed their family law. The

1993 reforms respected the overall thrust of the law in existence in each country. In contrast to the actions of the 1950s, which occurred in the absence of feminist demands, the reforms of 1993 involved in both countries place pressures on the political system from women's associations and women's rights advocates who demanded greater rights in family law (Charrad 1997). The changes were substantial in Tunisia and satisfied in large part the concerns of women's rights advocates. In Morocco the changes came considerably short of what women's rights advocates wanted.

The first and major step of the 1950s started on divergent paths in Tunisia and Morocco. Tunisia made drastic legal reforms that had the consequence of changing the legal status of women in substantial ways and of expanding their individual rights with respect to family life and personal status. In contrast, Morocco preserved the *status quo* by reiterating the principles of the *shari'a* while presenting them in a more concise and formally organized code. In this process the basic personal rights of women were not recognized. Instead, the power of lineages and the privileges of men were preserved.

Following the *shari'a,* the Moroccan *Mudawwana* enacted in 1957–58 retained the role of the matrimonial guardian as the person representing the bride in the marriage contract. The matrimonial guardian, who had to be a man (usually the father or a surrogate chosen by relatives), was to express his consent to the marriage on behalf of the bride. In principle he had no legal right to force the woman into marriage. The law opened a loophole, however, in making the following exception: the power of the matrimonial guardian was restored if the woman had engaged in "bad conduct" with a man, in which case her matrimonial guardian could coerce her to marry. These provisions meant that a woman did not possess the individual right as a citizen to give her consent directly to her own marriage. She also lacked the right to marry a person not approved of by the guardian.

The *Mudawwana* also retained repudiation, or the husband's privilege to terminate the marriage at will without a court decision. The repudiation simply had to be recorded by two witnesses. Polygamy was maintained, and a man could thus have as many as four wives. By enacting the above provisions the newly sovereign state of Morocco in the 1950s gave men and women highly unequal citizenship rights with respect to both entering and terminating marriage.

The Moroccan reforms of 1993 made only minor changes. They brought a slight modification to polygamy and repudiation, both of which continued to be legal. With respect to polygamy, the reforms introduced the stipulation that the notaries in charge of writing the marriage contract should receive a written statement from a judge who would authorize a polyga-

mous marriage only after having considered fairness to all the women involved. The 1993 reforms maintained repudiation and thus the unilateral
right of the husband to end the marriage at will. The revised law now required, however, that a man repudiate his wife in the presence of a judge
and after arbitration.

Although marriage continued to require the presence of a matrimonial
guardian, the Moroccan reforms of 1993 reduced his power a little. The
matrimonial guardian (the father or a surrogate), in effect is the voice of the
patrilineage and the symbol of its power over women. The 1993 reforms
kept the provision according to which a woman could not enter into marriage without being represented by a matrimonial guardian who would consent to the marriage on her behalf. Article no. 12 as modified by the reforms
of 1993 indicated, however, that the matrimonial guardian could agree to
the marriage only with the woman's consent (Chafi 1996, 30). Expressing
the view that the Moroccan reforms of 1993 did little to improve women's
citizenship rights with respect to family and personal status, Najat Razi, the
president of the Association Marocaine des Droits des Femmes (Moroccan
Association of Women's Rights) declared that, "[d]iscrimination [was]
maintained and the *Mudawwana* [was] still in part contrary to international
conventions" (*Le Monde* 1993). Even after the reforms of 1993, Moroccan
law continued to sanction the supremacy of the patrilineage. The codification of kin-based patriarchy remained and so did the limitations placed on
women's basic personal rights.

By contrast to Moroccan law, the Tunisian *Majalla* of 1956 shifted to a
considerable degree the construct of self from a member of a lineage to an
autonomous individual with basic personal rights. In one of the most dramatic provisions in the Islamic Middle East, the *Majalla* of 1956 outlawed
polygamy. This meant that men and women had equal citizenship rights to
contract a marriage. The *Majalla* also abolished repudiation and matrimonial guardianship altogether. A divorce could now only occur in court, and
the law allowed women to file for divorce on the same grounds as men. The
Tunisian reform has increased women's ability to terminate marriages in
practice (Charrad 1994; Chater 1992, 235).

By suppressing matrimonial guardianship, the *Majalla* redefined marriage
and placed the woman in charge of her own marriage contract. The right to
marry thus was shifted from the patrilineage to the individual as a basic
personal right. The abolition of the matrimonial guardian's prerogative undermined the legal control that men used to have over their female relatives
and defined compulsory marriages as illegal. In ending the unilateral privilege of the husband to terminate the marriage by repudiation, the *Majalla*
offered women some protection from the whims of their husbands in regard

to the dissolution of marriage. Tunisia law thus reduced the power of men over women and increased women's citizenship rights with respect to entering and terminating marriage.

The amendments that appeared in Tunisia over the years after the critical step of 1956 modified particular points of the code and brought clarification. A significant amendment appeared in 1981 in regard to divorce and guardianship of children. It made it possible for a woman to receive lifelong alimony after divorce instead of the lump sum that was previously the rule. The law of 1981 made the mother automatically the guardian of a child in case of the father's death, something that had not been true earlier. Guardianship in this context is different from custody, which refers to day-to-day care. The former consists of legal responsibilities for the child, such as signing school papers or authorizing a passport. Before 1981, if the father died, the mother usually had custody but not guardianship. The law previously in effect required the judge to select a guardian among a wide range of relatives. Judges usually chose a male relative to serve as the child's guardian. The law of 1981 brought custody and guardianship together in case of the father's death and made the mother the recipient of both. It challenged the supremacy of the paternal line and, thus, of the patrilineage.

The next important phase in Tunisia, represented by the reforms of 1993, answered in part demands by women's associations and women's rights advocates. The amended Tunisian Code of Personal Status of 1993 dropped an earlier offensive clause according to which a wife had to obey her husband. The reforms of 1993 also increased a mother's chance to obtain guardianship once she had been granted custody after divorce. Previously, the father had guardianship (or legal power over the child) after divorce, even when the mother had custody (or day-to-day care). Now, a mother could obtain guardianship if she could show to a judge that the father did not respect the best interest of the child or that he misused his guardianship privileges. This gave a divorced mother a legal recourse in case of serious conflicts with her former husband, who no longer automatically obtained guardianship. The reform called into question the power of the patrilineage over children.

Some of the Tunisian reforms have in common that they lessen the power of men as members of patrilineages at the same time as they increase the rights of women as individuals. Beyond the specific provisions, and considered from a broader perspective, the two bodies of legislation offer very different constructs of self. Moroccan law locates the self essentially in the patrilineage, whereas Tunisian law gives greater space to individuals with their own rights and responsibilities. In accordance with these different constructs of self, the law continues to legitimate kin-based patriarchy and the power of lineages in Morocco, whereas it challenges them in Tunisia. As a result, women have greater basic personal rights in Tunisia.

Rights in the Constitution:
Voting and Public Office

I now turn to a third arena of citizenship represented by voting and eligibility to public office. In both countries the constitution adopts universalistic values in declaring equal rights before the law for all citizens including women. The respective constitutions of Morocco and Tunisia gave women the right to vote in 1959. The two countries were part of a general worldwide trend in which the discourse on universal rights increasingly included women as inclusive models of citizenship came to predominate. An earlier historical pattern that prevailed in Western Europe, the United States, and many countries in Asia and Latin America involved separate steps, with national independence occurring first, then male suffrage, then female suffrage.

In the mid–twentieth century, however, postcolonial nation-states tended to establish male and female suffrage at the same time. Ramirez, Soysal, and Shanahan (1997) suggest that these developments are attributable to world models, international standards, and transnational influences rather than to local or national forces. They write that "[t]he franchise has become institutionalized worldwide as a taken-for-granted feature of national citizenship and an integral component of nation-state identity" (Ramirez, Soysal, and Shanahan 1997, 735).

The Moroccan Constitution currently in effect, revised and approved by national referendum on 13 September 1996, gives equal rights to men and women with respect to the franchise. It also states the obligation for all Moroccans to defend the kingdom. The text reads as follows: "All Moroccans shall be equal before the law [art. no. 6]. . . . Men and women shall enjoy equal political rights. Any citizen of age enjoying his or her civil and political rights shall be eligible to vote [art. no. 8]. All citizens shall contribute to the defense of the Country" (Kingdom of Morocco 1996, art. no. 16, 6–9). Moroccan women also have the right of eligibility as article no. 13 indicates that "[o]pportunities for . . . public offices shall be uniformly open to all citizens."

In the same vein the Tunisian Constitution, amended on 12 July 1988, makes the following provision in article no. 20: "Every citizen who has had the Tunisian nationality for at least five years and who has attained twenty years of age has the right to vote" (République Tunisienne 1998b, 10–11). Tunisian women also are eligible for public office. Similar to the phrasing of the Moroccan Constitution, the Tunisian Constitution (art. no. 6) states: "All citizens have the same rights and the same duties. They are equal before the law" (quoted in Chamari 1991, 114).

One indicator of the extent to which some of the citizenship rights abstractly granted in the Constitution are implemented in practice is women's access to public office. Such access reflects women's participation in decision-making positions within the state apparatus. The more women there are in public life and in government positions, the more there is a possibility for women's issues to receive attention in circles of power. The presence of women in parliament, in decision-making positions in government ministries, and in top-level managerial posts also helps forge an image of women as holding authority. It contributes to undermining prevailing notions of female identity as anchored only in family and kinship.

On this dimension, too, Tunisia does better than Morocco, and the difference is considerable. Data are available for both countries in 1994 (United Nations 1995, 172–73, 183–84). Women occupied 7 percent of parliamentary seats in Tunisia against 1 percent in Morocco. The difference between the two countries is even greater with respect to ministerial and subministerial level positions. The publication of the United Nations that I use as a source for this information defines ministerial level positions as ministers or equivalent and subministerial level positions as including deputy or assistant ministers, secretaries of state or permanent secretaries, deputies of state or directors of government. The same source indicates that women held 3.6 percent of twenty-eight ministerial posts in 1994 and 14 percent of thirty-six subministerial positions in Tunisia. By contrast, Morocco had no women in either a ministerial or subministerial post. Among high-level administrators and managers, a category that includes legislators, senior officials, and corporate managers, women represented 9 percent in Tunisia in 1992. No equivalent information is available for Morocco on this particular point in the United Nations source.

◆   ◆   ◆

I compared Morocco and Tunisia in three major arenas of citizenship. In all three the evidence suggests that women have greater individual rights in Tunisia than in Morocco, even though differences between men and women persist in Tunisia. With respect to conditions for membership in the political community of the nation-state, patrilineality, or male descent, occupies a more prominent place in Morocco than in Tunisia where mothers can much more readily pass nationality to their children. Wives find themselves in a slightly better position to pass nationality to their foreign husbands in Tunisia than in Morocco. In the arena of basic personal rights as

defined in family and personal status law, the differences between the two
countries are even more dramatic. In Morocco the law continues to sanction kin-based patriarchy in that it legitimates the power of lineages and
curtails women's basic personal rights to marry, divorce, and have guardianship of children. Tunisian law, in contrast, challenges the power of lineages
and establishes individual rights and obligations for all, including women, in
several aspects of the law. In the third arena, voting and eligibility for public
office, women in both countries have the same formally granted rights as
declared in the Constitution. In actuality, however, women have greater
access to public office in Tunisia than in Morocco.

The divergent forms taken by citizenship are the outcome of a different
relationship between the state and political forces anchored in kin-based
formations. The latter continue to occupy a significant place in Moroccan
society and politics, whereas they lost ground in Tunisia during the period
when the sovereign national state developed at the end of colonization. As
the site where issues of citizenship are played out, the nation-state defines
the forms taken by citizenship in each country.

Differences in forms of citizenship between Tunisia and Morocco emerged
with key policy orientations implemented when each newly formed state
equipped the country with a national body of legislation after the achievement of national sovereignty in the mid-1950s. Once the basic policies were
in place, the die was cast for the following decades. In Tunisia, the newly
formed sovereign state had an interest in transferring the allegiance of the
population from particularistic loyalties to itself, and attempted to undermine traditional kin-based groups. In Morocco, the state maintained particularistic loyalties by placing them under a supra-authority (Charrad in press,
1996, 1990).

The society where lineages historically have played a greater political role
and where patrilineality occupies a more prominent place in the law is the
one where women have more limited citizenship rights. When the law cod-
ifies patrilineality and kin-based patriarchy, as most of it does in Morocco,
women's citizenship rights are restricted. When the law challenges patrilineality and kin-based patriarchy, as most of it does in Tunisia, there is a
greater chance for the enfranchisement of women as citizens in the nation-
state. Becoming a citizen as understood in today's world involves the acquisition of individual rights. Patrilineality and kin-based patriarchy reinforce
each other to prevent women from becoming full citizens and from gaining
individual rights.

The cutting edge of debates on citizenship in different regions of the
world reflects the key issues involved in the future of each region. Currently
in the West, issues of equal rights and liberties for all are central to debates

that consider citizenship in relation to social class, ethnic diversity, welfare, multiculturalism, multilinguism, and immigration (Young 1989; Orloff 1993; Tilly 1996; Shafir 1998; Soysal 1994). These issues are at the heart of the character of Western societies in the future. In the Maghrib and most of the Middle East, some of the sharpest debates center on gender and the incorporation of women into the body politic. The future character of Middle Eastern societies and states in effect is being contested when women's full integration into the political community is debated. Issues of women's rights in that region unavoidably involve questions about the fundamental place of kinship ties in the social fabric and the role of kin-based social formations in politics. These issues call into question what has been at the very heart of social organization in the Maghrib and the Middle East.

5

The Islamic State and Gendered Citizenship in Sudan

SONDRA HALE

LIKE MANY FORMER COLONIES of Africa or the Middle East, Sudan (said to bridge "Arab" and "Black Africa") is the product of colonial invention. As a country with artificial boundaries that function to contain some 582 ethnic groups and more than 110 languages, the process of defining *citizenship* and of *Sudanization* has been strenuous.

In the immediate preindependence era of the 1950s, the term *Sudanization* described Sudanese nationals taking over jobs held by expatriates (mostly British). Now, as Paul Doornbos argues, the term refers to "the process of conversion of ethnically diverse population groups living in the Sudanese periphery to the dominant and prestigious lifestyle of the central Nile valley region" (1988, 100). In the past one might have used the term *Arabization* to describe the above process. In reality, much of the interaction of diverse people in Sudan more accurately can be called *Islamization*. Yet this is a term the current northern Muslim-dominated government has backed away from, just as it has backed away from "Arab" as its centerpiece ethnic identity.

Somehow, in building an Islamic nation (*umma*), Sudanese state authorities and Islamist ideologues must move forward with an Islam that is pan-Islamic, one that has the power to subsume ethnic identities, and one that is the primary tool for forging a unified nation. In such a situation, *nationality* and *citizenship* in the nation become salient rallying points. I propose that this particular task of forging a unified nation cannot be accomplished without molding a woman citizen of the Islamic state and that this has been recognized by the Islamists in power.

As the only Sunni Islamic Republic in the world (since 1989), the northern-dominated Sudanese state is pioneering a number of experiments related to identity, citizenship, nationality, and religious law and their intersections.[1] The intentional and unintentional/indirect gendering of some of these experiments has highlighted institutions, legal apparatuses, attitudes, and the like, which were heretofore seen as "gender neutral" or simply not analyzed in terms of gender. An exploration of the contemporary Sudanese state's experiments with religious law and political power may shed some light on previous eras, enabling one, for example, to contrast colonial and "postcolonial" discourses about women. Such an historical excursion is not, however, the goal of this chapter.

Although the focus of this chapter is on the contemporary era, it is useful to mention that northern Sudanese society has experienced many shifts in essentialist views of women and men and their relationships. A Sudanese notion of "woman" as an autonomous entity, a female being, separable from men and from family, has little or no reference in preindependence Sudan. British colonial discourse introduced the concept of woman-as-other-than-man (a central idea in modernist discourse), which ultimately generated gender-identity politics. In mimicking the colonial ideology, "mother" emerged as an essentialized category, and "motherhood," as a glorified status. Later, the colonial state and its successors constructed (through radio and later, television) the "working woman," an appropriate role for educated women in the modernizing/modernist Sudan.

Islamists today are attempting to abrogate some elements of colonial and postcolonial state gender ideologies while retaining others. Although they may interpret the relationship of men and women in *shari' a* (Islamic law) as complementary, because of the state's need to control the gender division of labor and to repudiate Western values and deny Western imported goods, the representation of woman as a separate entity is now conflated into

1. Fieldwork for this project was partially funded by a grant from the University of California, Los Angeles, (UCLA) Center for the Study of Women and the G. E. von Grunebaum Center for Near Eastern Studies. I thank my research assistants, Amal Abdel Rahman and Sunita Pitamber in Khartoum and William Young and Sherifa Zuhur at UCLA. Fieldwork in Eritrea was funded by the UCLA James S. Coleman African Studies Center, the Center for the Study of Women, and International Studies and Overseas Programs.

Here I use some of the field data first published in chapter 6 of my book and in a related article (Hale 1996a, 1996b). I have relied on data from several segments of my fieldwork in Sudan, extending from 1961 to 1988, and on recent dialogues I have had with exile communities in Addis Ababa, Ethiopia, Asmara, Eritrea, and Cairo, Egypt (in 1994, 1996, 1997, and 1998). The examination of the National Islamic Front (NIF) (successor to the *Ikhwan*) is based primarily on research in Khartoum in 1988.

woman/family and sometimes woman/family/*umma* (Islamic nation). These parallel representations of women may be contradictory: the modern woman as the embodiment of the Islamic nation (bearing and rearing children, tending the hearth, and purportedly, but not in actuality, acting as the moral gatekeeper) must also carry out the tasks of nation building (earning wages, perhaps holding a minor office, driving a car, getting an education, and the like). Thus, she becomes the modern "Islamic woman," in line with National Islamic Front (NIF) ideology. But these are not always roles of complementarity, and the identities may be abstract, that is, without much relationship to the daily lives of women nor to their expressions of "belonging" or alienation.

I focus on the contemporary era that began with the 1989 military-backed Islamist (NIF qua Muslim Brotherhood) overthrow of the 1985 elected government and is limited to an analysis of *northern* Sudanese society. I have been exploring the invention of the "ideal" Sudanese citizen as "modern Muslim" and the ways in which women are crucial to this construction.

For Sudanese women this is a crucial juncture in their historically variable relationships to the state, to the NIF, and to the oppositional National Democratic Alliance (NDA). The NIF is, de facto, the government; the NDA is, in essence, a government in exile in Asmara, Eritrea. This era is also a delicate point in the relationship of northern and southern Sudanese women.[2]

The mobilization of radical political Islam in the 1980s and 1990s was relatively unchallenged and successful. Success came easier because for centuries northern Sudan had been dominated by mainly Sufi sectarian politics, with frequent intervention of, or in collaboration with, the military. Part of the recruitment and mobilization success was also a result of the mobilization of public consciousness about citizenship in an Islamic state, so much broader than localized Sufism. That this citizenship is increasingly and more conspicuously being *gendered* is the main theme of this chapter.[3]

2. In this chapter, however, I will *not* deal with the complicated north/south conflict, the problematic relationship of women from the two regions, and the ambiguous concepts of "citizenship" and identity as these apply to southerners.

3. To analyze the shift in identity construction of the woman citizen–mother, Muslim, worker, soldier—I have used INTERNET sources and recent interviews and dialogues with Sudanese in exile. The regime has especially been reacting to the 1995 establishment of the National Democratic Alliance (NDA) in Asmara, Eritrea, and to 1997–98 military attacks along its eastern borders and on the southern front. Additionally, I have relied on recent informal fieldwork material on the NDA collected in Asmara and Cairo (in 1996, 1997, and 1998). Another of my sources on recent conditions and activities of Sudanese women is Fatima

I comment first on the difficulties of defining "Sudanese," what it means to have legal citizenship and how particular groups and categories of people have, de facto, been deprived of citizenship. The nature of contemporary Sudanese society is a reflection of a long history of shrinking and expanding states, political entities, and ethnic/language identities. "Sudan" as a concept and as a contiguous, official political territory was constructed by colonials. After carving out and claiming one large entity, the British then administered the north and south differently, sharply defining a "Black Christian/Pagan, African south" and an "Arab/Muslim north" when in many ways such a distinction is spurious. Within these artificially constructed political and ethnic boundaries, the British imposed their own *gender* constructs as these served them. Until the 1960s, however, women were undefined as legal entities in British common and civil law, which became Sudanese civil law. Only in *shari'a,* and in the 1980s constitutional reflections of *shari'a* were gender constructions, to some extent, spelled out. "Permanent" and "transitional" constitutions carved an image of Sudanese women as entitled to rights but vulnerable and in need of protections.[4]

In the 1990s, against a backdrop of "radical/political Islam," a number of potentially transformative processes took place. In fact, not only was Sudan's revolution one of the most active and seemingly successful Islamic movements in the world, but the NIF was attempting to transform national identity.[5] The Islamic state has been employing a number of strategies to effect cultural hegemony. One tactic is the manipulation of identity politics (including gender), which includes the invention of the "New Muslim Woman" and some women's resistance to being "reinvented." Resistance may include collaboration in the reinvention of national identity as "Muslim," as it is disaggregated from "Arab," a striking departure from the vigorous putative claims to Arab genealogy that have characterized Sudanese identity quests for many decades. The two categories ("Arab" and "Mus-

Ahmed Ibrahim. Ustaza Fatima has headed the Sudanese Women's Union (WU), affiliate of the Sudanese Communist Party (SCP), for more than forty years. See Hale 1991, 1993, 1996a. Ustaza Fatima spent one year with me at UCLA (1996–97) where she was a Fellow at the Rockefeller Institute for the Study of Gender in Africa.

4. See Hale (1996a, 137–39) for a summary of Osman (1985) and an analysis of the protective nature of Sudanese constitutions with regard to women.

5. In 1971 the progressive factions within the military, in coalition with civil society, carried out an abortive coup d'état. In reaction, military dictator President Jaffar Nimieri (who had come to power as a leftist) began to move to the right, embracing Islam personally and politically as his deus ex machina. By 1983 he had imposed the notorious "September Laws," harsh versions of *shari'a,* setting the stage for the 1989 installation of an Islamic state. *Shari'a* has remained intact.

lim") had historically been conflated but are now being treated as discrete. A second process is the legitimizing of the Islamic state through a process of "authenticating" the culture; women are key to that authentication.

As one might expect, however, women are resisting; they are both embracing and rejecting one of the main mechanisms men in power are using to create and maintain hegemony, that is, trying to position women to serve the culture not only as the carriers of culture but of morality as well. Following Virginia Sapiro:

> Regarding women as the carriers of both culture and morality but, at the same time, as having an essentially weaker grasp than men on culture and morality may appear a logical contradiction at first blush, but it is no cultural contradiction. It is a cornerstone of the views of women found in diverse pillars of cultural explanation, in Islamic, Christian, and Jewish theology, in Aristotle, and in Freud. (Sapiro 1993, 52)

Women, therefore, are fashioned through the media, the schools, the legal apparatuses, and community organizations to develop an "authentic" Sudanese culture based on an "original" Islam. As women leaders have fashioned it for themselves, however, this is to be an Islam separate from, although connected to, "Arab" culture. In fact, I have been determining to what degree it is the women themselves, as primary actors in their own story, who are creating (inventing) their own identity apart from an Arab culture that many women see as patriarchal and oppressive and to what degree they collaborate in their placement by men as the nexus and embodiment of the culture.

Within the overarching framework of state construction of citizenship and identity, I account for (1) the Sudanese state's manipulation of religious ideology; (2) the reinvention of cultural identities to conform to state ideology; and (3) the centrality of gender in this process. These processes are, of course, dynamic, reflecting the changing interests of international capital and the collaborating bourgeoisie. This is a gendered process, not only with consideration for the impact on women and gender arrangements but for the importance of women and men, as self-interested gendered actors in the process.

The "Authentic" Citizen

Most scholars and observers of social or historical aspects of Sudan dwell upon, or at least mention, the social and cultural diversity of the area.

Sources also stress the parade of ethnic migrations, invasions, displacement, and mixing of populations. The categories "Arab," "Afro-Arab," "Nubian," "African," and the like have been debated for some time within and without twentieth-century Sudan: as self-labels (sometimes chauvinistic or xeno-phobic); as imposed categories (oftentimes to exclude or dominate); and as putative claims. Nonetheless, until recently northern Sudan's "Arab" iden-tity prevailed in the literature and in terms of the culture of dominance.

For complex reasons, state figures are drawing new distinctions between "Arab" and "Muslim." The former Speaker of the Assembly, philosopher/politician Hasan al-Turabi, has made public statements that construct a fine distinction as did a number of the Islamist women interviewed for this research.

I explain the centrifugal/centripetal strategy related to Arab identity and the forms of identity manipulation the current regime is using. The implicit state rationales are as follows. First, emphasizing Arab identity hinders north-south integration under Islam. Simply, it is easier to "become" a Muslim than to become an Arab. A distance from Arab identity also allows the history of Arab slaving in the south to be minimized. Second, women, a necessary force in the "Islamic Trend," are more willing to see themselves as potentially liberated from certain patriarchal Arab customs upon a return to "pure" Islam. Third, acceptance by the outside world, especially the Arab/Middle Eastern world, as integral to the "Middle East" is facilitated by Sudanese becoming participants, even leaders, in the region's Islamic move-ments; whereas, being embraced as "authentically Arab" had always been problematic. The contradictory elements in these three strains are evident.

A fourth reason for building identity and citizenship around Islamic rather than Arab identity relates to gender constructs as well. It is significant that Islam can be used for militaristic mobilization and that women can be embraced as an integral part of that. Thus, the necessity of building a *mou-jahadeen,* a holy army, supported by the citizenry of the Islamic nation has included recruiting both men and women and adjusting gender constructs accordingly.

Citizenship, Gender, and the State

Two distinct but intertwined concepts are relevant to women: (1) citi-zenship and women's rights of citizenship and (2) issues of nationality. Above I mentioned the decades-long campaign of the dominant culture (Arab/Nubian riverain culture) to build a unified nationality. Upon inde-pendence (1956), Sudanese "nationals" fleshed out the first Nationality

Law (1957) in which nationality was to be granted to or confirmed for an individual based on the nationality of the father. That nationality was itself predicated on the father having been in Sudan since 1924. Only a child with an unknown father could claim the nationality of the mother.[6]

The 1993 Nationality Act made very few changes. Again, the only way a woman can pass on her nationality to her children is when the child is born out of wedlock. If a woman is married to a foreign national, she cannot pass on her nationality to her children—even if her spouse consents. The child remains a foreigner until adulthood. A husband can pass on his nationality to his wife, but not the reverse. In short, "A woman is not accorded equal rights under the Nationality Act (1993)" (EqualityNow 1997).

This is a striking set of circumstances in a country in which a drive for women's rights started as early as the 1940s, reached many goals by 1957, and achieved significant rights of universal suffrage, to work, of equal pay for equal work, to run for office, and some advances in family law (El-Sanousi and El-Amin 1994, 679; Hale 1996a, chapter 4).

After years of government claims to have appointed a committee to draft a constitution, and making reference to a constitution in some of its pronouncements, there is now a ratified constitution with little to say about women. The constitutions of 1956, 1964, and 1973 have all been repealed, and there were attempts to fill the vacuum with "Constitutional Decrees" (the 7th and the 13th). While the 13th Decree gives absolutist rights to the central government, it does not mention women's rights (EqualityNow 1997).

The combination of these Constitutional Decrees, *shari' a,* and the new Penal Code (based on *shari' a*) places women securely in a disadvantageous position: in the courts, with respect to land rights, and at work. A new section of the Public Service Act now undermines the 1974 statute. EqualityNow calls attention to two discriminatory measures: certificates of maintenance (*kafala*) and residential land plots. The first is a situation whereby a woman is not allowed to claim her spouse as a dependent; only a man can claim his wife and his children. Therefore, only men can receive stipends allocated for children (as part of salary). The residential plots assigned to those in public service and some other professions may not be allocated to a woman if her husband owns a plot. If the husband does not already own a plot, the one she applies for is given to him. She is, thus, deprived of her civil right to ownership of land/property (EqualityNow 1997).

6. Information from Sudanese lawyer and human rights activist Asma Abdel Halim. Personal e-mail correspondence, 5 Jan. 1998. Abdel Halim is also the primary author of the Equality Now Report cited below.

The new decrees and other "laws" (many are not technically in existence but are, nonetheless, applied) do not state that women have *rights* as citizens, only that they have *privileges*. Women's right to work was undermined by the Personal Status of Muslims Act (1991) in which it was stated that a woman may not work if it is against her husband's will (EqualityNow 1997). This is consonant with my 1988 interviews with Islamist women in which they insisted that a woman "is allowed to work only if it is necessary." And women cannot travel outside the country without the consent of a male relative (*mahram*), a rule enforced by a Women's Committee with no women members.

The citizenship of non-Muslims is seriously compromised. The U.S. State Department has recently issued a report on human rights in Sudan. It contends that:

> Children who have been abandoned or whose parentage is unknown—regardless of presumed religious origin—are considered Muslims and can only be adopted by Muslims. Non-Muslims may adopt only other non-Muslim children. No equivalent restriction is placed on adoption by Muslims. Foundlings or other abandoned children are considered by the State to be Sudanese citizens and Muslims and therefore can only be adopted by Muslims. In accordance with Islamic law, Muslim adoptees do not take the name of their adoptive parents and are not automatic heirs to their property. (U.S. Department of State 1997, pt. 3, 4)

AfricaWatch, in condemning the new Islamic Penal Code of March 22, 1991, contends that under the *shari'a* penal code, "women are treated as legal minors" (AfricaWatch 1991, 7).[7]

---

7. This is not specifically a chapter about women's rights and the status of women. If it were, one would underscore the lack of political participation, the declining enrollments in schools, the relegating of women to particular professions, and the like. In terms of political leadership possibilities for women, however, the diverse opposition parties share one notable feature with each other and with the Islamists: they are nearly devoid of visible women's leadership (not to be confused with active women's *participation*). It is significant, in fact, that women are not singled out in the new NDA document, referred to popularly as the "Asmara Declaration," except in the process of protection from religion: "The NDA undertakes to preserve and promote the dignity of the Sudanese woman, and affirms her role in the Sudanese national movement and her rights and duties as enshrined in international instruments and covenants without prejudice to the tenets of prevailing religious and noble spiritual beliefs" (National Democratic Alliance 1996, 11, 25). This is in line with the protectionist attitude toward women in all of Sudan's regimes.

Serving the Islamic Republic

The same women whose rights as citizens are being curtailed are being exhorted to serve the nation "as only women can." Some of the ways that women are being asked to serve, including some of the jobs they are asked to take or vacate have everything to do with Sudan's changing class profile. Islamism is as much about Sudan's changing class structure as it is about religion. The Islamists, mainly of the newly emergent urban middle-class, are walking a precarious line between a regime that obliquely seeks to meet the needs of international capital with its ideology of liberalism at the same time that it is militantly trying to avoid cultural imperialism.

The cultural positioning of women is relevant to the Sudan situation; that is, women are seen as the embodiment of the culture and are being expected to serve the culture/society through particular forms of labor. Women and the family unit, therefore, are integral to the state's response to the continuing crisis of Sudan's economy. Examining women's domestic and wage labor and political participation in the 1990s is revealing (Hale 1996a).

On the surface, women may not seem to be leading different lives. They have access to many types of jobs, to education, benefits, and political participation, and in many areas they are taking advantage of their opportunities and options. Women are becoming public people, which used to be seen (and probably still is by some) as a threat to the economic and social order but is now a necessity to keep the Islamic state alive. In fact, the Islamic state has had to expand its notion of the "New Muslim Woman." The needs of the expanding state have become militarized, and women are now being reshaped to fulfill both *specific* and *androgynous* roles: mothers, members of militias, students, social reproducers of Islamic values, political organizers, and citizens.

The NIF's attempt to look "modern" or *be* modern has meant reference to institutions we would generally consider secular, although they function in an "Islamic way," e.g., Islamic banking, Islamic insurance companies, appeal to potential constituencies through the media (e.g., missionary work on T.V. and televised weddings), and the like, but most importantly, the military and paramilitary.

Such has been the modernist and careful approach of the NIF. Women should only work if they do not have children and only if their income is needed by the family. This means, of course, that working-class women need to work. Islam and *shari'a* make allowances for them. But there are limits. The jobs women have should not threaten the power structure and should be "appropriate," that is, when possible, jobs should be extensions of their domestic labor.

Turabi argues that Islam is very democratic toward women: "The Islamic movement in Sudan chose not to allow women's liberation to be brought about by Westernized liberal elites or communists or whatever. It took the lead itself. . . . [I]t evoked religion against custom. . . . [T]here is no bar to women anywhere, and there is no complex about women being present anywhere" (Lowrie 1993, 46–47).

In general, the debate on women's rights has been coopted by the activist voices of the Islamists and conservative wings of old sectarian parties. These organizations have used vocabulary such as helping working women, fighting sex discrimination in employment, extending maternity leave, offering free transportation for women workers, organizing women in the informal sector, and the like, that is, coopting the liberal and left discourses. But the main goal is expressed in familiar essentialist language: to build an image of the "ideal Muslim woman."

Islamic welfare work was certainly a dominant function of the women's organizations registered under the Ministry of Social Welfare in the 1980s,[8] and almost all the twenty-some organizations aimed to educate women about Islam; create nurseries; work on childrearing, health and nutrition; build awareness of Islam and the nation; "eradicate bad customs," build an image of the "ideal Muslim woman," and teach *Islamic citizenship*.

In the 1980s individual resistance to these attempts to remold Sudanese women to fit an ideal image of the Muslim woman was expressed during my interviews. Although many women of the middle class with whom I spoke expressed doubt that anything would change in their everyday lives if *shari' a* were implemented, there were outcries from very religious working-class women.

As for a "secular" voice of the Sudanese Women's Union wing of the Communist Party, this organization countered with no more than a liberal portrait of a (Muslim) woman: practicing Islam in private, being literate, holding a job or participating in an "income-generating project" or something like a sewing cooperative, supporting the Communist Party, and shedding such "backward" customs as the *zaar*.

One of my interviewees, however, was Suad Ibrahim Ahmed, a long-time communist activist. Her dissident voice, now relatively quiet for reasons of personal safety and her state of health, railed against the insidious gender resocialization obvious in the national secondary school curriculum by the 1950s.[9] As an educator active in school reform, her testimony pointed to the

8. I obtained this typed registry in July 1988 from the Ministry of Social Welfare in Khartoum (n.d. [1985–88?]).

9. Interview, 1988, Khartoum, Sudan, 25, 26 July. According to a number of newspaper

notion that not only the spirit of Islamism, but its acts, were taking place decades earlier. According to this progressive, the influence of the *Ikhwan* on school curriculums was considerable even before independence. But because much of what was being promulgated was directed at the image of women, not much notice was taken, even by the Communist Party. In a society where males and females attend segregated schools until university, it is easier to manipulate the curriculum for women, molding them to fit Islamic ideals and mobilizing them to serve their country.

Noted legal analyst and Republican activist, Batoul Mukhtar Muhammed Taha, wrote a series of provocative newspaper articles in the 1980s, one of them challenging the right of the two NIF women representatives in the People's Assembly to represent all women. She claimed that society needs to value women as human beings, "not as a mere type, the 'Female'" (Taha 1988, 8).[10]

NIF ideology about the nature of woman and the ideal role of Muslim women had permeated middle-class urban society from University of Khartoum students, 70 percent of whom were wearing some form of *hejab* (Islamic dress) by 1988, to professional men and women.[11] But the most striking fact of mid-1980s urban Sudanese society was that members of the population who opposed the imposition of *shari'a* and the molding of the "ideal Muslim woman" were not offering an alternative invention, for example, the contemporary Sudanese woman, except in the vague liberal terms I just mentioned from the Women's Union.

Therefore, by the late 1980s, image invention was coopted by Islamist voices, especially the voices of politically active women. In the mid-1980s the most visible Islamist woman activist was Suad al-Fatih al-Badawi, one of only two women representatives in the People's Assembly, both of whom were NIF members. In her statements to the press, she took great effort to

---

and INTERNET sources, Suad Ibrahim Ahmed, in her late sixties, was among some fifty women arrested at a demonstration in Khartoum in December 1997; she was not only jailed but flogged.

10. She repeats some of these ideas in a written interview with me, Khartoum, Sudan, 3 Aug. 1988.

11. This information on the *hejab* is from a 17 July 1988 interview with Mohamed Osman at the University of Khartoum. He had taken a survey of students for his unpublished paper on social and political aspects of the veil. Sudanese have told me recently that fewer university students are now wearing *hejab*. I have not confirmed this information. In 1997, however, students from Ahfad University for Women were stopped and pulled out of a bus; those who were not dressed appropriately were flogged (numerous reports in periodicals and on the Internet [e.g., Sudanese Listserve, 7 Sept. 1997, SUDAN@LISTSERVE.CC.EMORY.EDU, posted by Muaz M. Ataalsid]).

be forward-looking and open, stating, for example, that, "We [NIF] are not opposed to corrections and changes [in the current *shari'a* laws] so long as . . . [they do not] take us back to the English laws" (al-Badawi 1986). Moreover,

> I do not believe in separatist roles [for men and women] in the construction of the nation. Men and women complete and perfect each other. . . . It was an obligation for . . . women [to make] the representation of women *authentic* and *real*. . . . Those women who have attained a high level of consciousness which is *progressive* and *untainted* by blind imitation of both the East and the West must not be stingy with their intellectual effort. . . . This era is marked by issues of development which the *enlightened vanguard* must struggle to solve in a fundamental way. (al-Badawi 1986, emphases mine)

The Muslim woman, essentialized, is presented as modern, forward-looking, dutiful, and enlightened, yet moral and authentic—a truly modern Muslim.

Nevertheless, the dark side of the image of devout and dutiful Muslims remained: the fact that men oppressed women through various patriarchal customs. A strategy had to be worked out whereby Islam could be the *deus ex machina*, a method for rescuing women from oppression. To do that, it would be more effective to demonize some aspect of the population, not necessarily men, but a category of men.

Many Islamist women contended that men oppress women, then conflated *men* and *Arabs*. They argued that Arabs (meaning "Arab men") have a low opinion of women and cannot be trusted in that they try to give a false idea to women about their rights under *shari'a*. *Shari'a* judge Nagwa Kamal Farid commented, "Sudan is still a man's society. . . . The man is the boss." Wisel al-Mahdi (Turabi's spouse and Saddig al-Mahdi's sister), in commenting on a very conservative group (she did not say "Muslim" or "Islamic group"), *Ansar al-Sunna*, which opposes any public activity by women, said, "They are against women. . . . They think a woman's voice is like women's breasts showing." She repeated it in Arabic, "*Sawt al-mar'a 'awra*, a woman's voice is a private part that must be concealed."[12]

Wisel al-Mahdi, Hikmat SidAhmed, and Nagwa Kamal Farid, three elite Islamist women, engaged in a chorus of abuse toward Sudanese Arab men, saying that "Any man in the street can be your boss" (Wisel al-Mahdi). Nagwa added that, "They [Arab men] do not have good ideas about women." Wisel added that "they think women are loose. And they have

---

12. The quotes by Wisel al-Mahdi, Nagwa Kamal Farid, and Hikmat SidAhmed are all from a group interview in Khartoum, Sudan, 12 July 1988, at the home of Hasan al-Turabi and Wisel.

very bad ideas, like the ideas of *the Arabs before Islam*." In agreement, Hik-mat referred to Sudanese Arab men as *jaahiliin* (ignorant, pagan). In re-sponse to the word *jaahiliin*, Wisel commented: "Yes. Because they are *Arabs*, actually. And these instincts have come to them for these last fifteen thousand years, and still it's there. In North Africa, in Saudi Arabia, in *any Arab country*. They have the same things against women. And that is why we are much against them. . . . We are against them [Arabs], and we think they are presenting a *false idea about Islam*" (emphases mine). Wisel al-Mahdi was keen to tell me that they (NIF women and sympathizers) want Islam to rule their lives, to enter all aspects of their personal and public lives, and to be the basis for their citizenship in the Islamic nation.

As for their position on "*feminism*," a question often asked of Sudan's elite Islamist women because of their seeming militant pro-women stance, Suad el-Fatih, at an International Women's Forum in Khartoum, 1996, was both evasive and adamant. To quote Margot Badran, who attended the conference:

> At a press conference, Suad al-Fatih spoke of women's need to communicate with the wider world. When asked if feminism might function as a common language, she gave a firm no. When asked if what had been going on at the Khartoum Forum could be called a kind of Islamic feminism, she gave another no, and added that "Islam would push feminism into a corner." She added, ". . . men historically have been more advanced. Women must be brought to the same level." If her words started to have a feminist sound, she abruptly shifted gears: "We have *taqwa*—piety. If we understand *taqwa*, we will never have feminism in Islam." (Badran 1996b)

Yet the appropriation of the feminist rhetoric, with regard to women's rights and with regard to oppressive Arab customs, could not be mistaken, whether delivered before the Islamic revolution of 1989 or in post-Beijing.

Islamist men, too, seemed to draw a distinction between being "Arab" and being "Muslim," but I found more militancy and defiance in the pos-ture of the Islamist women, especially in their insistence that Arab customs and patriarchy have oppressed them—not Islam.

Turabi, however, has made many comments in which he seems, simul-taneously, to be appealing to women, appeasing Muslim feminist critics, and distancing himself from the (Arab) past. For example, he has remarked that "Segregation is definitely not part of Islam. . . . [T]he *hareem* quarters, this is a development which was totally unknown in the model of Islam, or in the text of Islam; it is unjustified" (Lowrie 1993, 36). He combined these statements with comments about Sudan and Arab culture: "[T]he North is not Arab. . . . They speak Arabic, but they are not Arabs; they are part of

East African people. . . . [T]he Sudanese are Arab in culture . . . but all of them are colored peoples, unlike the Arabs who are very fair, very different" (Lowrie 1993, 66–67).

His spouse, Wisel al-Mahdi, was confident that when the Islamists came to power in Sudan, the plight of women would improve immensely.[13] After all, it was the *Arab* customs and traditions, not Islam, that had been oppressing women! As if to underscore that belief, she and others founded the International Organization for *Muslim* Women in 1989.[14]

Most of the other Islamist women I interviewed agreed that women would have a higher status, more rights, be more respected under *shari'a*, and be more included in the nation. At the same time women would be able to maintain their difference from men, for example, their emotionality, their sentimental nature, and their "femininity." As Wisel al-Mahdi exclaimed, "We are women after all!" Islamists worked on the notion that women could have it both ways: so long as they dressed respectably and acted appropriately, they could work and have careers yet be dutiful wives and mothers, the cruxes of the family. That such a life was only possible for those who could afford servants was rarely ever mentioned.

Besides, a sense of belonging was developing, perhaps for the first time. One Islamist woman expressed it this way: "I never understood what it meant to be 'Sudanese' before this [the rise of the Islamic Republic]. People talked about 'Sudanese,' but I did not have any feeling for that word. I did not think of us as a nation, only as an unfortunate collection of people thrown together by the British. I think that is how a lot of people felt. Now I know that we are an Islamic nation and that I am doing my duty in it."[15] This expression of belonging is in stark contrast to one of my interviews with a Nubian woman (Halfawiyya, from Wadi Halfa) in 1972: "You have asked me about 'Nubian identity' and whether or not I call myself 'Nubian,' 'Halfawiyya' [from the town of Wadi Halfa], or 'Sudanese.' Really, I don't call myself any of these. This is something that men do. I am married to a Sudanese man and that makes me 'Sudanese.' But I don't feel it. Women don't feel these things. It is my family I look to and my neighborhood [in Khartoum]."[16]

The NIF expended great effort to draw in women, and the recruitment has brought rewards, especially at a time like this when the state is so em-

13. The "Permanent Constitution" (no constitution has been ratified) was banned as soon as the Islamists came to power in 1989; an Islamic constitution was recently developed. A new Nationality Act of 1992 does not change the situation for women's citizenship; it is still an extension of one's father's citizenship.

14. This organization has been dissolved in deference to a new international umbrella organization.

15. Name withheld by request, interview, Khartoum, Sudan, 17 July 1988.

16. Awatif Mohamed [pseud.], interview, Khartoum, Sudan, 8 Jan. 1972.

battled. Women were the nexus of the NIF in the 1980s and continue to support the regime in large numbers. They are among the active organizers in the schools where women constitute the majority of teachers, in neighborhood medical clinics, in NIF nursery schools in the mosques, as consumer/producers, and so on. The NIF has strong appeal to women at a number of universities. Women are active in the student unions and in the recruitment of students into the government militias. To symbolize their citizenship in the new Islamic nation, many university women have been wearing the *hejab* for more than a decade.[17]

In the summer of 1996, Sudanese Islamist women, who had been very active in Beijing, organized an International Women's Forum, attended by some 150 women from forty countries. The welcoming remarks were delivered by Turabi, and Wisel al-Mahdi was the leading force. Her organization, the International Organization for Muslim Women, was the central organizing tool. Suad el-Fatih, elected president of the newly formed International Islamic Union of Women, led the *sahwa islamiya* ("Islamic awakening") of women toward the development of an Islamic global gender networking and proselytizing. Egyptian writer, Safinaz Kazim, in a plenary address, maintained that Muslim women have two identities: one is androgynous (gender neutral?); the other (gender) specific:

> The project of the organizers was to politicize women and mobilize their public energies toward helping achieve the establishment of Islamist states. But, at the same time women must be reminded that their first and highest duties were as wives and mothers, and their primary arena the home. The comingling of the rhetoric of the *ungendered Muslim* with the rhetoric of women's specificity juxtaposed the rhetoric of equality (of the androgynous Muslim) with the rhetoric of equity (the complementarity of the two sexes). In *time of need* the androgynous Muslim (woman) must be activated; in "ordinary circumstances" (when women are not needed politically) they must be repatriated to the sanctity of the home. (Badran 1996a, 12, emphases mine)

This is clearly a "time of need." In the most recent developments, women (and men) have been recruited into the Popular Defense Forces. Until recent months, the local and national militias have been called upon mainly for a show of force, commitment to the Islamic regime, and public service work. Young women in *hejab,* with khaki camouflage, carrying guns, is now a familiar sight, I am told. At a workshop and some meetings in Beijing, one of the young women of the *moujahadeen* offered photo displays

---

17. As I said above, at the time of my fieldwork in 1988, some 70 percent of the women students at the University of Khartoum were wearing the *hejab*. See n. 11.

of all-women militias training for the defense of the nation. She articulated a battle cry that could only raise a smile on the faces of liberal or radical feminists in the United States. In actuality, now that the Islamic state is under military attack from the east and the south, these young people have been forced to leave school (the universities, all thirteen of them, were closed for a time so that students could be moved to the front, poorly trained, for the most part) and join the military struggle. Women militia members, however, are fulfilling the jobs that are extensions of their domestic labor: nursing, preparing food for the soldiers, communications, raising the next generation of soldiers, and the like. They are the Greek chorus.

It is far too early to tell if this "military service" will instill ideas of emancipation in the minds of militia women and others serving the state. And, in fact, to back away from that statement, most of the Islamist women I have talked with consider themselves "emancipated" already. There have not yet been any women martyrs to buoy the image of the woman warrior. But an element that will be very important to women after the war(s) is that they have been absolutely necessary in the war effort.

For the work of socializing the young with Islamic values, women have received a great deal of public praise and attention. The resuscitation of the complementarity approach to gender is serving the NIF/the state in its ability to have a flexible labor pool, that is, to move women in and out of the work force and in and out of appropriate and inappropriate jobs in the name of helpmates but also in the image of the woman as creator of life and nurturer of the society. The NIF has pointed to the public activity of NIF women in answering the clichéd charge that the NIF-controlled government will ultimately send women back into the home. Instead, the government boasts, women serve in all capacities: in the homes, in schools, in the work force, and in the Popular Defense Forces (the militias). Women's work, however, serves class interests.

One of the NIF's important tasks is the control of human resources partially through the reconstruction of the gender ideology. Now economic crises and their solutions can be articulated in religious terms, and women have been positioned to respond appropriately. The prescriptive nature of Islam (and most religions) regarding sexuality, reproduction, the gender division of labor, and the family are useful in protecting class interests. Class interests, of course, are rarely acknowledged. Islam, after all, is presented by those in power in the new theocracy as "classless."

◆   ◆   ◆

The argument that I propose is that gender and citizenship are being renegotiated in the new Islamic Republic. In the militaristic surge toward integration under Islam, new distinctions are being drawn within the Islamist movement between "Arab" and "Muslim," and this is a significant and gendered process. Turabi has made public statements that construct a fine distinction as did a number of the Islamist women interviewed for this research. What was also striking, from all reports of the International Muslim Women's Forum in 1996, is that the designation "Arab," so long a source of northern/national/international pride, did not surface.

The most significant process in effect relates to the constantly changing construction of the "authentic" Muslim woman and her role in the new and now embattled Islamic nation. That women are more willing to see themselves as potentially liberated from certain patriarchal Arab customs upon a return to "pure" Islam sets the stage for their leadership in this form of identity negotiation. For many women there are no contradictions in their performance of prescribed "domestic" tasks (themselves constantly redefined) while wearing a *hejab* and camouflage, and carrying a gun.

Meanwhile much of the violence and violation of women's rights as citizens in the name of "public order" (the Public Order Act) is aimed at women who have not thought of themselves as "citizens of Sudan": non-Muslims, southerners and other "racial minorities," some socially and politically disaffected, and the severely economically disenfranchised.[18]

18. See "Legal Aid, New Laws and Violence Against Women in Sudan" 1997.

PART THREE

EASTERN ARAB STATES

6

Civic Myths, Citizenship, and Gender in Lebanon

SUAD JOSEPH

Civic Myths

CITIZENSHIP LAWS create and are created by civic myths, Rogers M. Smith (1997) argues. Although always contested, citizenship may be seen as "that set of practices (juridical, political, economic, and cultural) which define a person as a competent member of society, and which as a consequence shape the flow of resources to persons and social groups" (Turner 1993c, 2). Citizenship laws designate the criteria and prerogatives constituting political membership by defining political purpose, assigning status, and distributing power (Smith 1997, 30). "A civic myth," Smith details, "is a myth used to explain why persons form a people, usually indicating how a political community originated, who is eligible for membership, who is not and why, and what the community's values and aims are" (1997, 33). For Smith, civic myths are riddled with contradictions and conflicting themes. Civic myths, codified in citizenship laws, often also work through informal agreements, which, constitutive of the very nature of the political community, may appear to achieve legal status. Understandings such as the "social contract," "national pacts," and the like so inform their political communities that their logic may underwrite critical aspects of political/legal rationality.

All states have multiple civic myths that may bolster or challenge each other. Citizenship laws reflect the divergent themes scripted in competing or compatible national narratives rather than uniformly representing a single coherent story. In Lebanon multiple civic myths overlay each other and manifest themselves in different legal arenas—myths of economic liberalism, of social conservatism, of communalism, of individualism, of the autonomy of state and religion, of the state as a patron of religious institutions, of gender equality, of the primacy of patriarchal authority, and the like. The hegemonic civic myth of the Lebanese nation, however, has been the myth of sectarian pluralism. In this chapter I focus on a civic myth, glossed by the hegemonic civic myth of sectarian pluralism, yet critical to the laws and practices of citizenship in the Lebanese state, and, indeed, critical to the civic myth of sectarian pluralism—the civic myth of extended kinship. The civic myth of extended kinship, which has undergirded the Lebanese social order, has contributed critically to the disenfranchising of women and ju- niors through the complex and paradoxical operations of a "care/control" paradigm supported by the state and religious sects.

Citizenship laws in Lebanon were viewed as codifying a civic myth of sectarian pluralism long before the rise of multiculturalism with its post- modern and feminist advocates and critics (Binder 1966; Suleiman 1967; Hudson 1968; Joseph 1978). Variously described as a "fragmented political culture" or as a "consociational," "confessional," "sectarian," or "plural" political system,[1] the Lebanese civic myth has been told as a story of a nation composed of multiple natural communities organized on the basis of reli- gious sects. In this view of the civic myth, the religious sects existed before the Lebanese state and were presumed to have sustained a continuity of sectarian communal culture and cohesion. The historical governance of the population through the loosely religiously based millet system of the Otto- mans and the more narrowly sectarian system of the French Mandate (to- gether lasting for almost half a millennium), have been taken, by the sectarian pluralists, as evidence of the historical continuity of these "natural communities."

Kinship is also a myth, a myth constitutive of communities with history, relatively coherent rules of membership, codes of behavior, moral impera- tives for rights and responsibilities, and disciplinary powers to enforce its codes. Stimulated by David M. Schneider's (1984) critical studies of kin- ship, many anthropologists and sociologists have theorized the constructed- ness of kinship (Yanagisako and Collier 1987; Thorne and Yaom 1992; Yanagisako and Delaney 1995). Kinship recruits its members on the basis of the naturalization of an imagined biologically based system of recruitment. Kin groups create imagined communities upheld by the power of "nature,"

---

1. For ease of reference I refer to these views of the civic myth as "pluralism."

usually sanctified by the authority of God, and, in weak states such as Lebanon, often assimilated into and institutionalized by the laws and practices of citizenship. Like the civic myth of citizenship, kinship myths are riddled with contradictions (prescribing patrilineality, for example, while subsidizing matrilineality).

In Lebanon, I suggest, the hidden hegemonic civic myth has been the myth of extended kinship. The civic myth of extended kinship, subsidized by the state and sanctified by religion, has told a story of a nation composed of multiple, large (as opposed to small, nuclear), "natural" groupings based on biological (blood) relatedness, descended through male genealogies. One is "born" into kin groups in Lebanon. Kinship creates "birth groups." Kin groups have been seen as primordial, existing before the state, bequeathing members their primary identities, and claiming the a priori allegiance of their members. They have operated through a "care/control" paradigm in which the nurture of members is supported by their assimilation of the structures of patriarchal kin authority and standards of behavior. In the civic myth of extended kinship, the state has been seen as weak, unreliable, and unable to afford citizens protection from social, economic, and even political insecurities. The state has been decentered from critical social action. To the degree that the state has been seen as having agency, it is often negative. The state has existed for the extraction of resources. Most citizens have felt they have to guard against the state for its arbitrary and corrupt uses by others, and kinship has been seen as their primary protection against the state (as well as their primary conduit into the state).

Citizenship laws in Lebanon have codified the control of extended kin groups over their members as much, if not more than, codifying the control of religious sects over their members. That the patriarchal extended kinship system that has been so codified has disproportionally disenfranchised women and juniors has been central to the state's organization of political society and has been recognized by scholars of Lebanon. Less-acknowledged and scarcely theorized is the role kinship has played as a generic institution of control and discipline of all citizens of the weak state. Although patriarchal extended kinship clearly privileges males and seniors, in Lebanon patriarchal kinship disciplines males and females, seniors and juniors.

Western feminist theory on gender and citizenship has largely glossed extended kinship for historical and political reasons specific to Western states and to Western feminism. Western feminists have focused primarily on the nuclear family and the conjugal relationship of husband and wife. Theorized as the "sexual contract" (Pateman 1988) or "vulnerability by marriage" (Okin 1989), the conjugal relationship has been seen by many Western feminists as the greatest barrier to women's equal citizenship

(Vogel 1994). Rather than the conjugal relationship, I focus on extended kin relationships. Rather than vulnerability by marriage, I focus on vulnerability by "birth." Rather than the sexual contract, I focus on the "kin contract." It is the mobilization of patriarchal extended kinship, as a venue of social control, and the state's mobilization of religion to sanctify extended kinship that has been the most significant deterrent to citizenship equality for women in Lebanon, I suggest.

The hyperfocus on the civic myth of sectarian pluralism by scholars and activists has made it more difficult to understand the centrality of the myth of extended kinship in Lebanese citizenship laws. The hyperfocus on women's subordination to men in kin groups (rather than on the "care/control" paradigm that systematically and simultaneously has nurtured and disciplined members) in feminist studies of kinship has made it more difficult to understand why women would subscribe to kinship as emphatically as they do in Lebanon and why Lebanese feminists focus more on the problems of sectarianism than on the problems of kinship. The hyperfocus on the nuclear family and the husband/wife relationship in Western feminist scholarship (understandable in the political history of Western family/state relationships) has diminished the cross-cultural transportability of some Western feminist theory concerning gender and citizenship.[2] Citizenship laws in Lebanon, I contend, reflect the centrality of extended kinship to the civic myth of sectarian pluralism and the centrality of the civic myth of extended kinship to the reproduction of order in the political system.

Civic Myth of Sectarian Pluralism

Nearly all states encompass persons and populations differentiated by language, religion, ethnicity, and race, besides class and gender. No modern state consists of a homogeneous, stable, "natural" national community residing within never-contested political boundaries. Yet the "imagined community" (Anderson 1983) of the nation legitimates itself through stories that constitute its members as belonging to a shared political collective with an imagined common history. Civic myths of citizenship are appealing because they "create the most recognized political identity of the individuals they embrace" by supporting citizenship laws that "literally constitute—create with legal words—a collective civic identity" (Smith 1997, 31). A

---

2. Pateman has been careful not to claim that her theories apply to Third World societies. The argument presented in this chapter is not a critique of Western feminist theories of state and citizenship (which have been inspiring) but a recognition that theories are required for culturally specific conditions.

civic myth of citizenship tells a tale of an a priori foundational unity, woven through acknowledged and unacknowledged differences, of which the state, its laws, and its leaders are its political embodiments.

For previously colonized states, civic myths and citizenship laws invariably import culturally alien ideas. As Bryan S. Turner (1993b, vii) observed, the idea of citizenship is not only modern it is Western and intrinsically tied to the development of urban civil societies. Although many people would like to believe in the seamlessness of the society to which their citizenship weds them, Smith (1997, 33) contends civic myths, like citizenship laws, are shot through with tensions and contradictions reflective of ongoing conflicts and divisions among the multiple and changing, contending interests both within and outside the polity and conflicting sources of civic myths. As civic myths include some, they exclude others; as they empower some, they disenfranchise others; as they ennoble some, they demonize others. The excluded, disenfranchised, demonized need not be external to the political society and, indeed, are often "members," "citizens," of the state.

The civic myth of sectarian pluralism has described the formal logic of representation and governance in Lebanon. The assumption has been that the sects are "natural" communities characterized by cultural dynamics so fundamentally different from each other that only members of the sect can adequately represent the views and interests of the sectarian "community." With sectarian pluralism as the legitimating civic myth, seats in the Lebanese parliament have been, since independence in 1943, allocated according to the legal fiction of the distribution of religious sects in the population. Political parties to a large extent have been and have been expected to be largely uni-sect. Goods and services channeled from the state to citizens have been distributed along lines that appear sectarian.

The sectarian pluralist civic myth is a modern myth that legitimates itself by reference to historical continuity with the Ottoman millet system or even earlier systems of governance. The Ottoman millet system grouped all citizens into loosely defined religious categories. The categories were the basis for taxation, codes of attire and behavior, rules of deference, and the like. Critical to the civic narrative, the millets were given authority over family law. The millets were not coherent religious "communities," however. In the sixteenth century the Ottomans established only four millets, despite the existence of dozens of religious sects in the empire: Muslim, Christian Orthodox, Armenian, and Jewish. The Muslim millet subjected all Muslims— Sunnis, Shi'a, 'Alawites, and others, across national boundaries—to the authority of the Ottoman state. Orthodox sects from different nationalities were grouped under the Christian Othodox millet. The Armenian millet included non-Orthodox Christian sects such as the Roman Catholics, the

Maronites, and other Eastern Christians, even though they were not ethnically Armenian. Jews of all traditions were in the Jewish millet. The millets
under the Ottomans, therefore, were homogeneous "communities" in neither national, ethnic, nor religious terms. Nor were they stable, as millet
group membership, identities, and their rights and liabilities changed over
time.

The eighteenth through twentieth-century competition among the colo-
nizing Europeans states escalated the use, by European and Ottoman states,
of the millets for footholds within the Ottoman empire, and the manipulation of classic "divide and rule" strategies (Ofeish 1996, 122; Abu Jaber
1967). The French claimed the Maronites as their protected community;
the English claimed the Druze; the Russians, the Greek Orthodox; the Ottomans, the Sunnis—with each state vying to privilege their client "community." From these politically designed religious categories emerged elites
willing to be constituted and to constitute themselves and their "communal" institutions in terms of the shifting grounds of political sectarianism
that was emerging (Ofeish 1996, 120).

During the nineteenth century a series of civil uprisings in the Lebanon
region, beginning as peasant protests, were resolved by the Ottomans, with
European intervention, by the institution of governance on increasingly nar-
rower sectarian bases (Harik 1968). By 1914, under pressure from European
powers, the Ottomans had increased to seventeen the number of millets recognized in Lebanon. The seventeen sects were the basis for the formulas of
governance under the French Mandate after World War I. The Lebanese
Constitution of 1926, written under the French Mandate, formalized representation in the Lebanese government by religious sects, privileging the
French-protected Maronites. With little modification this Constitution was
adopted by the Lebanese Republic, founded in 1943. Article 95 of the Constitution, requiring representation in parliament and government agencies on
the basis of the seventeen recognized religious sects, stated: "As a transitory
measure and for the sake of even justice and concord, the communities shall
be equally represented in public posts and in ministerial composition, without
damage to State interest resulting therefrom."

The Christians were given the majority of positions (six Christian seats
for every five Muslim) with the Maronites allocated the single most. The
distribution of parliamentary seats and offices in government agencies was
based on the 1932 census, which has never been officially updated and
which upheld the legal fiction of a Christian majority until the Taif Agreement in 1990. The National Pact, an informal agreement made in 1943
among the leaders of the newly independent Lebanese state, allocated the
major state offices on a sectarian basis: the president to the Maronites; the

prime minister to the Sunni; the speaker of parliament to the Shi'a; the deputy speaker to the Greek Orthodox. Parliamentary seats were allocated to the largest sects in each district. And positions in government ministries and agencies were to be allocated proportionately according to the sectarian distribution claimed in the 1932 census. The Taif Agreement, which formally ended the Lebanese Civil War of 1975–1990, reauthorized the sectarian basis of political representation in Lebanon. However, it increased the seats in parliament, changed the balance of sects in parliament to 50:50 for Muslims and Christians, and increased the power of the prime minister (a Sunni position) relative to the president (a Maronite position).

Sectarianism in Lebanon has had a contested and nonlinear history. What constituted a sect, which groups were recognized and allowed representation, the distribution of power among the sects within and outside the state, the methods of distributing state resources, what legal authority the sects were permitted, what liabilities and privileges sect membership entailed, the relationship of each sect to the state and to external states—all have changed over time. Governance has not been based on "natural" sectarian communities so much as succeeding states have constructed political sects to facilitate governance.

Despite this variegated history, sectarian pluralism became a foundational myth of the independent Lebanese state. The hegemony of the civic myth of sectarian pluralism in Lebanon is seen in its repeated deployment to explain Lebanese history, state structure, politics, social organization, and citizenship laws (Binder 1966; Hudson 1968; Suleiman 1967). It has been used to justify what has been done, what can be done, and what cannot. The "National Pact" has been taken, by sectarian pluralists, as acquiescence to the power of sectarianism in Lebanon. Further proof, for advocates, of the centrality of the myth of sectarian pluralism has been seen in the state's delegation of family law (personal status laws), to religious courts rather than legislating a unified civil law. Scholarly and popular explanations of the Lebanese Civil War (1975–90)—and earlier social conflicts—center stage sectarian conflict. And arguments against legal reform for gender equality are most frequently rationalized as limited by the constraints of the sectarian system—either in terms of respect for or inability to surmount religious differences.

Many Lebanese feminists and feminist research on Lebanon often have taken sectarian pluralism as the primary source of patriarchy and gender inequality in Lebanon (Joseph in press). That the hegemony of sectarian pluralism has been seen by many Lebanese feminists as the critical obstacle to gender equality is evidenced by the high legislative priority they give to enacting a unified civil family code (Zalzal 1997; Bizri 1997). Even activists who have focused their lobbying on other legislative priorities for women often explain their strategies as steps toward weakening the grip sectarianism has over women's issues (Laur Mogheizel, personal communication). A unified civil family code *is* critical for achieving gender equality in citizenship laws. Many feminists in Lebanon, however, have focused on family law as an issue of sectarianism, overlooking it as *also* an issue of kinship. They have regarded family law as reflective of their control by men of the religious communities (Sharara 1978; Mogheizel 1997) rather than also indexing their control by men of their extended kin groups. They have correctly observed that legal pluralism in family law has diminished the power of the state in their lives. Although the call for a civil family code is critical to women's equality before the law and there is no recourse but for women to turn to and lobby the state for its intervention in legal arena, it has also been the case that the state has relied upon legal pluralism to shore up the extended kinship system that is central to the structure of its control over the citizenry. The hyperfocus on sectarian pluralism, however powerful and material its appearances and realities, has glossed the critical kinship dynamics that have underwritten pluralism (legal, social, and cultural), resulting in the gendering and aging of citizenship laws and practices.

Civic Myth of Kinship

Historically, state and kin groups have competed for control over their members (Balibar and Wallerstein 1991, 101). Most Western states have succeeded in appropriating the functions of kin groups, leaving kin groups with diminished authority over their members, diminished capacity to discipline their members, limited in their claims to the loyalty of their members, and reduced in their household normative form to nuclear family structures. Jack Goody's (1983) provocative history of family and marriage in Europe has suggested that the Catholic Church, acting as a state, systematically transformed European kinship. Before the consolidation of the Catholic Church into an institution of state governance, the kinship system and the position of women in Europe, he argued, was more similar than different from that of the Middle East. Beginning in the fourth century (against much resistance), the church subsidized the emergence of the "modern" European kinship system by prohibiting close cousin marriage, adoption, polygyny, wet-nursing, divorce, widow/er remarriage, concubinage. By supporting the individualization of choice, mutual consent for marriage, monogamy, the reduction of authority within the family (including male authority), and the child-oriented "elementary family," the Catholic Church, Goody contended, fostered an ecclesiastic kinship in which the church became an heir to the property, allegiance, and membership of the previously powerful kin groups—very much as states might try to do.

Goody's account has been controversial (Schneider 1984), but suggestive (Joseph 1988). Although kinship systems in Europe and the Middle East may have been, earlier, more similar than different, they developed different relationships to state systems that were critical in shaping their political outcomes. Middle Eastern states, like European states, tended, at times, to consolidate and stabilize certain forms of extended kinship at the expense of others (Joseph 1999a). Middle Eastern states in general, and the Lebanese state in particular, however, reinscribed the discipline of extended kinship in citizenship laws and practices. They have tended to absorb kinship systems into the structures of governance, thus subsidizing the reproduction of extended kinship and the continued control of extended kin groups over their members. This difference in the relationship of Western and Middle Eastern states to kinship systems may help to explain a crucial difference in points of departure between Western and Middle Eastern feminists.

Western feminists have tended to focus on conjugal relationships in the analysis of gender inequality in kin groups. Although Western feminists may analyze other kin relationships, husband/wife relationships have been privileged in the analysis of gender inequality. Almost completely absent in Western feminist theorizing of gender inequality have been analyses of extended kin—grandparents, uncles and aunts, cousins, male or female. An important exception to the nuclear/conjugal family bias has been the research on Afro-American families, which often has been couched in discussions or critiques of dysfunctionality (Stack 1974). That the ground-breaking Western feminist critique of citizenship and state theory, Carole Pateman's (1988) work on the sexual contract, should have focused on the conjugal relationship can be seen in light of Western kinship systems in which extended kinship (indeed, kinship in general) had come to be seen as having significantly diminished relevance for gender and state hierarchies. Pateman argued that the patriarchy that emerged from the classical liberal contractarian political theorist was a "fraternal patriarchy" in which the power of men as brothers, men as men, supplanted the power of men as fathers. Thus, it was the "sexual contract" hidden in the conjugal relationship that was critical to women's exclusion from citizenship and civil society (Pateman 1988). Similarly, Susan Moller Okin (1989) contended that "gender-structured marriage *involves women in a cycle of socially caused and distinctly asymmetric vulnerability*,"[3] producing an unjust family and what she calls "vulnerability

---

3. Italics in the original.

by marriage" (1989, 138). Ursula Vogel has concluded, "We can say that 'vulnerability by marriage' is still the strongest among the many barriers that hold back women's claim to equal citizenship" (1994, 86). That the conjugal relationship has been seen by many Western feminists as the critical obstacle to equal citizenship for women provides a crucial point of departure for analyzing differences in the gendering of citizenship in Lebanon.

In Lebanon it has been not only the "marriage/sexual contract" that has made women asymmetrically vulnerable but also, and perhaps more so, that the "kin contract" has been built on a patriarchy subsidized by and absorbed into the state and sanctioned by and codified in religious law. The civic myth of extended kinship—founded on the "kin contract"—has located the foundational unity of Lebanese social order in the rights and responsibilities of kinship (rather than citizenship). The state has codified patriarchy and patrilineality and attempted to stabilize them (Joseph 1999a). So central has extended kinship been to the political order that the boundaries between the public (state), civil society (nongovernmental sphere), and the domestic (kinship) have been purposefully and necessarily porous (Joseph 1997). Extended kinship has generated idioms, moralities, and relational dynamics for Lebanese in the polity, economy, religion, and society. That Lebanese women and men, juniors and seniors generally have subscribed so emphatically to the patriarchal, patrilineal, extended kin social order has been rooted in the balance of nurturance and discipline that I call the "care/control" paradigm.

The Kin Contract: The Care/Control Paradigm

Kin Care

The "kin contract" in Lebanon has been about the ideal of family love organized within a patriarchal structure of rights and responsibilities. The kin contract has extolled the ideals of family love, mothers' and fathers' unconditional sacrifices for their children, children's unwavering respect for their parents, the love and care of grandparents, uncles, aunts, and cousins many steps removed. It has been about the love of siblings for each other, especially the love of sisters and brothers (Joseph 1994b). The romantic lure of the kin contract has been grounded in material realities in which kin relationalities have been, for the Lebanese, the core of social identity, economic stability, political security, and religious affiliation and the first (often last) line of security—emotionally, socially, economically, and politically. It has been the kin who care. It has been kin against whom one has had irrevocable rights and toward whom one has had religiously mandated (at times legally prescribed) moral responsibilities.

Kinship has been the central social identity. The kin group has been seen as the primary identity and loyalty for any Lebanese—superseding national identity and loyalty to the state and competing only with religion. To a question of "who" are you, Lebanese have typically responded with the name of the kin group to which they belong, not their national or religious identities. Lebanese have defined themselves through kinship genealogies. Although genealogies are deeper for elite families, Lebanese generally have claimed membership in known kin groups, charting themselves within socially recognized genealogical locations. It has been the extended kin that has been inscribed in this national cartographic practice, not just the household or the nuclear family. Grandparents, uncles, aunts, cousins several steps removed, all have been mapped in the social geography of who is who in answer to the question of "Who am I?"

Persons have identified themselves through genealogies in which male persons have been coded as the primary ancestors. Rights and responsibilities have been defined in terms of lineages recruited through the father's line (patrilineally) although matrilineal kin also have had rights in and responsibilities toward each other. The longevity and historical continuity of kin groups, in this civic myth, has been documented through written and oral accounts of kin groups. The myth of kinship solidarity has been captured in the still-cited Arab *mathil* (proverb): "I against my brother; my brother and I against my cousin; my cousin and I against the world."

In Lebanon, the strength of extended kin relationships historically has been coterminous with relatively weak conjugal relationships. Natal kin have continued to demand the loyalty and allegiance of its members long after marriage. Sister/brother, mother/son, father/son, brother/brother, grandparents, uncles, aunts, and other natal relationships often have been seen to compete with husband/wife relationships, with especially sister/brother (Joseph 1994a) and mother/son (Barakat 1985) relationships often seen to "win" over the husband/wife. For women, the attraction toward natal kin has emerged partly as a result of social rules requiring patrilineal kin to remain responsible for their female lineage members even after their marriages. Men of the patrilineage have been seen to be responsible for the honorable behavior of their women more than their husbands (Meeker 1976). In the civic myth of extended kinship, women are supposed always to be able to return to the houses of their fathers, brothers, paternal grandparents, and even fathers' brothers in times of crises.

The extended kinship system has been reinforced by marriage practices favoring kin endogamy. The marriage preference for Muslims in Lebanon has been patrilineal kin endogamy. Although Christian churches technically forbid close kin endogamy, it has been widely practiced among Christians as well. For both Muslims and Christians, kin endogamy has, in fact, been both patrilineal and matrilineal. The dynamics of kin endogamy have been extensively analyzed elsewhere (Murphy and Kasdan 1959; Khuri 1970; Joseph 1999b). What is critical for this analysis is that kin endogamy has tended to reinscribe the power of kinship in the lives of kin members.

On the surface, kin endogamy can seem to be a practice of sect endogamy because kin members are usually members of the same religious sect. When marriages have occurred within the kin group, a strong kin allegiance can take on the appearance of a strong sect allegiance, yet it has been the kin bond that has underwritten the sect bond. But kin groups often have crossed religious sects after intersectarian marriages. Intersectarian marriages among Christians (Maronites, Greek Orthodox, Roman Catholics, etc.) have been very common as have intersectarian marriages among Muslims (Sunni, Shi'a, Druze, etc.). When kinship has coincided with the larger religious rubrics (Muslim/Christian), the allegiances have also appeared to translate into religious differences (rather than smaller sectarian differences). Fewer marriages have crossed these larger religious rubrics, however, so it has been easier to gloss kin allegiance as religious allegiance for the larger religious rubrics. Even when endogamy has been village or neighborhood (rather than kin) based, it has strengthened the authority of resident kin. Given the tendency toward patrilocality (residence following the child's father), endogamy has contributed to generationally reconstituting kin group in the sites that empower patrilineal patriarchy, reinforcing the primacy of kin identity.

Endogamy and patrilocality have been important because they have facilitated the primacy of extended kinship over the conjugal relationship. Perhaps the conjugal relationship became a more critical determinant of women's status in the West because of exogamy and nucleation. Where nucleation has not been normative and where endogamy has been encouraged (even if not always practiced), the extended kin have come to have more significant care/control functions than the conjugal relation.

Further reinforcing the primacy of kinship and kin identity have been the practices of religious affiliation (subscribed to by the state). Religious sects in Lebanon all presume that children belong to the kin group of their fathers and that they will follow the religious affiliation of their fathers. Religious sects have operated to reinforce kin relations and the patriarchal kin structure by supporting the authority of kin males and elders over females and juniors. Interventions by clerics into domestic issues almost always have reinscribed patriarchal authority. Religious clerics have strongly encouraged sectarian endogamy and condoned the practices of kin endogamy, even among the Christians where close kin endogamy is technically prohibited. Clerics (especially Christian clerics) have been referred to through the use of kin idioms ("father," "brother"), and have referred to sect members in kin terms ("son," "daughter," "brother," "sister"). Clerics, perhaps more than other public figures, have called upon Lebanese to care for kin—to attend to the needs of kin, to respect and defer to the authority of elders, to fulfill obligations toward kin, and to hold sacred the mantle of kinship. Clerics have deployed kin values, codes of behavior, and principles of discipline in their relationships with sect members, thus anointing kinship with the blessings of sacred authority.

Kin groups have been crucial to the economic security of kin members. In much of rural Lebanon land, handed down through generations, often has remained undivided. The result has been to wed descending generations of sibs and cousins to their kin as common property holders. Women, even when they are entitled to, often have not (or are not permitted) formally to inherit land. The rationale has been that because men of their patrilines remain responsible for them, leaving their land in the hands of their brothers repays the patrilineage of the protection they offer their women. Although many women do inherit and register land in their own names, many Lebanese women, Muslim and Christian, have indicated to me in interviews that they do not want to take the land from their brothers, that ultimately they may come back to their brothers, or that the father's land should stay in the father's line. Women have served their brothers and their sons. Many women have been used and abused by the patrilineal males who are responsible for their care. Yet their security has been tied to their patrilineal kin and their sons more than to their husbands, even if husbands have ultimately cared for them in old age. In the civic myth of kinship women, in Lebanon, have been expected to feel they can come "home" (home being the site of patrilineal kin—fathers, brothers, paternal uncles).

In a striking example of the notion of kin care and particularly the responsibility of the brother for the sister came from an urban middle-class informant. A seventy-year-old never-married Christian woman who has worked all her adult life sacrificed her own education to work to support her siblings. Her family has not subdivided their land for several generations. She will have a one-time payment from her employer when she retires that could support her for only a limited time. I asked her how she will support herself. Her answer was that her younger brother would take care of her. "*Majbur fiyyi*" (he is obligated to me) she calmly stated. The utter certainty of her sense that she will be cared for even though she will have no ongoing retirement income was astounding. She had given much to her brothers and their families all her life. She was peaceful in the knowledge that she was entitled to their care.

Men also often have not subdivided property inherited from fathers/ grandfathers. Indeed, male kin often further invest with each other in businesses. Brothers often jointly build multistoried buildings in which each may occupy an apartment at marriage. Lebanese regularly have turned to kin in times of need for loans, networking, *wasta* (brokerage), references, jobs, housing, and other financial assistance.

The power of kin groups as sources of economic security is directly reflected in the rise of the phenomenon of "family associations" in Lebanon. Family associations provide loans and other forms of financial savings and aid, networking, and political connections for their members. Between 1991 and 1996 more than five hundred new family associations were legally recognized by the Lebanese government in Beirut alone (Salem et al. 1996). Helping each other, particularly their poorer members, the family associations operate as nongovernmental organizations(NGOs), entering the sphere of civil society and offering services that the state either cannot or will not deliver or that the citizens have not been and do not expect to be offered by the state.

Kinship has also been central to the political identity and security of Lebanese. Lebanese have had as their primary allegiance loyalty to kin and not to the state. Historically, Lebanese have relied upon kin rather than the state for protection and security. The political community, to the degree that a community has been experienced, has been underwritten by kin relationships. Patron/client relationships, the motor force of Lebanese politics (Huxley 1975; Joseph 1990), have been built on the blocks of kin relationships. Many kin groups have owned allegiance to specific political leaders and their patrilineal successors (*zu'ama'*) for generations, passing political identities, affiliations, and loyalties through their patrilineages.

Historically, the state has been seen as ineffective in providing critical social services and protection. The state has not effectively competed with kin groups to offer alternative communities and services. During the Civil War (1975–90) some political groups (parties, militas) became more effective competitors to kin groups for the loyalties of the young. That they were somewhat successful can be seen in the cry shared by many parents that their worst enemies during the wars were the parties and the militias. Parents, in my study of a Christian village east of Beirut, were both vocal and articulate in specifying that the political parties tried, and at times succeeded, in taking their children away from them. But the failure of the war, the exposed corruption of many of the militias and parties (including some of those organized by religious sects), and the devastation wrought upon the country led many Lebanese to plead, "*badna ad dawli*" ("we want the state"—rather than militias and sectarian groups). The call for the state to reinstate order, however, was asserted in opposition to violence and chaos rather than in support of state authority over kin.

Kin Control

The care of kin has been conjoined with the control of kin. Kinship has been as much about accepting the structures of patriarchal authority and the demands of kin responsibilities as it has been about receiving the benefits of kin nurturance. Social control has been achieved in Lebanon largely through the discipline of extended patriarchal kinship. I define patriarchy as the privileging of males and seniors (including senior women) and the rationalization of male and senior privilege in the idioms and moralities of kinship sanctified by religion (Joseph 1993a). Kin groups in Lebanon have been seen as organized along gendered and aged structures of authority legitimated by religious authority.

The Lebanese state not only has not effectively competed with extended kin groups for the loyalty and allegiances of its citizenry it has relied upon and mobilized extended kin groups on behalf of the political order it has been attempting to construct. The state has been unable or unwilling to constitute citizenship without mobilizing kinship. Political pluralism, the National Pact, the delegation of family law to religious courts, and the consequent gendering and aging of citizenship have not been only evidence of gender and age biases but also the outcomes of the centrality of extended patriarchal kinship in the civic myth of the national order of a weak state. The state has assimilated the logic of kinship as an institution of governance. Kinship has been a site of subject making for the state, a site in which the state has constituted its citizens.

The use of kinship—both their own and that of their followers—by *zu'ama'* (political leaders) has reinforced the utility of kinship in the lives of ordinary citizens and underwritten the civic myth of sectarian pluralism that has glossed it. Given that Lebanon has not been a law state, a rule state, relationships have determined access to resources. The better situated the set of relationalities based in kinship, the better situated the citizen in terms of access to state and other public resources. Kin have been the basis of networks, *wasta* (brokerage), patron/client relations. As a result, there has been little public morality to make leaders accountable to the general public or to make the state accountable to its general citizenry or to make citizens loyal and accountable to the state, beyond the morality of the highly personal relationships legitimated by kin moralities. Kin groups have been the primary (although not the exclusive) recruiting groups for the followers of *zu' ama'*. Kin groups often have remained attached to the same family of *zu' ama'* for generations, with son/client following father/client in loyalty to the same father/son series of political leaders. Leadership and followership have been built on kinship relationships although never limited to it.

Zu' ama', for their part, have used lineage leaders and kin elders to link with kin groups, further reinforcing kin structures of authority. *Zu' ama'* have mobilized their own kin as political bases, recruiting their sons not only as followers but as heirs to their political leadership. Indeed, kinship has been the gateway to political office in Lebanon for men and for women (Kahhaleh 1997; Moawad 1997)—a venue found even in the United States (Kim 1998; Hess 1966). *Zu' ama'* have used the idioms and morality of kinship to legitimate relationships with their followers, calling a follower "*ibni*" or "*binti*" (my son, daughter), "*'ammi*," "*khalti*" (my uncle, aunt), "*khiyyi*," "*ikti*" (my brother, sister) to evoke the loyalties of kinship. *Zu' ama'* have used their positions within the state to extract state resources and services for their personal followings. These highly personalized venues for citizenship claims have easily elided with sectarian venues because patron-client relationships tend to be same-sect.

Political parties have not been so much sectarian in the sense of representing the interests of particular sects as a whole as they have been the personal followings of individual leaders (*zu' ama'*) rooted largely within specific sects and organized around highly personalized patron-client relationships (*za'im-zilm*) (Suleiman 1967). Patrons have been willing to receive any potential client and clients have been willing to seek out multiple patrons, depending on circumstances (Joseph 1990). These patron/client relationships, the heart of the political "party" system in Lebanon, have tended to have few ideological underpinnings and fewer yet systematic religious rationalities. Within every religious sect there have been multiple political leaders competing with each other as much if not more than with leaders of other religious sects for claims to the personal loyalties of followers. That kin groups, however, have tended to coincide with sect membership or be subsumed within sects (given kin and sect endogamy) has facilitated the translation of kin-based mobilization into sect-based mobilization.

For the sake of political order, it has been kin groups that have had to be kept together. Pivotal kin institutions have mobilized to solidify the loyalty of kin and authority of kin males and seniors over kin members. *Wasta*, mediation by kin brokers (usually kin elders, male and female) have put moral pressure on kin members to resolve disputes and maintain kin civility.

Kin patriarchs often have been able to strengthen their personal and kin positions vis-à-vis political leaders by disciplining kin members to vote, in local and national elections, in a block for the same leader. *Zu'ama'*, for their part, have courted kin patriarchs and attempted to funnel resources from the state to their clientele through kin elders. In this manner the interests and actions of political leaders and kin elders often have coincided to reinforce the political advantages of kin solidarity.

Public order has not been just about keeping women in their place (Vogel 1994, 80). It has also been about keeping men in their place, junior men and senior men. Patriarchs have had control over females and juniors, but they also have had responsibilities for them. The kinship system, by tying males and seniors to their responsibilities to females and juniors, has acted as a form of discipline over those it has empowered. The kinship system has constrained the males and seniors it has privileged. It has cared for the females and juniors it has controlled. Kin has provided a structure of governance, a form of discipline (Deleuze 1997), policing members into hierarchical structures of gendered and aged authority from which political and religious leaders constitute their "imagined" "natural" "communities."

The codes of duty, the honor of obligations, have been critical to the discipline of kinship and to the control mechanisms of the care/control kin contract. To the Lebanese the first line of duty has been to kin. Obligations to kin have far exceeded obligations to the state. Most males and seniors have felt a sense of responsibility to their kin and those in their charge. If the extended kin culture has given brothers authority over sisters, it has also given brothers responsibilities for sisters. If elders have had rights over juniors, their rights have been conditioned with obligations. Grandparents have been involved in raising grandchildren; uncles and aunts have raised nieces and nephews. Brothers have shared finances, work, and homes with each other. Modesty has been expected of both men and women. Obedience (*ta'a*) to elders has been expected of junior males and females.

In Lebanon, as Vogel (1994, 84) cites for the West, the penalties for disobedience for women have been much higher. The weight of kinship work has fallen on women in Lebanon, as Micaela di Leonardo (1987) has argued for ethnic women in the United States, but it has also fallen on men. In the example above of the seventy-year-old never-married Christian woman, the brother indeed has felt responsible for her welfare. He had purchased a summer apartment for his family near her summer apartment with the intent that they would live near each other in retirement. The stories of older brothers sacrificing their own education for the education of younger siblings (including younger sisters) are rampant in Lebanese society. In my ongoing study of a Christian lower middle-class village near

Beirut, a man in his forties took over the head of household functions after the death of his father more than a decade ago and after his elder brother emigrated. The siblings—all adult—(including a married sister, her husband, and children) continued to live together, with the mother formally in charge of the household but the second-oldest son providing the financial and moral cement. He confided to me that none of his working siblings contributed financially to the cost of supporting the household. He bore the financial burden. Yet, he gladly drove one and one-half hours to bring home special food for the mother to cook for his sibs, paid for his sister's education, helped his brothers establish their businesses, and regularly took his youngest sister to "*shammimha al hawa*" (let her smell the wind—take her out).

Another example comes from the same village. There, a teenage girl ran away with her young sweetheart in an effort to force her parents to let her marry her suitor. It was her brother and her father's brother (*'amha*) who went to find her and negotiate with the kin of her suitor. Her paternal uncle, in this highly endogamous kin group, was also her mother's father's mother's sister's son (maternal grandmother's sister's son). When the paternal uncle proclaimed that he knew the suitor's kin and that they were an honorable and acceptable match, her parents finally accepted and allowed her to marry the suitor. Although they might have agreed anyway, the voice of the *'am,* the girl's strongest protector after her father and brother, gave the marriage the moral authority of the kinship system.

Kin responsibility disciplined males and seniors into moral obligations to care for women and juniors. It also gave them authority over those for whom they were responsible. The siblings of the man in his forties discussed above usually asked his advice on major ventures. His sister had to ask his permission, when she was younger, to go out. The mother turned to him for household decisions. The mother summed up his position to me: "He is everything."

Females and junior have suffered disproportionately in this extended patriarchal kin system. Politically, however, the system has been designed to discipline and control kin members, regardless of gender and age, while caring for and nurturing them. To mobilize kinship in the service of control and care does not, in itself, require gender inequality. The kinship system in Lebanon appears to have been fluid historically and in many respects remains so. Women kin members have been critical social actors in the kinship system, particularly as they have gained the authority of age. In the civic myth of extended kinship patriarchy has been upheld by the system of patrilineal descent for Muslims and Christians. For most Lebanese the matrilineal line (the mother's lineage), however, has been important and has been deployed situationally to make claims not only to resources but also to identity. Although the myth of kinship has focused on the patrilineal kin and on the male members of those lineages, the reality has been that matrilineal uncles, aunts, grandparents, cousins have played critical roles in the lives of the children of mothers—expanding their brokerage networks, offering financial and political assistance, giving moral support, and offering marital possibilities. Matrilineal kin have often undermined or challenged the authority and control of patrilineal kin over their members. The day-to-day involvement of matrilineal kin has increased the power and influence of women of those lineages (Joseph 1993a). That matrilineal kinship has also been gender and age hierarchical, however, has meant that matrilineality has not challenged patriarchy.

The reality is that kinship has been very diverse in Lebanon. Patriarchy, like all aspects of kinship, has always been a struggled for and struggled against institution (by both women and men, juniors, and seniors). The lived kinship system has always been complex and contested. Kin have not always taken care of their own. They can be very competitive and hostile to each other. Contrary to the famous proverb, kin have often allied with strangers against each other. Although the reality of kinship has been full of contradictions, kinship has remained the center of social and political action in Lebanon.

Citizenship Laws

Citizenship laws are designed to create the legal subjects of the state, subsidizing a process of "subject-ification" (Foucault 1983; Ong 1996). In Lebanon citizenship laws have codified rules and supported practices further institutionalizing the extended patriarchal kinship that underwrites them. The primary vehicle for reinscribing extended patriarchal kinship has been the privileging of patrilineality (Joseph in press c) and the nesting of kinship within the realm of the sacred through the delegation of family law to religious institutions.

The basic Constitution of Lebanon was written in 1926 during the French Mandate. In their final forms articles 7, 12, and 21 laid the basis for formal equality of genders before the law. Article 7 states: "All Lebanese are equal before the law. They enjoy equal civil and political rights and are equally subjected to public charges and duties, without any distinction whatever" (Butros 1973). Article 12 asserts, "All Lebanese citizens are equally admitted to all public functions without any other cause for preference except their merit and competence and according to the conditions set by law" (Butros 1973). Article 21 gives the formal franchise to Lebanese:

"Any Lebanese citizen aged 21 who meets the conditions of the electoral law is entitled to vote" (Butros 1973). The Representative Council, from which the Constitution was developed in 1926, considered adding clauses in articles 7, 12, 21 to specify the application of each clause equally to men and to women or to all religious sects or to all citizens regardless of regional affiliation. But each clause was defeated with the argument that the application of each clause to each of these categories was already clear and, therefore, specification was not necessary (Mogheizel 1985). Laur Mogheizel, a pioneer for women's legal rights until her death in 1997, argued in her important study of Lebanese laws that the Lebanese Constitution and Lebanese laws have generally been written in gender-neutral language and that when the legislature intended for a particular article or law to apply only to men, it specified "male" after "Lebanese." The Constitution, however, does not have an article specifying equality of women and men before the law or the equality women and men in economic, social, and cultural rights.

Although the intent may have been clear at the framing of the Constitution, the conditions to be met for voting eligibility were left to be defined by regular legislative law. Electoral laws issued by Decree no. 1307 on 10 March 1922 and by Decree no. 2 L. R. on 2 January 1934 referred to Lebanese generically, making no reference to gender-specific exclusions. But the Election Law issued 10 August 1950, superseding the 1934 decree, denied women the right to vote and to be elected to public office. The exclusion of women's franchise was achieved by limiting voting rights to Lebanese registered in electoral lists that included only male Lebanese citizens above the age of twenty-one (Mogheizel 1985).

Lebanese feminist organizations actively lobbied, held conferences, organized demonstrations, wrote petitions, and campaigned through all forms of public media from the 1930s on behalf of women's equal political rights. Legislative Decree no. 6 on 4 November 1952 ordered that women be "gradually" given their political rights by first being included in the election lists of municipal elections and later in the national election lists. Initially, women were required to have an elementary schooling degree, but later this condition was dropped. Voting was made obligatory for men, but not for women. This gender distinction was eliminated in the 24 April 1957 Electoral Law, which dropped the obligation of voting for men and asserted that all electoral lists include the names of both Lebanese women and men (Mogheizel 1985). The Electoral Law of 26 April 1960 consolidated women's political rights by stating that every Lebanese woman and man age twenty-one and older can vote and run for office if he or she is on the electoral lists, with the electoral lists required to include both women and men.

In 1953 Emily Fares Ibrahim was the first woman to run for parliamentary elections; she ran in several elections but was not elected. Between 1953 and 1972 seven women ran for Parliament with two running twice and one running three times (Mogheizel 1985). In 1960 Mirna al-Boustani al-Khazan Hikma was elected to complete the remaining eight months of the term of her father, Emile al-Boustani, who had just died. In the 1996 elections three women were elected to Parliament, one the wife of an assassinated president, one the wife of a deceased member of parliament, and one the sister of the previous prime minister. Although more women eventually have run for and achieved office, the Lebanese Parliament has never managed to have more than a handful of women members. In 1998–99 three women were serving in Parliament. Some women have also run for and obtained seats in municipal councils in a number of Lebanese cities and villages.

The Lebanese Constitution deferred to the Parliament the defining of avenues for obtaining Lebanese citizenship. Lebanese citizenship laws were devised largely during the French Mandate period and significantly reflect the influence of French law on Lebanese citizenship laws. French legal tradition had been based on the Roman legal principle that men, but not women, could own property (Jreisati 1997). Classical Western contractarian theory defined the citizen as a property owner. As property owners, only "free men" could be citizens. Carole Pateman (1988) argued, men were seen to own property and to own property in themselves and their dependent women and children. In French law, men were also seen as having property in their persons (Pateman 1988). That Lebanon followed French law in this gendered philosophy has meant that women, in Lebanon, came to be seen as properties of men (Sharafeddine 1997). Whereas Pateman argues that the property-owning franchise criteria classically meant that men were seen as autonomous individuals, the Lebanese state, I suggest, has regarded even males primarily as members of families rather than as individuals. The state, however, has granted males more "individual" status than females. Lebanese women can own property (and since the Lebanese Civil War they have had the legal right to own businesses), but in many ways they have been seen as less-individualized citizens than have men. This gender-differentiated view of female and male citizens has been inscribed in Lebanese laws regulating the acquisition of citizenship.

The principal stake in the acquisition of citizenship has been whether citizenship has been passed through blood or land. During Ottoman rule, which lasted until World War I, citizenship had been based partly on one's connection to the land and partly on one's inheritance of blood (which included mother's blood). By 1925 Ottoman law was allowing women to pass citizenship on to their children if their children were born on Ottoman land (Makdisi 1997). French law at that time (changed in 1960) defined citizenship predominately through blood (patrilineal blood exclusively). Following French law, Lebanon, since 1925, has allowed children to obtain citizenship only through their fathers, except under unusual circumstances (Makdisi 1997; Mogheizel 1997). The commitment to this patrilineal principle of citizenship was largely responsible for Lebanon's refusal to ratify the United Nations Convention to Eliminate All Forms of Discrimination Against Women, which specified that women have the right to pass citizenship on to their children (Mogheizel 1997).

The patrilineal principle of citizenship acquisition was conditioned partly by the conjugal relation for a time. Before 1960, Lebanese woman marrying foreign men lost their Lebanese citizenship, whereas foreign women marrying Lebanese men lost their previous citizenship and became Lebanese nationals. This ruling preserved the patrilineal passage of citizenship to children. It also had loomed as a threat to women who contemplated marrying nonnationals, outside their patrilineally defined political community. After 1960, citizenship laws permitted Lebanese women to choose their nationality after marriage. Lebanese women who followed the nationality of their foreign husbands have been able, since 1960, to reclaim their Lebanese citizenship upon the deaths of their husbands.

Lebanese women, however, have not had the right to pass Lebanese citizenship on to their husbands, except under very limited circumstances. A foreign husband who has obtained Lebanese citizenship through his Lebanese wife may pass Lebanese citizenship to their children. Linkage by land has allowed children born on Lebanese land of unknown parentage (unknown mother or father) to obtain Lebanese citizenship. Children born on Lebanese land of a known mother but an unknown father also have been able to obtain Lebanese citizenship.

Lebanese men, though, have the legal right to pass Lebanese citizenship to their foreign wives. Foreign wives who have been naturalized Lebanese have had the right to pass Lebanese citizenship to their minor children if their Lebanese husbands died. Lebanese women, reclaiming their Lebanese citizenship after the deaths of their foreign husbands, also have had a right to pass Lebanese citizenship to their minor children. This inequity in the citizenship laws has led to the plea by Lebanese women's rights activists that Lebanese women should be given the same rights that the foreign wives of Lebanese men have to pass citizenship to their children (Mogheizel 1997).

As Collier, Maurer, and Suarez-Navaz (1995) have observed, blood and land can both be naturalized and essentialized. That Lebanese citizenship laws have followed French, rather than Ottoman law, in privileging blood over land was influenced by the active role of the French in writing the Constitution in 1925. Cultural premises biologizing kinship no doubt also facilitated the privileging of blood. That blood was defined as patrilineal was, at the time, consistent with both French and Lebanese cultural systems. The linkage of blood, kinship, and nation has been central to the gendering and aging of citizenship in Lebanon. That linkage has been particularly discriminatory toward women and children, who more than men and seniors have been defined more through kin and religious structures. The most dramatic site of this gendered and aged linkage of women and children with kin and sect has been the sectarian family laws.

The Civic Myth Codified: Personal Status Laws

If, as I have argued, extended kinship has been central to the social order of the state, it would follow that the state has needed to ensure the sanctity of kinship. Kinship evokes the highest moral authority in Lebanon, second only to religion. So central has kinship been to the political order that the state has sanctified kinship by reinscribing it in religion, which both authorizes and claims exclusive domain over kinship. The centrality of kinship in the Lebanese social order partly rationalizes the state relinquishing, to religious sects, the critical domain of "family law." The delegation of "family law" to religious sects, I suggest, testifies not only to the centrality of the civic myth of sectarian pluralism but also to the sanctification of kinship in the political order. The blessings of the divine has further enhanced the power of kinship in the lives of Lebanese.

Article 9 of the 1926 Constitution guaranteed freedom of religion and the rights of sects to observe their own family (personal status) laws. "Liberty of conscience is absolute. By rendering homage to the Almighty, the State respects all creeds and guarantees and protects their free exercise, on condition that they do not interfere with public order. It also guarantees to individuals, whatever their religious allegiance, the respect of their personal status and their religious interests" (Butros 1973). Article 10 afforded sectarian communities the right to establish their own schools, further empowering religious sects in an arena critical to kinship—the socialization of children: "Education is free so long as it is not contrary to public order and to good manners and does not touch the dignity of creeds. No derogation shall affect the right of communities to have their schools, subject to the general prescriptions on public education edited by the state" (Butros 1973). But it was Decree no. 60/L. R., put into effect by the French High Commissioner de Martel on 13 March 1936, that gave religious sects the critical right to devise their own family laws and to establish religious sectarian courts to adjudicate matters of family law (Dib 1975, 11). Decree no. 60/L. R. provided for the possibility of legislation of a civil family law for those religious sects not formally recognized by the state and, therefore, not entitled to their own family laws and courts. Lebanon, however, following a pattern typical of most Middle Eastern states (including Israel), has not developed a civil personal status code. Members of religious sects not recognized by the state, therefore, must either submit to the laws and courts of one of the recognized sects or leave the country to marry, divorce, or deal with other matters of family law.

Family law, also called personal status law, regulates marriage, divorce, child custody, and inheritance. The delegation of legal authority over matters of personal status to religious institutions has institutionalized a legal pluralism consequent to the civic myth of sectarian pluralism. Legal multiculturalism has meant that Lebanese citizens have not shared a common legal culture around issues crucial to women, children, and civil rights. Nor have they had recourse to a shared body of civil law in disputes over marriage, divorce, inheritance, or child custody. The state has marginalized itself in the arena of family law, making itself legally unavailable to its citizens in these critical matters. Fifteen family codes have been authorized by the state, for the eighteen legally recognized religious sects. Fifteen different legal cultures condition the experiences of Lebanese citizens around kinship issues. Which legal code applies to any particular citizen has been determined by descent, designated by "birth group"—by kin affiliation, by religious descent designed through the patrilineal line. That such pivotal matters of law have been determined by prescriptions of birth has been one of the most profound testimonies to the power of the civic myth of extended kinship.

The nesting of family law in religious sects has empowered the clergy to define the boundaries of the marriage community—who and how Lebanese can marry and divorce. They have been empowered to decide the lives and futures of children, not only in custody matters after divorce but also through education. They have had a critical role in economic matters dealing with property—the allocation of inheritance. All this has given religious sects a role in constituting the character of the "subject" of the state in legal terms.

Historically, most clerics in Lebanon have defined the boundaries of their marriage communities rather narrowly. Whereas religious endogamy today focuses on the larger religious rubrics (Muslims and Christians), in the past, as recently as the early twentieth century, religious endogamy meant marrying within the smaller religious sect. Maronite clergy frequently forbade or discouraged marriages to Greek Orthodox and vice versa, for example. In the 1970s I documented numerous cases of Armenian Orthodox priests intervening to prevent marriages of Armenians to any non-Armenian Christians (Joseph 1983). Druze clerics discouraged marriages to Shi'a, and so forth.

The legal pluralism in family law has led to an absence of an "equality before the law" standard in Lebanon. Women and children of different religious sects face very different legal choices and possibilities in terms of marriage, divorce, child custody, and inheritance. Sunni women, in practice, have not been able to inherit from their fathers, but Christian women have. Muslim women may have to face a marriage with co-wives, but Christian and Druze women have not. Muslim women have not been given alimony on divorce, but Christian women have. Greek Orthodox, Shi'a, and Sunni women have been able to divorce, but not Catholic women (Zalzal 1997).

Women and children have been disproportionally disadvantaged by the delegation of family law to religious sects. Women are more likely than men to forfeit their religious heritages when they marry out. Women, although not legally required to do so, have been expected to follow the religion of their husbands. Women who marry out of their religious community may not pass on to their children their own religious heritages—a right reserved for men.

For Muslim women exogamy is more problematic. Muslim family laws have forbidden Muslim women to marry non-Muslims. Non-Muslim men must convert to Islam to marry a Muslim woman. These laws have prohibited Muslim women from abandoning their patrilineally ascribed religion. The extraordinary measure of prescribing that a woman follow her Muslim father's religion rather than her non-Muslim husband's probably emerged from the recognition that women have been the weak link in patrilineal extended kin. The religious exogamy of a woman would lead to the loss of children for the religious sect—losses to the patrilineally defined religious community—whereas men's religious exogamy would recruit children away from other sects—and other patrilineages.

Sectarian family law has upheld the extended patrilineal kin's authority over and custody of children. In cases of divorce, death, or absence of the father, family law in most religious sects has privileged the father's lineage over a mother's claim or the claims of the matriline to children. Religious institutions have often upheld the rights of patrilineal grandparents, uncles, and aunts over those of the mother for child custody cases. In divorces, Muslim women may have custody of their children in the children's early years but may lose custody of children to their husbands and the husband's lineage as the children grow older. Typically, Muslim women may keep their boys until they are seven years old and girls until they are nine years old, at which point physical custody may revert to their fathers or the fathers' lineages. Given the specter of estrangement from their children, some women remain in unwanted marriages to retain access to their children. Muslim women who remarry after divorce may also lose custody of their children to their ex-husbands or the ex-husband's male kin. But Muslim men do not lose custody of their children if they remarry. Women who convert to another religion or who did not convert to Islam to marry a Muslim man would not be given custody of their children upon divorce (Yakan 1997).

Carole Pateman (1988) has argued that classical contractarian political theory drew a line between the public and private (domestic, kinship) in which the public was the realm subject to state regulation and the private was subject to natural law. In Lebanon the state drew a line between the public and private in which the private (domestic, kinship) was subject to religious law. By delegating kinship to religious law and funneling citizenship through religious membership, however, the state erased the line it drew between the public and private. It made religious laws, in effect, the laws of state, requiring citizens to follow religious laws to exercise their citizen rights. The state assimilated the rules of extended patrilineal kinship codified by sectarian family laws into the codes and practices of Lebanese citizenship.

◆   ◆   ◆

Ursula Vogel (1994) has argued that in Western liberal democratic theory, from Hobbes to Rousseau, women were targeted as the population to be controlled (through the institution of marriage) to ensure order. "Nothing less than the permanence of the legal order and, indeed, the immortality of civil society are staked upon the presumption 'that every child can be considered the son of the mother's husband'" (Vogel 1994, 81). In Lebanon, I have argued, disproportionate control over women and children has been critical to the disciplinary mechanisms subsidized by the state. The extended kinship system fostered by the state and sanctified by religion, however, has controlled men and women, adults and children. If the basic requirement of the state has been to achieve social order and community structure has been central to social order, then the kinship system has been the crucial strategy for achieving social order. Lebanese are embedded in extended kinship relations—legally, politically, socially, economically, and religiously. Extended kin relations succor and sacrifice them.

Vogel has suggested (1994, 86) that the idea of the "individual" (as the "abstract figure of the moral agent and rights bearer") has been based on the assumption of men's dominance in the West. In Lebanon the notion of the "individual" as an autonomous self has coexisted with the notion of a "connective" self that has not been gendered but which, when combined with patriarchy, has created an asymmetrical vulnerability for women and children (Joseph 1993a). The bearer of moral agency in Lebanon has not been the autonomous individual but the kinship network. The kin network has shared moral agency—not as a corporate collective, but a shifting set of intimately connected others, including patrilineal and matrilineal kin (while privileging patrilineal kin). Vogel (1994, 87) further has suggested that women's citizenship has aligned itself with the idea of a civic public built on recognition of heterogeneity and plurality. In Lebanon plurality has too easily slipped into the sectarian pluralism, which has subsidized and been subsidized by extended kinship.

The logic of law has been to construct the subject of law (Collier, Maurer, and Suarez-Navaz 1995). Citizenship laws literally have constituted persons as "citizens," as the bearers of the collective civic identity. Aihwa Ong has argued, citizenship is "a cultural process of 'subject-ification,'" in the Foucaldian sense of self-making and being-made by power relations that produce consent through schemes of surveillance, discipline, control, and administration" (Ong 1996, 737).

The civic myth of sectarian pluralism inscribed a legal fiction based on a myth of homogeneous religious communities with stable cultures continuous over time. The national symbol of the civic myth has been the National Pact. The popular understanding that the National Pact was a bargain cut between political leaders of religious sects to preserve the relative autonomy of their "communities" captures only part of the civic myth. To use Deniz Kandiyoti's (1988) term, it was also a patriarchal bargain cut between men as heads of extended kin groups in alliance with men as heads of religious sects to discipline men and seniors and women and children as well. Karen Sacks (1975) argued early on that control over women and children was the reward the state gave to men in exchange for its control over their labor. In the weak state extended kin groups became part of the political organization of politics. That extended kin groups were patriarchal was crucial to the structuring of discipline in the newly formed Lebanese state.

In the National Pact the political leaders concluded a gentlemen's agreement, their own social contract, based upon the kinship contract. They enshrined their gentlemen's agreement in the realm of the sacred by elevating religious family laws to state laws. Women and children were the invisible chips with which the political and religious leaders bargained. Women and children were very much a part of the national pact, but as part of extended kin groups. The National Pact, as civic myth, was concluded at the disproportionate expense of women and children, yet it also disciplined men and elders. Hidden in the civic myth of sectarian pluralism has been the civic myth of the extended kinship system, sanctified by religion.

I have argued that insofar as extended kinship has supported and been supported by religion, it has lent itself to be glossed by religion. Disaggregating kinship from religion is critical for feminist analyses of the gendering and aging of citizenship in Lebanon. Recognizing the separateness or relative autonomy of kin and sect will help reveal the processes that differentiate the gendering and aging of citizenship in Lebanon from other societies, particularly Western societies. The difference in the relationships of Western and Middle Eastern states to kinship systems may explain why, to understand the gendering of citizenship in Lebanon, it is necessary to isolate the role of kinship in underpinning sectarian pluralism and patriarchy. Sectarianism cannot be taken on its own terms as the undiluted point of departure in analyzing the gendering and aging of citizenship. Nor can one conflate kinship with sectarianism or gloss kinship under sectarianism.

Targeting kinship realigns feminist analysis of gender inequality from a focus on conjugal relationship to a culturally specific critique of extended kinship and the culturally specific weave of kinship in the body politic. For example, I have suggested that, in Lebanon, the hypervulnerability of women and children has been less a result of the conjugal relationship and more the outcome of rules and dynamics nested in the extended kin structure—particularly patrilineality. Disaggregating kin and sect also will expose the social reality that kinship in Lebanon has not been only about the power of males and seniors. It has also been about the disciplining of males and seniors. The hyperfocus on gender subordination in the study of kinship has made it more difficult to understand why women would subscribe to kinship as emphatically as they do in Lebanon. Kinship has been powerful because it has cared for and controlled its members. Given the weakness of the state, the care of kin has been critical for survival. Disaggregating kin from sect also will help demonstrate the processes by which kin and sect groups have interests that may not always coincide. During the Civil War, many religious sects attempted to wrest control of their members away from extended kin groups—with some success. But in the devastations of the war kin also drew closer together for survival. The postwar discrediting of many religiously based political groups destablized their grip on their members while other religiously based political groups have continued to consolidate the loyalties of their members, at times at the expense of kin loyalties.

The civic myth of extended kinship has been crucial for understanding the structure and dynamics of patriarchy and the gendering of citizenship in Lebanon. The investment of the state in kinship has come not only from a concern to control women as women but also from the concern of a weak state for sustaining social order in general, including controlling the very men and seniors empowered in the gender hierarchal system. Control of women's sexuality and certainty of patrilineal genealogy has been an important feature of the Lebanese legal system as has been the general control of all social actors. Generic allegiance and submission to the rules and authority of the kinship has been primary to the script of the national civic myth.

I have argued that the kin contract has been the hidden civic myth behind the gentlemen's agreement designed in the National Pact. The kin contract has operated through a care/control paradigm in which kin members have received nurturance in a system that simultaneously has required their internalization and embracement of patriarchal moralities, structures of authority, and codes of behavior. In the face of a weak state that offered few civic alternative services and projection, which assimilated kinship dynamics into political processes and which reinscribed the power of extended kin in the lives of Lebanese citizens through the codification of religious family law as defacto state law, extended kinship has consolidated its force, has obtained legal stature, and has been blessed by sacred authority.

I have argued that men and seniors have also been the subject of kinship discipline. It has been, paradoxically, the relative success of the kin contract to discipline males and seniors into their responsibilities and obligations, to manage their labor, to commit them to their families, that has led to the asymmetrical vulnerability of women and juniors. Barbara Ehrenreich (1983) has argued that the women's movement did not destroy the American family. Rather, she contends, American men abandoned their families in droves in the 1950s and 1960s. Women, left with elevated financial, social, and moral family responsibilities, she argued, responded, by the 1970s, by demanding rights concomitant with their responsibilities. I might suggest, as a logical deduction from Ehrenreich's argument, that if, in the United States, it was the weakness of men's commitment to the family contract that gave rise to the women's movement, in Lebanon, paradoxically, it has been the capacity of the extended kin contract to discipline both men and women into the rights and responsibilities of kinship that has dampened the movement for women's rights and responsibilities as citizens.

In Lebanon, relative to the United States, men have not abandoned their kin responsibilities. The culture of kinship is alive to the responsibilities of men to their wives, children, parents, siblings, and extended kin. Men, generally, have been expected and have expected themselves to work, and even sacrifice, to support their kin. Many men may have not carried out their culturally prescribed responsibilities. But there has been no cultural ambiguity, no social debate as to what and whether they have extended kin responsibilities. Men's rewards for the obligations and duties of their roles has been the authorization (legal and religious) of their power over women and children.

Similarly, women have largely embraced kinship. Even though some may contest specifics of their culturally prescribed roles, few women in Lebanon would argue for more "American"-style kin relationships. Women and children have paid a price—acceptance of the structures of patriarchal authority. Their rewards have been the socially supported expectation of the care of kin. Women, in addition, have had the possibility of a kind of respect for their kinship roles not available to many women in the United States. Lebanese kin culture has worshiped "the mother," even iconized her as the true idea of all that is good in society. There have been far more songs, romantic poetry, and essays written about the "mother" and the love for and of the mother in Lebanon than there are about the father. Women strut their pregnancies in public streets. As they have sons and age, they usually come to have material power among their extended kin, including their husbands. The elevation of and mythologizing of the role of the mother, itself operates as a form of discipline to recruit women into these roles. Many Lebanese women have challenged and resisted specifics of kin relationalities; yet they have generally embraced their extended kin as the central site of their senses of self, identities, responsibilities, and rights.

In this chapter I have not challenged the civic myth of sectarian pluralism as a central story of citizenship in Lebanon so much as I have exposed the hidden civic myth at stake—the centrality of extended kinship to the reproduction of the sociopolitical order and the complex and paradoxical deployment of a care/control paradigm of extended kinship to achieve order. The civic myth inscribed a legal fiction of a kinship system based on imagined homogeneous kinship groups with stable identities over time. Extended kinship has been constructed through social, political, legal, and sectarian processes. It has also been contested. Lebanese have never been the passive recipients of edicts of the state or religious sects. Kinship structures have changed, identities transformed, loyalties shifted, and membership has been fluid. Lebanese culture shifts; like all cultures it has never been stable or fixed. Boundaries of communities have changed; people have moved, and values, mores, rules constantly contested, revised. Women and children, just as men and elders, have negotiated, manipulated, and struggled within as well as against the kinship system. While the reality has been constantly changing and the kinship system has constantly been challenged and transformed, the state codified the "myth" of extended kinship" hidden within the National Pact and sectarian pluralism. It has been as much the hidden civic myth of extended kinship as it has been sectarian pluralism that has inscribed gender inequality in Lebanese citizenship laws and practices.

7

Transit Citizens

Gender and Citizenship under the Palestinian Authority

ISLAH JAD, PENNY JOHNSON, AND RITA GIACAMAN

MORE THAN FOUR YEARS after the signing of the Declaration of Principles between Israel and the PLO in September 1993 and more than two years since the election of a Palestinian Legislative Council in January 1996, Palestinian citizenship remains a vexed question, both in its legal definition, in emerging governmental policies, and in daily transactions between the Palestinian Authority (PA) and individuals and groups in Palestinian society. An examination of gender and citizenship in Palestine must, therefore, begin with a basic question: Are there Palestinian citizens, and, if so, what is the nature of their citizenship? Indeed, "Palestine" itself is fundamentally at question, existing at present as a nonstate entity with noncontiguous territory, limited authority, and even more limited sovereignty, both external and internal limits on its legislative abilities, and an unresolved state of occupation by Israel.

In the optimistic view, Palestine, during the "transitional period," is an emerging nation-state and is in the process of developing the rights and obligations of citizenship. In a pessimistic view, Palestinian citizenship, legally speaking, remains a glorified Israeli identity card because the Israeli stamp of approval is required before any Palestinian identity card or passport can be issued. Even the basic human right to family reunion meets some of the same obstacles today as in the period of direct Israeli military occupation. The perilous state of final status negotiations at present between Israel and the Palestinians reinforces the view that the present transitional arrangements may harden into a new form of apartheid.

Both views are partial truths, and both fail to provide an adequate framework to examine the complicated and contradictory transformations taking place on the ground. The establishment of a Palestinian Authority, the return of the external Palestinian leadership, and the election of Palestinians representatives have profound political implications. The terrain of citizenship—as rights, claims and obligations based on membership in a community—is fluid and in formation through a wide variety of factors, including ideologies of nationalist entitlement, networks of political patronage, changing social, political, and economic relations, the formulation and implementation of new policies and changing patterns of political participation, and the limits of the Oslo Agreements. All of these factors have significant gender dimensions.

When examining the question of gender and citizenship in Palestine in transition, we thus take a multifaceted approach. We examine the legal rules that govern citizenship, including the initiatives to formulate a Basic Law, and their implication for gender equity in Palestine. But we also look at citizenship in its active dimension through an analysis of the strategies and activities of the Palestinian women's movement and briefly review emerging governmental population policy as an area crucial to women.

Post-Oslo: Features of Authority

Before we examine these aspects, it is useful to highlight several features of the post-Oslo period that influence the formation of citizenship, in general, and gender and citizenship, in particular.

Militarization and Security

The Oslo Agreements were security-led agreements.[1] Israeli security, control of anti-Oslo opposition among Palestinians ("internal security"), and regional stability and security—an overriding concern of the United States and other Western powers—guided the terms of the formal agreements and their unpublished annexes and confidential side agreements. In the Declaration of Principles (1993) and the Interim Agreements (1995) the creation of "a strong police force" was one of the few clear Palestinian prerogatives and one that the Palestinian Authority (PA) took up with alacrity. At least seven to

1. The Oslo Agreements refer to the Declaration of Principles on Interim Self-Government Arrangements (DOP) signed on 13 September 1993 by Israel and the Palestine Liberation Organization (PLO), and the Interim Agreement on the West Bank and the Gaza Strip (IA) signed by Israel and the PLO on 28 September 1995. For a legal analysis of the agreements, see Raja Shehadeh 1997.

nine separate security, police, or army agencies are currently functioning, with personnel variously estimated at fifty to eighty thousand, making the police to civilian ratio one of the highest in the world. At the same time, Israel retains overall security powers, which are exercised through closures, arrests, and even house demolitions. Given that the political structure of the Palestine Liberation Organization, strongly reflected in the PA, already had many military elements, a militarization of Palestinian politics was inevitable, leading one political analyst to observe that the security services "monopolize the whole of public space" (Bishara 1998, 214). This monopolization has a number of implications for women's citizenship and empowerment, specifically in that nationalist entitlements—such as positions in the Authority—are primarily given to males who are part of the militarized hierarchy of the major political organization, Fateh, and more generally in that internal security takes precedence over democracy, the rule of law, and citizens' rights. On the positive side, women's issues are necessarily a part of the struggle for democracy, broadening the context and allies of the women's movement.

State and Civil Society

Before the Palestinian Authority, the Palestine Liberation Organization in exile, one analyst pointed out, had a "unitary model" in which state and civil society were conflated; "a pluralistic civil society in the making" was "lodged within the confines of a proto-state" (Giacaman 1998, 8). Thus, the PLO contained unions for workers, women, students, and other groups, besides economic enterprises, research centers, and other nongovernmental organizations (NGOs). Transposing this model, the PA "envisions society organized into 'General' and 'Higher' Unions at the top of which, after Oslo, the Palestinian Authority presides" (Giacaman 1998, 6). The NGO movement, including the women's movement, has vigorously opposed this model, and the Palestinian Authority veers between attempts to control NGOs and to use their capacities for service delivery and their other resources. To date, it seems incapable of using the potential of NGOs and of emerging civil society as a strategic asset for community mobilization for societal development and for an equitable final status solution to the Israeli-Palestinian conflict.

Struggle Against Israel Versus Struggle for Democracy

Israel is still an occupying power, which continues to expand Israeli settlements, insists on sovereignty over both West and East Jerusalem, and enormously affects Palestinian life through its "security" policies (the effect of border closures that restrict movement of workers and goods into Israel and between the West Bank and Gaza on the Palestinian economy being one outstanding issue). This policy means that Palestinian organizations and movements, including the women's movement, continue to focus on the struggle for national rights besides the internal issues of democracy and citizen's rights. Indeed, a focus on internal human rights issues has been criticized, and sometimes punished, by the Palestinian Authority as sabotaging the national cause and serving Western imperial powers. In this climate and under these conditions, the women's movement has the difficult task of building a women's agenda that confronts both the problems of democratization and occupation.

Palestinian Authority Versus the Islamist Opposition

The primary opposition to the Palestinian Authority and the Oslo accords has come from the Islamist opposition, particularly Hamas (an acronym for the Islamic Resistance Movement), which has conducted both suicide attacks against Israel (primarily Israeli civilians) and developed a strong political and social infrastructure in the West Bank and Gaza. The Palestinian Authority's support for the women's movement is influenced by its aim to contain Hamas while the Authority also hesitates to alienate conservative religious sentiments for fear of strengthening the Islamic opposition. At the same time, Hamas's opposition to the women's movement aims to strike a blow to the Authority. The Authority is, thus, an uneasy ally of the women's movement at important times (such as the model parliament described below), and the women's movement has generally been effective in using whatever political space that opens opportunities with the Authority to lobby for women's representation and rights. Some emerging features of state feminism can also be identified, such as women leaders becoming government officials and the blurring of the boundaries between governmental and nongovernmental activities.

Donor-Driven Agendas

Barely two weeks after the signing of the Declaration of Principles on 13 September 1993, the U.S. government hosted approximately forty donor states and institutions in Washington where $2.4 billion was pledged to support the fledgling Palestinian Authority and the Palestinian people in the West Bank and Gaza. The logic was clear: for the peace process to work, the Authority had to be able to function, and the living conditions of Palestinians had to improve. Shortly after, the World Bank became the main coordinator of donor funding, with the United Nations cochairing the local coordination and joint liaison committees and the International Monetary Fund (IMF), World Bank, and United Nations cochairing sectoral working groups (Pederson and Hooper 1998, 14). Although the United Nations has had a long-standing presence on the ground, many of the major donors, including the World Bank and IMF, were new to Palestine. Unlike in some parts of the world, the World Bank, in particular, showed little interest in gender issues (Kuttab 1995 et al.; Taraki 1995), and the crisis in male employment caused by Israeli closures led donors to focus in the first years on short-term employment generation programs that absorbed males as day laborers. Closures and other measures also caused Palestinian per capita income to fall and unemployment to rise, and the economic promise of the peace process was severely tarnished. At the same time, other donors, such as the United Nations and a number of European states, had "gender agendas," which led to the support of women's movement's demands for gender units in ministries, and some valuable projects, such as a successful gender statistics unit at the Palestinian Central Bureau of Statistics. The upsurge in donor funding also created severe imbalances in the resources and programs of women's groups as donor interest in training and workshops—often focused on the "hot" topics of democracy and citizenship— were reflected in a superabundance of such activities, some productive, and others activity for activity's sake, while other interests of women were relatively neglected. Donor support, as elsewhere in the world, is a two-edged sword that the women's movement needs to wield carefully, particularly as it has lost some of its grass-roots base in the era of demobilization of nationalist resistance.

Toward Equal Citizenship?
The Case of the Basic Law

The Declaration of Principles (DOP) instructs the Palestinian Authority and its elected Legislative Council to promulgate a Basic Law—the only primary legislation clearly mandated to the council in the interim agreements as a whole although still subject to an Israeli veto. Numerous drafts of the Basic Law have been proposed, both before the establishment of the council and by the council itself. As of this writing, the council has approved a Basic Law in its third reading, but there is no indication that President Arafat will sign this law into effect.[2] The delay reflects both a sharp conflict

2. Palestinian Legislative Council member Hatem Abdul Qader wrote in a 1998 publication, "We have been waiting for the Basic Law to be endorsed by the Executive, headed by Arafat, since 31 November 1996" (Abdul Qader 1998, 78).

between the legislative and executive, whereby President Arafat has considerably weakened the authority of the council (Abu Amr 1997), but also the structural problem of legislating in a transitional period in which the political form and orientation of the emerging "state" is unclear. For example, significant amendments of existing Jordanian legislation in the West Bank would contradict confederation with Jordan. In addition, it throws a strong spotlight on the problems posed to the Authority by the restrictions of the Oslo accords. For example, President Arafat is probably unwilling to face an Israeli veto, but neither is he prepared to weaken the council's provision in the Basic Law that "Jerusalem is the capital of Palestine," among other contentious issues that would be unacceptable to Israel. Thus, not only the Basic Law but no other significant piece of legislation has been passed by the council and ratified by the president, with the possible exception of a Local Governments Election Law (which regulates one-time municipal elections, several laws to establish governmental agencies, and a Law to Encourage Investment, which essentially bypassed the council).[3]

A previous document embodying Palestinian aspirations, the Palestinian Declaration of Independence, proclaimed in Tunis by the Palestine Liberation Organization on 15 November 1988, guarantees equality between the sexes. As several writers have noted, however, the declaration affirms "equality and non-discrimination in the public rights of men and women," implying that private rights, or rights within the family, are excluded (Rishmawi 1992). Before the establishment of the council, the final of four successive drafts of the Basic Law, reflecting, according to the chief drafter, Anis al-Qassem, "discussions with representatives of the Palestinian women's movement" (al-Qassem 1996) does not contain this qualification. Instead, article 10 stated: "Women and men shall have equal fundamental rights and freedoms without any discrimination."

This provision was also included in a draft produced jointly by the Law Center at Bir Zeit University and Al-Haq, a prominent Palestinian human rights organization. The council's latest version of the Basic Law, however, eliminates this provision and places women's rights in the more-general and less-powerful antidiscriminatory framework: "All Palestinians are equal before the law and the judiciary, without any discrimination between them in respect to rights and obligations, because of race, ethnicity, sex, race, religion, political opinion or disability" (art. 9).

Because this antidiscrimination provision also existed in the earlier drafts by al-Qassem, one can assume that the elimination of an additional provi-

3. In the period between the election of the council in January 1996 and the end of 1998, the Authority, in its official publication, lists only thirteen laws.

sion on equality between women and men was a conscious de-emphasis of gender equity by the council's drafters in the Legal Committee.

Of, perhaps, even greater importance for the gendering of citizenship in Palestine, is the council's addition of clear provisions affirming Islamic law (*shari' a*) and the role of religion in public life. Although all drafts prohibit religious discrimination, the previous drafts of al-Qassem are silent on the status of *shari' a* law and the question of state religion. The council's draft Basic Law affirms in article 4 that "Islam is the official religion of Palestine with respect accorded to the sanctity of all other religions" and that "the principles of Islamic *shari' a* are a principal source of legislation." The use of "a source," rather than "the source," is a deliberate choice because this issue was raised in various debates. The language as a whole reflects a pronounced tendency to adopt the language and practice of other Arab states rather than to differentiate Palestine from them, probably as part of a project of legitimizing the emerging Palestinian state in the region and among Islamic states, and appealing to local constituencies. In this vein, we can also see that the dilemma of gender and citizenship in Palestine is shared with other Arab states: the "complementary" status of men and women in *shari' a* and in personal status law throughout the region, which regulates "family matters" such as divorce, marriage, and inheritance in tension with the status of equal citizens in public life as can clearly be seen when these domains interface, such as in passport regulations or permits to travel abroad. It is interesting that these last items have been particular concerns of the Palestinian women's movement, as noted below.

Among the numerous matters of concern to the women's movement is the question of nationality. The Palestinian National Charter of 1964 derives Palestinian nationality through the father, and not the mother. In contrast, the Palestinian Election Law, which governed the January 1996 elections to the Palestinian Council, defined Palestinian nationality through either parent. An early draft of the council returns to the charter version, affirming: "Palestinians are Arab citizens who were residing normally in Palestine until 1947. Every son [and daughter] to a Palestinian Arab father is considered a Palestinian" (art. 9). The present draft, however, states merely: "Palestinian citizenship shall be regulated by law" (art. 7). The council here has adopted a nonformulation, probably in order to escape acknowledging the restrictions of the interim agreements, whereby Palestinian citizenship is essentially limited to residents of the West Bank and Gaza and a highly select group of returnees. The council thus avoids separating Palestinian nationality and Palestinian citizenship, which would be a very difficult turning point for the Palestinian national movement. Further debates on a nationality law may raise these very prickly questions in which gender issues are subsumed.

Although the Basic Law is a "transitional" law, applicable only in the transitional period before final status and although the experience of many authoritarian states show that constitutional rights may not be enforced, the debate and outcome are important because they indicate competing visions of society and the weight given to them.

The Palestinian Women's Movement and Political Participation

The Palestinian national movement has fluctuated between a discourse of modernity and a discourse of tradition in its positions and practice toward women and women's activism. Similar to other national movements in the Third World, advancing a "modern" role for women was viewed as important to widen political participation and resistance. At the same time, the role of woman as custodians of Palestinian identity and heritage was a linchpin of nationalist ideology reinforced by the loss and idealization of pre-1948 Palestine. The platforms of Palestinian political organizations reflected, and continue to reflect, this dualism, and the nationalist movement has generally contained the women's question inside and for the benefit of nationalist and organizational politics.

The 1964 Palestine National Charter, which founded the Palestine Liberation Organization, has no overt treatment of women's issues nor of any other social group in Palestinian society. "Palestinian" has a unitary meaning, and the public is addressed by general and abstract expressions such as "the Arab Palestinian nation," which is the legal owner of the land (art. 3), or by "eternal Palestinian characteristics." As in other national movements, the main contradiction (here "between the Palestinians and Zionism and colonialism") is seen as primary, and any "contradictions between Palestinian forces are a secondary question" (art. 8). On closer scrutiny, however, eternal Palestinian identity seems also eternally male defined. Fathers pass on Palestinian identity to their sons (art. 4), and a Palestinian is defined as "every individual who was born to an Arabic Palestinian father after the year 1947, either inside or outside Palestine" (art. 5).

The takeover of the PLO in 1968 by the new nationalist guerilla organizations changed the field of political activism with important implications for the women's movement but did not transform the unitary definition of Palestinian identity. The most significant nationalist organization, Fateh, in fact, implemented this definition in practice with a powerful "nonideology" which emphasized national unity above all else. Promoting social unity, rather than addressing social interests, which was essential to mobilizing all nationalist forces (al-Hassan 1972), was given additional weight because of the actual fragmented circumstances of Palestinians in the diaspora or under direct Israeli control in Palestine. An extreme version of this nonideology was pointedly delivered by founding Fateh leader Munir Shafiq in a 1977 article where he affirmed that men and women have identical political interests, denied any specific women's oppression and belittled activist women (Peteet 1991, 161). Although popular unions were founded for women, students, workers, professionals, and refugees, their duty lies in mobilizing their ranks for the nationalist cause, rather than representing their interests. The fact that these groups were based in exile (membership in PLO unions was illegal under the Israeli military occupation) obviously heightened the national, rather than the social, identity of these unions.

Women then had the central task of mobilizing for national liberation—but even in this mission, the burden was on women themselves. Despite PLO slogans on political participation, no policies were put into place that took into account the obstacles facing women and effectively encouraged their participation. The establishment of the General Union of Palestinian Women, the mobilization of women for armed resistance, the establishment of women's committees in the Occupied Territories in the 1970s, the mobilization of women during the *intifada* (Jad 1990), and the publication of women's rights platforms in the 1990s were primarily initiatives of the women's movement itself.

Thus, with the 1991 Madrid Conference and the launching of the Palestinian-Israeli peace process, the women's movement found itself more prepared than other popular movements among Palestinians to take its own serious and realistic initiatives to respond to these changes and take steps to ensure the role of women in the formation of a Palestinian independent state. A directive of the PLO in Tunis, to establish approximately 100 technical committees in the West Bank and Gaza to prepare for statehood, provoked an immediate response. None of the committees dealt with women's issues. The women's movement moved quickly and successfully to demand (and raise funds for) a "women's affairs" technical committee, which, ironically, is the only committee that has survived until the present. The Women's Affairs Technical Committee (WATC) is currently a major coordinating and advocacy group for the local Palestinian women's movement and has an unequivocal nongovernmental identity.

The women's movement was, thus, aware of the necessity of women's participation in state building from the inception of state formation. Indeed, by necessity, Palestinian women had to be "active citizens" (as in the civic republican tradition) in order to be citizens at all (Lister 1997b). As has been frequently the case in Palestinian history, women themselves created their new role with no decision from the political leadership.

The Palestinian Women's Charter was one of the first initiatives of WATC in cooperation with the General Union of Palestinian Women in Tunis. Published in Jerusalem in August 1994 and endorsed by all women's committees and most major nongovernmental organizations concerned with women, the charter was based on the equality provisions in the 1988 Palestinian Declaration of Independence and on relevant United Nations conventions, including the Convention on the Elimination of All Forms of Discrimination Against Women (CEDAW), and placed "equal opportunities for women in rights and obligations" squarely in the framework of building a democratic society. The charter attributes existing "discrimination and inequality against women" to the many colonialisms imposed on Palestine, "ending with the Israeli occupation," reinforced by prejudicial "customs and traditions" (GUPW 1994, 1).

The charter is also a response to and a critique of the first draft of the Basic Law, then issued in Tunis, which contained no provision for gender equality. The charter thus asserts the "principle of equality between women and men in all spheres of life must be included in the constitution" (GUPW 1994, 1). After discussions with the drafter, Anis al-Qassem, such a provision was included, as noted above. The charter also shows a strong concern with the right of women to political participation, including holding political office, and "equal opportunity with men in political parties" and nongovernmental organizations. Women's past and present subordination in Palestinian political parties has been clearly recognized and contested by the Palestinian women's movement; looking to the future, women activists expected to meet some of the same obstacles.

Another clear concern was nationality. The charter went into detail: "To grant the women her right to acquire, preserve or change her nationality. Legislation must also guarantee that her marriage to a non-Palestinian or a change of her husband's nationality while married, will not necessarily change the citizenship of the wife. . . . Women should also be granted the right to give citizenship to her husband and children, be guaranteed the full freedom to move, travel and choose her place of residency" (GUPW 1994, 2). Significantly, nationality issues have both rallied the women's movement and have offered concrete, if small, successes in changing administrative regulations, such as for the issuance of a passport (abolishing the need for a male guardian), and the equality of women and men as Palestinians has been argued effectively from a sense of nationalist entitlement.

Although the principles and strategic thinking behind the charter have been of great importance, the document itself has not been an object of further campaigns for wider ratification. The Jerusalem conference announcing the draft charter experienced factional struggle as anti-Oslo women's groups protested the appearance on the speaker's authority of a member of the Palestinian Authority. Although the factional aspect has been healed, the problem of governmental and nongovernmental women's representatives remains unresolved and is part of the larger question of state and civil society in Palestinian politics raised earlier whereby the conflation of state and civil society in PLO organizations, such as the General Union of Palestinian Women, leads to a state-dominated vision of society. The General Union of Palestinian Women itself, which has a number of leaders from PLO cadre returning to Palestine, is in conflict over its identity with one trend pushing for a clearer nongovernmental character.

The charter also affirms a number of specific economic rights but leaves personal status issues at the most general level, demanding "the guarantee of women's full equality regarding issues of personal status" (GUPW 1994, 3). In the period after the charter, personal status issues, however, became central to a cumulative number of gender and law initiatives undertaken by the women's movement. The history of these initiatives shows both the strengths and problems of the "equality" approach that has dominated the strategic thinking of the Palestinian women's movement.

Gender, Legislation, and Government

The question of personal status laws (and the status of Islamic *shari'a*) came into sharper focus with a series of important activities undertaken by the women's movement to review existing legislation and propose amendments and new legislation within a framework of gender equity. Workshops reviewing legislation in the summer of 1994, a major conference, Women, Justice, and the Law (coordinated by the Palestinian human rights organization Al-Haq), in September 1994 (Al-Haq 1995), regional workshops on gender and legislation in 1995 (WCLAC 1997), and a series of regional and national activities in 1996 and 1997 culminated in an elected model parliament (coordinated by the Women's Center for Legal Aid and Counseling (WCLAC)and a steering committee of women's organizations), which debated and voted on model legislation concerning women in four regional sessions in early 1998. These activities all contributed to a greater understanding of the inequities in existing law and to an emerging consensus among a range of women's organizations, and what might be termed the Palestinian democratic movement in general, on priorities for legal reform.

In these initiatives women and men considered labor law, social welfare and education, criminal and public law, among others, and effectively used the principle of equality to discover gender inequities that should be addressed and recommended special provisions for women's rights on such issues as maternity leave and child care at the workplace and violence against women.

Applying the principle of equality in personal status laws, however, was much more difficult for participants in these forums, given that the *shari' a* has a legally defined model of family and gender relations based on complementary male and female roles rather than equality. Rights and obligations are seen as equivalent, rather than equal: the husband's responsibility for "maintenance" of his wife is exchanged for female "obedience" in the exercise of her marital and child-raising duties in the home. This ideal model is, of course, often at variance with the multiple strategies employed by actual Palestinian households to meet changing economic, political, and social circumstances. Palestinians are also governed by personal status laws that are not of their own making (the Jordanian Personal Status Law of 1976 in the West Bank) and are outdated (the 1954 Gaza Law of Family Rights in Gaza). Both are applied in religious courts, with Christian denominations having their own religious courts.

The workshops preceding the model parliament included a broad spectrum of community activists and leaders—not only the cadre and supporters of the women's movement—and, thus, several different approaches emerged to the question of reform of existing personal status law. (The model parliament included eighty-eight elected representatives, like the Palestinian Legislative Council, with both female and male representatives). A number of women's activists consistently advocated applying the principles of gender equality in the Palestinian Declaration of Independence and United Nations resolutions and pushed for a civil family law and civil courts to adjudicate family law. A second trend responded with an almost blanket endorsement of *shari' a* without further interpretation and reform except by religious authorities. A third essentially compromised between the two by advocating reform within *shari' a* law and affirming that Islamic law is responsive to change that reflects the needs of contemporary women and society.

An important outcome of these workshops was a book used as the main document for discussion at the model parliament. "The Law and the Future of Women" (Khader 1998) combined specific recommendations for amendments to existing *shari' a* law with a general recommendation for a unified Palestinian family law to be applied in civil courts with jurisdiction over the whole population. Arguing that Islamic jurisprudence considers the marriage contract as a civil contract rather than a sacrament and that men have monopolized knowledge and interpretation of the *shari' a*, the author, attorney Asma Khader, advocated a "unified Palestinian family law," noting that the 1995 workshops show support for such an initiative. The law would treat all Palestinians as equal, respect the principles of religion and "sources of Palestinian legislation . . . including Islamic *shari' a*," make the civil authorities responsible for marriage contracts and other matters not requiring judicial intervention, and place family disputes and cases in special sections of the civil courts. Interestingly, Khader uses Palestinian unity to show that the present situation of ecclesiastical and *shari' a* courts violates the "principle of equality between citizens," besides allowing nonelected individuals to make laws, violating the principle of the independence of the judiciary (Khader 1998, 112–17).

When these recommendations came to the first regional parliament session to consider personal status laws, held in Nablus in March 1998, an influential *shari' a* judge intervened in the discussion to castigate the parliament as having no authority even to speak on issues of *shari' a*, sparking heated discussions and debates (seen in newspapers, on campuses, and on television) between representatives of the women's movement and Islamists, often unofficial "spoke-sheikhs" for Hamas. Leaflets circulated, calling activists in the women's movement and the model parliament agents of a Western conspiracy (and advocates of adultery and other immoral behavior), causing in turn new defenders of the parliament to speak out in public. By the time personal status issues were debated in Gaza, however, in late April, a more healthy atmosphere prevailed and the session successfully addressed a range of personal status issues. One of the consistent demands of the women's movements—raising the marriage age to eighteen for both men and women—passed easily, and indeed, has met little vocal opposition to date. Early marriage is increasingly seen as a problem in Palestinian society, with 25 percent of females in a 1994 court record sample marrying at sixteen or under (Welchman forthcoming). The prohibition of polygamy, however, passed by a narrow margin of forty-two for, thirty-two against, and five abstentions, reflecting the problem that polygamy is positively sanctioned in the Koran and thus, resistant to change. A number of other useful recommendations, increasing women's rights in child custody and divorce and protecting her rights to dowry and inheritance, were also offered in the Gaza session (*al-Ayyam* 1998).

Among other lessons, the women's parliament showed clearly that the rights of women and their standing as equal citizens before the law requires not only identifying and advocating principles, but developing highly specific understanding of local institutions and strategies that are responsive and intervene concretely in these local institutional settings. At the same time, post-Oslo women's activism has found varying responses from the Islamists, the Palestinian Legislative Council, and the Palestinian Authority Executive.

The Islamist Response

In the post-Oslo period, Islamist organizations have made it clear that the preservation of *shari' a* is a "redline" in their relations with the Palestinian Authority. Women's initiatives to review legislation, including personal status law, gathered steam, particularly in the last period of the model parliament. With this review, Islamists, especially Hamas (in the West Bank more than Gaza), responded by organizing attacks in mosques and public meetings, denouncing women's organizations, targeting those involved in the parliament. Publications circulated widely, slandering women's organizations as part of international conspiracies, indicating that they were outside the nationalist dialogue, thus inciting violent attack, certainly in speech and possibly in action. Indeed, one such publication, "The Palestinian Women and the Conspiracy of Secular Feminists" (Al-Hoda 1998), published on 28 March 1998 in response to the model parliament, was the first publication of the Islamic women's organization, Al-Hoda Women's Society, founded the year previously with the aim of providing a counter to the Palestinian women's movement and its programs. Another new Islamic women's organization, Al-Khansa Islamic Association, was established in February 1998. Both assert that Islam gives women her full rights but may be open to dialogue on issues where these rights are not implemented by society.

The Islamists are clear that personal status law is exclusively the province of religion, and have recently put forward the demand that it be removed as a subject of consideration by the Palestinian Legislative Council and mandated to religious authorities. The fact that West Bank and Gaza personal status laws differ may, thus, allow for some reform, but only within the religious structures.

The Palestinian Legislative Council

In general, there is a positive atmosphere in the Legislative Council toward women, but the constraints on the council's legislative powers, as discussed above, are such that the council was not able to undertake any significant legal reform of family law in the transitional stage—the model parliament was more capable of passing legal amendments than the real parliament. The council has lent its support to the women's movement in such matters as canceling regulations requiring women to have a male guardian's permission for a passport. In draft labor and civil service legislation, the council unified the retirement age for men and women at sixty-five and extended maternity leave for working women from six weeks to three months. These two provisions, although not formally enacted, have come into force in practice in the public sector and a number of other institutions.

Five of the council's eighty-eight members are women who have a relatively effective role in the council's proceedings. In the wider sense, the council's battle to exercise its powers as elected representatives of the people is part of the process of democratization that is also vital to the women's movement.

The Palestinian Authority Executive

Some of the considerations of the Palestinian Authority Executive in delineating post-Oslo features of authority have been set forth above. The predominance of security over democracy and the unitary model of state and civil society have negative implications for gender equity and women's active citizenship. At the same time, the Authority's relatively secular stand vis-à-vis the Islamist movement, its desire to modernize, and the influence of donor agendas, besides, perhaps, a sense that women have entitlements through nationalist struggle, allow openings for lobbying and advocacy for women's rights.

One pronounced negative development, however, is that the priority of the Authority, and particularly of President Arafat, to establish political control through mechanisms of political patronage, among others, has used and revived clan and kin networks to the detriment of women and individual citizen's rights. The accompanying revival of customary law—deployed by district governors at times and less-official bodies—reserves arbitration and judgment largely for male elders and raises the specter of sanction for such illegal acts as honor killing. In October 1995 President Arafat established a presidential office for clan affairs, and one month later, an association called "The Descendants of the Bir Saba Tribes" was authorized, among whose members is the minister of justice (Frisch 1997). The appointment of municipal councils in 1997 throughout the West Bank and Gaza took into consideration clan networks and leadership and, thus, largely excluded women. In the municipality of Abu Dis, women activists gathered one thousand signatures demanding women's representation and gained an appointment (Boulatta 1998). A number of other public protests came from women activists,[4] but in all, only about ten members of municipal councils (with membership in all municipal councils numbering in the hundreds) are currently women. An oral agreement between the WATC and the minister

---

4. See "Saut al nisa'" (Voice of women), a regular supplement on women's affairs in *Al-Ayyam* newspaper, 5 Mar. 1998, for a report of the protests of a group of women from the town of Beit Jala to the Ministry of Local Government and the governor of the Bethlehem District over the refusal to allow women to attend town meetings, the rejection of women candidates, and the suggestion of two female candidates. One was appointed.

of local governments stating that at least one woman should be included in each council was not honored in all cases.

At the ministerial and sectoral level, however, gender issues are at least present as part of policy making. The establishment of a Gender Planning Unit in the Ministry of Planning, headed by veteran women's activist Zahera Kamal, and the establishment of Gender Units in about ten ministries has had uneven effects on governmental policies, depending on the institutional context of each ministry. Limited access to information, decision making, and power are pronounced. Although two of twenty-five ministers were women until July 1998 (the ministers of social affairs and higher education), women are even more poorly represented among deputy ministers and are in a small minority among directors general. In a study of six ministries, the Women's Studies Center found no women deputy ministers, and four women, in contrast to thirty men, were directors general (Women's Studies Center 1996). Gender awareness is more difficult to judge: although some ministry officials see "gender" as a donor-imposed plot, others are particularly sensitive to the needs and interests of women and girls—as reflected, for example, in a Ministry of Education instruction to allow young married women to remain in school.

Gender and Policy Making

The legislative impasse described above makes it particularly important to examine governmental policymaking to better assess emerging concepts of citizenship, citizen's entitlements, how these might be gendered, and how they impact women's lives and futures. At the policy level it also becomes clear that developmental arguments can play a role in advancing the status of women as citizens while the inclusion of women's rights and needs can make policies more effective. A full examination of Palestinian Authority policy is beyond the scope of this chapter—and, indeed, requires much research—but a brief case study of population policy[5] shows problems in both conceptualizing and including women's rights in policymaking and the potential for change.

Population Policies

In the first Palestinian national demographic survey, the Palestinian Central Bureau of Statistics (PCBS) assessed the total fertility rate (TFR) for the

---

5. For a more detailed gender analysis of fertility and population in Palestine, see Giacaman 1997. The following section is derived from her report.

West Bank and Gaza, excluding East Jerusalem, at 6.24 (the average number of children born alive to a woman during her lifetime in prevailing fertility conditions) (PCBS 1996). Sizeable regional variations were found between the West Bank and Gaza; the TFR for the West Bank was 5.61, and the TFR for Gaza was 7.44. Gaza, thus, has one of the highest fertility rates in the world. Only Oman and Yemen in the Middle East and several countries in sub-Saharan Africa register similar or higher fertility rates (UNDP 1996).

When this report was released to the public, the Palestinian press highlighted an interview with PCBS officials during which Palestinian high fertility in Gaza was termed a "time bomb" because of its potential effects on development, social and economic progress and stability. This view of Palestinian fertility reflects the current agenda of building a viable Palestinian economy and state: persistent high fertility, in this perspective, restricts the use of human resources and hampers the ability of the labor force to support an overwhelmingly young population. This position stands in contrast to an earlier but ongoing discourse that sees Palestinian high fertility as an element of Palestinian survival in the face of Israeli occupation and assault on Palestinian national identity. In both positions, women are essentially viewed as objects with a singular role—reproduction. In the context of this ideological battle, women's rights and the effects of persistent high fertility on women's life opportunities tend to disappear from the picture. Yet the expansion of rights, opportunities, and entitlements for women may well be the key to an effective Palestinian population policy.

Trends in Population Policies

From the years of occupation to the present, mainstream nationalism contained a stated pronatalist policy using population growth and demographic pressure as an instrument through which to achieve liberation (Tamari and Scott 1991). Such a policy was concretized in the development of a very low-cost clinic infrastructure under the rubric of maternal and child health but, in fact, focused on children's health and generally neglected women's health needs. Although women were exhorted to have more children—with prizes occasionally awarded to super-mothers, it was the profound absence of social security, political crisis, and highly restricted and gendered labor markets that were more dominant factors in keeping fertility high. A slight and gradual decline did occur, particularly in the West Bank, in the 1970s and until the *intifada* when fertility rates again rose. Given the conditions of Israeli occupation, children (particularly sons) remained perceived and actual resources for family survival, old-age security, and prosperity.

An alternative policy evolved from the health movement in the West Bank and Gaza that developed in the late 1970s and early 1980s. By the middle 1980s, influenced largely by health considerations, some NGOs had already developed a new policy that reconsidered the impact of high fertility on the well-being of mothers and children. Such groups introduced family planning services within primary health care clinics, again at very low cost, and focused on the provision of adequate pre- and postnatal care. With practice, some of these groups incorporated the notion of the right of couples to choose their ideal family size and the notion of the rights of women to health as part of their stated policy and, to some extent, their practice (Najjab 1994).

The third type of policy is that of the United Nations Relief and Works Agency (UNRWA) that is mandated to provide service for Palestinian refugees. Until recently, UNRWA provided basic medical and health care in the West Bank without any form of family planning services while providing a cautious mix of advice and family planning services in Gaza. The primary reason for the caution apparently pertains to an expected negative political reaction to such family planning service implementation, given the prevailing strong nationalistic pronatalist ideology. UNRWA today provides family planning services in its clinics on a large scale.

The fourth and most recent type of population policy is antinatalist and/ or implicitly oriented toward population control; it is upheld most recently by some international aid agencies operating, or beginning to operate, in Palestine. Although these different agencies formulate their policies within the framework of women's reproductive health, safe motherhood, and child spacing, the point of departure is the same—a problem of overpopulation in the area that requires immediate intervention. This "problem" is implicitly framed in political and developmental terms of reducing the conditions of political strife and increasing political stability. In this view, overpopulation results in a massive increase in people living in poverty in contrast to an alternative view that overpopulation is a consequence of poverty, inequality, and insecurity (Meillasoux 1983). The activities of such aid agencies in family planning project implementation is likely to widen considerably the family planning service network in the country, especially because new projects are being developed in conjunction or close coordination with the Palestinian Authority. That is, they are likely to have a positive impact on women's choices and access to services.

There is a danger, however, that family planning program implementation without adequate attention being paid to other key issues, such as improving the quality of health and family planning care, and decreasing early marriage, increasing employment, and developing social security would translate into family planning services with limited impact and expenditures that could be better deployed in a more multifaceted approach that links with policies promoting women's rights and social and economic development. The fact that international aid is present in Palestine in large amounts, but for a limited time, increases the tendency for some donors to view fertility reduction in Palestine as a quick fix for developmental (and political) problems that have been generated over decades. Such a view usually translates into inadequately conceived programs that primarily aspire to achieve fertility control through the introduction of contraceptive services and in which the reasons for persistent high fertility in Palestine are not seriously addressed or women's rights and family welfare systematically considered.

A "rapid deployment" in the context of family planning services is particularly problematic given that the Palestinian health care system is dilapidated, lacking in human resources and infrastructure. In this context international agencies with preset plans and preset large budgets to spend, despite good intentions and principles concerning women's health, can move more quickly than is wise for women's safety and rights. Evidence on this ground suggests an expansion of family planning with an increase in services and their use, but problems in systematic examination of risk, early detection of problems, and follow-up, for example, of rates of infection and intrauterine device (IUD) insertion. Given existing patient overload, lack of space and staff, and problems in such areas as recordkeeping, Palestine faces a problem familiar in the developing world: in the absence of follow-up, family planning can introduce new health problems for women. Other key services of government clinics, such as prenatal care, appear to be suffering in some regions; in four clinics in the northern region of the West Bank, the number of attendants at the family planning clinic during the past year increased systematically, as the numbers in the prenatal care decreased.

Existing PCBS data, and other studies, show clearly that Palestinian women use existing family planning services and contraceptive technologies, in increasing numbers. Patient data from the four clinics above shows, however, that the average age at which a woman appears at a clinic to start contraception is thirty years. With an average early marriage age of eighteen, women may turn to contraception after reaching what is considered (whether by the woman, husband, or family and kin) the "ideal family size." According to PCBS's initial demographic survey, 63 percent of women preferred a family of four to six children, with 32 percent of married Gazan women and 27 percent of married West Bank women reporting more than six children as ideal (PCBS 1996); continued son preference is also clear and can drive fertility higher. While women's actual wishes and needs deserve much more study, this continued opting for relatively large families must be considered in an integrated population policy that takes into account women's needs and rights and the structural (and cultural) reasons for large families as well.

The Palestinian Ministry of Health is sensitive to the problems raised above but is also dependent on donors for much of its budget (particularly for new hospitals and programs). An active Women's Health and Development Directorate in the Ministry and the coordination of the Ministry with Palestinian health NGOs also has the potential to address women's rights, women and family survival, and socioeconomic needs. The two are related and have an important impact on fertility. As a World Bank 1995 report on fertility in sub-Saharan countries (a region of persistent high fertility) stated:

> When women's legal rights are insecure, they demand more children. If women cannot own land, do not have rights to property when their husbands die or if they divorce, or are legally treated as minors, then children provide them with their only security. Unless women's legal status is strengthened, they will demand large families as insurance against future uncertainty. Laws must be enforced to ensure women's right to acquire, own and dispose of property, and to protect them from discrimination. Customary laws and practices that inhibit women's rights and opportunities must also be addressed. (Scribner 1995)

The application to Palestine, where insecurity has been the prevailing condition and where women, and men as well, have had little opportunity to exercise legal rights, is clear. Indeed, one demographer, pointing to the rise in fertility during the Palestinian *intifada* and the small, but significant, decline in Palestinian fertility since 1993, has linked fertility to political conditions in a broad definition (Courbage 1997). Effective change that takes into primary consideration the rights of women to control their own lives and the right of families to make the choice of their ideal family size is possible with consultation and cooperation, as well as the initiation of public debates and building national consensus from the bottom up. Such an approach to the population question can achieve dramatic results in a short period of time. Within this framework, key legal changes and the improvement in the status of women through education, employment, social security, and the provision of equal rights, are critical elements for success which require the exercise of citizen's rights and entitlements.

In Transit to Citizenship?

The population policies example illustrates that at the level of sectoral policies, key unresolved questions of citizenship, among other problems, arise in the Palestinian context. Policy-making requires a vision of citizen's rights and a vision of Palestinian state and society in order to be effective, integrated, and sustainable, and also needs active citizen involvement. In this sense the people involved in the women's movement have taken a leading role as active citizens in putting forth for public debate a vision of Palestinian society based on equality and applying this vision to legislation, state-building, and societal development. Whereas women activists in other contexts have often argued for inclusion in citizenship, under the particular circumstances of Palestine in transition, the women's movement must create the conditions of citizenship. This is both an opportunity for engendering citizenship, and an enormous challenge, which the women's movement addresses within the context of the democratic movements in Palestine.

8

Gender and Citizenship in Jordan

ABLA AMAWI

IN HM KING HUSSEIN'S Speech from the Throne at the opening of the thirteenth Parliament's first ordinary session, HM stated that "The family or the tribe in our country . . . is one of the cells of society, which make up the entire people. It maintains society's lofty ideals, protects its noble values, and moves its beautiful traditions and generous customs forward. The family—like the tribe—has always been a source of . . . honor and pride. It has never been . . . a burden or a source of blemish, nor has it been a shortcoming or a censure" (*Jordan Times* 1997, 7).

The king's speech underpins the notion of the centrality of the family unit within Jordanian society and that Jordan is built on the concept of *al-usra al-wahida,* the single or united family, and by extension, the tribal families. The king usually refers to the Jordanian people by depicting the nation as a collective family with the king at its head. From this concept emanate all other notions of national cohesion, the articulation of the rights and obligations of members of the family within the context of society as a whole, the interrelatedness between the patriarchal family and the patriarchal state, and the promotion of allegiance around these symbols of family and tribe solidarity in support of the state.

Moreover, the speech also reflects another dimension of the question of gender and citizenship in Jordan, namely, the conflict the state is facing between two opposing forces. On the one hand are the forces of rapid socioeconomic and political change that modernization has been causing with its concomitant impact on modes of societal interaction and structures and, on the other hand, the desire to preserve traditions and maintain the status quo of the social order and, by extension, the basis of state cohesion.

In this chapter I approach the question of gender and citizenship by delving into the concept of citizenship within the context of the Jordanian state and the way the state, through its attempt at nation building, has articulated the relationship between the citizens and the state. More precisely, I examine the way it has articulated male-female relations as grounds for excluding gender from citizenship.

The Notion of Citizenship

It is difficult to provide a precise definition of the term *citizenship*. As Charles Tilly notes, "the word 'citizenship' causes confusion" (Tilly 1995). It has been used to designate a mutual relationship between citizens and the state, interrelationships among citizens emerging from their relationships with the state, a set of rights and entitlements, or "those people who are included in a given state's circle of full political participation" (Lipset 1960 quoted in Tilly 1995, 8).

Tilly provides a very useful definition of citizenship, noting that "a tie qualifies as citizenship insofar as it entails enforceable rights and obligations based on persons' categorical membership and agents' relation to the state" (Tilly 1995, 8). He further elaborates that this citizenship is not a uniform category but can "range from thin to thick: thin where it entails few transactions, rights and obligations; thick where it occupies a significant share of all transactions, rights and obligations sustained by state agents and people living under their jurisdiction" (Tilly 1995, 8).

This definition of citizenship offered by Tilly is very effective when used to describe the relationship of gender and citizenship in Jordan. It delineates simply that citizenship is a *direct legal relationship between the individual and the state,* and, secondly, it renders *an image of a continuum* whereby "impenetrable" citizenship can be identified on one end and "fragile" citizenship on the other.

It is argued here that the Jordanian woman has a "diminished" citizenship. She does not enjoy "thick" citizenship status in Tilly's notion, ensuing from the fact that her relationship with the state is not direct but is articulated through a mediator. This intermediary is her husband, her brother, her father, and, by extension, her family or tribe. The state grants women rights as citizens; these rights, however, can only be actualized through the males in the family, who have control over women's actions and conduct.

Moreover, women's citizenship status in Jordan fits the concept of "fragility" in Tilly's view, as opposed to that of Jordanian males. This is notably the case if one perceives citizenship to constitute (1) equal rights and entitlements of all citizens, whether males or females, vis-à-vis the state, and (2) full membership in a community encompassing equal civil, political, and social rights and responsibilities.

I analyze here the question of gender and citizenship in Jordan by examining the right to citizenship, to a passport, and to a family registry, the relationship within marriage (the Civil Code and the personal status law), the broader concept of citizenship, and the notion of equality as citizens.

The Right to Jordanian Citizenship

The Jordanian Citizenship Law dates back to the days of the British Mandate imposed on Jordan in accordance with the decision of the Council of League of Nations in September 1922. The Transjordanian government under the mandate adopted the Ottoman Code and accordingly set up a system of courts.[1] It also issued a Travel Document and Regulations Law in 1927, and enacted a Nationality Law in June 1928, which followed the provisions of the Treaty of Lausanne (Report by His Britannic Majesty's Government on the Palestine Administration 1923).

The Nationality Law addressed the inhabitants of Transjordan not in terms of individuals but as Ottoman subjects. It granted Transjordanian nationality to all Ottoman subjects who were residing in Transjordan on 6 August 1924.[2]

This law was amended in 1954 with the issuance of the Jordanian Nationality Law,[3] which states that "Jordanian nationality shall be defined by law" (*Official Gazette* 1954, 105). It was modeled after British Nationality

---

1. These courts include a court of appeal, courts of first instance, four civil magistrate courts, *shari' a* courts, and a Department of Tribal Administration to deal with intertribal disputes and cases between the Bedouins (Annual Report by His Britannic Majesty's Government on the Palestine Administration 1923).

2. Article 1 of the Jordanian Nationality Law provides that all Ottoman subjects habitually resident in Transjordan on 6 August 1924 shall be deemed to have acquired Transjordan nationality; articles 2 and 3 of the law deal with persons who acquired Transjordan nationality under article 1, that is, who were Ottoman subjects habitually resident in Transjordan on 6 August 1924 and who decided within a period of two years to opt instead for Turkish nationality or for the nationality of one of the states previously in the Ottoman empire in which the majority of the populations was of the same race as themselves; article 4 persons who acquired Transjordan nationality under article 1, but who opted for Turkish nationality, for the nationality of one of the states previously in the Ottoman empire in which the majority of the population is of the same race as themselves, shall be obliged to leave Transjordan (Report by His Britannic Majesty's Government on the Palestine Administration, submitted to the Council of the League of Nations 1929, 143).

3. Jordanian Nationality Law no. 6 for 1954, *Official Gazette,* no. 1171, p. 105, 16 Feb. 1954.

Laws in which nationality stemmed from the establishment of paternity. A British mother was unable to pass on her nationality to her children, and if she married a non-British subject, she and her children lost their nationality. The children of British men and non-British wives would be automatically British, however, as would the non-British wives.[4]

The Jordanian Nationality Law of 1954 and its further amendment in 1987 stipulated that nationality can be granted to the following persons (Jordan Nationality Law 1987, art. 3): anyone who has obtained Jordanian nationality or a Jordanian passport under the terms of the Jordanian Nationality Act of 1928, as amended, or Act no. (6) of 1954, as amended by Act no. (22) of 1987; anyone carrying a Palestinian passport issued before 15 May 1948—provided that he is not Jewish—and habitually residing in Jordan during the period of 20 December 1949–16 February 1954; anyone born to a father holding Jordanian nationality; anyone born in the Hashemite Kingdom of Jordan to a mother holding Jordanian nationality and to a father whose citizenship is unknown, or who is stateless, or whose paternity has not been legally established; anyone born in the Hashemite Kingdom of Jordan to unknown parents, insofar as, failing evidence to the contrary, any foundling discovered in the kingdom is deemed to have been born there; and all members of the northern nomadic tribes referred to in article (25), paragraph (2) of the Provisional Electoral Act (no. 24) of 1960, and who are actually resident in the territories that were incorporated in the kingdom in 1930 (*Official Gazette* 1987, 1623).

The law also stipulated that a Jordanian man can grant the Jordanian nationality to his non-Jordanian wife provided that certain conditions are met, such as residing in the country for a period of three years if she carries an Arab nationality, and five years if she carries the citizenship of a foreign country.[5]

Other provisions in the law work to constrain the conduct of women and to preserve the "cohesiveness" of society as "one unity." Because nationality is passed only through the male, a Jordanian woman marrying a non-Jordanian cannot pass her nationality to her "foreign" husband.[6]

---

4. N. 25 quoted in Massad 1995, 472. Some of these laws were changed in 1981 and 1985, whereby British women won the right to transfer their citizenship to their own children born abroad.

5. Article 8 of the Nationality Law. This article corresponds to the U.N. Agreement Concerning the Citizenship of a Married Woman (29 Jan. 1957) published in the *Official Gazette*, no. 3829, p. 1003, 1 June 1992. The Jordanian cabinet approved this U.N. agreement published in the *Official Gazette*, no. 3829, p. 998, 1 June 1992.

6. Amendment no. 22 for 1987 published in the *Official Gazette*, no. 3496, p. 1623, 1 Sept. 1987. This amendment differs from the previous provision, which stated that "the wife of the Jordanian is a Jordanian and the wife of a foreigner is a foreigner."

To bypass the citizenship restrictions placed on women, the non-Jordanian husband must fulfill specific conditions, including investments in the country, residence for at least four years with the intention of permanent residency, and legal means of employment that do not compete with Jordanians for employment in the same occupational field (*Official Gazette* 1963, nos. 1675, 290).

Moreover, the foreign husband of a Jordanian woman can acquire a residency permit only if he (1) possesses a work permit that does not compete with Jordanians (which must be verified through official ministries); (2) has a viable income source; (3)invests in the country; and (4) has academic or professional qualifications that are not matched in the country.[7]

What is more problematic is that a Jordanian woman marrying a non-Jordanian cannot pass her nationality to her children and cannot even grant them residency permits, whereas the children of a Jordanian man married to a non-Jordanian wife can pass his nationality and residency status automatically to his wife and children. The Law of Residency and Aliens Affairs[8] authorizes the minister of interior to grant a residency permit for a period of five years to any alien wife married to a Jordanian husband. The minister also has the authority to grant a residency permit for the same period to any alien who has resided in the kingdom for ten years in a legitimate way.

Because the Nationality Law is paternally and not territorially based, the children of a Jordanian male are Jordanians wherever they are born (Nationality Law, art. 9), and a minor (less than eighteen) whose Jordanian father acquires a foreign citizenship can retain his/her Jordanian citizenship (Nationality Law, art. 10). The children of a Jordanian woman, however, cannot acquire her nationality or residency status. Consequently, these children are deprived of all rights, including enrollment in the school system, social entitlements, and/or political rights.[9] Indeed, they are not even registered in their Jordanian mother's passport, which is stamped "Children are not included due to the different nationality of the father."

The Nationality Law provisions reflect the conception that nationality is based on blood ties established only through the father and is not tied to the land or to the nation; that is, unless the concept of the nation fits the image of a paternal society. It is ironic that the only way maternal ties can be

---

7. Article 26 of the Residency Law and Foreigners' Affairs. Sa' di Abdeen, Musoat al-Jaib lil-Tashira' wa al Qada wal-Figq, The Residency Law and Foreigners' Affairs, no. 24 for 1973. Dar al-jib lil Nashir wal-Tawzea, Amman, 1991. The Residency of Foreigners Law published in the *Official Gazette,* no. 2426, p. 1112, 16 June 1973. Latest amendments no. 10 for 1991 published in *Official Gazette,* no. 3740, p. 73, 16 Jan. 1991.

8. No. 24 of 1073, as amended by law no. 5 of 1991.

9. In accordance with article 75 of the Constitution.

used as the basis for nationality is in the case of illegitimate children whose mother has been killed by her kinsmen in an "honor" killing before she has even applied for citizenship for them.

Activists in Jordan, including the Jordanian National Committee for Women, have issued a recommendation to add a paragraph to article 13 of the Nationality Law, which would grant the Council of Ministers the right to grant the children of Jordanian mothers married to non-Jordanians the Jordanian nationality if the council finds such action suitable. This change would ease the situation of many women because it would be reviewed on a case-by-case basis rather than as a result from a blanket change, which the government would probably reject.

The restrictions to full gender citizenship rights that the Jordanian government has made were confirmed in the reservations it registered to the United Nations (UN) Convention on the Elimination of All Forms of Discrimination Against Women (CEDAW) adopted by the UN General Assembly on 18 December 1979. The government signed CEDAW on the third of December 1980 and ratified it on the first of July 1992. A declaration of reservations regarding article 9/2 (Nationality of Children) was made upon signature and confirmed upon ratification (among other reservations mentioned later) (Nasser 1997).

Jordan did not state the basis for its reservations at the time of signature. In a later memorandum submitted by the Ministry of Foreign Affairs, it affirmed its reservations and stated that these reservations will not be withdrawn because they conflict with the provisions of the *shari'a* and with the Jordanian Citizenship Law. In justifying the government's position, Sheikh Khayyat notes on the article, "If this means that the children should follow the nationality of their mother—in the sense of being traced to her—this is rejected by Islam. Almighty God says: 'Call them by the names of their fathers: that is [more just] in the sight of God' (Sura 33, verse 5)" (Khayyat 1992, 8).

A closer examination of Jordan's reservations indicate that these reservations are not solidly based on the *shari'a*, but on a masculinity-based nationalism. There is no contradiction between article 9/2 of CEDAW and the *shari'a* provisions. This paragraph stipulates that "states parties shall grant women equal rights with men with respect to the nationality of their children." The *shari'a* did not address the issue of nationality, but that of "*Nassab*," which is establishing paternal linkages of a child to his father and not to the mother. In fact, it seems that the government's apprehension is unjustified because article 38 of the Jordanian Civil Code emphatically stresses that "every person shall have a name and a surname and his surname shall be attached to the names of his children." Therefore, paternal linkages based on blood ties to the father would not be denied if the mother passed her citizenship to her child who holds the surname of the father.

If one can refute the notion that the reservation is religiously based, then what are the other bases for the reservation? Many officials claimed that the reservation is based on the need to address the "higher national interest" of the country (Nasser 1997). According to this argument, opening up nationality entitlements would be politically unwise probably because of the Arab-Israeli conflict and the fear of depopulating the Occupied Territories and the fear of increased constraints on the state's meager resources.

What is ominous in the provisions of these restrictions is that they do not grant Jordanian women equal citizenship rights before the law. In the hypothetical drive to protect the "national interest," these reservations may reflect an assumption that Jordanian women do not possess the intellectual capacity to discern the intentions of their suitors. Even if one assumes that this is the case, should the women's children be penalized for the rest of their lives because of their mother's supposed "intellectual inadequacy"? If this capacity is in question, then one should seriously scrutinize women's right to vote, to occupy a seat in Parliament and other administrative posts, to choose a marriage partner, and, most critically, their entitlement to motherhood itself! These provisions pose deeper questions engulfing not just the reasoning capacity of Jordanian women but also their loyalty to the nation as well.

This masculinity in the Nationality Law resonates in other laws as well. Most importantly, it reflects the underpinnings of a paternally based citizenship with its main function of reproducing the nation. Moreover, it underlies the fact that the direct relationship between the citizen and the state is based on the type of citizen, a male, rather than on a citizen per se. Accordingly, that citizen is the one entitled to a direct relationship with the state and through *him* the relationship of the *lesser* citizen is mediated. This is clearly demonstrated in the passport law, the family registry book, and the personal status law.

The Passport Law

The discrimination in terms of the Nationality Law reflects a deeper subordination of Jordanian women that is also evident in the passport law (Passport Law 1969, no. 2) and the family registry book. According to the passport law, a Jordanian wife cannot obtain a separate passport without her husband's written permission and neither can the children under the age of sixteen. If those children are to be included in their mother's passport, the husband's permission for that inclusion is required. Interestingly enough, a female child can obtain the passport upon reaching the age of eighteen years without the consent of her guardian, but once she marries, she has to obtain her husband's permission.

The incongruity in the limitations inherent in the passport law are apparent if one examines article (4/a) of the law, which grants a woman the right to leave the country provided she has a valid passport. Paradoxically, she has the right and freedom to travel, yet this right is diminished by the prerequisite of a husband's permission to obtain the passport, thus precluding the woman from enjoying a direct relationship with the state.

Indeed, these restrictions imposed on women's right to travel have been confirmed in Jordan's reservation to article 15, paragraph 4 of CEDAW, which stipulates that states parties will accord to men and women the same rights with regard to the law relating to the movement of persons and the freedom to choose their residence and domicile. Jordan's reservation was said to be based on the articles' conflict with the *shari' a* (Nasser 1997).

One can argue that there is no contradiction between article 15, paragraph 4, of CEDAW and the *shari' a* provisions because the wife can stipulate to the husband in the marriage contract where she wants to live. Under *shari' a* law a woman can exercise her right to choose her residence and domicile vis-à-vis her future husband. This condition must be honored by the husband, otherwise a wife can apply for the cancellation of the marriage contract without prejudice to her marital rights. In fact, the *shari' a* court of appeal expanded the exercise of this right when it ruled that such a condition should be applied even if not stipulated in the marriage contract, provided that the wife proves that the new place is not safe and secure for her.

It is ironic that the only way a woman can bypass her husband's permission is through the agreement of the Passport Department director, who can grant her a passport for a one-year period (Nationality Law, art. 13). This freedom, however, is limited in practice, especially for Jordanian mothers who were abandoned with their children in Jordan by their non-Jordanian husbands. The yearly provisional renewal makes it difficult for the children to move and travel and increases the burden of the mothers, who must go through the tedious process of passport renewal with all the expenses that entails.

The Family Registry Book

The registry is another example of the limitations placed on women's control over their lives and the imposition of an intermediation between them and the state. The registry is a document that has been increasingly used, instead of the passport, as required documentation in all administrative procedures in Jordan.

The registry is issued in the name of the head of the household (father, brother, husband), and it lists all other female members and children. The dilemma posed by the registry format is that it assumes that the head of the household is the male, and all transactions or entitlements from the state must go through the mediation of the male. These entitlements range from the bread subsidies (cash in lieu of bread), voting cards, any documentation required by the government, and registration of children in schools, all of which require the presentation of the registry.

This assumption has been very problematic, particularly in instances in which the male spouse who supported the household is dead, lost, continuously or periodically absent, or has given up Jordanian nationality. In such cases the wife or widow left behind becomes unable to acquire her own registry or to benefit from her entitlements as a citizen.

The registry regulations are an obstacle to Jordanian women married to non-Jordanian husbands. Because the family they constitute is not entitled to full citizenship rights, it is also not entitled to acquire its registry. Thus, women who do not conform to the accepted behavioral norms and, instead, marry outside the family, tribe, or nation are marginalized, and the families they form are not considered units in the legal sense. With their multiple diminished rights, they do not even qualify to be characterized as citizens.

A recent amendment to this law made it possible for divorcees and widows to acquire their independent registries; they cannot, however, include their children, who are included in their father's registry. Yet, the affliction of Jordanian women married to non-Jordanian men does not end if they divorce the "outsider." The women are accepted back into the "fold" and can, according to the recent amendments, acquire their own registries independently. Their children, however, the offspring of the inadmissible marriage, cannot be included in their mother's registry and, thus, remain outcasts without any entitlements due them from the state.

These citizenship/passport/residency provisions lead one to examine the relationship between gender and citizenship in terms of inclusionary and exclusionary criteria. One cannot view the relationship of women's status as citizens solely from the Nationality Law angle. Women's status in the public domain as constructed by the state is merely a reflection of its construction of relationships in the private domain, namely, relationships within marriage and relationships within the family as a unit. This public/private dichotomy is culture specific and leads to a discussion of Jordan's Civil Code and the personal status law.

Jordan's Civil Code

The civil code in Jordan is based primarily on the Mejelle, or the Ottoman Civil Code.[10] This code was based, in principle, on the Hanafi jurist school, provisions from other schools of jurisprudence, and European models (Nasir 1990, 4).

The civil code regulates the relationship between the citizens and the state. This is articulated through legislation, including the constitutional, administrative and financial laws, the penal code, and private and public international laws (*Official Gazette* 1976, no. 2, 645, 1 Aug.). As stated, however, in section 2, no. 2 of the civil code, "If the Court shall find no provision in this Code it shall decide by the rules of Moslem jurisprudence which are more adaptable to the provisions of this Code, and if there is none then by the principles of the Moslem *shari' a*. And if there is none then by custom, and if there is none then by the rules of equity" (*Official Gazette* 1976, no. 2645).

The problem with customs and traditions is the elastic definition of what constitutes *established customs*. The Jordanian Civil Code defines *custom* as "general, ancient, stable and continuous and shall not contravene the provisions of the law, public order, or morals. But if custom is that of a certain town it shall be applicable in that town" (*Official Gazette* 1976, no. 2645). The difficulty in this vague adoption of custom is that in many cases it impinges on the rulings by judges who, more often than not, rule in favor of the males.

The issue is much more complicated for religious minorities. There are eleven recognized Christian denominations in Jordan.[11] The courts for these denominations are recognized by the Constitution (art. 108) and handle all personal status cases (Jordanian Constitution, art. 109), much like the *shari' a* courts for Muslims (marriage, divorce, custody, etc.). They do not, however, handle issues that are considered part of the public interest (inheritance, citizenship, passports, etc.).

The problems in the jurisdiction of these churches are several. Because many of them are extensions of churches elsewhere (Rome for the Catholics and Syria for the Roman Orthodox), many of the judges do not even speak Arabic. Moreover, in cases requiring appeal in higher courts, the couple must take their case outside of Jordan to a higher court for their denomination. This recourse not only infringes on the sovereignty of the Jordanian

10. The Ottoman Civil Code (A.H. 1293, A.D. 1876) comprised 1,851 articles.
11. Lawyer Asma Khader, interview, 31 Jan. 1997, Amman, Jordan.

state but makes the church an added level of intermediation between the woman and the state and compounds the level of intermediation already existing between her and the state through her husband. Consequently, many couples convert to Islam in order to have their cases heard in the *shari' a* courts, or if one of them rejects appealing to the church court, then the only option is the *shari' a* court (Jordanian Constitution, art. 105).

The Personal Status Law

Article 2 of the Constitution stipulates that Islam is the state religion; accordingly, all personal status cases for Muslims are handled in the *shari' a* courts (Jordanian Constitution, art. 105). The first personal status law (PSL) operating in Jordan was the Ottoman Family Rights Law of 1933, which remained in application until 1951 when a Jordanian law was promulgated (Jordanian Family Rights Law 1951).

The latest PSL was promulgated in 1976.[12] This law deals with marriage and betrothal, marriage contracts, the dowry, repudiation, dissolution of marriage by order of the court, *iddat* (the period after the breakup of the marriage until there is proof no pregnancy exists), parentage, foster age, custody, maintenance for kin, and provisions dealing with missing persons and wills.

The PSL is based on the Islamic *shari' a,* which is based on Qur'anic provisions, the *Sunna* (the Prophet's practices and saying), *ijtihad* (informed opinion on legal and theological issues), and *qiyas* (deriving judgment from similar cases based on the three sources stated above). In terms of the application of the *shari' a* in Jordan, article 183 of the PSL refers to the most authoritative Hanafi opinion in matters not covered by this law.[13]

The existing interpretation of *shari' a* provisions in Jordan, such as the ones incorporated within the PSL, and the influence of traditional customs

12. The law was issued as Provisional Law no. 61 of 1976. It was provisional because it was issued under article 94 of the Consitution in the absence of a parliament since it was suspended by the king.

13. The Hanafi is one of the Sunni juristic schools and is named after Abu Hanifa al-Numan (A.H. 80–1560 circa A.D. 700–767). Abu Hanifa was meticulous about ascertaining the authenticity of any tradition attributed to the Prophet, making ample use of analogy and *istihsan,* that is, giving preference to a rule other than the one reached, confined only to factual questions but including hypothetical cases that might arise and would require a religious ruling. "Legalistic devices" (*hiyal shariya*) are essential characteristics of his doctrine used in an attempt to compromise between the legal, the ideal and the real, to bridge the gap between jurisprudence and reality, stressing the fundamental pragmatism of his own doctrine and that of the Sunni doctrines in general.

and the patriarchal structure, which left their imprint on the penal code, have opened the door for many to attack the *shari'a* as the intellectual guiding source of these laws. It must be noted, however, that many other discriminatory laws are not based on the *shari'a* but were influenced by the traditional customs and the patriarchal structure, which left their imprint on the penal code.

Specific issues in the PSL that are flagrantly discriminatory and are discussed here are guardianship in marriage, or the need for a *wali* to act as mediator for the woman in concluding her marriage, the issue of suitability/ equality (*kafa'a*) of the husband, marriage outside the faith, the relationship between a husband and a wife, and custody of the children. The penal code deals with issues of disobedience and discipline within marriage and control over female behavior and conduct.

Guardianship in Marriage

According to the PSL, marriage is a contract between a man and a woman; she is legally his to establish a family and procreate (PSL, chap. 1, art. 2). The woman does not, however, possess the full capacity to conduct her own marriage, owing to the restrictive limitations placed on her right. This right has to be mediated by a male (a member of her family) who figuratively, and literally, passes the mediation role to another male, the future husband.

This need for a guardian—whether the woman is eighteen or fifteen years old—underscores a contradiction between the various provisions of the PSL and other laws, most prominently the civil code. For example, the PSL stipulates that the legal capacity for marriage is sixteen years for the bridegroom and fifteen years for the bride (PSL, art. 15), whereas the civil code fixes the age of maturity at eighteen Gregorian years (PSL, art. 43, para. 2). The legal age for marriage not only contradicts international conventions on children's rights but also deprives female children of the right to educational attainment, increases the chances of high divorce rates, and diminishes the chances for the women to face future challenges, especially in terms of employability.

Despite the fact that a woman possesses legal capacity, a guardian, or *wali,* is needed to conduct the marriage. The *wali* is usually the father of the woman or, in his absence, the brother, uncle, or any of the closest kin. The Jordanian law stipulates that a woman needs the permission and approval of her guardian to contract a marriage, except in the qualifying provisions. The PSL stipulates that a virgin female more than eighteen years of age needs the permission of her *wali* to conduct a marriage (if she has denied the presence of a *wali*) (PSL, art. 22). If, once conducted, the *wali* does not object or has weak reasons for objection, the marriage is sustained. If, however, the *wali* has legitimate grounds for objecting to the suitability/ equality (*kafa' a*) of the suitor, then the judge must approve the dissolution of the marriage provided that the woman is not pregnant (Temporary Law 1976, no. 61). *Kafa' a* is defined as equality in status as a condition for marriage, especially in terms of the ability of the husband to afford the advance dower and the wife's maintenance (PSL, art. 20).

A previously married woman more than eighteen years old can marry herself without her *wali*'s approval (PSL, art. 13). Similarly, the judge has the right to conclude a marriage if approached by a virgin woman who has completed fifteen years of age to marry a man of her equal in terms of suitability if the guardian's objection is based on illegitimate grounds, provided that the guardian is not the father or grandfather (PSL, art. 6). If the guardian is the father or grandfather, her application will not be granted unless she has completed eighteen years of age and the guardian has no legitimate grounds for his objection (PSL, art. 6).

This provision for a *wali* highlights the discriminatory concept of women as less equal emotionally, economically, and intellectually. The *wali*, therefore, stands as the mediator between the woman and the state in issues related to her private life. Moreover, a woman can never be a guardian, which underlines the whole concept of the role of the male *wali* as the only one with the capacity to decide for a woman's life. As al-Hibri argues, the need for the *wali* to act as a mediator has been based on the need to ensure male/female segregation, the need to protect women from any hideous intentions by men, and the patriarchal view of women as needing protection (al-Hibri 1994). This provision for a *wali* assumes that women lack the ability to make free choices and, thus, are not to be trusted. Subsequently, her opinion and will are canceled and substituted by that of the *wali*.

The significant need for a guardian is predominant even in cases where the Hanafi jurisdiction, and the law, stipulate that a woman can bypass the authority of the guardian. In these cases, social customs predominate and the woman often delegates her right to the guardian to conclude the marriage. Because the family's "honor" is tied to the female's behavior, women feel obliged not to tarnish the family's reputation. There is also the fear that she will be disowned and deprived of the family's financial and moral support, both of which are needed in a society structured around family networks. These networks not only maintain the solidarity of the family but also serve important functions as well. These networks translate into connections that guarantee access to state services, social relationships, and other fringe benefits that emanate from a society based on patron-client relations.

To disassociate herself from her family is synonymous with disassociating herself from the web of beneficial linkages within society.

Marriage Outside the Faith

The right to choose a spouse and enter into marriage with women's own free and full consent is emphatically denied in the case of a difference in religion. Marriage by a Muslim woman to a non-Muslim man is void, unconditionally and regardless of whether it was consummated (PSL, art. 33). This decision also applies in instances where the husband recants his Islamic faith or a non-Muslim wife of a non-Muslim man converts to Islam (PSL, art. 51). In these cases the two parties must separate, otherwise their married situation constitutes "adultery."[14] For such a marriage to be valid, the man is obligated to convert to Islam.

A Muslim man, however, can marry a non-Muslim woman if she is of the three monotheistic religions (Islam, Judaism, and Christianity). The discrimination in this case is said to be based on guarding the family's Islamic beliefs. It is feared that a Muslim woman married to a non-Muslim will be prohibited by her husband from practicing her religious duties, and the offspring of such marriage will follow their father's religion and not Islam. It is assumed, however, that the offspring of a Muslim man married to a non-Muslim woman will automatically follow their father's religion.

The Relationship Between a Husband and a Wife

Much like in the public domain, the state, through its laws, regulates the details of the private domain. In fact, the state reproduces the patriarchal structure within the family. Obedience is transferred to the head of the family, the patriarch. It is he who enjoys the prerogatives of demanding obedience, dissolving the marriage, regulating the behavior of family members (especially women) and, most importantly, constitutes the wife's direct link to the state.

These sets of controls are articulated in the PSL. Article 39 of the PSL states that the husband must treat his wife kindly and that she is to obey her husband in legal matters (*mubah*). This obedience has been interpreted within the Jordanian context (following the Hanafi jurisprudence) as related mainly to the concept of *nashiz*, or the woman who leaves the marital home without a legitimate cause or accepts employment without her husband's

---

14. In accordance with PSL, art. 43.

approval (PSL, art. 68). The mandated punishment for this disobedience (*noshoz*) is the loss of alimony entitlement (PSL, art. 37).

The husband is also granted the right to end the marriage (art. 83). He can demand that the wife not seek employment without his approval and join him if he is employed out of the country. Although this is contrary to the Constitution's stipulation granting every citizen the right to travel and prohibiting forced stay, provisions in other laws also deny women that right. As stated, a woman requires her husband's agreement to acquire a passport; she is prohibited from traveling without the husband's approval, and she can be legally forced to reside in his place of employment.

It must be noted that some provisions in the PSL grant women certain rights. A woman can dictate special conditions in the marriage contract.[15] As stipulated in article 19 of the PSL, the only conditions she can include are her preference to remain in her country of residence, her objection to the husband taking a second wife, and her right to divorce him (PSL, art. 87). She can ask the judge for a separation in specific cases, including lack of financial support by the husband, ill-treatment or his absence for an extended period (PSL, arts. 113–33). These conditions stipulated in the contract are considered valid and binding. The failure to honor them gives the wife the right to apply for the dissolution of the marriage without prejudice to any of her marital rights.

Despite the fact that these "progressive" rights can somewhat protect women, they are rarely used by them. Most women are ignorant of the laws, in what has been termed "legal illiteracy." Thus, they are unaware of their rights. Even in instances where a woman is aware of her rights, the presiding judge and the family often discourage her from using them. Within Jordanian traditional structures, if a woman demands her rights, especially the right to seek divorce, it is considered a shameful act that dishonors not only the woman's family but also the husband, who would be regarded as "not man enough."

As stated, interfamily relations are all delineated in the PSL and other laws. Even when a woman can establish a direct relationship with the state and is protected by laws, traditional structures and cultural norms work to de-link direct relations and again mediate through the male.

Custody of the Children

Similarly, a woman's right to custody of her children is also constrained, and the male's right predominates. In accordance with Abu Hanifa inter-

---

15. Guidelines stipulated in Temporary Personal Status Law, Provisional Law no. 61, of 1976, art. 19, para. 1–3.

pretation, the civil code states that a mother has the right to the custody of her children (Jordanian Civil Code, art. 154). The age of custody for a boy ends at nine years and for a girl at eleven (Jordanian Civil Code, art. 161).

The law also stipulates several conditions to regulate custody, all of which work to diminish the right of the mother to custody. The mother must have a certain set of characteristics to be worthy of the task entrusted to her, characteristics that are not at all required of the father as a custodian. She must be "trustworthy," dedicated to her trust, must not have anything distracting her from her obligation, must be able to raise the children, and must not be remarried (Jordanian Civil Code, art. 155). If she remarries, she forfeits her right to custody (Jordanian Civil Code, art. 156). Even if she does not remarry, her custody rights expire once the children reach maturity (Jordanian Civil Code, art. 162). She can, however, retain her right to custody once any of the causes for the marriage's dissolution are annulled (Jordanian Civil Code, art. 158). Under these custody conditions, she cannot travel with the child outside the kingdom without the approval of the *wali* (who is usually the father or the paternal grandfather) (Jordanian Civil Code, art. 166).

Thus, the issues of guardianship, custody of the children, obedience within the marriage, and the passport law all reflect a set notion of male superiority. This male superiority as currently interpreted in the *shari' a* rests on the notion that men occupy a higher step (*daraja*) above women because they are charged with their financial maintenance. In return, women owe obedience (*ta' a*) to men. The notion of the man's legal obligation for family support as inscribed in the PSL and the assumption of women's economic dependence on men has proven dangerous for women. It did not factor in the socioeconomic changes impacting families and women's lives. Women are increasingly entering the labor market. Many families currently can only exist on the contribution of both partners. The laws regulating work and other issues, however, were not amended to reflect women's contribution; social security, insurance, and income tax benefits continue to reflect the belief that a woman is not legally obligated to support the family. This view of dependence in the law contributes to the marginalization and subordination of women's status and equality.

Despite the fact that personal freedom is guaranteed in the Jordanian Constitution (art. 7), women are deprived of their full civil rights, whether to choose a partner, to conduct a marriage contract, to acquire a passport, to have custody of their children, and so on. One can argue, therefore, that because women are deprived of their full civil rights, they adequately fit the description of those defined in the civil code as not entitled to exercise their civil rights because they lack mental powers or because of "minority, idiocy, or lunacy" (sec. 44).

Moreover, as stipulated, then it is befitting to argue in conformity with the civil code that those who "lack capacity or whose capacity is incomplete as the case may be shall in respect of the provisions relating to guardianship, curatorship or custody be subject to the stipulations and rules prescribed in the law" (Jordanian Civil Code, art. 43). Otherwise it would be difficult to comprehend why a woman would need a "guardian" or "protector" to mediate between her and the state and to regulate every aspect of her life, unless there is a predisposed assumption of her intellectual inadequacy. Even if these assumptions are only hypothetical, the need for a guardian, which diminishes a woman's right to make free choices, contradicts provisions in the Constitution that state that "no person shall be allowed to disown his personal freedom or capacity or to amend their provisions" (Jordanian Civil Code, sec. 47).

Adopting this dependence/superiority dichotomy has left its negative impact on women's status within the family. This impact can be observed most prominently in issues handled by the penal code, including disobedience and discipline within marriage and control over female behavior and conduct.

The Penal Code

Disobedience and Discipline

On issues of domestic violence there is some vagueness. The PSL stipulates that a husband must treat his wife with kindness and she is to obey him in allowed matters (Personal Status Law 1976, no. 61, art. 39). It also grants the wife the right to seek separation if she is subjected to violent treatment (Personal Status Law 1976, no. 61, art. 132). In cases, however, where she is considered a *nashiz* (interpreted in the Jordanian provisions to mean she has left the marital home without any legal reason or has not allowed her husband to enter the household), she forfeits her right to alimony, except in cases of battering in which alimony is assured.

Jordanian Criminal Law no. 6 for 1980 was clear on the issue of domestic violence, stating that beating is a act punishable by law, except in cases where there is an exercise of a right, a performance of duty, or what is allowed in the law. The law mentions disciplining children but does not mention wives.

The *shari'a* provisions granted the husband the right to discipline his wife—if she disobeyed him (*noshoz*)—after he followed incremental steps, including providing advice, distancing himself, and then beating. Jurists disagreed on the need to follow the incremental steps, the extent of beating for disciplinary measures, the motives for it, and other disciplinary measures (al-Hibri 1994).

Many Jordanian men extrapolate from the *shari'a* concept of *nashiz* and assume that it is acceptable for the husband to discipline his wife because he is her legal protector and financial provider (Massad 1995). Moreover, if she resorts to the police, unless the battering is severe, she is told that it is a "family matter" and, thus, outside the mandate of police interventions. It is alarming that this control over behavior has been institutionalized in the law in addition to accepted traditions.

Control over Behavior and Conduct

Jordanian Criminal Law is based on the Ottoman Law of 1858, which is based on the French Criminal Law of 1810. For crimes related to women the French law stipulated two punishments: an "exonerating excuse," which relieved the criminal from any tough penalty but adhered to some precautionary measures (French Criminal Law, art. 96), and a "light penalty," which replaced the death penalty or life imprisonment with hard labor and at least one year imprisonment (French Criminal Law, article 97).

In 1960 Jordan issued Criminal Law no. 16 based on many of the provisions of the Lebanese Criminal Law of 1943. The Lebanese Criminal Law stipulated the same provisions as the French Criminal Law regarding penalties for crimes committed against women (Lebanese Criminal Law, art. 562). The Jordanian law differs only in one respect from the Lebanese law. Whereas the Lebanese law was more equal by using the term *zawjaho,* or spouse, to delineate both the husband and the wife in terms of crime and punishment, the Jordanian law only refers to the wife, *zawjataho,* caught in adulterous situation.

The Jordanian law addresses murders deemed crimes of "honor" in two ways. The exonerating excuse based on the stipulation that "he who discovers his wife or one of his female relatives committing adultery and kills, wounds, or injures one or both of them, is exempted from any penalty" (Jordanian Penal Code 1960, art. 340, no. 16), and the "light penalty" based on the stipulation that "he who discovers his wife, or one of his female relatives with another in an adulterous situation, and he kills, wounds, or injures one or both of them, benefits from a reduction of penalty" (Jordanian Penal Code 1960, art. 340, no. 16).

Moreover, the husband/brother/father receives lenient punishment based on the excuse that the "anger" felt as a consequence of the adultery situation in conformity with article 98 of the law, which states that "he who commits a crime in a fit of fury caused by an unrightful and dangerous act on the part of the victim benefits from a reduction of penalty" (Jordanian Penal Code 1960, art. 98, no. 16, and 1988 amendment, art. 98, no. 9).

Rulings in these cases, especially those related to reducing punishment, are based either on the cause of the crime or the excuse. In the first instance the judge can reduce the punishment in accordance with the situation leading to the crime, whereas in the latter instance the judge can examine the cause of the crime and determine punishment accordingly.[16]

The discrimination in the penal code is clear. Whereas it dictates lenient punishments for crimes committed by males against their female relatives or wives and provides ludicrous justifications, such as the "anger" or "fury" felt by the male, it has no equal provisions for the woman who equally has justifiable causes and can equally become emotionally charged with "fury" as a result. In fact, if she kills her husband, she would not benefit from any reduction of penalty and would receive at least three years in prison (Jordanian Penal Code, art. 98).

In most cases, accused men benefit from the leniency of these laws and are sentenced only to six months to three years in prison. Consequently, there has been a marked increase in the number of these crimes of "honor" in recent years. Most of them are not even based on actual facts or hard evidence but on mere suspicion. Many argue that in some cases the motives for the killing may be economic rather than for immoral acts. According to police records, "honor" crimes ranked highest among the total number of reported homicides in Jordan. There were twenty reported crimes of honor in 1995, which represented 23.5 percent of the total homicides committed that year (Husseini 1996).

The question here is whether the provisions of this criminal law are compatible with the provisions of the Jordanian Constitution, the *shari' a,* or international conventions. The answer would seem to be resoundingly negative. The Jordanian Constitution guarantees equality to all Jordanians (males and females) in rights and responsibilities, whereas the *shari' a* provides no basis for discriminatory treatment of adulterous males or females. The *shari' a* stipulates equal punishments for both. Similarly, international conventions such as the International Declaration of Human Rights clearly emphasize equality and no discrimination based on sex (General Assembly of the United Nations 1967, arts. 1, 2).

The implementation of this discriminatory law, therefore, contradicts the Jordanian Constitution and the *shari' a,* both of which have supremacy over a law passed by Parliament. To adhere to its application demonstrates only

16. Article 340 of the Jordanian Penal Code of 1960 and article 95, which states that "there is no excuse for a crime except in cases specified by the law."

the impact of traditional values on these laws that aim to prolong the sub-jugation of women.

The application of the provisions of this law has been very harmful to women because the rulings are based on the convictions of the judge about what constitutes "sufficient" cause and the allowed degree of "anger." Examining some rulings in the court system only affirms this bias (Kaddoumi 1997). The element of surprise and the anger resulting from it has been very elastic in terms of application so that the anger over the knowledge of adultery can stretch from one instantaneous minute to two days (Kaddoumi 1997, ruling no. 66/112). Such laxity about the lapse of time, in fact, makes the crime look more like premeditated murder than a "flash of anger" on the part of the husband or male relative. What is most worrisome is that in many cases the crime is considered self-defense because it is in the defense of "honor" (Jordanian Penal Code, art. 98).

To grant women equal citizenship status before the law, they must be perceived as human beings equal to men in terms of feelings such as anger and in terms of dignity. If, therefore, there are exonerating provisions, they must apply equally to both, and punishment should be equal for both males and females. Activists in Jordan have been demanding amendments to article 340 of the law to no avail. It must be noted, however, that by advocating for equality in "honor" killings for women, it sounds as if there is implicit support for "honor" killing in general, which is not the case. This crime must be totally outlawed on the basis that justice can only be achieved via due process of law and not through individuals who are empowered to act on behalf of the state. The question that begs here is what the ramifications of a comprehensive application of gender equality in Jordan would be.

Whether discrimination is biologically based or gender based, it leads to the same conclusion, namely, that there is discrimination in the way the law applies to men and women. Does, however, this discrimination imply by definition a lesser status of "citizen" relegated to the female? It is argued here that Jordanian women not only face a diminished notion of citizenship when it comes to their status within the family based on the PSL, or in their relationship with the state based on the nationality law, but a broader discrimination that engulfs almost every aspect of gender roles in Jordanian society. This bias can be seen clearly in the provisions of laws that regulate the workplace and social benefits.

Broader Concept of Citizenship

Citizenship can mean, narrowly, the right to carry a specific passport, but here I examine the concept in broader terms to analyze the relationship between the individual and the state or, in other words, the access and rights of different categories of citizens to the state.

There is an apparent contradiction in the laws that regulate socioeconomic life in Jordan. On the one hand, there are bases for establishing equality mandated in the Constitution, the National Charter, and the labor laws. Yet, on the other hand, this equality is impaired by provisions that fall short of full equality in terms of entitlements.

The Constitution stipulates that all Jordanians are equal before the law[17] and the National Charter affirms this equality in terms of rights and duties and in terms of opportunities, education, training, employment, and guaranteeing a satisfactory working environment for both males and females, regardless of gender (National Charter, chap. 1, para. 8; chap. 2).

Based on these precepts of equality, the labor law affirms the right of every citizen to employment. It also specifies the terms for women's employment; it prohibits working on night shifts and in dangerous jobs and gives women the right to resign and receive their end-of-service compensation.

Recent amendments to the law (1997) granted working women more rights. These rights include extending maternity leave from six to ten weeks with full pay rather than half pay; made it mandatory for firms that employ more than twenty women to provide day-care facilities for employees' children who are less than four years old; granted women one hour a day for breast-feeding; prohibited firing of women because of pregnancy; and allowed women one year off, without pay, to care for their newborns.

Despite the progressive aspects of the law and its amendments, in practice many loopholes facilitate discrimination. For example, the law did not guarantee equal pay for equal work; it excluded from its provisions all workers in the agricultural, domestic, and seasonal work sectors, which have high employment of women who are low paid, if at all; it did not emphasize the need for equality in employment opportunities and training, and it did not stipulate stiff penalties for violations (approximately thirty dollars for each violation). All these factors contribute to discrimination within the workplace.

Similarly, the civil service law of 1988 stipulated the equal rights of all Jordanians in terms of occupational scales, titles, and work leaves. In practice, however, women do not fare well in the labor market. Males constitute 68 percent of the labor force, females only 32 percent. Most females are employed in low-paid secretarial and teaching jobs, whereas almost all top

17. In Article 6 of the Jordanian Constitution, the state guaranteed employment and education within its means to all citizens equally. Moreover, Article 22 of the Constitution stipulated that each Jordanian has the right to assume public posts in accordance with the special conditions set in the laws and regulations.

administrative posts are occupied by males and women constitute only 2 percent. Moreover, women are also offered fewer opportunities to benefit from training and scholarships abroad. Companies tend to invest in their male workers, which is regarded as more cost-effective in the long run because many females tend to drop out of the labor market when they marry (Kaddoumi 1997, 10).

Jordan has signed the International Labor Conventions. Of significance are those related to equality in pay, nondiscrimination in hiring, equality in social security benefits, and equality in employment policies (United Nations International Labor Convention 100, 111, 118, 122). Jordan, however, did not sign the agreements guaranteeing equality in opportunity and treatment nor the agreement guaranteeing protection of motherhood (United Nations International Labor Conventions 3, 103, 156). As lawyer and activist Asma Khader notes, "The reservations Jordan has made can only reflect the traditional view of women the state still upholds because it did not wish to enforce the need to facilitate women's employment by providing protection for motherhood. This reemphasizes the woman's role as the primary caregiver and increases her marginalization within the family and society further."[18]

Despite the fact that women are increasing as a percentage in labor market statistics, albeit slowly, the income tax law and the social security law remain discriminatory at best. Indeed, only the husband enjoys exemptions in income taxation. He can waive these exemptions to his wife, especially in cases where she is the sole provider for the family, but the decision remains his alone and is not mandated in the law. Finally, it is assumed that the husband is the sole agent responsible for the family and, therefore, all forms must be submitted in his name, and he is responsible for all tax procedures and estimations.

The social security law exhibits gender biases as well. A female can retire at the age of fifty-five and the male at the age of sixty. As an employee, her rights and entitlements are prejudiced. Upon death, her family cannot benefit from her social security benefits, unless they can prove that she was the sole provider; old age benefits accrue only to the husband on the assumption that he is the sole provider; and she cannot combine her retirement benefits with a salary (she can only take one of them) (Jordanian Civil Service Law, art. 24). These restrictions also characterize the health insurance law, which deprives the female from being included in her husband's health insurance if she is employed and excludes her family from benefits from her health insurance (Jordanian Civil Service Health Insurance Law, 1993 amendments, arts. 8, 3).

18. Lawyer Asma Khader, interview, 31 Dec. 1997, Amman, Jordan.

From the above, it becomes clear that the exclusion of women from the broader sense of citizenship, particularly as it relates to socioeconomic entitlements and male-female relationships, has contributed to enforcing the supremacy of the man as head of the family. Discrimination within the broader citizenship entitlements have their basis in the *shari'a* as interpreted in Jordan, in customs, and in the legal system. Male superiority and female subjugation as mandated in the PSL and enforced by traditional values have left their imprints on other laws regulating women's lives.

I return to the question of what the ramifications of a comprehensive application of gender equality in Jordan would be. A discussion of the notion of equality in Jordanian discourse and a broader view of the various laws that discriminate against women and deprive them of enjoying full citizenship status may illuminate the fact that, within the existing legal provisions and the patriarchal structures, it would be difficult to imagine a concept of women other than as subordinates to men.

Equality as Citizens

The Jordanian Constitution guarantees equality to all Jordanians before the law with "no discrimination among them in terms of duties, responsibilities even if they are different in terms of ethnicity, language or religion" (Jordanian Constitution, art. 6, item 1). Another translation of equality stipulated in the Constitution is that of the state guaranteeing employment and education "within its means . . . and equal opportunity to all Jordanians" (Jordanian Constitution, art. 6, item 2).

The Jordanian Constitution, however, does not specify that there will be no discrimination on the basis of sex, a fact that many activists regard as providing avenues for discriminatory clauses within existing laws.[19] Indeed, this loophole within the Constitution was irksome enough to constitute an important element of the National Charter of 1990.

Although the charter has no binding legal power, it represents the unanimous consent of various political, ideological, and social trends in Jordan and served as the grandiose proclamation to the incipient liberalization period in Jordan, which began in 1989. All signatories reached consensus on the need to remove any misunderstandings regarding equality between the sexes that characterized Article 6 of the Constitution. Article 8 of the charter stated that "Jordanians are equal before the law with no discrimination among them in rights and responsibilities although they may differ in ethnicity, language, religion, or sex" (Khader 1996).

19. Vivian Habash and Ghada Humeidan, interview, 28 Dec. 1997, Amman, Jordan.

When discussing the notion of equality in Jordan, one has to contend with the existing discourse that distinguishes between equality and equity. This issue was raised at the Fourth World Conference on Women in Beijing (1996) where the Jordanian delegation emphasized their preference for the usage of equality rather than equity.

Among women activists in Jordan, the accepted definition of equality between men and women is one that guarantees equal opportunities, equal pay, and equal treatment in the workplace, and enhances women's access to all decision-making levels (*Star* 1991). Equity is understood as obliterating the distinctions between males and females.

What is at stake here is not only the rejection of the term *equity* but what is regarded as a cultural battle of authenticity in the face of alien concepts and notions. Adherents of these views argue that their notion of equality stems from the Islamic faith and Arab traditions that stress specificity of individual biological characteristics. By juxtaposition, they claim that the West is trying to ignore these cultural beliefs in its push for the notion of equity (Suleiman 1995). As Nawal al-Fauri of the Islamic Action Front Party notes, "Equality is understood by some to mean 'total equality.' It is an effort to force alien concepts on the peoples of the area, and in the Western sense this equality implies the impersonation of roles, which neglects the biological and psychological differences between men and women as opposed to Islam, which focuses on the specificity of characteristics" (al-Fauri 1995).

The Jordanian government has not shown any inclinations to amend the PSL, which might alter the balance of power within the family and, thus, engender equal status for both males and females. In fact, it has stated its reservations vis-à-vis the CEDAW Articles that call for ending discrimination against women within the marriage and the family.[20] The ramifications of this dependence/superiority of the male is a deformed notion of the *family* within Jordanian society. This presents a paradox because within Jordanian state and society discourses there is a heightened emphasis on the centrality of the family.

---

20. CEDAW 1997, art. 16. Jordan had expressed its reservation about sections C, D, G of paragraph 1 of this article (art. 16/1, marriage and family life). "States parties shall take all appropriate measures to eliminate discrimination against women in all matters relating to marriage and family relations and in particular shall ensure, on a basis of equality of men and women"; (C) The same rights and responsibilities during marriage and its dissolution; (D) The same rights and responsibilities as parents, irrespective of their marital status, in matters relating to their children; in all cases the interests of the children shall be paramount; (G) The same personal rights as husband and wife, including the right to choose a family name, a profession, and an occupation.

Originating from the notion of *al-usra al-wahida*, or the united family, the state propagates the notion that the family unit constitutes the basic and integral part of Jordanian society that must be protected.[21] The problem here is that many who stress the centrality of the family argue that this and attaining women's rights are mutually exclusive. Advocates of women's rights contend that only by respecting women's rights and the rights of all family members can family solidarity be guaranteed; otherwise, the family will break up and disintegrate (Khader 1995).

Within Jordanian Law, the "family" has been defined very broadly. The civil code stipulates that the family consists of the individual's relatives of a common ancestor, those of direct relationship (between ancestors and descendants), and the relatives of each spouse (Jordanian Civil Code, chap. 2, secs. 34, 35, 37). The centrality of the family within Jordanian society was also reflected in the Jordanian National Charter of 1990, which stipulated that "the family is the main unit in the Jordanian society structure, and it is the natural environment in which to raise the individual, educate him, and build his personality; the state with its formal and informal institutions must provide for the family the means for its establishment, solidarity, and good living" (Jordanian National Charter 1990, Dec., chap. 5, para. 3).

By precluding any progressive amendments to the existing laws that are based on in-built inequality, the status of women will remain marginalized within the family and, by extension, within society. The discriminatory laws are actualized in ways that deprive women of being equal partners within the family unit. The law assumes that a woman is incapable of making decisions or being trusted. As a result, her husband is the direct link with the state not only on her behalf but also on behalf of the children. As a "full" citizen, only through him can they acquire their names, nationality, passports, bank accounts, and place of residence; be registered in the family registry; acquire health insurance, social benefits, and marriage of the girls within the family; and, by extrapolation, become citizens themselves. These combined inequalities only work to subordinate the status of women within the family and society. Within the family a woman's role is enforced as the caregiver who cannot equally manage the family's affairs.

A woman's marginalization as a citizen does not end by delinking herself from the male in her life, whether the father or brother before marriage or the husband during and after marriage. Once she is widowed or divorced, she acquires more rights, including her right for an independent family registry, her right to social security benefits, the right to marry without a guardian's permission, and her entitlement to the state's social welfare system.

---

21. Princess Basma speaks at the Beijing Women's Conference, 7 Sept. 1995.

Her inclusion, however, is only based on the perception of her marginalization in society. She is grouped within the "*vulnerable groups*" that need the state's protection, including the "elderly, widowed, and divorced" (National Assistance Fund Eligibility Criteria). In all of this legislation, her rights cannot be enjoyed by her children, who are kept out of her family registry, out of her health insurance entitlement, and so on.

♦   ♦   ♦

Jordan, like other developing countries, has been undergoing a process of rapid socioeconomic change. Women's enrollment in education and their participation in the labor force has increased dramatically in the past three decades. The only justification for the discriminatory laws, either in text or in practice, is the desire to maintain the status quo of the patriarchal structure within the family and, by extension, within the state.

Those who step out of the demarcated boundaries, such as women marrying non-Jordanians or those who do not conform to the existing norms in the preservation of family honor, female respectability, and obedience, become marginalized, and their rights to equal citizenship are denied.

Empowering women may shake the foundations of the dominance and superiority of males within the family and the tribe. The state is facing two juxtaposed forces—on the one hand, its need to modernize in a globalized and competitive world and, on the other hand, the forces that this modernization may unleash. The attempt to reconcile these forces is seen in the contradictions in Jordanian laws.

Change may unsettle the existing pattern of social control, the distribution of power and authority within society, and, by extension, community security. These patterns have been protected by the legal system, by the existing interpretations of religious texts, by the practices within the judicial system, and by the traditional norms within society. Although these changes are impacting society as a whole, the battle is played out only in the field of women's rights because it constitutes the base for the supremacy of male dominance.

The diminished citizenship of women stems from multiple sources, including the family status law, the patriarchal structure that gives supremacy to the male head of the family and the tribe at the expense of women, women's economic dependence as a result of their low percentage in the labor market, and the absence of women in decision-making positions that would enable them to impact changes themselves.

The centrality of the legal system and its power over the lives of individuals make it natural to argue that the first step to improve women's lives is through a change in the laws. The laws as they currently stand regulate interfamily relationships and designate the rights and status of each member within the family. This is not to belittle the force of traditional values and cultural norms that contribute to the subordination of women, however; laws that guarantee equal rights to all citizens can impact changes in existing modes of interactions.

It would be difficult to reconcile the state's pronouncements of equality, at least in the public domain, and the inequality existing in the private domain. Empowering women in the public domain through socioeconomic changes and the forces of modernization cannot occur without a simultaneous empowerment in the private domain. The focus on struggle to bring about equality must be directed toward both the private and the public; it must be directed at bringing about a precise definition of the private and public domains.

The conclusions reached here not only require attacking the expected discourse but may also require "shaking off" the shackles of existing gender relations. The image of *al-usra al-wahida,* or united family, is built around the articulation of a cohesive structure, of family relations based on obedience to the male head of the household (the patriarch), mutual obligations, and respect for the elderly. A very interactive symbiosis is created between the patriarchal family and the patriarchal state. The Jordanian society as a whole is depicted as a united family with all its members owing allegiance to the regime.

Consequently, preservation of the structure regardless of whether that means contradictions in the legal system, leniency in application of human rights provisions, and the absence of adherence to international conventions calling for equality for women has been tolerated. To encourage change an affirmation of Jordanian women's equal loyalty to the state, equal entitlements, but most importantly, equal mental and emotional capacities must be stressed. Ignoring this only works to perpetuate the gender concept of self dehumanized as a citizen and as an individual.

9

Gender and State in Iraq

JACQUELINE S. ISMAEL AND SHEREEN T. ISMAEL

IN THIS CHAPTER we examine the state of women in Iraq in the context of state/society relations. It is argued that the patterns of women's lives in Iraq are contextualized in terms of the intersection between the institutions of modern patriarchy and politics. Post-Gulf War Iraq illustrates the supranational character of modern patriarchy and confirms the dictum that women's rights are human rights.

Institutions of Patriarchy

The concept of patriarchy generally refers to the empowerment of males over females in the social organization of everyday life. Modern patriarchy may be defined as a system of male privilege in the social order that functions as a recompense to men for their disempowerment vis-à-vis the state. The principle of male sacrifice for the state and female sacrifice for the family, symbolized in different ways by different times and cultures in terms of honor, duty, love, and so on, is a cornerstone of the modern nation-state system. No matter how it is culturally symbolized, however, it boils down to a coercive principle: females live and die at the behest of males, and males live and die at the behest of the state.

Although the dynamics of race and class create inequalities within genders in terms of context, nevertheless, the coercion women experience has its locus in the private sector, traditional patriarchy's domain of male dominance, whereas the locus of coercion men experience emanates from the public sector, modern patriarchy's domain of state dominance. This relationship between gender, patriarchy, and state is disguised by discourses that delink the processes of state from the coercion inherent in patriarchy and delink the coercion inherent in the state from the processes of patriarchy. The case of post-Gulf war Iraq, however, renders the patriarchal nature of the state system and the supranational character of its enforcement naked.

Before the twentieth century, women's lives in Iraq, as in the rest of the Middle East, were regulated by the traditional patriarchal family. The private sector of family life was the domain of women and children where they were unlikely to interact with non-kin in the patterns of everyday life. The public sector, composed of institutions where non-kin interacted, was the preserve of men. At the boundaries between public and private sectors, women were sequestered behind walls and veils. A story associated with the founding of the first Women's Grammar and High School in Iraq in 1899 illustrates the struggle of women in Iraq to transcend these boundaries. As reported by Sabiha al-Shaikh Daud (1958) in her invaluable history of the women's movement in Iraq:

> The *wali* of Baghdad, Namiq Pasha, sought the advice of the Baghdad Wiliyat Council of Education on the founding of the girls' school. The council blessed the idea but spent countless hours debating the structure and location of the building, finally putting forth the following conditions:
> It should not be lower than nearby buildings
> Its windows should not open onto the street
> All nearby homes should not have high trees
> After a long inconclusive discussion [about an appropriate site for the school], one of the council members, Jamil Sidqi al-Zahawi, sardonically suggested that there was one building that could meet all the conditions. The *wali* asked where, and Zahawi [a well-known philosopher/poet] replied, "This building has to be the balcony of the Suq al-Ghazil mosque minaret as it is the highest edifice in Baghdad. No other surrounding building is higher than it, and women can get to it unseen as there aren't any windows. In addition, when they talk, no one will hear them." They all laughed, and a building for the school was allocated, a female principle and three female teachers appointed, and ninety students admitted. (1958, 159)

The founding of the school, in fact, marks the initiation of women's entrance into the public sector through the doors of education. On 14 November 1911 a school for Jewish women opened; and on 25 January 1913 one opened for Muslim women (Daud 1958, 48). When the British occupied Iraq in 1918 after the defeat of the Ottoman empire, they attempted to discourage further development of schools for girls on the grounds that "there is no need for women in government offices; there are not enough female teachers; the people are fanatic and do not want to send their daugh-

TABLE 1

Female Enrollment in Schools in Iraq, 1920–1958

Year	Grammar School Enrollments	High School Enrollments
1920–21	462	0
1925–26	4,053	0
1930–31	7,046	176
1935–36	17,765	832
1940–41	23,329	2,475
1945–46	28,068	2,693
1950–51	42,249	10,558
1957–58	124,704	12,285

Source: Daud 1958, 242

ters to school" (Daud 1958, 48). In spite of British opposition, however, in 1918 Zahra Khidhir opened a school consisting of three grades and enrolled forty female students. This was particularly significant because it was the first voluntary action by a woman and, thus, marks the initiation of women's entrance into civil society.

Thereafter, the number of grammar schools for girls increased rapidly, jumping from 3 in 1920–21 to 27 by 1925–26, 45 by 1930–31, 121 by 1935–36, and 145 by 1940–41 (Daud 1958, 61). The development of high schools followed suit, as reflected in table 1.

The rapid growth in primary education resulted in the development of teacher training institutes for girls. By 1930–31 there were 36; these increased to 65 in 1934–35, 112 in 1940–41, and so forth. By 1957–58, there were 12,885 teaching education institutions for women. The opening of higher education to women was much slower. It was not until 1938–39 that the first female student graduated from university in Iraq. In 1955–56, 276 graduated (Daud 1958, 240–41).

The involvement of women in the public sector through their participation in voluntary associations had its roots in the education sphere. Nadi al-Nadha al-Nisayah (Women's Renaissance Club) was founded in Baghdad in November 1923 to educate women and prepare them "to become active members of their society" (Daud 1958, 6). It concentrated its activities in three areas: literacy courses for women; distribution of clothing to poor women; protection and education of female orphans. Opposition to women's ingress into the public sphere was manifested in "complaints about the activities of the club to the government" (*Al-Bilad* 30 Nov. 1930). The veil, which symbolized the sequestration of women in the family, became a focus of struggle. Reflecting the nature of this struggle, in the 1920s, the first prime minister of Iraq, Abd al-Rahman al-Naqib, forbade his household to walk within the house without a veil for fear that a plane might pass overhead and reveal the females of his family (Daud 1958, 96). In spite of the resistance, however, women's associations continued to develop (Daud 1958, 175). In 1933 the Red Crescent Society was established as a branch of the Red Cross (and became independent in 1945); in 1937 Jamaiat Mukafahat al-Muskrat, an association to combat alcoholism; in 1947 the Association for the Protection of Children. In an attempt to regulate the activities of women's associations, in 1945 the government established the Union of Women (*Al-Itihad al-Nisae*) with the aims of increasing coop-eration among Iraqi women and strengthening relationships with national and international women's organizations. By 1954 the number of women's clubs and associations had grown to forty.

The entrance of Iraqi women into civil society soon transcended national boundaries. The first international women's meeting in which Iraqi women participated was the First Eastern Women's Congress held in Damascus 3–10 July 1930. Aminah Rahal, one of the two Iraqi delegates at the congress, was a student in the teachers' training school for women. In her presenta-tion to the congress, Rahal declared: "The social conditions of Iraqi women do not differ from the conditions of her Arab sisters. She strives for the same social objectives as are sought by other Arab women. . . . What we hope for is that women will concentrate their efforts and aspirations on liberating her Arab brethren from their condition [of exploitation]" (Daud 1958, 159).

Rahal and her colleague followed up their participation in the Damascus congress with organization of an Arab Women's Conference in Baghdad 23–26 November 1934. This was held under the auspices of King Faisal of Iraq. The Ministry of Education formally requested that all teachers' col-leges and cultural organizations work to ensure the success of the con-ference. In her report to the conference, the Iraqi delegate, Rose Yusuf Francis, declared: "Iraqi women just woke up from their passivity. . . . Is there any better proof of this than the holding of this Arab conference in our country for the first time?"

From 1930 on, Iraqi women participated in almost every major regional and international women's conference. Thus, they had ventured far from the seclusion of home since their first tentative steps into classrooms in 1899. This movement, however, was confined to the urban upper classes. Rural women and the urban poor (who together constituted more than 90 percent of Iraqi women) had no opportunities for education or participation in society outside the home. Noting this, the Iraqi delegate to the Second Eastern Women's Congress, held in Teheran in December 1932, noted in her opening statement to the congress: "The movement for the education of Iraqi girls has been expanding greatly. . . . If we are able to be optimistic about the future of women in cities and towns, I am sorry that I cannot be optimistic at all about the future of peasant and working-class women" (Daud 1958, 163). The conditions of rural women in Iraq in the 1940s were described by one observer accordingly:

> Women's position in rural Iraq is painful. . . . She shares with the [rural] man his misery; she helps him in his difficult tasks, in addition to her house and maternal duties. . . . Women, particularly in the tribal communities of the south, shoulder a great burden and have much greater pressure on them than men. She shares with her husband the agricultural work; harvesting, weeding the land . . . getting up early to milk the cows, feed the cattle, and clean their stalls; then she leaves to collect wood, carrying her baby. When she returns to her hut, she kneads the dough, bakes and prepares food for her husband. In addition to all that, she is up at night grinding the grain, fighting sleeping with chants and songs. In addition, women sometimes work, husking rice in factories at night after the family has gone to sleep—and delivering [their] wages to [their husband[s]. . . . Some of them support their lazy husbands by selling feed or milk. With all that, when the husband gets upset for the least of things, he kicks his wife out of the house. He may even beat her mercilessly. (Khayat 1950, 43)

Table 2 reflects the country's rapid population growth and, in effect, mirrors the absorption of women's lives in the family-centered tasks of procreation, nurturing, and sustenance, the lot in life for all but a small privileged class of urban women. As the table reflects, in a span of just fifty years, Iraq's population jumped from less than three million to more than twelve million. Social, economic, and political changes in this period were as dramatic as the population explosion. From a primarily rural, agricultural society with a quasi-feudal, quasi-tribal social structure in 1927, by 1977 Iraq had been transformed into a modern urban-based society. In 1947, 64 percent of the population was rural and 36 percent urban. By 1965 the rural-urban distribution had shifted to 49:51, and by 1977, to 37:63 (Ismael 1980, 239). These demographic changes were driven by the economic transformation from an agricultural to rentier economy based on oil exploitation, and by the political transformation from a colonial backwash of the British empire to a militarizing dictatorship hellbent on self-aggrandizement.

Dramatic as these changes were, they did not significantly alter the pattern of life for rural women. Oil wealth brought only marginal improve-

TABLE 2

Population of Iraq, 1927–1977

Year	Female No.	Female Percentage of Pop.	Male No.	Male Percentage of Pop.	Total
1927	1,456	49.0	1,512	51.0	2,968
1934	1,692	50.1	1,688	49.9	3,380
1947	2,559	53.1	2,257	46.9	4,816
1957	3,155	49.8	3,185	50.2	6,340
1965	3,964	49.0	4,133	51.0	8,097
1970	4,686	49.6	4,754	50.4	9,440
1971	4,840	49.6	4,910	50.4	9,750
1972	5,000	49.6	5,074	50.4	10,074
1973	5,169	49.6	5,244	50.4	10,413
1974	5,343	49.6	5,422	50.4	10,765
1975	5,521	49.6	5,603	50.4	11,124
1976	5,710	49.6	5,795	50.4	11,505
1977	5,805.5	48.3	6,224	51.7	12,029.7

Source: Republic of Iraq 1978, 35.

ments to the rural standard of living as reflected in lowered infant mortality rates (in 1973–75, 104.5 per thousand in rural Iraq), but this merely increased the burden of child care because fertility rates remained high (more than 7.8 children per family in rural areas) (Annual Abstract of Statistics 1977, 37). Whereas the countryside benefited only marginally from the substantial increases in oil wealth in the seventies, cities benefited directly. Improvements in the urban standard of living, reflected in a widening differential between urban and rural infant mortality rates (88.7 compared to 104.5 per thousand for the 1973–75 period), brought expanded educational opportunities to females (Annual Abstract of Statistics 1977, 37). Between 1968–69 and 1977–78, female enrollment in primary institutions increased from 29.4 percent of total enrollments to 37.4 percent (Annual Abstract of Statistics 1977, 206); in secondary institutions, from 24.7 percent to 29.6 percent (Annual Abstracts of Statistics, 210). Most of this growth was in urban areas because resistance to female education in rural areas was deeply entrenched and not seriously challenged by government policy.

Perhaps even more indicative of the changes in the patterns of women's lives in urban areas was the expansion of advanced education and employment opportunities. Between 1970–71 and 1977–78 female enrollment in universities, colleges, and technical institutes increased from 22 percent of total enrollment to 31 percent (Annual Abstract of Statistics 1977, 226). The number of women working in industry increased from 7,000 in 1968 to 20,000 in 1976; the proportion of women employees in government offices increased from 12.4 percent of the total in 1972 to 15.4 percent in 1977 (Annual Abstract of Statistics 1977, 248).

While Iraqi women, like women throughout the Arab world, struggled to transcend the boundaries of patriarchy, the institution itself was undergoing fundamental transformation in the form of modernization (that is, Westernization). Traditionally, the institutions of patriarchy were based on the primacy of family roles in the social organization of society. Modern patriarchy is based on the primacy of public roles. Family and state, key institutions in the transition from traditional to modern patriarchy in the West, functioned to gender the segmentation of public and private sectors and to subordinate the private sector to the public sector in industrializing society. In the Arab world, historically, family roles were gendered in the context of tribal organization. Public and private sectors, distinguished in terms of kin and non-kin relations, were closely coupled by strong social bonds of community, not segmented; and the public sector was subordinate to the private sector.

The imposition of the Western model of social organization on the Arab world, typified in the concepts of modernization/Westernization, was initiated with its political subordination to the Western nation-state system in the aftermath of World War I. Imposed by the League of Nations, the mandate system in effect subordinated the private sector (essentially the whole of society in a kin-based society such as the Arab world) to the supranational public sector of modern patriarchy. The devolution of the nation-state system onto the Arab world over the next several decades effectively entrenched the dominance of the public sector, represented in the state, over the private sector. The result was the distortion, not displacement, of traditional patriarchy and the malformation of the state by the integration of the public sector with kin-based tribal social dynamics. Under what has been called neopatriarchy (Sharabi 1988), public and private sectors are neither segmented nor loosely coupled, but fragmented, resulting in various distortions of state and family dynamics throughout the Arab world.

Institutions of Politics

Government, the central institution of politics, is conceptually distinguished from the state. Whereas government is temporal, the state is perceived as a symbolic entity, spatially located but temporally transcendent. It exists as a legal fiction invented in the Treaty of Westphalia in 1648 to vest, legitimate, and perpetuate political power in territoriality (manifested symbolically in the myth of nation). Government, then, may be conceived as the operational arm of the state, its temporal representative empowered by the powers that be (by the international community of powerful states) to exercise power on behalf of the state for the good of the state. In the West, where the nation-state system evolved from the Treaty of Westphalia, the distinction between state and government has served to entrench the doctrine of sovereignty in international relations, which in effect legitimates a government's right to do what it will within the bounds of its own territory.

As a myth, the concept of the nation-state imbues the exercise of politics with metaphysical qualities. In the tumultuous upheavals that rocked European political establishments in the eighteenth and ninteenth centuries, the myth served to buttress centralized political power against the forces of democratization. Outside the West the emergence of the nation-state system has been untempered by the processes of historic evolution, which in the West produced a compromise between centralized power and democratic anarchy. The devolution of the nation-state system onto the rest of the world in the aftermath of World War II, however, established governments with nearly absolute domestic power. It is unchecked internally by the countervailing forces of historic evolution and guaranteed externally by the supranational organizations of the nation-state system.

The nation-state system promotes ethnic and gender privilege in government. Political struggles against these tendencies have been manifested in women's and minority struggles for political participation and nonpartisan struggles for human rights. In the political turmoil that swept across the Arab world in the aftermath of World War II, the issue of women's rights became a slogan not only for the established women's associations but also in the new radical political groups that emerged. In Iraq, in an effort to gain some control over the volatile political activism of the period, in 1954 the government moved to require licensing of all public groups.

The Communist and Baathist parties in Iraq represented the political trends of socialism and nationalism dominant in the post–World War II Arab world. Their diagnoses of the women's issue reflects the fundamental differences in ideology between the two movements. The diagnosis of the Iraqi Communist Party was highlighted in a program of action proposed by the party in the mid-fifties. This program emphasized the party's commitment to "seek legislation which will give women comprehensive political and economic rights and eradicate oppressive social injustices; and to work to ensure that women have active roles in the building of Iraqi society, in which women make up no less than half" (*Al-Qaidah* 1955).

The League for the Defence of Women's Rights, a clandestine association established by the Iraqi Communist Party, is an example of the party's activism on the issue of women's rights. After the 1958 coup in Iraq, which toppled the monarchy, the league initiated open operations and established branches throughout the country with a membership of twenty thousand. In January 1959 it was formally licensed under the name Rabitat al-Mara al-Iraqiyah and held its first congress the following March under the slogan "Safeguarding the Republic and Women's Rights." General Abdul Karim Kassem, prime minister of the new republic, personally opened the congress. The association committed itself to struggle for (1) safeguarding the republic; (2) education for all women; (3) progressive personal status laws; (4) expansion of literacy programs; (5) expansion of day care, kindergarten, and educational locations; (6) development of women's occupational skills training and employment centers (Khairy 1981, 211).

The accomplishments of the league in the initial years of the republic, before it was banned by Kassem in 1963, were impressive. It published a women's journal, *Majalat al-Mara;* established 87 literacy centers with 7,503 students taught by 605 volunteer members; established 111 centers to teach sewing and domestic skills; and opened a number of health clinics. The league championed reform of the personal status laws. In 1959, Law 188 of the personal status code removed the regulation of family affairs from religious control and placed it under civil control. Perhaps more significant was the abolition of tribal custom law that allowed the killing of women to eradicate shame (Khairy and Khairy 1984, 322–24). So successful was the league in mobilizing women that by the time its second congress met in 1960, it had a membership of 43,000 (*Itihad al-Shaab* 1959, 16 June).

The league's fate provided an indication of the ethno-tribal and patriarchal nature of political dynamics in the new republic. In an attempt to divide the league, in 1959 the Itihad Nisa Kurdistan (Union of Kurdish Women) was licensed. The league, however, moved to coordinate its activities with the new association, and on 16 June 1959 both organizations announced that their basic aim was to unify all Kurdish and Arab women of all political persuasions in their struggle to support the new republic. The official organ of the Communist Party of Iraq observed:

No doubt, women's political views, especially after their liberation and the spread of democracy, differ according to their political persuasions. . . . Differ-

ences in views and political ideas reveal the progress of women and Iraqi society. . . . On this basis, women must strengthen their solidarity and unify their
efforts within a democratic association whose aim is to unify all Iraqi women,
regardless of their national origins, political views, or social class. Those lofty
aims carry the struggle to protect the republic and fight for the rights of
women and children. . . . The League for the Defense of Women's Rights and
the Union of Kurdish Women believe in the necessity of uniting with the the
Union of Kurdish Women believe in the necessity of uniting with the women's
movement in Iraqi Kurdistan. (*Itihad al-Shaab* 1959, 16 June)

In 1961 the Kassem government, by then at odds with the Iraqi Communist
Party, encouraged the establishment of an organization to rival the league and
reduce its power in the women's movement. The government withdrew its
support from the league and licensed the *Munadhamat Nisa al-Jumhoriyah*
(Organization of Republican Women). In 1963 the league was banned.

In contrast to the ideological position of the Iraqi Communist Party, the
patriarchal chauvinism inherent in nationalism was reflected in Baathist prescriptions on the nature of women's problems. Article 12 of the Constitution of the Baath Party, for example, declared "The Arab woman shall enjoy
the full rights of a citizen, and the party is struggling to raise her level so
that she may deserve to enjoy these rights." Elaborating on this, in 1963,
the party issued a definitive statement on the issue: "Women's liberation . . .
is a democratic necessity, in addition to being a human one. A disrespectful
view of women is a part of feudal-tribal ideology. . . . The socialist society
[of the Baath] is the only avenue that can provide the objective conditions
to liberate women. . . . The party and the revolutionary government must
combat negative views of women and work to eliminate the vestiges of
these reactionary outlooks" (*Nidhal al-baath* 1963).

Within Iraq's Baath Party, responsibility for the political mobilization of
women was delegated to the Al-Itihad al-Aam li Nisa al-Iraq (General Federation of Iraqi Women) as the central organization for women's participation in the political structure. Created after the 1968 Baathist coup, the
federation functioned as an umbrella organization to bring women's professional, union, and cooperative associations under the tutelage of the Baath
Party and to subordinate the women's movement to the regime's ideological objectives (Ismael 1980, 243). At the party's eighth regional congress in
January 1974, Saddam Hussein gave clear expression to the party's patriarchal orientation toward the women's movement: "Women will not be liberated by women's assertions. . . . Women can only be liberated by
liberation of the entire society, political and economic. Since the Arab Socialist Party is the leader of social change in every sphere and activity, the

main and vanguard responsibility falls on its shoulders" (Regional Command, Baath Party 1974, 116–17).

The nature of this patriarchy was made clear in January 1976 in response to a federation draft proposal for changes in the personal status laws pertaining to women. In response to the draft, Saddam Hussein essentially killed the proposal by cautioning that change in this area must be very gradual because "when we deal with legal issues pertaining to women, we should be sensitive to . . . the experience of not only this country but to the Arab nation as a whole. . . . We should not ignore our Arab nation in any decision we make or action we take. . . . We must ensure that our nation . . . comprehends our steps" (*Al-Thawra* 1976).

In the Baathist government in Iraq generally, and Saddam Hussein's regime in particular, the nation-state's inkling toward fascist formation became manifest, undaunted by the necessities of political compromise or niceties of liberal temperance. First stipulated in the provisional Constitution of 1968 and reconfirmed in subsequent revisions, including the latest, the draft Constitution of 1995, officially the Baath Party governs Iraq through the Revolutionary Command Council (RCC), which exercises both executive and legislative authority. The very structure of government, including the constitution and judiciary, provides for an environment of "widespread and systematic violations of human rights" (United Nations 1995, 6). Official reports to the U.N. Human Rights Commission have noted that "the politico-legal organization of the Republic of Iraq constitutes of itself a systematic cause of human rights violations" (UNESCO 1994, 58). In 1990, *Middle East Watch* observed that in Iraq there was "a system of government wholly devoid of checks and balances, one in which many fundamental rights and freedoms are guaranteed in word but are routinely trampled in deed" (UNESCO 1994, 22).

In reality, Saddam Hussein governs Iraq. Effectively employing the instruments of Baath power—subterfuge, terror, and purge—he reduced the party to an instrument of his power. As president of the republic, prime minister, chairman of the RCC, and secretary-general of the regional command of the Baath Party, Saddam Hussein consolidated Baath power in his hands. He is an archetypal patriarch and embodies the state. Consistent with Baath ideology, the party is the state, and the leader is the party (al-Jaza'iri 1994, 46–49). Thus, public policy, law and order, life and death are all subject to Saddam Hussein's whim and fancy.

The human rights record of the regime is fathomless and notorious. Upon briefly seizing power in 1963, the Baath regime initiated bloody purges of all opposition—potential, perceived, and imagined. All leftists—communists, independent Marxists, and humanists—were specifically targeted. In the regime's nine-month reign of terror (from 8 February 1963 to 18 November 1963), it is estimated that up to ten thousand people were killed, five thousand from the ranks of the Iraqi Communist Party alone (Zaher 1989, 32).

> Bands of the National Guard roamed the streets and carried out summary executions, arbitrary arrests and savage torture. Sports grounds, military camps and schools were turned into concentration camps and interrogation centres for tens of thousands of people from all walks of life. At the top of the list were leaders, cadres, and activists of the trade unions and the mass democratic organizations, including the Iraqi Women's League and the General Union of Students of the Iraqi Republic. (Zaher 1989, 31)

With its resumption of power in 1968, the new Baathist regime disdained the flagrant use of violence exercised in 1963 for subtler forms of intimidation and repression. A network of secret police agencies was constructed to spy on the population and on each other (al-Khafaji 1994, 20–21). At the same time, the Baath Party initiated an aggressive recruitment campaign to transform the party into a mass organization. Through employment of a combination of intimidation, terror, and rewards, the party penetrated all facets of Iraqi society and subordinated it all to Baathist patriarchy. Through repression, the regime sought to enforce the population's absolute compliance to its authority. According to a *Middle East Watch* report on Iraq:

> In Iraq of the 1970s and 1980s, the victims of repression came from a broad range of groups—conservatives, liberals, non-Baathi Arab nationalists, Communists, Shias, Kurds, Assyrian Christians, Jews, students, intellectuals, military personnel, and even Baath party members and senior figures of the regime. Large numbers of journalists, writers, intellectuals, . . . doctors, students, and academics . . . were arrested, executed or disappeared in the late 1970s and early 1980s. (*Middle East Watch* 1990, 3)

This repression went on in full view of the international community. The problem of oppressive regimes, after all, is commonplace, especially in the Third World. The international community, manifested in the United Nations in general, the Security Council in particular, was duty bound by the U.N. Charter to protect the sovereignty of states, no matter how sadistic their governments. Such is the nature of international patriarchy that state rights are sacrosanct and inviolable (except by more powerful states). In fact, the member states of the Security Council competed with each other to court the favor of the Iraqi regime and arm it with the most modern tools of repression and massacre (Phythian 1997).

If politics is conceptualized as a contest among contending values, interests, and worldviews, then suppression represents a process of de-politicization. In Iraq under the Baath, values, interests, and worldviews that conflicted with Baathist ideology were systematically suppressed. With unfettered financial resources from phenomenally expanded oil revenues in the seventies, the state took control of both the public and private sectors, expanding its tentacles of surveillance into every home, school, business, and social association (al-Khafaji 1989, 74–82). Because the educated urban middle class of professionals, technocrats, and civil servants represented the most politically conscious element in the society, it was the primary target. As an urban phenomenon based primarily on the promotion of the advancement of women through education, the women's movement was particularly undermined because its leaders and advocates were among the ranks of political activists targeted in this period. By the end of the seventies, the society was effectively depoliticized.

In its suppression of political opposition and enforcement of submissiveness to the will of the state (personified in the person of Saddam Hussein), the Baathist regime (which by international standards constituted the legitimate government of Iraq and represented the state in international forums) detained, tortured, executed, and disappeared women as well as men. Feminist critiques on Iraq generally agree that in the Baathist program of repression, women in Iraq were "granted equal rights with men" (Cobbett 1989, 128). In addition, women became a tool of male repression through the agency of state rape, which was used "to crush the spirit of political prisoners, to recruit women into the internal spy network, and to 'break the eyes' [humble or dishonor] of families or communities" (Omar 1994, 66; Makiya 1993, 16–17). As reported by the Special Rapporteur of the United Nations' Commission on Human Rights:

Security personnel would sometimes rape a young women in order to later use her as an informant under the threat that her non-compliance would result in the revelation of her rape, thus subjecting her to public disgrace and ostracism. It has been alleged that some of these rapes were recorded on videocassettes to be given to the victim's family in the event of non-compliance. Other women were reportedly raped simply as an act of insult or vengance directed against their families. Testimony received from former Iraqi security officers corroborates these allegations. (UNESCO 1992, 24–25)

The human toll of domestic oppression in the seventies was dramatically escalated in the eighties with war, ethnic cleansing, and genocide. A summary of its major dimensions follows.

Iraq-Iran War

The initiation of the war in September 1980 set the stage for the decade. By the time it ended in August 1988, estimates of the total number killed on both sides ranged from five hundred thousand to more than one million (*Middle East Watch* 1990, 5). In addition to the general victimization women suffered as a result of the war, public policy targeted them for special indignities. In October 1982 the minister of defense ordered the arrest and detention of wives and children of deserters, and special grants were offered to men to marry war widows: "For marrying a woman with a middle-school certificate a man received a grant of 200 dinars, for a high-school graduate 300 dinars and for a university graduate 500 dinars" (Omar 1994, 63).

Forced Expulsions

With the initiation of the Iraq-Iran war, the government of Iraq initiated a campaign of terror against Iraqis alleged to be of Persian origin. In April 1980 eight hundred merchants were summoned to a meeting with the minister of commerce. When all assembled for the meeting, they were herded onto trucks and summarily taken to the Iranian border (Shaban 1994, 224). Their families were subsequently evicted. Justifying the expulsions, in June 1980, the general director of security stated that "there are some who are Persian by citizenship, and there are others who are Persian by loyalties" (Shaban 1994, 224). In April 1981 the Revolutionary Command Council issued a decree (no. 474) offering financial compensation to Iraqi men married to women of "Iranian nationality" to divorce their wives or send them out of the country. As reported by the Special Rapporteur of the U.N. High Commission on Human Rights, the decree was followed by "a campaign directed against persons of 'Persian origin' during which thousands of (often Shiah) men were arbitrarily arrested (many of whom have subsequently disappeared) and their families deported to Iran" (UNESCO 1994, 29).

About three hundred thousand people were evicted, with a large proportion women and children, as many of the men were among the disappeared (Shaban 1994, 224). Shi'a elite—merchants, *ulama*, professionals, and intellectuals—were initially targeted. Deported to Iran, they have languished in Iranian refugee camps since. Not officially recognized as refugees by the United Nations High Commission for Refugees (UNHCR), they were dumped in Iran and left dependent on Iranian largesse. Those who survived the trauma (and many probably did not), exist on the fringes of Iranian society (Immigration and Refugee Board, Canada 1996).

Anfal *Campaign*

In 1987 a program of ethnic cleansing of the Kurdish population of northern Iraq was initiated with the destruction of Kurdish villages near the Iraq-Iran border and resettlement of their populations in southern Iraq. By early 1988 the program had expanded into a project of genocide as a final solution of the Kurdish problem. By the end of 198, about forty-five hundred Kurdish villages in northern Iraq had been destroyed and between seventy thousand and one hundred thousand Kurds—men, women and children—killed (*Middle East Watch,* 1993). Table 3 presents the details of the campaign as reported by the Special Rapporteur of the U.N. Commission on Human Rights.

During the conduct of the Iraq-Iran war, chemical weapons had become a regular part of Iraq's military arsenal. In March 1984 both the United States and the United Nations publicly denounced Iraq for its use of chemical weapons (*Middle East Watch* 1990, 81). Nevertheless, the major powers gave tacit approval and assistance to Iraq's development of a major chemical weapons industry, and by 1985 Iraq was producing mustard gas and at least two types of nerve agents (Phythian 1997; al-Kharsan 1993, 189).

In spite of mounting evidence of Iraq's use of chemical weapons against the Kurdish population in northern Iraq throughout the spring and summer of 1987, the international community (as represented by the big powers and the international organizations they dominate) disregarded the issue of genocide and quibbled over the evidence of poison gas usage.

> Only when pictorial evidence of the horror of chemical warfare against defenceless civilians became available, following the poison-gas attacks on the Iraqi Kurdish town of Halabja near the Iranian border on 16 and 17 March 1988, did the world take serious notice. Western television crews filmed ghastly scenes of bodies strewn along Halabja's streets, families locked in an embrace of death, lifeless children, doll-like with blackened mouths, eyes, and nails, and the upended carcasses of domestic animals. (*Middle East Watch* 1990, 83)

TABLE 3

The Anfal Campaign

| Operation | Chemical Weapons Use | | | | Effects | | |
	Dates	Place	Specific Locations	Number of Incidents	Men	Women and Children	Elderly
Anfal 1	2/23/88 to 3/19/88	JaffatiValley	Sergalu, Bergalu, Yaghsamer, Haladin, Sekaniyan, Shanakhsch, and Gojar Mountain	Multiple and repeated	Most escaped; returnees disappeared	Most escaped; scores died during flight	Most escaped; some detained in Nugrat al-Salman Prison
Anfal II	3/22/88 to 4/1/88	Qaradagh subdistrict	Saywsenan, Balakajar, Dukan, Masoyi, and Zerda Mountain	Single attacks on the villages	Captured and disappeared	Suleim.: saved Kalar: disappeared or detained in Dibs	Suleim: saved Kalar: detained in Nugrat al-Salman Prison
Anfal III	4/7/88 to 4/20/88	Germian Plain	Tazasar Village (and two other possible locations)	Single attacks on villages and/or pockets of PUK (Kurdish Democratic Union) resistance	Captured and disappeared	Mostly disappeared or taken to Dibs	Detained in Nugrat al-Salman Prison

Anfal	Dates	Region	Villages	Attack pattern			
Anfal IV	5/3/88 to 5/8/88	Valley of the Lesser Zab	Goktap and Askar	Single attack on 5/3	Captured and disappeared	Most captured and disappeared or detained in Dibs	Detained in Nugrat al-Salman Prison
Anfal V	5/15/88 to 6/7/88	Valleys of Shaqlawa and Rawanduz	Wara, Balisan, Nazanin, Sheikh Wasan, Bileh, Seran, Garawan, Akoyan, and Faqian	Attacks on Wara on 5/15, followed by repeated attacks elsewhere on 5/23 and thereafter	Captured and disappeared	Captured and disappeared, or taken to Dibs	Detained in Nugrat al-Salman Prison
Anfal VI	7/30/88 to mid-August 88	Valleys of Shaqlawa and Rawanduz	Balisan, Malakan, Warta, Hiran and Smaquli Valleys	Multiple and repeated	Captured and disappeared	None	None
Anfal VII	mid-August 88 to 8/28/88	Valleys of Shaqlawa and Rawanduz	Balisan, Malakan, Warta, hiran and Smaquli Valleys	Multiple and repeated	Captured and disappeared	None	None
Anfal VIII "Final Anfal"	8/25/88 to 9/6/88	Badinan region	Large number of villages	Many villages on 8/25 only	Captured and disappeared	Captured and released in Baharka	Captured and released in Baharka

Source: Adapted from Commission on Human Rights 1994, 99–100.

Institutions of the Nation-State

It may seem ironic, but entirely consistent with the supranational nature of modern patriarchy, that the human toll of domestic oppression in Iraq was dramatically escalated in the nineties by the international community. Iraq's invasion of Kuwait in August 1990 set the stage. In response, the U.N. Security Council passed a number of sanctions against Iraq (see table 4).

Meanwhile, the United States orchestrated an international alliance ostensibly to liberate Kuwait, and in January 1991 initiated a massive air bombardment of Iraq, dropping more than one hundred thousand tons of explosives in the most intensive air bombardment in history. On 24 February U.S. led forces initiated a ground offensive, and within one hundred hours, the Iraqi army was routed from Kuwait. A cease-fire was declared on 28 February. Although the war destroyed Iraq's civil infrastructure, in effect catapulting the society back into a preindustrial mode of existence, the government of Iraq not only survived with its military prowess (the Republican Guard) intact, indeed, it was in effect abetted by international compliance with its violent suppression of a civil uprising against it (Ismael and Ismael 1994). As concluded by an eminent international law scholar, Richard Falk (1994a),

> Having continued the war to the point of provoking a breakdown of internal order, partly encouraged by President George Bush's call to insurrection, a distinct set of responsibilities ensued for coalition forces to remove the criminal regime in Baghdad from power and to uphold the human rights and the right of self-determination of the Iraqi people. In essence, the war was improperly initiated and was continued well beyond the basic UN mandate; however, after being so dubiously extended, it was perversely and prematurely terminated in a highly disruptive fashion that caused severe and massive suffering and devastation. (37)

Like the Iraq-Iran war, the Gulf War was fought by men in Iraq and suffered by women. Estimates of the number of Iraqi soldiers killed in the war range from seventy thousand to two hundred thousand (Cainkar 1993, 46) and of the number of civilians killed, about one hundred thousand (*Herald Tribune* 1991, 4 June; *Middle East Watch* 1992). Beyond the casualty figures, however, the toll on Iraqi women was profound, as definitively detailed by Louise Cainkar (1993), who concluded:

> Iraqi civilians inordinately bore . . . the social, economic, political, and health costs of the Gulf war and sanctions. Data show that women and children have been the most affected. With public services halted, trade in commodities at a

TABLE 4

U.N. Security Council Resolutions on Iraq, August 2–November 9, 1991

Resolution	Date Passed	Substance
660	August 2, 1990	Condemned Iraq's invasion of Kuwait and demanded that Baghdad withdraw its forces
661	August 6, 1990	Imposed stringent sanctions on all trade to and from Iraq
662	August 9, 1990	Declared Iraq's annexation of Kuwait null and void and demanded that Iraq rescind the annexation
664	August 18, 1990	Demanded that Iraq allow foreign nationals to leave Iraq and Kuwait and that it rescind its order to close diplomatic missions in Kuwait
665	August 25, 1990	Permitted states to use limited naval force to ensure compliance with the economic sanctions, including the right to inspect cargoes
666	September 13, 1990	Allowed food shipments to Iraq and Kuwait for humanitarian purposes but only if distributed by approved international groups
667	September 16, 1990	Condemned raids by Iraqi troops on French and other diplomatic missions in occupied Kuwait
669	September 24, 1990	Adopted a procedural measure entrusting its sanctions committee to evaluate requests for assistance from countries suffering because of the trade embargo
670	September 25, 1990	Prohibited air traffic with Iraq and occupied Kuwait except for humanitarian reasons
674	October 29, 1990	Reminded Iraq that it was liable under international law for any loss, damage, or injuries arising in regard to Kuwait and third states, their nationals, and their corporations. States were invited to collect information on their claims
677	November 28, 1990	Asked the U.N. secretary-general to safeguard a smuggled copy of Kuwait's preinvasion population register
678	November 29, 1990	Authorized states "to use all necessary means" against Iraq unless it withdrew from Kuwait on or before January 15

TABLE 4-*Continued*

Resolution	Date Passed	Substance
686	March 2, 1991	Reminded Iraq that all twelve resolutions would continue "to have full force and effect" until full compliance was effected
687	April 3, 1991	Demanded with a cease-fire resolution complete destruction and verification of Iraq's weapons of mass destruction before removal of sanctions

standstill, and incomes suspended, each household took on responsibility for human survival during the war. Since household management and labour is the responsibility of women, the burden of replacing the infrastructure destroyed by bombing and producing unavailable or unaffordable commodities fell largely upon the shoulders of women. Working nonstop and under primitive and unsanitary conditions, women forged human survival and saved lives. Without their work, civilian mortality and morbidity rates would have been much higher than they were. (43)

The war and sanctions not only devastated Iraq's civilian population generally and women particularly they also served to reinforce and strengthen state oppression. In particular, a genocidal campaign against the Marsh Arabs of southern Iraq was conducted unabated throughout the post-Gulf War period. According to the 1993 report of the Special Rapporteur of the U.N. Commission on Human Rights, the campaign "mirrors the Government's *Anfal* operations in the Kurdish northern area" (UNESCO 1993, 35). A 1996 human rights report to the U.S. Senate Committee on Foreign Relations noted that "Iraqi military operations continued to target Shi'a Arabs living in the southern marshes. In central and Southern Iraq the regime continued to divert humanitarian supplies to its security forces, the military, and other supporters" (U.S. Department of State 1997, 126).

Maintenance of the sanctions regime in the years since the war has in effect placed the people of Iraq in the direct cross fire between a repressive international system and an oppressive government. The sanctions regime imposed on Iraq in August 1990 has been reinforced with an additional twenty-seven Security Council resolutions after the cease-fire resolution from April 1991 to April 1998 as reflected in table 5.

Table 5 provides a specification of Security Council priorities that in ef-

TABLE 5

U.N. Security Council Resolutions on Iraq, April 1991–April 1998

Resolution	Date Passed	Substance
688	April 5, 1991	Human rights and humanitarian aid
689	March 9, 1991	Procedural matters related to implementation of resolution 687
692	May 20, 1991	Procedural matters related to implementation of resolution 674
699	June 17, 1991	Procedural matters related to implementation of resolution 687
700	June 17, 1991	Procedural matters related to implementation of resolution 661
706	August 15, 1991	Humanitarian aid
707	August 15, 1991	Condemnation of Iraq for "violation of a number of its obligations under section C of resolution 687," and for its noncompliance with weapons inspections regime
712, 715, 773	Passed between September 19, 1991, and August 26, 1992	Procedural matters related to implementation of resolution 687
778	October 2, 1992	Humanitarian aid
806, 833, 899	Passed between February 5 and May 27, 1993	Procedural matters related to implementation of resolution 687
949	October 15, 1994	Condemnation of Iraq for "recent military deployments . . . in the direction of the border of Kuwait"
986	April 14, 1995	Humanitarian aid
1051	March 27, 1996	Procedural matters related to implementation of resolution 661
1060	June 12, 1996	Deploration of "the refusal of the Iraqi authorities to allow access to sites designated by the Special Commission"
1111	June 4, 1997	Humanitarian aid
1115	June 21, 1997	Condemnation of Iraq for not allowing unrestricted access to the Special Commission
1129	September 12, 1997	Humanitarian aid
1134	October 23, 1997	Reaffirmation of resolution 1115, with threat of retaliatory measures

TABLE 5 – *Continued*

Resolution	Date Passed	Substance
1137	November 12, 1997	Procedural matters related to implementation of resolution 1134
1143. 1153	Passed December 4, 1997, and February 20, 1998, respectively	Humanitarian aid
1154	March 2, 1998	Procedural matters related to implementation of resolution 687
1158	March 25, 1988	Humanitarian aid

fect reflect the supranational nature of modern patriarchy: thirteen of the twenty-seven resolutions were related to implementation of punitive resolutions passed either in response to Iraq's occupation of Kuwait or the cease-fire; four were based on condemnations of Iraq for resistance to the stringency of weapons inspection; eight were based on humanitarian aid. Furthermore, thirteen of the twenty-seven resolutions reaffirmed "the commitment of all Member States to the sovereignty, territorial integrity and political independence of Iraq" (specified in resolutions 688, 949, 986, 1060, 1111, 1115, 1129, 1134, 1137, 1143, 1153, 1154, 1158). But only one resolution (688) addressed human rights, and then only tangentially, not directly, as a condemnation of the government of Iraq for "the repression of the Iraqi civilian population."

In its supranational character, modern patriarchy, like the proverbial patriarch, plays a disciplinary function in the family of nation-states. The operation of this function relies on punitive and disciplinary tools, tempered with charity. From this perspective the concept of patriarchy may be described as a metaphor that symbolizes polarized relations of power and dependence, control and submission, dominance and subordination. Equated with social relations, the poles describe the gender roles of patriarchy in the traditional family system: power, control, and dominance for male roles; dependence, submission, and subordination for female roles. Equated with international politics, the poles describe the status and roles of actors in the modern nation-state system: power, control, and dominance for the technologically advanced states of Europe; dependence, submission, and subordination for other states, particularly those outside the racial pale of Europe. On the racist character of the world order emerging in the post-Gulf War world, Ali Mazrui (1994) has identified it as a pattern of "global apartheid." Similarly, Richard Falk (1994b) observed:

> The Gulf War revived the plausibility of aspiring to master geopolitics and, with almost religious finality and patriarchal zeal, associated this vision of renewed Northern domination of the South with the militarization of space. Such a conception of order is content to witness the spread of Lebanonization in countries of the South, reserving an interventionary option for exceptional cases where crucial resources or strategic checkpoints are threatened by hostile forces or where a country in the South seems on the verge of acquiring the sort of military capability and political will that endangers the sense of Northern invulnerability. (547)

Viewed from this perspective, modern patriarchy is about race and power relations in the international arena. Powerful states (especially the United States) play a male role of dominance and control and expect weaker states to adopt female roles of dependence, submission, and subordination. When weaker states fail to follow the prescribed role-scripts, punitive and disciplinary tools are employed (as in Libya, Cuba, Panama, Iraq, Iran, Sudan).

The eight resolutions dealing with humanitarian aid were in response to the complex humanitarian disaster unfolding in Iraq as a direct consequence of war and sanctions. The resolute maintenance of sanctions in the years after the war extended and deepened the humanitarian crisis precipitated by the war. The impact of sanctions on the civilian population of Iraq has been monitored by the United Nations and international NGOs since the end of the war. Table 6 identifies some of the major reports released between the cease-fire in April 1991 and May 1998.

Complex humanitarian disasters are catastrophes of such scope and magnitude that the very fabric of human life (structure, context, and texture) is threatened (Orbinski 1996, 137–49). Monitoring the disaster that was unfolding in Iraq after the Gulf War and escalating as a result of sanctions, the international community was fully apprised of the situation. The resolutions passed by the Security Council in response to the escalating humanitarian disaster were at best token responses that gave the appearance of responding but actually contributed only marginally to disaster relief. In Iraq, as James Orbinski (vice president of Medecins Sans Frontieres International Canada) observed with regard to other complex humanitarian disasters, the Security Council used humanitarianism "as a substitute for legally defined political and military obligations under international law" (Orbinski 1996, 145).

A report prepared by the World Health Organization in March 1996, but

TABLE 6

Selected Reports on the Impact of Sanctions on Iraq, April 1991–May 1998

Date	Issuing Agency	Title	Author (and Publication Information)
March 20, 1991	United Nations	*Report to the Secretary-General on Humanitarian Needs in Iraq in the Immediate Post-Crisis Environment*	Martti Ahtisaari (doc. S/22366)
February 1991	WHO/UNICEF	*Joint Report: A Visit to Iraq, 16–21*	
May 1991	Harvard School of Public Health	*Public Health in Iraq after the Gulf War*	Harvard Study Team (photocopy)
July 15, 1991	United Nations	*Report to the Secretary-General on Humanitarian Needs in Iraq*	Sadruddin Aga Khan (doc. S/22799
1991	London School of Economics	*Hunger and Poverty in Iraq, 1991*	Jean Dreze and Haris Gazdar (subsequently published in *World Development*, vol. 20, no. 7, 1992).
September 21, 1992	Harvard School of Public Health	*The Effects of the Gulf War on Infant and Child Mortality in Iraq*	Ascherio et al., *New England Journal of Medicine*, vol. 327, no. 13.
April 1993	UNICEF	*Iraq: Children, War and Sanctions*	Eric Hoskins (photocopy)
March 1996	World Health Organization	*The Health Conditions of the Population in Iraq since the Gulf Crisis*	WHO/EHA/96.1

not released until 27 April 1998, documented the mounting scale of crisis in terms of quantum increases in infant and child mortality, in the incidence of infectious disease, in malnutrition. The report's conclusions left no doubt about the role of the Security Council's sanctions in Iraq's complex humanitarian disaster:

In an attempt to assess the impact of the United Nations sanctions on the quality of life of the population in Iraq, the following facts should serve as constant reminders in drawing overall conclusions regarding the humanitarian aspects of the sanctions:

1. The six-week war in 1991 resulted in the large scale destruction of military and civilian infrastructures alike. In general, civilian populations were subsequently more affected by the consequences of much destruction than the military populations, the latter of whom have tended to be more protected against the daily hardships ensuring since enforcement of the sanctions.

2. The sanctions imposed on Iraq and related circumstances have prevented the country from repairing all of its damaged or destroyed infrastructure, and whenever attempts have been made, these have been incomplete. This applies to electricity generating and water purification plants, sewage treatment facilities and communication and transportation networks. This has affected the quality of life of countless Iraqi citizens, especially those belonging to the mid and lower economic levels of the country's total population of 20 million, who do not have alternatives or options to overcome the effects of these ravages.

3. Iraq is an oil-rich country, which prior to the 1991 war was almost totally dependant on the import of two vital requirements for a healthy life— food and medicine. More than 70 percent of food requirements of Iraq, prior to 1991, were imported and the bulk consisted of staple cereals, legumes, cooking oils, sugar and tea, which are the major items in the daily diet of the average Iraqi citizen. *Financial constraints* as a result of the sanctions have prevented the necessary import of food and medicine.

4. Other items of the daily diet, especially animal products such as dairy products, chicken and beef, in which the country was almost self-sufficient, are now being sold on the open market at "sky-rocketing" prices, which only those at the highest income level can afford. The average Iraqi citizen depends on rationed foods, which supply one-third of the daily minimum caloric needs. Iraq has a disciplined rationing system, which, so far, has prevented a major famine. Animal products on the free market, due to their high prices, are not available to infants and children in most families, which is a source of protein they urgently need.

5. The vast majority of the country's population has been on a semi-starvation diet for years. This tragic situation has tremendous implications on the health status of the population and on their quality of life, not only for the present generation, but for the future generation as well.

6. The reduction in the import of medicines, owing to a *lack of financial resources,* as well as a lack of minimum health care facilities, insecticides, pharmaceutical and other related equipment and appliances, have crippled the health care services, which in pre-war years were of a high quality. Assessment reports rightly remarked that the quality of health care in Iraq, due to the six-week 1991 war and the subsequent sanctions imposed on the country, has been literally put back by at least 50 years. Diseases such as malaria, typhoid and cholera, which were once almost under control, have rebounded since 1991 at epidemic levels, with the health sector as a helpless witness.

7. Very rarely has the impact of sanctions on millions of people been documented. Severe economic hardship, a semi-starvation diet, high levels of disease, scarcity of essential drugs and, above all, the psycho-social trauma and anguish of a bleak future, have led to numerous families being broken up leading to distortions in social norms.

8. The impact of this unfortunate situation on the infant and child population in particular in Iraq needs special attention. It is not only the data on morbidity and mortality that tell the story, but equally important are the crippling effects of many of these morbidities which are often forgotten. The psychological trauma of the six-week 1991 war and the terrible hardships enduring with the sanctions since then, can be expected to leave indelible marks on the mental health and behavioral patterns of these children when they grow to adulthood. This tragic aspect of the impact of the war and conditions surrounding the sanctions is rarely articulated, but the world community should seriously consider the implications of an entire generation of children growing up with such traumatized mental handicaps, if of course, they survive at all. (World Health Organization 1998)

The concept of citizenship generally refers to the status or condition of a member of a political community (nation or state). Because status and condition are functions of context, they constitute important variable dimensions in the study of citizenship. To examine the status and condition of Iraqi women, we contextualized their status in terms of the intersection between the institutions of patriarchy and state and their condition in terms of the intersection between time and the institutions of politics. From this perspective, the status and condition of Iraqi women were examined in terms of the interaction between the relatively stable institutions of the international political order (patriarchy and state) and the changing institutions of politics at the national level (government).

This examination revealed that changes in the condition of women in Iraq have been significant over the course of the twentieth century. Taken in context, however, the condition of women is relative to the condition of society. Viewed from this perspective, the condition of women in Iraq is a function of the interaction between changing socioeconomic conditions in

Iraq and their relatively stable status. Socioeconomic conditions in Iraq, in other words, have undergone significant variation over the century, particularly the last half, and this has impacted substantially (although not uniformly) on the entire population; the status of Iraqi women relative to men, however, has not changed. Their status has remained subordinate to men in Iraq.

All this interaction is brought to the fore in terms of the conditions of Iraqi women at the close of the twentieth century. As citizens, Iraqi women are members of two political communities: the state of Iraq and the state in Iraq. They are subordinate members of a national patriarchy that is itself a subordinate member of an international patriarchy. The state, in other words, must be examined in context. International discourse on Iraq isolates it from the social, political, and economic context of the nation-state system, represented here as the system of modern patriarchy. In this discourse the government of Iraq in general, and Saddam Hussein in particular, are represented as gross anomalies of politics in an otherwise credible political world. In fact, however, among the plethora of oppressive governments and brutal dictators that dominate politics in the non-Western world, Iraq is not a unique case at all. Neither is Iraq a unique instance of international oppression, only one of the more extreme cases. In the globalized patriarchy of the postmodern world, sanctions are a common means to discipline wayward children in the family of nation-states and aerial bombardment the preferred means of punishment since the 1990 Gulf War.

PART FOUR

THE ARAB GULF

10

The Concept and Practice of Citizenship in Saudi Arabia

SORAYA ALTORKI

IN THIS CHAPTER I problematize the modern notion of citizenship in terms of its relevance for Saudi Arabia. Is the modern understanding of citizenship applicable as a concept and practice to this society? I maintain that the prerequisites and concomitants of modern citizenship are, in any case, notable by their absence for women (and, indeed, for men) in this country, and I offer a possible alternative to the mainstream model of citizenship. I argue that the family, and not the individual, is the basic unit of analysis that works toward women's participation in social life.

Citizenship, on the surface, seems like a good idea for any society. Yet at least in its *current Western meaning* that dates to the early nineteenth century, it rests on the notion of contract-making individuals who defend their interests in society. As a consequence, citizenship—the processes and practices by which contract-making individuals defend their interests in society—has brought in its train features that are problematical. Among these are, first, an individualistic, utilitarian ethic, as opposed to an ethic of ultimate ends based on the idea of shared rights and obligations. As Hann puts it, "The extension of citizenship in the modern world is based on the notion that individuals have sacrosanct rights. But this universalism is deeply prejudicial to the maintenance of trust and sociability in the realms where individuals interact" (1996, 4). At best, making the individual the focal unit of citizenship promotes indifference to others; at worst, it fosters selfish ambition (Heller 1986, 1–10).

Ironically, the early contributors to the concept of citizenship believed that it could and would advance the values of mutuality and the moral solidarity of the community. Their reasoning was based on the fact that eighteenth-century societies were basically small scale and that individual rights could be reconciled with the collective interests of the community. They believed that individuals could seek their own private interests in a responsible way, participating in activities that would simultaneously foster the needs of society as a whole. As societies evolved and became more complex, however, it became clearer that the emphasis upon the sacrosanct rights of the autonomous individual, increasingly isolated from others in the community, would undermine collectivist ethics based on voluntarism.

Another problematical feature of citizenship is the capitalist economic system of private property ownership with which it has been associated. This system sunders historical and traditional relationships and creates economic inequalities despite its advocates' belief that eventually, as the economy grows, these inequities will gradually disappear. These impacts have been all the more disruptive in non-Western societies, where mutualism and the ethos of moral solidarity of the community have historically been the primary values, not individualism.

Ultimately, then, the modern concept and practice of citizenship is associated with the process of modernization, a highly disruptive process at many levels: psychological, social, cultural, and economic. The idea that individuals have the right to have their contracts enforced on the basis of the fundamental principle of private property ownership is culturally specific to a tradition and system associated with the West.

After I discuss citizenship in its Western context and meaning, I examine the Saudi Arabian case by discussing social structure and tracing political developments associated with the monarchical system. In doing so, I show how the Western understanding of citizenship is not relevant for this country. Women's participation in Saudi Arabian life and politics can occur via the family and women's social networks in which mutuality, trust, and solidarity, rather than individualism, are the values advanced. In short, I offer a suggestion regarding women and citizenship in Saudi Arabia more informed by the cultural specificity of that society.

The Conceptualization of Citizenship

I define here the modern concept of citizenship and elaborate on some of its constituent elements. I disagree with those who have assumed that citizenship is a homogeneous, undifferentiated, universal category, and I argue that these conclusions do not apply to the countries of the Middle East in general, and most especially to a nation like Saudi Arabia, where the gender divide is sharply articulated.

The word, citizenship, comes from *civitas* (city); thus, a citizen was originally an inhabitant of a city or town. In such cities lived townspeople who were regarded as, in some sense, "free men." Formal citizenship for these individuals had to wait, however, for a shift in the balance against free men in favor of monarchs during the Age of Absolutism in Europe. The late eighteenth century revolutions in America and, especially, France brought the terms *citizen* and *citizenship* onto the stage of modern politics. This development reached its theoretical culmination in the document known as the Declaration of the Rights of Man and the Citizen (1789).

In the nineteenth century, citizenship acquired its current connotative and denotative meanings, and citizenship became a cardinal feature of European state constitutions. The development of citizenship in the West was given a classical formulation by Marshall in 1950. Marshall's formulation gives a concept that is homogeneous, undifferentiated, and universal; the critiques mainly focus on class, race, ethnicity, and gender—variables that he downplayed on the whole. Athough Marshall was aware that class differences were an impediment to full citizenship, he believed that the historical development of the nation-state would lead to the overcoming of such obstacles by disadvantaged groups.

The following extended citation is generally accepted as the starting point for further discussions about citizenship in the West:

[Citizenship has] three parts, or elements, civil, political and social. The civil element is composed of the rights necessary for individual freedom—liberty of the person, freedom of speech, thought and faith, the right to own property and to conclude valid contracts, and the right to justice. . . . The institutions most directly associated with civil rights are the courts of justice. By the political element, I mean the right to participate in the exercise of political power as a member of a body invested with political authority or as an elector of the members of such a body. The corresponding institutions are parliament and councils of local government. By the social element, I mean the whole range from the right to a modicum of economic welfare and security to the right to share to the full in the social heritage and to live the life of a civilized being according to the standards prevailing in the society. The institutions most closely connected with it are the educational system and the social services. (Marshall 1950, 10–11, quoted in Walby 1994, 380)[1]

1. Interestingly, this passage does not refer to obligations but only to rights.

Note that for Marshall these civil, political, and social rights accrue to the individual, who is regarded as the basic unit of society. That the individual was a white male should be underscored. Marshall's model is rooted in liberalism. Accordingly, citizenship rests on the notion that "human beings are atomistic, rational agents whose existence and interests are ontologically prior to society" (Dietz 1987, 2).[2]

Citizenship and State in Saudi Arabia

Upon first consideration, the modern concept and practice of citizenship—as expressed in Marshall's formulation—in a country such as Saudi Arabia would appear to be an improbability. Normally, the constitution of the state would be the primary venue for a discussion of the citizen and the rights and obligations of citizenship. Saudi Arabia does not have a constitution in the standard meaning of that term, for its fundamental law is the *shari'a*. One searches in vain to find references there to citizenship, and although the word *citizen* now is used in the media and even by regime officials, it is a neologism that does not sit easily. The use of this word by official spokesmen and documents is predicated on the need to reflect the requirements of the contemporary world, a world where invocations are routine in the media and elsewhere of the peoples' rights and duties. Even in states such as Saudi Arabia, where traditional usages and customs are privileged, it seems that officials feel the need to describe the relationship between the state and the people in terms of citizenship.

Nevertheless, official state practice reveals the ambivalence the leaders feel about citizenship. A mark of this ambivalence is the fact that an office in Cairo whose task is to supervise and assist the needs of Saudi Arabian nationals living in Egypt refers to these nationals as *ra'aya* (subjects [to be protected]).[3] This is a throwback to the Ottoman empire when administra-

2. The other features of liberalism in Dietz's helpful formulation are (1) the individual is free to pursue his own good provided he does not infringe the right of others to do the same. (2) All men must be considered equal. (3) Every individual bears *rights* that protect him from infringement by others and ensure him equal access to opportunities. (This point clears the way for a notion of the private vs. public dichotomy because sacrosanct individual rights refer to a private domain—including the domestic scene—that are immune from state interference. And for liberal thought, this private domain is the property of the male, so even the arena often attributed to women, the household, is the man's, and he can use it to deny the women within it access to public life.) (4) The free individual competes to pursue and maximize his interests (Dietz 1987, 3–6). Nouns and pronouns are masculine because this is the language in which liberalism was written.

3. *Ra'iyya/ra'ayya* originally meant literally "sheep" or "flock." But contemporary customary usage best renders it as "the ruled."

tors centuries ago stratified society into men of the sword, men of the pen, men of commerce, and the "flock," or the popular masses.

Indeed, in a book recently published in Riyadh and intended as a manual for the socialization of students in the nation's schools, the author, examining the principles of rule and the relationship between rulers and ruled cites Qur'an 4:59, "O you who believe, obey Allah, obey the Prophet, and those in authority among you." Additionally, he cites the *hadith* attributed to the Prophet: "You are all shepherds and responsible for your flock. The Imam is a shepherd responsible for his flock. The man is a shepherd responsible for his flock. The woman is a shepherdess in the house of her husband and is answerable to him for her flock" (Huqayl 1996, 95). The connotation of *ra'ayya* in this *hadith* is that of the ruler looking after or protecting his people. This is, of course, not the usual connotation of citizenship that one encounters in contemporary political discourses.

Yet *citizen* has now entered the vocabulary of the rulers, and even the king has routinely used the term. The following is a citation from late winter/early spring 1983: "there is no barrier between the state and the citizens [*muwatinin*]. Any citizen who has an opinion is called to present himself and reveal it. . . . Our press and the media must also be guided and seek assistance from men who can guide the citizen to that which is in the interest of his religion and worldly affairs" (Huqayl 1996, 84).

The king used the word *citizen* basically as a synonym for "subject," retrofitted, as it were, to suit the requirements of more modern speech. Those who have contributed to a theory of citizenship, however, normally begin with a reference to the individual's free "participation in or membership of a community" (Barbalet 1988, 2). In the main, that community has been assumed by writers on the topic to be the nation-state (Roche 1995; 716, 717, 721).

The nation-state idea, however, is a relatively new phenomenon in the Middle East. Because of the importance of families and the rudimentary nature of the Saudi Arabian political and administrative institutions for much of the country's existence, the population, it could be argued, has never really had a clear sense of statehood. In practice the people devalued statehood in favor of the much more relevant kinship, friendship, and economic networks that formed their notion and practice of community. In neither of these three social structures (kinship, friendship, or economic networks) is the individual given a central role. Joseph, following a standard observation of many scholars of the Middle East, has noted (1996a, 14) that in the Middle East the individual is not considered the basic unit of society. Rather, it is the family that bears this hallmark. Article 9 of the Basic Law on the Political System explicitly states this to be the case in Saudi Arabia: "The family (*usra*) is the core of Saudi society. Its members are raised on the basis of Islamic belief, the requirements of goodwill, obedience to Allah, His Prophet, and those in authority, respect for the law and its execution, love of the homeland, and glorying in its majestic history." And article 10 declares that "the state strives to strengthen the bonds of the family." It is, furthermore, the elder male who represents this family, both to its members and to the outside world. The state in its first three decades (1932–64) remained a relatively unimportant fact in the daily lives of the people. No doubt, the role of the state in society became much more pronounced as a function of the extensive socioeconomic programs underwritten by the enormous oil revenues of the 1970s to early 1980s. The state, nevertheless, still had to compete with traditional social structures for the people's terminal loyalties.

To the extent that states are born or consolidated, among other things, by wars that are perceived to threaten the community, some scholars have argued that certain elements of the population intensified their loyalty to the concept of a Saudi Arabian state in the aftermath of the 1991 Gulf War. Citizenship, according to this interpretation, began to acquire a measure of meaning for them as the war crystallized certain nascent feelings of patriotism for the territorial state, which now had become a contender for the people's affiliations alongside religious, family, friendship, and business networks. As people have come to express their loyalty to the territorial state, they have come to feel that they have more of a stake in it and how it is managed, organized, developed, what kinds of resources need to be mobilized for what kinds of purposes, and the like. Ultimately, opinions on these issues can be expected to differ, not only among the people but also among policymakers.

Although the above scenario may seem implausible to some, and it is probably too soon to evaluate it, there is no denying that the Saudi regime since the Gulf War has begun to behave as though the people were being stirred by desires of fuller political participation, that they were, in other words, making increasingly known their interest in their country as would-be citizens. Even before the Gulf War, in 1984, the king went so far as to declare that Saudi Arabia was a democratic polity and implied that the people were citizens who enjoyed equality with the monarch: "The method of rule in Saudi Arabia is based on democracy, and we consider ourselves a part of this people (*sha' b*). There is no distinction between the great and the small. The doors of the authorities are open to any citizen [*muwatin*]" (Huqayl 1996, 103).

This kind of political rhetoric, however, remained at a highly abstract level until the start of the next decade. Then, in the immediate aftermath of the Gulf War, the king made an important speech to the nation on 1 March 1992 in which he issued the Basic Law on the Political System and the Law on the Consultative Council. The latter was meant to be a deliberative body that would play an advisory role on policy. Whatever the motives behind this move, it was unprecedented in the country's history. It is true that commencement of the work of this council was delayed until August 1993 and that at any rate it had no power to make policy. But even if one considers it an initiative at the rhetorical level only, meant to deflect the current of dissatisfaction with the continuing monocratic system of rule, the fact that the king introduced it makes it a legitimate part of the public discussions on the future of the country.

It is worth mentioning that both the king's speech and the Basic Law on the Political System refer to the "citizen" (although not citizenship). Articles 6, 27, 31, 34, 36, 43, and 47 of the Basic Law each have a single reference to the word either in the singular or plural. The word, *homeland* (*watan*) appears once in each of articles 9, 33, and 34. *Citizenship* apparently is a more difficult concept for the authorities, but article 35 states, "The law will explain [the principle of] Sa'udi nationality" (*jinsiyya*, a word that can connote either nationality or citizenship).[4] Additionally, it may be pointed out that the Law on the Consultative Council implies a citizenship role at least for its appointed members.

Yet, even if it is conceded that the term *citizen*, is gaining a modicum of currency in official documents and speeches, the media, public discussions, and the writings of the opposition, very few, if any, of the requisite conditions and presumptions of citizenship as that term is ordinarily understood have been met. This is certainly the case for Saudi Arabia. As I will show, this alliance between the state and elder males of the family has significant implications for the full range of participation by women in the public, the private, and the domestic arenas.[5]

Yet it is my contention that it is precisely by preserving the family as the basic unit of society that the best chance for a truly meaningful concept of Saudi Arabian citizenship for women (and men) can be generated. Patriarchal relationships in the family are not crystallized forever. They are social constructions. Hence, the rules by which men and women interact in the family are subject to negotiation and renegotiation. To know that in earlier

4. The full texts of the Basic Law on the Political System and the Law on the Advisory Council may be found in *Al-Sharq al-Awsat* (London), 22 Aug. 1993, which appears in Huqayl 1996, 203–22.
5. Following the distinction made by Joseph (1996a, 33) between public (governmental), private (nongovernmental), and domestic (kinship).

centuries in cities such as Aleppo and Nablus, for example, women were socially prominent property holders (Meriwether 1993; Tucker 1991) suggests that a decline in that status in the intervening interval was a consequence of altering social constructions and reconstructions of their rights. If such alteration could happen in one direction in historical time, it could again move in the opposite direction in the future.

Because the family, not the individual, is the basic unit of Saudi Arabian society, and the civil and political rights outlined in Marshall's model are absent in this case, what warrant can there be for accepting the utility of that model? In fact, only the social "element," the bedrock of which for Marshall is education and social services, would appear to be relevant. And even here, given the fact that Saudi women are considered in theory and treated in practice as subordinate to men, whatever social rights attach to the former do so by devolution from the men who are their fathers or husbands. The social order is characterized by power asymmetry the crux of which is men's disadvantaging of women to the former's benefit. In other words, it is only as extensions of male kin that women could have access to state-administered economic welfare programs, to education, and to social services, such as health, transportation, and so on. It is, however, true, that widows or divorced women may qualify for a government loan to build a "house." Additionally, in earlier years when no universities existed in the kingdom, the government would permit young women to receive scholarships to study abroad.

To develop the argument it will be necessary to refer to the following features of Saudi Arabian history, politics, and society. Although the Ottoman empire extended its authority along the Western littoral of the peninsula by appointing a governor of the province of Hijaz, the region otherwise escaped the empire's writ. Consequently, the various reform measures known as the Tanzimat, in addition to the Mecelle legal provisions, which represented an attempt to "modernize" the *shari'a* by introducing concepts such as individual rights, had no impact on the peninsula. In the empire's last years at the turn of the ninteenth to the twentieth century, warfare between the Rashid and Sa'ud families resulted in the defeat of the former.

The state that came into existence in 1932 was really not a state in the contemporary sense although it did receive international recognition as one. Instead, it was a structure best considered a personal *dawla*, featuring the coming together, under duress and through the *bay' a* (oath of allegiance) to the Amir 'Abd al-'Aziz, of a number of tribal *amir*s, each of whom had previously enjoyed independence of action.

The relationship between 'Abd al-'Aziz and these *amir*s continued to be of the traditional kind: they regarded him with respect as a leader, and he accorded them a significant measure of autonomy. Over time, 'Abd al-'Aziz was able effectively to extend his writ throughout the peninsula, making him a very powerful figure. The people of his dominion, however, considered him a paternal leader and not an aloof monarch who relished the trappings and the pomp and circumstance of monarchy. That they had relatively easy access to him is something that has been established by historians. I maintain that the people not only believed it was their right to approach him and be heard but they regarded it as their right to be protected by him. I emphasize the word *right* in this context.

The rights of the people are at the heart of any concept of citizenship. Although referring to the people's participation in public life in the time of 'Abd al-'Aziz as "citizenship" may raise some eyebrows, it can be argued that in fact this is what it was.

After 'Abd al-'Aziz's death, matters began to change. Access became more difficult. The monarchy became routinized and the state increasingly bureaucratized. The old model of the king as a shepherd to his people gave way to a modern, rationalized neopatrimonial absolute monarchy based on centralization of power. It was, however, premature to talk of a successfully integrated Saudi Arabian nation-state at the end of the twentieth century.

It is true that many social and economic changes have taken place since the death of 'Abd al-'Aziz, including rising rates of literacy, the growth of professional and middle classes, substantial infrastructure development, the growth of the media, development of the country's educational facilities at all levels, the proliferation of social services, increasing commercial, financial, and industrial activities, administrative and bureaucratic rationalization, and the encapsulation of the economy into the international market economy. In many respects, however, very little has changed over these seventy years or so. Crucially, political participation has become more restricted. Socially, the society remains highly patriarchal at the national, provincial, regional, district, and family levels and at the functional level of the workplace.

Because of the social and economic changes summarized above, attempts had to be made to develop the legal system in civil and commercial domains. These attempts have distressed some activist '*ulama*' (referred to collectively as the "*salafi*" trend), who believe the boundaries of the *shari'a* have been stretched too far in the effort to facilitate the modern operation of certain financial and commercial enterprises, for example. But for many purposes, traditional Islamic law continues to prevail. As is well known, the Wahhabi-Hanbali interpretation of this law enjoys hegemony. Although sometimes observers have exaggerated the inflexibility of Wahhabism and Hanbali jurisprudence, it is fair to say that this school is strongly resistant to legal innovations.

Personal status, as again has often been remarked by scholars, is the area of Islamic law perhaps least resistant to change. Within this realm Wahhābi-Hanbali jurisprudence is the most conservative of all the schools. In matters of birth, marriage, divorce, inheritance, and custody, the law privileges males and renders females in a metaphorical sense the property of men. Women do, however, have the right to inherit and own property, an important quali-fication to the above gloss that they are treated as though they are the property of men.

In light of the above recapitulation, conditions for citizenship seem to be either highly attenuated or, at best, only potentially present. The Saudi Ara-bian population, rather than consisting of citizens with certain vested rights and responsibilities, is more akin to a group of subjects who take their cues from "those in authority among you."

The socialization process for Saudi Arabian subjects may be seen by ex-amining the curriculum books for schools. It is stressed that education in the kingdom must have as its objective the training of generations of stu-dents who are loyal to the values of the monarchy and the ruling house ("Al-Mamlaka al-Sa'udiyya al-'Arabiyya" n.d., 3). It is, of course, an offi-cially stated purpose of education that graduates be able to work toward the attainment of a life of fulfillment and prosperity, to live in cooperation with others, and to work for the general well-being of the country. But these objectives, according to the official version, cannot be met in the absence of the loyalty mentioned above.

"Citizenship"[6] is conferred by virtue of patrilineal descent. A person whose mother is Saudi Arabian but whose father is not may not acquire Saudi Arabian citizenship. The identity card issued to each Sa'udi Arabian national by the Ministry of Interior is called the *bitaqat al-usra* (family card), once again underscoring the family's core role in society. In rare cases a female Saudi Arabian national may marry a non–Saudi Arabian male, but she must first receive both the permission of her male kin and the state. This demonstrates the coalition that exists between family and state patriarchy. If she *does* marry a non–Saudi Arabian, she does not give up her Saudi Arabian nationality. As mentioned, however, none of her children would be consid-ered a Saudi Arabian "citizen." No non-Muslim males may marry Saudi Arabian females although Saudi Arabian (indeed, all Muslim) males may marry non-Muslim females. Recently, the state mandates that men, too, must apply to the Ministry of Interior for permission to marry non–Saudi

6. The word is placed in quotes to denote my dissatisfaction with its use in the context of Saudi Arabia.

Arabian women. Naturalization is only possible by a rare special dispensation issued by the government upon petition.

Because the country essentially escaped Ottoman rule and Western colonial intrusion, the legal source for the status of a national in Saudi Arabia is Islamic law. There are no elected state or governmental bodies in Saudi Arabia, so the question of the franchise has never been open to debate. Even the post-1991 demands for reforms (see below) have not resulted in the right to vote.

It is fair to regard the Gulf War of 1991 as a watershed in the country's history. If 1932–53 is the initial period of state formation, 1953–70 the period of uncertain internal development and embryonic administrative rationalization, and 1970–91 a period of "rush to development," 1991–present may be seen as the era of the emergence of participatory demands and halting political reforms. Of course, there had been earlier stirrings of reform in the nation's recent history. Perhaps the most famous was the "liberal princes" episode in the early 1960s before the accession of King Faysal. Part of the cautious reform proposals at that time was Prince Talal ibn 'Abd al-'Aziz's draft constitution, which advocated the creation of a parliament two-thirds of whose deputies would be elected and one-third appointed (*Arabia Monitor* 1992, 4).

Symptomatic of the new direction was King Fahd's speech, mentioned above, which he made on 1 March 1992. This speech was, in fact, a response to legitimacy challenges and an effort to explicitly restate the central role of the monarchy in the face of Iraqi challenges to the dynasty's claim to protect the holy places and growing expectations in society that some changes were needed (al-Rasheed 1996a, 361).

In December 1990, about four months after Iraq's invasion of Kuwait, forty-three prominent Saudi men presented a petition in which they requested a consultative assembly, rationalizing expenditures in the provinces, enforcement of equality of individuals before the law, judicial reform, an end to media censorship, revisiting the role of the morals police, and reforms in the affairs and status of women.

In February 1991, after the cease-fire, a group of '*ulama,* unhappy about what they perceived to be the diminishing role of the '*ulama* in society, also petitioned for a consultative assembly, insisted that the *shari'a* be restored as the foundation for the conduct of affairs, demanded an equitable distribution of public expenditures (cf. private wealth), urged a more activist "Islamic" foreign policy, stressed the need for a stronger military, and upheld a stronger role for religious institutions in the legal system (al-Rasheed 1996a, 362–63).

With both liberals and Islamists demanding a Consultative Council, it is not surprising that the king complied in his speech one month after the second petition. This body began its deliberations in August 1993 with the king's announcement of the names of its sixty members, in addition to its chairman. A profile of its membership shows that ten of its members are *'ulama'* (six of which are doctors of Islamic law, the remaining four, more traditional *shaykhs*), two are engineers, two are physicians, one is an attorney, seven are writers and journalists, twenty are administrators in government and private institutions, four are military officers, six are merchants, and nine are university professors. In July 1997 an announcement was made that its size would be expanded from sixty to ninety. Membership is appointed and restricted to men thirty years of age and older, each session is to be for four years, and its role is to be advisory only.[7]

In his speech the king confirmed that the country's constitution is the *shari' a* and stressed that the dynasty rules "by guiding principles, bases, and clear fundamentals . . . and statutes which stem from the *shari' a* and are regulated by it." Moreover, "the nation has always supported its rulers as a result of legitimate *bay' a* (oath of allegiance) which binds rulers and subjects [citizens?]" (al-Rasheed 1996a, 368, 369).

The term *citizen* appeared more than once in this speech. Thus, the king declared that "relations between citizens (*muwatinin*) and rulers (*wulat al-amr*) are based on . . . love, mutual respect, and justice." And further, "the King's *majlis* and the *majlis* of the Crown Prince are open to all citizens, because every individual has the right to address the higher authorities in regard to matters" (Musa 1992, 36).

In another part of the speech, the ruler used terminology that implied a potential citizenship role for these subjects when he declared that relations between him and the people are ordered by three concepts: (1) *tanasuh* (loyalty and sincerity in giving one another advice); (2) *muwalat* (contract of clientage); (3) *ta' awun* (cooperation). Although she is not interested in citizenship, al-Rasheed (1996a, 369) maintains that the first and third of these terms denote a mutuality and reciprocity, rather than the unidirectional notion implicit in the idea of an absolute monarch and his subjects.

Toward the end of his speech, the king placed more pronounced emphasis upon the word *citizen:* "The Saudi citizen (*muwatin*) is the basic pivot for the advancement and development of his homeland (*watan*)" And, intriguingly, he paid homage to the role of the individual in the nation's

7. Recently, members of the consultative council have invited some women to attend the meetings as observers.

future when he declared that the individual is the agent of "progress" and "advancement" (al-Rasheed 1996a, 370, 371).

Toward the end of the year, however, the king spoke to an assemblage of the country's *'ulama'* and made it plain to even the members of one of the country's most influential social forces that they must, in effect, not engage in a citizenship role. In this speech on 10 December 1992, he declared that the men of religion must adhere to themes of belief (*'aqida*) when they addressed the people. He declared his regret that some of their comments had been picked up by the foreign media and presented to their readers as criticisms of internal policies:

> Sometimes we read in the foreign press things that they print, attributing to well-known persons in the Kingdom. This is what is said. I do not want to name names. . . . I want to say that, *as citizens,* we should cleave to a single framework that is one of love for people, and not to open our doors. No gain comes from that except for him who wants to criticize the methods that sometimes exist, and I do not mean always but sometimes. (Khitab al-malik yakshuf 'ajz al-umara' 'an muwajaha al-tayyar al-salafi 1993, 14, emphasis mine)

Women and Citizenship in Saudi Arabia

It has been maintained that "the greatest advances [for women in the Arab world] have been made when women have agitated on their own behalf with their social and political agenda in hand" (Fluehr-Lobban 1994, 151). In a way, the citation is misleading because it seems to suggest that reformers, such as Hoda Sha'rawi in Egypt, could act "on their own" and make common cause with their sisters as rational, atomistic individuals, somehow detached from the family networks in which they were enmeshed. In fact, this notion of the contractualist individual is recent to Middle Eastern societies. Whatever successes achieved by these women reformers accrued to them, despite the fact that the basic unit of society was the family, and its momentum and trajectory set by its men, was not able to prevent women from advancing demands for and obtaining access to education, employment, and the like.

In short, the modicum of achievements by women in countries such as Egypt and Turkey were made in the context of the patriarchal organization of society and government. Earlier, I defined patriarchy as the disadvantaging of women by men for men's benefit. The concept, however, needs to be unpacked to show how patriarchal assumptions and modes of operation in the society as a whole dovetail with the regime's patriarchal conduct and policies. Hence, the workings of patriarchy in society and the regime's patri-

archal conduct toward the people may come to be seen as an almost seamless web of mutually reinforcing mechanisms and processes.

A helpful conceptualization of patriarchy is presented by Walby (1989,
220–29), who discusses the concept and practice in terms of six structures
and three forms (state, public, and private). The first structure is what she
calls the patriarchal mode of production, featuring the expropriation of
women's labor in the household by her husband (or, as in Saudi Arabia, by
elder males in the case of extended families).[8] The second structure is patriarchal relations in paid work, featuring a blockage of access by men against
women—either total blockage or segregation and discrimination if access is
partially accorded. The third structure is the patriarchal state. Women are
prevented from access to its resources and its power.

The fourth structure is what she terms male violence, which could be
psychological besides physical, latent besides actual, and which produces
what she terms "well-founded expectations of its routine nature" among
women (Walby 1989, 224). The fifth structure is what she calls patriarchal
relations in sexuality, which orients women to marriage as desirable but a
marriage in which double standards are allowed that subjugate women. The
final structure is what she terms patriarchal culture, which is made up of "a
relatively diverse set of patriarchal practices . . . and discourses which are
institutionally rooted" (1989, 227) and in which religions play a leading
role.

One can see from this capitulation that the disadvantaging of women in
arenas that do not directly involve the state has a way of assisting their
disadvantagement by the state in its own arena. In other words, patriarchal
inferiorization of women at the domestic level reinforces it at the state level
and vice versa. In this context, article 9 of the Basic Law on the Political
System makes the family the central unit in the kingdom, and article 10
commits the state to strengthening the bonds and relations characteristic of
it. "Male dominance is most visible in societies in which complementarity of
powers has given way to an enhancement and expansion of institutionalized
male authority accompanied by simultaneous diminution of women's domestic, sacral, and informal authority" (Elshtain 1992, 116). Put this way,
one could argue that the situation in Saudi Arabia does not represent the
least favorable case. It could be argued that women's influence in the domestic realm has increased over the last generation or two (Altorki 1986,
passim).

8. I should observe that Walby is dealing with industrial societies and, specifically, Britain.
Hence, she is unaware that the extended family can provide some limited advantages to
women, for example, the care of their children by relatives when they are otherwise occupied.

Yet signs of disadvantagement continue. It is true that women have the right to enter into marriage and commercial contracts. But they do not participate in the *social* contract, whereby individuals relinquish their rights temporarily to a ruler or to political institutions but remain the repository of those rights (Joseph 1993b, 23). As observed earlier, this does not mean that women lack legal rights in Islamic law. In fact, Western observers have often failed to acknowledge that the *shari' a* does contain provisions extending a measure of legal independence to women. Thus, the right to own property is rooted in all four schools of Sunni law and in Shi'i law. This aspect of the status of women compared favorably to the status of women in the West for many centuries until legal codes were modernized there in the last two centuries. Ironically, though, ownership of property for Saudi women has not extended to ownership of their persons. Nothing could be further from the Lockean idea that one's property is an extension of one's free self.

Accordingly, despite the stipulated *shari' a* provisions entitling women to own material property, and certain other provisions, such as *mahr* (a dowry provided to the bride as a hedge against destitution should her husband divorce her), legal, cultural, and social disabilities continue to attach to the status of women in the Arab world, generally, and Saudi Arabia, specifically. In saying this, let me immediately acknowledge that class variations require some modification of this statement.

In 1956, because of the keen interest of then Crown Prince Faysal's wife, two private schools for the education of girls were established in Jidda. In 1960 a state school for girls was opened in Burayda, a step that created such a stir that the government had to send security forces to implement the new policy of providing access to education for girls. In 1962 women were allowed to attend universities ('Ar fi al-Bayt al-Sa'udi 1992, 40; Altorki 1986; AlMunajjed 1997, 62). Of course, the educational facilities for girls and women were and are strictly segregated.

Gradually, under very restricted conditions, women began to enter the work force. According to data provided by Khalidi and Tucker (1992, 4), a survey of government positions in 1987 revealed that there was one female decision-maker in the ministries.[9] By comparison, Kuwait had five, Bahrain four, Tunisia three, Algeria one, and Oman one. Surprisingly, none of the other Arab states had any female decision-makers in the government ministries in 1987, including Egypt, Iraq, and Syria.

Employment and education data for women are generally more impor-

---

9. *Decision-maker* was defined as a minister, a deputy minister, an assistant minister, a secretary of state, or an assistant secretary of state.

tant than information about women in high political decision-making roles. These two areas constitute the core of virtually all women's reform movements in the Middle East in this century. In 1990 Saudi Arabian women constituted about 7 percent of the total labor force, and only the United Arab Emirate (UAE) scored lower (Khalidi and Tucker 1992, 5).

Data on education show major gains for Saudi Arabian women relative to men. Thus, in 1970, the ratio of females to males in primary schools was 40 percent, whereas in 1985–87, the ratio was 80 percent; comparable figures for secondary schools in these two time periods were 24 percent and 64 percent. In 1986–87, the ratio of females to males in postsecondary institutions was reported as 65 percent (Khalidi and Tucker, 1992, 4–5). A 1992 U.S. State Department report, however, depicts a more favorable picture for women relative to men at the university level, showing that Saudi Arabian women graduates from the nation's universities constituted 55 percent of the total, that is, more women have graduated from universities than men ("Intihakat" 1993, 32). AlMunajjed (1997, 69) reports that, according to the Saudi Arabian Ministry of Planning, in 1990, 64 percent of university graduates in literature, 66 percent in education and economics, 70 percent in paramedical [nursing] studies, and even as many as 47 percent in medicine were women.

In the mid- to late 1980s, the data shows that Saudi Arabian trends in female education compare favorably with Egypt and Tunisia, for example, in primary and secondary education and considerably better in postsecondary education. The country does less well, however, in a comparison with the small Gulf states.

No professional or technical training programs are open to women (Al-Munazzama al-Huquqiyya al-Amirkiyya 1992, 33). Because most of them major in humanities or social science subjects, this absence of opportunity for professional/technical education is a serious obstacle to their potential as prospective employees.

If the employment data are correct, these educated women are not able to enter the job market in proportions suggested by their school enrollments. Of course, these are general trends, which may break down in particular cases. Female employment in Saudi Arabia is disproportionately high in the teaching and nursing fields. Even in these fields, though, the government is reported to impose a quota for female hires (Al-Munazzama al-Huquqiyya al-Amirkiyya 1992, 33). Indeed, the royal decree of 3 August 1985 specifically stipulates that the state "prevents the Saudi Arabian woman from working in all spheres except teaching in female schools and nursing"; and proclaims that "it is prohibited under any circumstance to integrate adolescent girls and women with men in places of work or facilities attached to them." It is estimated that about one million Saudi Arabian women who are capable of working are unemployed (Al-Munazzama al-'Arabiyya 1993, 25–26). Those who do work earn less than men in comparable jobs despite having the same level of education and qualifications ('Ar fi al-Bayt al-Sa'udi 1992, 41).

The foregoing information does shed some light on the involvement or participation of Saudi Arabian women in the social and economic realms. Field research, for example, a study of the provincial town of 'Unayza, in Najd Province, shows that women can and do own businesses and are relatively successful at it, sometimes by themselves and sometimes in partnership with men (Altorki and Cole 1989, 187–93). Indeed, this kind of research has shown that businesswomen were able to succeed even before the introduction of schools for females in the country.

It is also important to point out that women are entitled to certain social benefits. The government requires businesses to extend maternity leave to them. They may not be forced to work overtime or to maintain regular work hours at night. And, when they do travel or take leaves, their husbands will not lose their jobs by accompanying them. Additionally, divorced or widowed women may qualify for government loans to build a "house."

Still, Saudi Arabian women are disadvantaged by many legal and customary restrictions. Their testimony is worth half that of men in courts of law, and they inherit much less than do males. It is easier for men to divorce them; women must endure a lengthy, complicated process to initiate divorce, losing custody of their children to their former husbands at the ages of five (boys) and seven (girls). They may not travel without their husband's permission, and then they must be accompanied by a male relative whom they may not legally marry. They are subject to physical abuse by men and have no recourse to the government, which declares that such matters are an internal family affair.

Sometimes, newspapers run "Islamic Advice" feature columns advocating the "severe disciplining" of women, which is understood to suggest a degree of physical punishment, as a way of maintaining a good marriage. According to observers, hospitals record a growing number of cases of women patients seeking treating of injuries caused by beatings at home ("Intihakat" 1993, 32).

The "Morals Police," known as the *mutawwa'un* are known to accost women in the streets for alleged violations of the dress code. As a way of controlling women's conduct, the government holds the men of the household liable for punishment if women of the household commit infractions of norms and legal injunctions. Ultimately, it reserves the right to imprison these women if their menfolk are deemed unable to restrain them ('Ar fi al-

Bayt al-Sa'udi 1992, 39). These procedures reinforce the patriarchal cooperation that exists between state and family in the kingdom.

To summarize, Saudi Arabian women are increasingly educated; participate minimally in the work force, although in large numbers in certain specific fields; and enjoy certain employment benefits. On the whole, however,
one may conclude that the evidence is not supportive of the notion of
women in Saudi Arabia representing a citizenry in Marshall's understanding
of that term: civil, political, economic, and social enfranchisement.

Although the third development plan (1980–85) called for "the expansion of the principle of work for women in a way that will increase human
productivity" and use of the media "to change society's positions by directing women's work and participation in the growth and progress of the
country according to our Islamic values" ('Ar fi al-Bayt al-Sa'udi 1992, 41),
conservative groups have succeeded in using their interpretation of those
values economically to disenfranchise Saudi women. In 1980 some women's
Islamic banks were established, offering women an opportunity to work for
the first time in the field of finance, although the employees, in contrast to
men in the nation's regular banking sector, did not have the experience or
the capital to make major headway in this area.

If it is true that women's advances there must come on the heels of their
own efforts, then, perhaps, the consequences of the "driving incident" in
1990 is instructive. Saudi Arabian women, under customary law ('urf) were
not permitted to drive automobiles. As is well known, when a group of
forty-seven of them, highly educated, some with doctorate degrees, and apparently with valid licenses issued in other countries, defied the ban in Riyad
on 6 November 1990, they were arrested, their licenses were revoked, and
they lost their jobs. As a result of the protests of the 'ulama', the minister of
interior, Prince Nayif, issued a law prohibiting women from driving. Consequently, what had been forbidden as a matter of custom now became a
prohibition under force of law (Al-Munazamma al-Huquqiyya 1992, 33). A
year or so later, the women were compensated for the period during which
they had lost their salaries, and their jobs were restored to them. But those
who had worked for the government remained out of work for a longer
time and were only recently reinstated ("Taqrir Wizarat al-Kharijiyya al-
Amirkiyya li 'Am 1992" 1993, 32).

Saudi Arabian women are able to seek financial restitution or compensation for wrongs done to them, but only as individual supplicants. It is reported that women are allowed to present petitions to the amir of the
weekly *majlis* for redress of financial grievences. But they may not attend
the session and must proceed through a female relative of the amir. In the
Eastern Province, it is reported that women may send written petitions to

the prince in charge of the provincial weekly *majlis* there ("Intihakat al-hukuma al-Sa'udiyya li huquq al-insan" 1993, 31).

The king's speech of 1 March 1992 did not introduce new ideas that, if implemented, would alter the status of women. The closest the Basic Law on the Political System came to touching on women's status was the the declaration, as paraphrased by one observer, that "the state protects human rights according to the *shari'a* and provides for the citizen and his family in case of emergency, illness, incapacity, and old age, supports the social security system, facilitates the scope for work for each person capable of working, facilitates regulations protecting the worker and the employer, and makes readily available public education and health care for every citizen" (Al-Munazzama al-'Arabiyya 1993, 22).

◆   ◆   ◆

There are at least two ways of conceptualizing power. On the one hand, power is exercised when X gets Y to do something that Y otherwise would not do. On the other hand, power is "the ability of X to limit the scope of political decision making to considerations of only those issues that X finds non-threatening" (Elshtain 1992, 112–13). Powerlessness is a matter of degree, to be sure. But the combination of having to do others' bidding when one otherwise would not do so with the fact that the only legitimate discourse is the one that does not threaten patriarchal authority tells a great deal about the status of women in this country. Although social conditions are never frozen in time and place, Saudi Arabian women—the Y in the above example—can draw no great measure of comfort from the realization that the international history of citizenship is that it is achieved over the long haul. It has sometimes been asserted, especially in the West, that "Islam" is responsible for the marginal status of women in Saudi Arabia. This ahistorical contention, however, flies in the face of the fact that her inferior position results from cultural and social constructions by men and not from formulations in sacred texts.

As discussed in the central sections of this chapter, the modern concept and practice of citizenship is alien to Saudi Arabia despite the increasing currency of the word in its political discourse. The Saudi Arabian opposition has tried to induce the state to make good on its pledges about democracy and the role of citizens, and it is largely in the discourse of that opposition that the concept is being developed and crystallized in the kingdom.

Yet what is the meaning of "full citizenship"? Must Middle Eastern women generally, and Saudi Arabian women specifically, aim to emulate the model of Marshall or even his model as corrected by his critics? Is it only when they find themselves in full harmony with the Western view of citizenship that they may regard themselves as fully enfranchised? To recall that view: individuals are atomistic rational actors who are free to make contracts based on ownership of their persons and whose interests they may advance basically without hindrance by the state or other citizens.

I contest this model for at least two reasons: (1) the ideal type presented by Marshall and his critics has been shown by feminist scholars to have failed women in the West itself; (2) the positive aspect of family must be valued, and, in any case, it is not going to go away any time soon in countries such as Saudi Arabia. Some feminists (e.g., Hooks 1984) have shown that the family, for some groups in the West, can and has played a supportive role for women who are in the toils of subordination by patriarchal structures in the state and society. Accordingly, it may be necessary to evolve a model of Saudi Arabian female citizenship that upholds her traditional interaction in a dense network of relationships with relatives and near-relatives.

I have already hinted in this paper that the extended family can provide some important support for the Middle Eastern and Saudi Arabian woman. Elsewhere (Altorki 1986), I have argued that Saudi Arabian urban women have increased their "strategic capital" by negotiating greater rights with their husbands in regard to the education of their children and certain other domestic matters, including their own access to education and jobs. Given this, it is realistic to hold that the expansion of access to political, social, and economic resources for Saudi Arabian women can occur through her use of resources rooted in the domestic scene.

To put it in other words, it is unrealistic to think that coalitions in Middle Eastern societies can be formed to foster and promote the interests of their members by making a clean break with family structures and processes. This is particularly so in the kingdom. The logic of the situation is that women must work from within family networks to achieve access to the resources mentioned above. Of course, recognizing the importance of the family in this endeavor does not mean one should be oblivious of the problems of power asymmetries that are reflected there. It means, however, that those asymmetries must be addressed over time and through creative adaptations of traditional structures and processes.

Some Western feminists, such as Ruddick and Elshtain, believe that this is what must happen in the West before women there become full citizens. The same argument may be made for the Middle East, more generally, and Saudi Arabia, specifically. The argument is that they can negotiate changes in their status (as they have begun to do in Saudi Arabia) by drawing upon their moral authority as mothers and nurturers. I am not saying that changing relationships between husbands and wives in the family will lead directly to changed relationships between men and women in society at large and between ruler and ruled. Instead, I argue that as women successfully renegotiate their rights and status in the family, their success will inevitably become part of the national agenda as more men of the younger generation accede to women's demands at home for more effective authority. As the relationship begins to equalize in the family, it will begin to have an effect on other domains.

Signs of women seeking to extend their rights outside the family are becoming evident. Reports circulating in Saudi Arabia suggest that as a consequence of denied access to many occupations and the ease with which men can divorce them, some Saudi Arabian women have begun to pool their financial resources as a hedge against insecurity ("Intihakat" 1993, 32). This modest form of collective action, like the experiment in establishing women's banks, is a small step toward Saudi women building protections for their interests through existing traditional networks. They are also breaking new ground; for example, many women are active members of the chamber of commerce in Jiddah and make use of the many services it provides. Women, however, can only vote by proxy to men. Moreover, as the incident of women trying to assert their rights to drive cars shows, a frontal challenge to established patriarchal rules is bound to be rebuffed.

The government itself has begun to respond to these fledgling stirrings of activity outside the family circle by women, going as far as to broaden women's access to social and economic resources. For example, the Fifth Development Plan (1990–95) stipulates that the government offer financial incentives to women to start new businesses; study the possibility of increasing women's participation in the public sector; consider the possibilty of allowing women to teach boys in the early grades; examine the possibility of creating a women's chamber of commerce; look into the possibility of establishing venture capital company operations managed by women to help women-run enterprises find loans and provide investment advice and facilitate investment of capital by these women; and periodically reassess occupations deemed suitable for women's employment and publicize its findings in the media (AlMunajjed 1997, 100–101).

Again, even if the government reneges on these commitments, its proposals have now entered public discourse, and they may be legitimately discussed. At the very least, the proposals can be used as markers for the further elaboration of expectations that women have about their rights. In other words, they become part of the social reconstruction of their reality.

At the end of the day, however, if citizenship is to be meaningful for those to whom it attaches and who claim it, a great deal of work remains to be done. The work is all the more complicated by the necessity to make creative adaptations to norms and processes that have no "track record" in Saudi Arabia while using traditional structures and networks to make it a central part of social and political life. Even then, it will be informal and uninstitutionalized forms of power that women will enjoy, in comparison to the culturally embedded and legitimated statuses and authority attributed to men. But that in itself would be a major development.

11

Citizenship, Gender, and the Politics of Quasi States

HAYA AL-MUGHNI AND MARY ANN TÉTREAULT

KUWAIT is a rapidly modernizing country where women are visible in a number of public arenas and hold important positions in the government. Kuwaiti women, however, enjoy inferior citizenship rights as compared to Kuwaiti men. They are able to participate in the administration of local cooperative societies by standing as candidates or voting for co-op board members but are not allowed to run for the national legislature nor to vote for any of its members. The struggle for women's political rights has been an important issue in Kuwaiti politics since the 1962 Constitution was adopted and the first law governing elections under its aegis was passed (al-Mughni 1993; Tétreault and al-Mughni 1995a, b). Although the Constitution outlines substantial citizenship rights that, at least theoretically, apply to women as well as men, the state formally has excluded or failed to extend equally many such rights to female citizens. The rejection of Kuwaiti women's reasonable request for equal rights was repeated once again in 1999, a turbulent year that saw the first legal dismissal of a sitting parliament, the promulgation of an amiri decree conferring full political rights on Kuwaiti women, and the rejection both of that decree and of a member-initiated measure identical to it by what arguably was the most liberal Kuwaiti parliament elected since the body was redistricted in 1981.

In this chapter we examine the contradictions between the notion of citizenship as envisioned in Kuwait's Constitution, and the role and status of Kuwaiti women—citizens in name but seldom in fact. We show that, not only with respect to political rights but also with respect to many civil and

237

social rights (Marshall 1950), the status of Kuwaiti women lags behind that of Kuwaiti men. We argue that the continued subjection of Kuwaiti women is part of a strategy to legitimate and support a neopatriarchal state. We argue as well that resistance to democracy is embedded in gender inequality and that it serves the interests of many Kuwaiti political groups: Islamist, tribalist, and liberalist alike. In Kuwait, as in other states, sex-gender systems direct not only the reproduction of the family but also the reproduction of the state (Stevens 1999).

States and Quasi States

The term *quasi state* comes from the work of Robert Jackson (1990) who uses it to refer to many developing countries that formally are recognized as sovereign entities by one another and by international organizations such as the United Nations General Assembly, the Organization of Petroleum Exporting Countries (OPEC), and the Arab League. Like older nation-states, quasi states enjoy "negative sovereignty" (Jackson 1990, 27), the principle that every formally recognized state has equal rights under international law, including the right to be free from external interference in its internal affairs. Unlike most older nation-states, however, quasi states are deficient in "positive sovereignty." Each fails to some degree to meet the criteria that characterize states as compulsory political organizations that claim a monopoly on the legitimate use of force to execute their orders over a specific territory, in other words, the capacity to govern plus the consent of the governed (Weber 1978; Jackson 1990). Although some of the deficiencies of quasi states can be attributed to external intervention (Weber 1995), most are the result of a lack of internal legitimacy (e.g., Hudson 1977).

Kuwait arguably enjoys a much higher level of positive sovereignty than many other states in its region (Tétreault 2000). It has an almost three-hundred-year history of existence centered on what is today its capital city and has been ruled by members of the same family since 1752 (Rush 1987). The quality of governance began to change in the late 1890s, however, when Kuwait's only ruler, who achieved power through a coup against his predecessor, forged a cliency relationship with Britain that lasted until 1961 (Crystal 1990; Tétreault 1991). The transfer of substantial resources from the ruler's external patron allowed the power of the ruling family to grow at the expense of domestic social groups (Gasiorowski 1991), chiefly the merchant class which, until then, had enjoyed a nearly equal status with the ruling family (Crystal 1990; Rush 1987; Tétreault 2000). Even before the cliency relationship between Kuwait and Britain came to an amicable end in

1961, Kuwaitis had begun to demand political rights from what had become an autocratic regime (Crystal 1990; Tétreault 1991, 2000).

The coming of oil gave Kuwaiti rulers external resources that allowed the state to be more autonomous with respect to its domestic policies than either the British patron or Kuwaiti activists preferred (Crystal 1990; Tétreault 1991). Kuwait became an "allocation" state, rapidly developing a model welfare program that raised the living standards of all Kuwait residents, particularly Kuwaiti citizens, to very high levels (Kuwait Ministry of Guidance and Information n.d.). Jill Crystal (1990) argues that Kuwaiti rulers transferred substantial financial assets to the merchant class as a quid pro quo for the merchants' agreement to leave politics to the ruling family. Kuwait's liberal Constitution, however, reflects a more democratic social contract than many members of the ruling family find palatable. This Constitution was suspended twice by Kuwaiti rulers: the first time from 1976 to 1981 and the second from 1986 to 1992. During these interregnums, civil and political rights were severely curtailed and the regime suffered so much domestic criticism that domestic stability was threatened (e.g., Tétreault 1990).

Kuwaiti rulers attempt to moderate citizen demands by deflecting discontent from themselves onto domestic social groups, pitting one group against another in a divide-and-rule strategy (Naqeeb 1990). They also seek to boost their legitimacy by appealing to neopatriarchal principles that enjoin subordination to social and political superiors (Sharabi 1988). In this kind of group politics, women are at a disadvantage. Neopatriarchy and neofundamentalism (Roy 1994) both cast women as socially and politically inferior, making women's demands for equal treatment appear to be anti-Islam. The already tenuous legitimacy of women's demands for political equality was weakened during the late 1970s when the Kuwaiti monarchy sought to harness religion to its campaign to weaken the democratic opposition in Kuwait (Tétreault and al-Mughni 1995a). Yet liberals among the political opposition also proved to be unreliable supporters of women's rights, particularly disappointing in the case of the 1985 parliament, many of whose liberal members were elected with the help of Kuwaiti female activists.

The growing prominence of Islamists in the Kuwaiti parliament, beginning in 1981 (Gavrielides 1987), and the experience of the 1990–91 Iraqi invasion and occupation during which women were highly visible in the resistance while Kuwaiti *badu*, those Kuwaitis who came from a recently nomadic tribal background, acquired a collective reputation as cowards and slackers (Tétreault 1994), increased antagonism between these two groups. At the same time, Islamist movements increased in stature inside Kuwait and outside as well. The key role of the mosque in the resistance is the reason most often cited for the enhanced reputation of Islamists after liberation (e.g., al-Essa 1992) which contributed to the election of large numbers of Islamist candidates to the 1992 National Assembly (Tétreault 2000). Throughout the 1992 parliament, Islamist and tribal representatives claiming religious validation for their politics challenged the regime and the liberal opposition directly on gender issues, eventually winning some important victories (Tétreault 1997, 2000).

Gender and the Nationality Debate

Concerns over nationality and the social role of foreigners have been intense in postwar Kuwait. In 1993 a special program on the reform of the Kuwaiti Nationality Law, sponsored by the Kuwait Graduates Society,[1] was aired on Kuwait Television. Guest speakers included members of the parliament who argued in favor of reforming the law so as to dissolve distinctions between Kuwaitis and to ease naturalization procedures for non-Kuwaitis. The Nationality Law of 1959 and its various amendments[2] establishes three categories of Kuwaiti nationals: Kuwaitis by descent, by birth, and by naturalization. Kuwaitis by descent are those who were residents of Kuwait before 1920 and maintained residence there until the Nationality Law was promulgated. Kuwaitis by birth are those born to a Kuwaiti father, whether inside or outside Kuwait. In addition, a child born in Kuwait or outside to a Kuwaiti mother, so long as her/his relationship to a non-Kuwaiti father has not been legally established, is deemed to be a Kuwaiti national. Kuwaiti women, however, can neither confer their nationality on their legitimate children nor transfer their nationality to their foreign husbands although Kuwaiti men can do this for their foreign wives and the children of such marriages. Indeed, recently, some parliamentarians have demanded that foreign wives of Kuwaiti men be given Kuwaiti nationality after giving birth to a first child rather than having to meet the present fifteen-year residency requirement for obtaining nationality.

Nationality by naturalization may be conferred on those who were not registered as Kuwaiti citizens under the provisions of the Nationality Law but who have maintained residence in the country for at least fifteen years

---

1. The Graduates Society is a voluntary organization with liberal politics and a strong interest in human rights. During the 1992 parliamentary election campaigns, the Graduates Society sponsored one of two debate series enabling candidates to speak publicly on human rights issues.

2. Kuwaiti nationality laws are discussed at length in Longva 1996b.

and fulfill other requirements before applying for nationality. Such requirements include having knowledge of Arabic, being capable of earning a living, and being a Muslim. Kuwaiti nationality also may be granted to those who have rendered useful services to Kuwait, provided that they are Arab nationals, and to illegitimate children, including foundlings born in Kuwait of unknown parentage.

Reforms of the Nationality Law advocated by middle-class and tribal groupings focus on naturalized (male) individuals and *bidun*, stateless persons—from the Arabic *bidun jinsiyya*, meaning "without nationality"— Kuwaiti subjects who are not also Kuwaiti citizens. Extending the rights of Kuwaiti women to bestow their nationality on their children was not a feature of the early debate on nationality law reform. The interests of middle-class and tribal reformers in limited changes centered on naturalized citizens and *bidun* lie in the fact that, unlike the merchant class, which long practiced endogamy, many are partners in mixed marriages with such individuals. These liaisons—within the context of a social organization based on the purity of descent (*asil*)—have impeded the unequivocal access to social and economic power desired by ambitious members of middle-class and tribal groups.

Naturalization is among the most complex aspects of Kuwaiti politics. It is tied to issues of national identity and social preservation. The influx of foreigners and their families, beginning in the 1950s, quickly rendered Kuwaitis a minority in their own country: by 1965, Kuwaitis made up only 36 percent of the population (Kuwait Ministry of Planning 1992, 27). During the 1960s, the government initiated a number of measures intended to increase the Kuwaiti population. They adopted a two-pronged strategy, a pro-natalist policy with regard to those already citizens of Kuwait, and naturalization of Bedouins and Arab nationals who had rendered useful services to the country.

To encourage Kuwaitis to have large families, the state initiated a program to provide financial incentives to marry and to have large numbers of children. These incentives include interest-free loans to build homes, generous maternity leaves (up to two months at full pay with an additional four months at half pay), family allowances, and day-care services for children aged three to six years. This last policy is designed to enable working mothers to meet their responsibilities toward their children.

The nationality law limits the number of naturalized persons to fifty per year, but the number of persons naturalized was actually much higher. According to a report published by the Economist Intelligence Unit (1979) between 1973 and 1977, eighty-nine hundred persons were naturalized in Kuwait. Shafeeq Ghabra (1997) calculates that the number of persons naturalized between 1965 and 1981 was two hundred and twenty thousand. Almost 80 percent of those naturalized were of tribal origin.

Traditional Bedouins were presumed to be more loyal to the regime than urban Arab nationals (Naqeeb 1990; Ghabra 1997). Thousands were nationalized before the 1981 election, which followed the end of the first suspension of the Kuwaiti Constitution. This action swelled the number of the regime's supporters in a large number of election districts (Gavrielides 1987).[3] The high rate of naturalization of tribe members, however, turned out to be economically costly. New towns had to be created to accommodate each tribe in a way that preserved its traditions and genealogical cohesion—its tribal coherence and organization. The majority of the Bedouins who belong to the 'Aneiza tribe, for instance, were settled in Jahra' in limited-income housing provided by the government. Their large families contributed to a growing demand for additional housing units, putting considerable strain on the national economy and forcing many young people to delay their marriages. In spite of repeated efforts to accelerate the rate of construction, the government continues to fall short of the housing demands of the Kuwaiti population. A 1997 estimate by Hamid Shuaib, the chief engineer of the Kuwait municipality, stated that five new satellite towns were needed to cope with population growth (*Arab Times* 1997, 21 Oct., 3).

The state also provides all citizens, naturalized persons included, with free education. Even so, the larger portion of the tribal population remains confined to low-wage occupations. Young men of tribal origin demonstrate a continuing preference for serving in the police force, an occupation chosen by many of their fathers. Military service also was regarded as a desirable occupation by the newly settled tribes, in part because it was seen as a demonstration of their loyalty to their country; many persons of Bedouin origin were attracted to that profession.

Not all Bedouin residents of Kuwait were naturalized, however. Many were denied citizenship at the time they applied, whereas others refused to accept "naturalized" citizenship (generally referred to as "second-category" citizenship) because it did not come with voting rights (Ghabra 1997, 365). Before 1986, when enforcement of regulations requiring Kuwait residents to show documentary proof of their nationality were tightened, the children of such persons attended state schools and, subsequently, took jobs in the police and military. As a result, what had been intended as a relatively liberal policy toward tribal immigrants led to the emergence of a large stateless

---

3. The election districts also were redrawn, emphasizing the impact of tribal voters even more. See Gavrielides 1987; Tétreault 2000.

class of persons. Today, approximately one-third of male working-age *bidun* residents of Kuwait are employed by the Ministry of Defense (*Arab Times* 1997, 25 Oct., 5).

In reaction to the horrors inflicted on the civilian population, many of the *bidun* who had remained in Kuwait during the Iraqi invasion and occupation, the government has been pressed to come up with a solution to this aspect of Kuwait's nationality problem. A special committee attached to the Ministry of Interior was set up to assess the situation and to recommend ways to regularize the status of Kuwaiti *bidun*. Before the invasion, the number of *bidun* had reached approximately 226,000 persons. Afterward, their numbers were estimated as between 42,000 (*Arab Times* 1995, 26 Aug., 3) and 150,000 (Al-Shall Economic Consulting Group 1997). The decrease in the number of *bidun* in Kuwait is owed in part to their dispersion among the refugees fleeing Kuwait during the occupation, the naturalization of those who met the criteria specified under the current law, and the reduction in the number of stateless citizens from the large number of those who provided documentation attesting to their country of origin. The shrinkage of the *bidun* population, combined with widespread support for finding some accommodation that would grant citizenship to many thousands on the grounds of their service to the state and/or their blood relationship to Kuwaiti citizens, strengthens the likelihood of achieving a solution that will be generous to the *bidun* remnant.

Engendering Citizenship

Nationality is not synonymous with citizenship. Nationality is a top-down concept that refers to an identity and a set of entitlements conferred by states on persons according to bureaucratic rules. The development of nationality as a political status began in the nineteenth century as states attempted to increase their control over selected populations during a period characterized by proliferating nationalist movements and extensive voluntary and involuntary migration across political boundaries (Guy 1992; Manzo 1996). Nationality is a claim that a person belongs to a particular state, but it was developed to exclude from state entitlements refugees, formerly colonized persons, and other "illegal aliens," who presumably belonged to some other state (Manzo 1996). Nationality also affirmed a state's authority over former residents living abroad whose behavior and treatment were thought to reflect on the reputations of their country of origin (Guy 1992). From these beginnings, it is not surprising that nationality today does not confer automatic entitlement to political participation or to distributions by the state.

The electoral law passed by Kuwait's first postindependence parliament restricted the right to vote and run for office to Kuwaiti men more than twenty-one years of age. In Kuwait, until quite recently, naturalized Kuwaitis and their children were not entitled to vote or to run for elective office. In 1994 the election law was amended to allow the sons of naturalized citizens who were born after their fathers had become Kuwaiti citizens to vote and run for office. In 1999 access to the public sphere of formal politics seemed within the reach of Kuwaiti women. On 16 May, in a historic move, the amir of Kuwait, Shaikh Jabir al-Ahmad al-Sabah, issued a decree to grant Kuwait women the right to vote and to run for office "in recognition of their vital roles in building Kuwaiti society and in return for the great sacrifices they had made during various challenges the country faced" (*Kuwait Times*, 18 May 1999, 1).

An amiri decree issued when parliament is not in session has the same force as a law passed by the parliament, but under article 71 of the Constitution, such a decree must be approved by parliament when it reconvenes. The decree granting full political rights to women was promulgated shortly after the amir had dismissed the parliament and called for new elections. Opposition to the measure was immediate, coming mainly from members of Sunni Islamist groups who argued that such rights are against Kuwait's Islamic tradition. Only a few years earlier, the government itself had taken this position. When Kuwait signed the Convention on the Elimination of All Forms of Discrimination Against Women (CEDAW) in 1994, it incorporated reservations on a number of provisions, including one giving equal rights to men and women with respect to guardianship and adoption of children, saying that they conflicted with Islamic law. To Ann Elizabeth Mayer, the government's position seemed more political than Islamic:

> Kuwait added further confusion when it . . . entered reservations that were substantially different from other Arab Muslim countries. Kuwait [also] objected to the provisions that gave women political rights . . . [and the right to] give their nationality to their children. . . . Kuwait's reservations did not follow a particularly Islamic pattern, even though Kuwait's personal status law is theoretically based on *shari'a* law. Seen in relation to the laws in other Muslim countries, the reservation on women's voting rights seems particularly odd, since even a self-proclaimed Islamic state like Iran allows women to vote. On the matter of passing on nationality, Kuwait and Tunisia differed, too, for in 1993 Tunisia had changed its law to allow Tunisian nationality . . . to be passed on by the mother under certain conditions. (Mayer 1995c, 115)

Similar values underlie the unequal distribution of other rights and entitlements. Economic, or what T. H. Marshall (1950) refers to as social rights, also are limited for Kuwaiti women. In Western countries women constitute the majority of recipients of social services and benefits awarded to families with dependent children. In Kuwait, however, the state's extensive welfare system is designed to meet the needs of low- and middle-income families headed by men, *rab al 'usra* (heads of families). These programs include public housing, rent subsidies, and subsidies for water and electricity. The state also offers low-interest loans to encourage Kuwaiti men to build their own homes. As compared to their male counterparts, Kuwaiti women who receive welfare assistance must be unemployed and demonstrate an absence of male support. Working women and those with husbands or fathers judged able to support them are not eligible to receive welfare assistance. In 1992 alone, 308 applications submitted by women declaring their need for state support were rejected on the grounds that the women were either employed or should obtain assistance from a male relative (personal communication to Al-Mughni from Ministry of Social Affairs and Labor, Kuwait 1993). Gender differences in social benefits also extend to the wage sector. Nasra Shah and Sulayman al-Qudsi (1990) report that even when women have higher educational qualifications than men, their wages still fall below the male average. In addition, Kuwaiti men working in the public sector receive a monthly child allowance that is added to their salaries, a benefit that is denied to Kuwaiti working women unless their husbands are unemployed or work only in the private sector.

Female beneficiaries of public assistance receive monthly income support as well as rent subsidies. In 1996, 6,057 divorced women and widows received such benefits (interviews by al-Mughni 1997). A large majority of these female heads of household live in isolated residential blocks, characterized by high rates of violent crimes (Tétreault and al-Mughni 1995b). Women on welfare are required to live in state-owned apartments rather than in houses, access to which is granted only to families headed by male citizens. The women's stay in these apartments is seen by the authorities as ephemeral and not permanent, that is, that they will stay there only until their financial situations improve or they remarry. After that, the state ceases its financial support, including housing benefits.

Kuwaiti women are forbidden by law to marry non-Muslims, a prohibition not enjoined on men. Neither women nor men are forbidden to marry non-Kuwaitis although women who marry outside of the national community cannot rely on the protection and support either of the state or of their male peers. The children and non-Kuwaiti spouses of Kuwaiti women are defined and treated as expatriates: they have no right to remain in the country unless they receive residence permits from the state, and they must qualify for these permits on the same basis as other foreigners seeking Kuwaiti residence. The children of Kuwaiti women and non-Kuwaiti men are denied admission to government schools although the children of Kuwaiti men and non-Kuwaiti women are entitled, as are the children of two Kuwaiti parents, to attend these schools. In 1978 Kuwaiti women married to non-Kuwaiti men were denied the right to apply for government housing although such persons already benefiting from state-subsidized housing were allowed to remain in their residences. But even on those whose housing installments were regularly paid, the state refused to confer the ownership rights granted to Kuwaiti male heads of household. In 1993 the right of Kuwaiti women married to foreigners to receive housing loans was rescinded.

After the war, more than eighty families, many of which were cases of Kuwaiti women married to non-Kuwaitis and of widows and divorcees with children, occupied the empty flats of Sawaber, a government residential complex. The government ordered these families, who were referred to in the press as "illegal tenants," to vacate the premises. When they refused to leave, drastic measures were applied, including service with eviction notices, power cuts, and a final ultimatum in the summer of 1994 requesting them to leave before force would be used. The housing rights of Kuwaiti women married to non-Kuwaitis were debated in the 1992 National Assembly. Opposition was fierce. Many who objected to equal entitlements for women did so on the grounds that "after [the Kuwaiti woman's] death, her non-Kuwaiti husband and children would inherit the property" (*Arab Times* 1995, 26 Aug., 3). Current housing regulations allow the foreign children of Kuwaiti women to continue to live in their mother's house after she dies, but only until the girls are married and the boys reach twenty-six years of age. After that, the government repossesses the house.

By 1996 only 630 families of Kuwaiti women married to non-Kuwaiti men were receiving welfare benefits (personal communication to al-Mughni from Ministry of Social Affairs and Labor, Oct. 1997). The "chilly climate" for Kuwaiti women married to non-nationals has pushed some of them to leave the country. In 1993 it was estimated that 7,970 Kuwaiti women were married to non-Kuwaiti men. As a result of state policies, by 1995 almost one-third of these women had emigrated to Western countries in search of better lives for their children (al-Makhawi 1994). In addition, at least twenty female Kuwaitis renounced their nationality and had their names published in the official gazette. These women were denounced by the Islamist writer al-Shibani (*Arab Times* 1995, 3 Sept., 6) as "traitors" and "anti-Islam" without any reference to the severe discrimination they faced along with their families. Despite individual and collective attempts by Kuwaiti women to secure some rights for their non-Kuwaiti spouses and children, the government has remained impervious to their demands. Equally deaf to their pleas has been the all-male National Assembly, content to keep unchanged existing social laws that marginalize women and deprive them of their citizenship rights.

Women, Family, and Citizenship

Embedded in the gendered construction of citizenship is the assumption that women are not individuals in their own right but are family members whose rights and duties are defined in relation to their kinsmen. It is the duty of men, not the state, to protect and support women. Men are envisioned as the protectors and keepers of women, ensuring that their honor is preserved and their sexuality remains under control. It is this understanding, that a woman's political, social, and economic existence is entirely subsumed under that of the male head of her household, that leads to the assumption that a Kuwaiti woman married to a non-Kuwaiti man has, by her action and its consequences, ceased to be a Kuwaiti.

Many Kuwaitis find it difficult to conceive of women existing without the protection of men, having an identity of their own, being fully in charge of their own lives and not merely living for others or subordinating themselves to the interests of the family. In fact, nothing can be more damaging to a woman's reputation than leading her own life and taking control over her body and mind as a free individual disconnected from family obligations. Indeed, the term *free* carries negative connotations. It is associated with immoral, loose behavior. A free woman is referred to as *wasika*, which means dirty, unclean. A free woman loses her self-respect and also finds herself socially marginalized with neither men nor women wishing to associate with her.

Kuwait's personal status law, drawn up in accordance with the Maliki interpretation of Islam and enacted in 1984, legitimized male protection and control over women. As interpreted by Kuwaiti attorney Badria al-Awadhi, this law requires husbands to support their wives and children. In return for their right to *nafaqa* (maintenance), women must obey their husbands and rear their children. The law, however, does not give the husband an absolute right to *ta'a* (obedience). If a wife feels that she no longer can live with her husband and leaves her husband's house, a judge cannot force her to obey her husband's demand that she return. Under these circumstances, however, the wife will lose her right to maintenance and the court will support her husband should he refuse to pay (al-Awadhi 1998). Social norms also restrict Kuwaiti women's behavior. Unmarried women, regardless of their age, are expected to live with their families. Kuwaiti women cannot even travel outside the country or visit friends at night without consulting their parents or husbands.

In Kuwait a man may divorce his wife without her consent and is only responsible for her maintenance during the three-month period of *iddah* during which a woman is secluded in order to determine whether she has been impregnated and, if so, to ensure that only the husband could be the father of her child. Consistent with Islamic law, a woman found to be pregnant is entitled to maintenance throughout her pregnancy. In addition, under Kuwaiti law, if a woman is divorced without her consent, her former husband is required to pay her maintenance for one year as a compensation. This is known as *nafaqat al-muta'a*. In other cases, a divorced woman is not entitled to maintenance for herself other than during the three-month *iddah*. Her husband, however, is required to provide her with an allowance for any children in her custody. Custody according to Kuwaiti personal status law is awarded based on the judge's estimation of what is in the best interests of the child (al-Awadhi 1996, 1998).[4] Thus, it is not unusual for a divorced woman to retain custody over her children until her sons reach fifteen years of age and her daughters marry although the mother loses custody if she remarries. This is a significant departure from most interpretations of Islamic law (Esposito 1982). Fear of losing custody of their children has led many Kuwaiti men to delay or eschew divorce.

Sanctioned by religious norms, parental control over children is left unchallenged. The state does not interfere in this domain. Rather, parental authority is unbounded, almost absolute. Fathers or husbands can forbid their wives or daughters to work outside the home, and there is absolutely nothing that Kuwaiti women can do under these circumstances to exercise their constitutional right to employment. The state does interfere in the area of sexuality, however. Homosexuality, along with premarital sexual relations, are considered criminal acts, and any attempt to induce abortion "without justifiable cause" also is a punishable crime. Although marrying outside the community is not a crime in itself, such marriages do have detrimental consequences for Kuwaiti women. This, however, has not deterred some women from marrying outsiders or from having extramarital relationships. Between 1993 and 1996 there were 2,551 marriages contracted between Kuwaiti women and non-Kuwaiti men. Infant abandonment, although very rare, is treated differently. Although the state refrains from protecting those who marry outsiders, it has taken on the care of the illegitimate children, who

---

4. There is only one personal status law in Kuwait, which applies to all Kuwaiti citizens. Shi'a, however, are at liberty to refer to *jaafari* laws (*mazhab*) administered by a Kuwaiti tribunal. There are no civil options for marriage, divorce, inheritance, and child custody in Kuwait.

as noted earlier, enjoy Kuwaiti citizenship with the same political rights and social benefits as other Kuwaiti citizens.

Men's privileges as citizens in the public political sphere derive from their dominant status in the private domestic sphere where male privilege is reinforced by social policy and laws. As elsewhere in the Middle East, the family is an important social institution. The Kuwaiti Constitution identifies the family as the basic unit of society, stating that "national laws should preserve the family structure, strengthen family ties, and protect motherhood and childhood." In official public speeches, women are addressed as mothers, wives, and daughters. The entire society is conceived as "*al-'usra al-waheda*" (a single family), which has become the dominant national symbol after liberation. First propagated in the 1970s, this concept of *al-'usra al-waheda* resonates with images of traditional Kuwaiti families whose members lived closely together under the wing of the family's patriarch. Kuwaiti children are taught to call the amir *baba Jabir,* that is, father Jabir, the head of Kuwait's one united family and the nation's sole authority to whom everyone owes respect, obedience, and loyalty.

The family as an institution is central to the social, political, and economic spheres of Kuwaiti life. Perhaps surprisingly to persons whose cultures are less family-centered, this strong and protected institution is a structure with significant autonomous political capacity.[5] The family's residence—the home—is the central metaphor for private space but, like other Kuwaiti institutions, the home cannot be confined by the analytical boundaries between public and private that are conventionally used in the West. The private character of the Kuwaiti home is reflected in constitutional provisions (Arts 38 and 44) forbidding state intrusion. The home is the only secular space with this status, making it an attractive site for political meetings when public meetings are restricted or banned. The Kuwaiti home has long been a primary venue of civil society through one of its major institutions, the *diwaniyya,* which is located squarely in the center of the public-private divide (Tétreault 1993).

The *diwaniyya* is the modern Kuwaiti analogue of the ancient Greek *andron,* a room in the home separate from the family's living quarters where unrelated men can be entertained without impugning the family's honor by exposing its women to public view (Walker 1983). In Kuwait the regular gatherings in such rooms also are called *diwaniyya*s. These gatherings generally include a core of relations who are not members of the household, a quality that, together with their locus in family homes, puts the *diwaniyya*

---

5. Material in this section comes from Tétreault 1993, 279–80.

in the private sphere and exempts it from the government permits required for other meetings. In practice, however, a *diwaniyya* also is a quasi-public event that includes nonfamily members.

The *diwaniyya* is the product of a merger between two traditional patterns of Kuwait social life: the practice of seafaring businessmen gathering to exchange information and the primary role of the family in social, economic, and political activities. Regular family visiting and the predominance of family businesses in the Kuwaiti economy explain the widespread practice of gathering together for typically Kuwaiti, family-based strategic planning and action. After the ratification of the Constitution, it seemed only natural that *diwaniyya*s became places where candidates went to meet potential constituents and to campaign for election. This began a process whose evolution ended in the use of *diwaniyya*s in 1989–90 as meeting places for pro-democracy activists working to restore the Constitution and the parliament (Tétreault 1990). The importance of private rights in protecting *diwaniyya*s explains why, although Kuwaiti feminists might want to restrict the ability of their fathers, husbands, and sons to control their lives, they do not want to invite the state to breach the protected space of their homes to do this. They prefer instead to have public status as political and moral actors entitled to social benefits and access to civil institutions such as the courts where they can defend themselves on an equal basis against violations of their constitutionally guaranteed civil rights.

Religious and Liberal Discourses on Women

Since the official Islamization of the state in the late 1970s (Tétreault and al-Mughni 1995a, 71), Kuwait society has witnessed an outpouring of religious fervor across all social classes.[6] Perhaps more accentuated among middle- and lower-income groups (Sharabi 1988; Roy 1994), the visibility and authority of *shaikhs* (learned religious men) has grown along with widespread female veiling and an obsessive attention to "moral" issues, many of which revolve around women's rights and female behavior. Until the late 1970s Kuwaiti supporters of the Islamic revival movement were more likely to be found among the lower classes. They tended to be members of large families residing in public housing that were headed by fathers with little education who worked in nonrewarding occupations (al-Thakeb and Scott 1982).

The two most influential Islamist groups in Kuwait, the *Jam'iyyat al-*

---

6. Here *Islamist* refers to political activists who cite religion as their authority, and *Islamic* refers to characteristics of Islam as a religion.

Islah al-Ijtima' iyya (the Social Reform Society, which is affiliated with the Muslim Brotherhood), and the *Jam' iyyat al-Turath al-Islami* (the Islamic Heritage Society, which is part of the Salafi/Wahhabi movement), initially concentrated their recruitment efforts on the less privileged. Postsecondary schools are primary venues for recruitment. Unlike their female peers, the young men at these institutions are disproportionately from among the socially and academically disadvantaged. Islamism in Kuwait claims the student body at Kuwait University as one of its strongest bases. Consequently, gender issues at the university naturally attract the attention of Kuwaiti Islamist leaders, and questions of personal status in the setting of the university have the power to unite (neo)fundamentalists and political Islamists (Roy 1994), Sunna and Shi'a, in their common pursuits of both political dominance over Kuwaiti secularists and new adherents to the Islamist movement.

The university is a focal point of Islamist politics because it is an economic gatekeeper—university degrees are passports to higher-paying and higher-status jobs—and, even more, because it is the place where large numbers of young Kuwaiti men first discover how poorly prepared most of them are to compete and win in a system that is not rigged in advance in their favor. Traditional patterns of child rearing in Kuwait place few demands and restraints on the behavior and performance of boys and male adolescents but many on their sisters. This translates into better work habits and superior academic performance by girls, a pattern that persists at the university where young women competing for admission to technical, high-status majors in medicine and engineering have an edge over young men if grades and performance are the primary criteria for selection and retention (Tétreault 1990).[7] Interestingly, the academic achievements of young women are considered to have been unjustly earned not only by the young men they leave in the dust but also by their own parents, professors, and peers. "Girls have to stay at home," said a father of a high-achieving daughter and a son who left the university because of bad grades. "What else can they do but study? It's not fair."[8]

---

7. These patterns also are class based. Upper-class families tend to restrict their male children more than other families, and are more likely to send them abroad for university training. At the same time, fewer women than men study abroad, regardless of social class. One result is that the population of Kuwait University has been about 60 percent female for some years and includes large numbers of young women who are highly able along with average and poor performers. The top performers among young Kuwaiti men of every social class tend to study abroad, leaving the less able in their age cohorts to compete against a pool of women whose intellectual ability and social skills are better than theirs.

8. The speaker is a manager at the Kuwait Oil Company who was interviewed by Tétreault

The conservative values of young Kuwaiti Islamists are reinforced by their social isolation from modern culture and a strong sense of injustice (al-Thakeb and Scott 1982) that comes not only from their own relatively disadvantaged positions but also from incessant haranguing by movement leaders. The majority of Kuwaiti Islamists come from the Bedouin community, which today accounts for an estimated 65 percent of the citizen population (Ghabra 1997). The growing involvement of recently settled *badu* in Kuwaiti political life contributes to what Shafeeq Ghabra calls "desertization . . . the transfer of the desert's customs, traditions, beliefs, dress codes, and mentality into the city" (Ghabra 1997, 367).

Desertization also has taken place within the National Assembly ever since the 1981 election. In the parliament, tribalists and Islamists—categories with significant overlap—join to push for further Islamization of society, primarily by imposing social and economic restrictions on women. Among the proposals submitted during the 1992 parliament were several to make *shari'a* the sole source of Kuwaiti law, and a law banning any Kuwaiti woman from traveling abroad unless escorted by a *muhram,* a male relation prohibited by Islamic law from being able to marry her. But the central role of the university as simultaneously a site and an object of contestation places regulation of faculty and student behavior at the top of Islamist concerns. During the 1992 parliament, proposals to do that included one permitting female students to veil at all times, even in laboratory settings where university officials regarded the practice as unsafe, and one to impose gender segregation at all schools and colleges in Kuwait. This last also would have required the replacement of male workers at cafeterias in girls' schools with female workers and the replacement of female nurses at boys' schools with male nurses.

Although the other proposals failed, a modified version of the gender-segregation bill was passed in July 1996, shortly before the parliamentary election campaigns began. Opponents succeeded in removing the segregation requirement from private schools, but all postsecondary institutions are to be gender-segregated within five years (Tétreault 1997a). In practice, this obligates the government to incorporate changes in the existing buildings used by Kuwait University and by the Public Authority for Applied Education and Training to ensure gender-segregation and requires these institutions to develop regulations regarding student conduct and dress codes that are in line with Islamists' definitions of Muslim morality and principles.

Parliament's gender politics also produced a less well-publicized law in

---

in April 1990. This rationale came up repeatedly in Tétreault's interviews with students, professors, and parents both before the invasion and after liberation.

1995 allowing working mothers to retire after fifteen years of service, regardless of their age. Submitted by Khaled al-'Adwa, a flamboyant Islamist
from the tribal area of Ahmadi who spearheaded many of the antiwoman
proposals offered in the 1992 parliament, the new law adds to the pressure
on Kuwaiti women to leave the work force (al-Rahmani 1996) in order to
make more jobs available for men in the overstaffed public sector.

The confinement of women to the boundaries of the patriarchal household is one of the objectives arduously pursued by Kuwaiti Islamist groups.
To support their argument for female domesticity, they complain about rising divorce rates, child delinquency, and family problems, which they insist
would not have occurred in contemporary Kuwaiti society had women stayed
at home and looked after their children. Departure from traditional gender
roles is blamed by these men for all the social problems currently besetting
Kuwait. Kuwaiti Islamist discourse is centered on such social problems,
which are often intentionally and intensely dramatized and exaggerated to
justify their proposals for "moral reforms" and for restrictions on women's
mobility and visibility. Relying on Islamic tenets that proclaim motherhood
to be the most sacred role for women and for the nation, they use religion
to mask their misogyny. Underlying their call for female seclusion is a barely
disguised fear of women's public achievements.

The participation rate of women of all ages in the labor force increased
from 2 percent in 1965 (Shah 1994) to 17 percent in 1997 (National Bank
of Kuwait 1997, 34). Kuwaiti labor participation rates for both sexes are low
because of the large portion of the population that is under age (the "child
dependency rate") and early retirement; Kuwaiti men may retire at fifty
years of age (interviews by Tétreault, 1990, 1992, 1996). The labor force
participation rate of Kuwaiti women between the ages of twenty and forty
years has been increasing at a faster rate than that of other age groups. "In
1989, 50 percent of women aged 20–40 were working and by 1997 their
percentage increased to 60 percent" (National Bank of Kuwait 1997, 34).
Women's educational achievements are equally remarkable. They compete
with men in all majors at the university and graduate at much higher rates
(Tétreault 1990, 2000). "[O]f the 22,373 net new jobs requiring university
or professional degrees that were occupied by Kuwaiti workers during the
past eight years, 62 percent were filled by females, while Kuwaiti males filled
the remaining jobs" (National Bank of Kuwait 1997, 36). Many women
have succeeded at traditionally male-dominated jobs. They hold managerial
positions in the private and public sectors and some have set up their
own businesses. Such involvement has given rise to assertive, independent-
minded women, many of whom have avoided marriage with its traditional
conjugal obligations and responsibilities. Such women are the focus of what

Kuwaiti Islamists bemoan as the "spinster crisis," but this crisis is less about women deprived of marriage and more about women who have begun to question men's authority in the realm of "domestic bliss" (Tétreault and al-Mughni 1995a).

Islamists also pursued the gender war beyond the halls of Kuwait's parliament. In 1997 Leila al-Othman, a liberal woman writer, was summoned and interrogated by the public prosecutor on charges of promoting moral corruption in society based on books she had published in the 1980s. Islamists charged her with blasphemy and apostasy for her depiction of sexual relations (*Arab Times* 1997, 2 Jan., 1). Even before the passage of the gender-segregation law, Islamists had launched continual attacks on the government in the press and parliament for permitting concerts, festivals, and fashion shows on the grounds that such entertainments violate tradition and Islamic law.

The Islamist upsurge prompted the government to reconsider its support for religious revivalism, realizing that political stability requires a balance between conservative and liberal forces. There was speculation that the May 1999 amiri decree granting political rights to women was part of a larger strategy to curtail the power of Islamists in Kuwaiti life. A government-Islamist alliance to defeat the incumbent Speaker during the July 1999 election of officers and committee members in the new parliament, however, along with the failure of the government to lobby members to support the measure until nearly all of them had taken public positions regarding their voting intentions, makes it doubtful that the aim of the decree was substantive. As one of us has argued elsewhere, the women's rights decree seems to have been "a cat among the pigeons," a device to distract popular and legislative attention from policy initiatives designed to reorganize much of Kuwait's domestic economy (Tétreault 2000). Even if the measure had, in the end, been ratified, the outcome would not necessarily have implied full citizenship rights for women. The state itself supports the subjugation of women to patriarchal control and insists on women's identity as family members to maintain a balance between modernity and tradition. During the 1970s, when rapid modernization resulted in social and political strains, women's traditional roles as symbols of national cohesion were reinforced (Tétreault and al-Mughni 1995b). The re-emergence of women's demands for full citizenship rights after the war, a consequence of their experiences during the occupation and as members of resistance movements (al-Mughni 1997), has evoked in the government, Islamist groups, and in upper-class women's organizations a felt need to revive women's traditional roles and, thus, a shift toward conservatism on many "women's issues."

Interestingly, although Kuwaiti liberals support the integration of women in the national economy and some take positions supporting the extension

of political rights to women, they do not advocate a female identity dissoci-
ated from the traditional role of women as mothers, wives, and daughters.
Like the Western libertarian John Stuart Mill (Okin 1979), Kuwaiti liberals
often draw the line at female emancipation at the threshold of the home.
For example, Hassan al-Essa, an outspoken liberal, called for a review of the
liberal position with regard to women's paid work, which he saw as putting
considerable strains on family life and child-rearing, and Abd al-Latif al-
Duaij, another liberal, insists that "we (liberals) are in favor of women's
dedication to their home and believe that motherhood is the highest social
occupation" (*Al-Qabas* 1995, 19 Aug. 31).

Liberals' concerns are complex, however. Not merely the result of male
gender interests (Molyneux 1985b), these concerns reflect, on the one
hand, liberal estimates of the relative political weight enfranchising women
would bring to Kuwait's various political groups and, on the other, a genuine commitment to human rights that includes women's human rights. For
example, a few political Islamists have supported women's political rights.
One of them, Shi'i parliamentarian Hasan 'Ali al-Qallaf, abstained in the
vote on the parliamentary measure, refusing to join his Sunni colleagues in
opposition to it but not sufficiently persuaded by the human rights argument to agree to full political rights for women. Yet, despite the failure of
the measure, Kuwaiti women can take some consolation in what the 30
November vote revealed. The distribution of the vote on the amiri decree
several days earlier, forty-one opposed and twenty-one in support, was influenced by parliamentary objections to the decree as unconstitutional. The
second vote, however, was taken on a measure initiated by members of
parliament and, therefore, comes closer to capturing the actual distribution
of sentiments on the issue. The results here were thirty-two opposed, thirty
in favor, and two abstaining (al-Najjar 1999). This reflects a significant
movement away from what had been the conventional liberal position,
which held that if women were granted the right to vote, the preponderance
of Islamist women would shift the balance of forces in the electorate in a
way that would be detrimental both to women's gender interests and to
their own political fortunes (Tétreault 1994, 2000). The 1999 vote shows a
shift in values away from this instrumental perspective toward a Kantian
position that regards the human being as valuable in her own right, as an
end, rather than simply as a means.

Looking Toward the Future

The unexpected successes of Islamists in pushing for restrictions on
women's rights in Kuwait have led many across the political spectrum to
reconsider the role of gender in politics along with the role of women in

Kuwaiti society. The state nurtures and promulgates an ideology of the family based on patrilineal descent that serves as a model for other social structures in Kuwait. This ideal of the family is supported by all classes and tribes making up Kuwaiti society because, in Kuwait, families reflect more than lineage and even more than class and status. Continuity of traditional customs such as the *diwaniyya*, the reciprocal exchange of *ziyyarat* (social visits), other ceremonies such as weddings and collective mourning rituals, all are evidence of the cohesion of Kuwaiti families as foundations for psychological security and individual identity. Family life is central to Kuwaitis, men and women. It penetrates deeply into their day-to-day activities. It is omnipresent, affecting their choices in life and their perception of themselves. Kuwaiti women are active participants in the promotion of familial ideology and in the preservation of indigenous traditions and customs. Their success balancing their commitments to traditional culture against the demands of a changing world has been a key stabilizing element against the disruptive pressures of modernization (al-Mughni 1997).

Not surprisingly, therefore, the rising rate of divorce, resulting from a breakdown of traditional marriages, and the consequent visibility of female heads of household prompt widespread public concern. In 1993 the state responded by creating a new division at the Ministry of Justice to provide counseling to couples seeking to dissolve marriages. In 1996 the Family Consultation Division managed to ward off 120 impending divorces. Jami'yyat al-Islah al-Ijtima'iyya set up *lajna al-huda,* a committee that offers advice on marital relations and family life. In addition, during the 1990s a string of conferences, public debates, and symposiums were sponsored by the state and by voluntary organizations,[9] all dealing with marital breakdown and family values.

In this context, and despite apparent inconsistencies, the position of liberals on gender issues is crucial and their support for a continuation of women's public role in the face of increasing Islamist pressure has been important for women. In 1997 this support grew significantly as a group of Kuwaiti liberals constructed a public role for female activists within the formal political sphere. The National Democratic Forum (NDF), a new "political group,"[10] included six women among its seventy-two *mu'assisin*

9. Voluntary organizations in Kuwait operate under government licenses and receive state support. Even so, as do offices and ministries that are official arms of the state, many display substantial independence from the positions taken by government officials (Ghabra 1991; Tétreault 2000).

10. Political parties are technically illegal in Kuwait, but elections are contested in part through the mediation of such political groups, voluntary associations whose main concerns deal with public policy.

(founding members), a total of 8 percent. In its manifesto the group out-lines its recognition of "women as a social force that must be dealt with in a framework of new civilized concepts" and "asserts the importance of devel-oping women's role and place in society, increasing their participation in public life, activating their status as citizens with full responsibilities, and modifying existing civil laws that obstruct their rights and duties in their political, economic, and social role" (translation by al-Mughni).

The NDF favors the extension of full citizenship rights to women and is exemplary for having put its ideals into practice from the start by accepting women as equals among the founders. The NDF is the first political group in Kuwait to have women as founding members. Islamist groups long have recognized the utility of mobilizing women to participate in political activ-ities, and most have established women's committees. Islamist groups, how-ever, did not include women among their decision makers. In contrast, the NDF elected two women, Mudhi al-Humoud and Sheikha al-Nusif, as members of its executive board.

During the 1999 parliamentary election, NDF members ran themselves and supported others who shared their pragmatic views. The closeness of the vote on women's rights reflects a significant shift in the social and ideo-logical base of liberal politics in Kuwait. One source of this shift is a grow-ing disenchantment with the militance of Islamist groups. In consequence, the government shifted its position away from its former strong support of Islamists, an act that allowed the formation of the new, liberal-sponsored political group as a means to counterbalance Islamist power. This shift was greeted with charges that the government is trying to "liberalize society." It evoked fierce opposition and resistance by conservative and religious groups, always ready to deploy the resources of the state to discipline and police society to ensure conformity to their norms and values.[11] The campaign mounted by Sunni Islamists against women's rights in the autumn of 1999 included charging the government with succumbing to foreign pressure from the United States.

Islamists also stepped up their ongoing efforts to strangle any sort of religious discourse not entirely managed by themselves. The trial and con-viction of Ahmad al-Baghdadi, chair of Kuwait University's political science department, on charges of blasphemy brought against him by an Islamist leader, was just the most visible manifestation of an intensive campaign to bring the government back into line with its sometime Islamist allies. How

11. For an examination of similar goals of Islamism in Egypt, see Goldberg 1992. The efforts of religious radicals to deploy state power to enforce their understandings of morality are also common in the history of Christian religionists; see, for example, Walzer 1965.

the government engages in coalition-building to mobilize support for policies embodied in other amiri decrees issued during the parliamentary interregnum thus will affect not only the substance of these proposals but also the climate for human rights, including women's human rights, in Kuwait.

The current situation in Kuwait with respect to gender and citizenship is fluid. This is clear in the conflict of interests between the state as an institution and the substantive impact of neopatriarchy on governance. Although the state supports tribal groupings and affiliation, it does not promulgate a tribal ideology or an identity in the sense of *qabila*, the identification of the nation with a particular tribe. Such an identity would be a negation of its own existence. Tribesmen are loyal to their particular tribe independently of territorial boundaries and a national identity centered on a community of residence. 'Ajman Bedouins, like members of other Kuwaiti tribes, perceive themselves as belonging to 'Ajman and focus their loyalty on their tribe. Politically, this was reflected in the practice by some tribes of holding primary elections,[12] which capitalized on the strong tendency for *badu* to vote for candidates representing their own tribes. Perhaps because of their divisive effects, however, such "tribal primaries" were declared illegal, and those holding tribal primaries in 1999 were arrested. Most of those charged with violating the new law against tribal primaries, however, were later exonerated, leaving the practical status of the law in some doubt.

For urban Kuwaitis, national identity is quite different. The English word *citizen* is derived from a Latin root, *civis*, "city," coming through the French *citoyen*, the egalitarian term of address used among "fraternal" French revolutionaries. This linguistic legacy reflects the history of citizenship as a concept embedded in the experiences of urban life. In the Kuwaiti urban experience as well, national identity is bound up with the connection between the citizen and the town (Longva 1996b; Tétreault 2000). As a result, despite a very different linguistic tradition, urban Kuwaitis share with Europeans a particular understanding of citizenship.

> Urban Kuwaitis . . . understand citizenship as *jinsiyya*, from the root verb *jns*, to make alike, to assimilate, to naturalise. . . . There is here an idea of similarity and horizontal solidarity. . . . *[J]insiyya* . . . does not posit a priori a supreme authority. In this sense, it is . . . [close] to the Western concept of citizenship. Although *jinsiyya* [carries] no connotation . . . [of] the city, the urban Kuwaitis relate this notion with a territorialised community . . .

---

12. The so-called "tribal primary" was institutionalized in the 1985 election to counter the loss of leverage of formerly dominant tribes in Kuwait that resulted from the 1981 redistricting; see Gavrielides 1987 and Tétreault 2000).

previously the town, today the nation-state, rather than with a particular leadership. . . .

[In contrast,] the tribes in Kuwait understand nationality and citizenship in the sense of *tabi' iyya*, which can be translated as "following" or "allegiance" to a leader. . . . The root verb of *tabi' iyya* means, among other things, to walk behind someone, to be subordinate to, to be under someone's command. The concept is clearly built on an idea of hierarchy and vertical allegiance. (Longva 1996b)

The electoral impact of the *jinsiyya* understanding of citizenship on hadhar Kuwaitis is, therefore, very different from the impact of *qabila* on the voting behavior of Kuwaiti *badu*. Khaled al-Sultan, for instance, a noted Kuwaiti Salaf from a prominent merchant family who has run several times for parliament, cannot count on receiving the votes of the members of his large extended family (clan). Voting and other forms of political participation are not simply extensions of family membership to urban Kuwaitis, for whom voting decisions depend on being attuned to a candidate's political agenda. This shift from *ta' abiyya* to *jinsiyya* underlies the genesis of modern political organizations such as the NDF.

The war experience, which found a disproportionate number of *badu* fleeing the country while a disproportionate number of *hadhar* remained in Kuwait, highlighted the national security drawbacks of an ideology of nationalism based on tribal norms. Kuwaiti officials are aware that to increase loyalty and respect for the state and its institutions is in the long-run interest of the state. To understand the rationale for this, it is important to avoid confusing state interests with those of the ruling family and the government. As both of us have observed on many different occasions, in Kuwait there is substantial independence among and even within these several institutions. Ministries develop policies that correspond to their mandates as organs of the state; these become options discussed in meetings with the prime minister and other ministers who are officials of the government. Even the ruling family is not immune to internal differentiation. It is neither a royal institution nor one whose members' interests necessarily coincide. In fact, in 1992 and in 1996, a few young members of the ruling family made public declarations of their intention to run for parliamentary seats, initiatives squelched at higher levels of the family but which provide evidence of the progress of modernization even within this quintessentially traditional institution.

Despite the deeply rooted presence of modern values in Kuwait, the situation of Kuwaiti women has lagged behind modernization in other areas of Kuwaiti life. It is ironic that women's involvement in the public realm as paid workers has had so little impact on their social position as dependents of men. Indeed, persisting views of women as first and foremost family members affect women's relationship to the state by placing them in an unfavorable position within the welfare system. We have argued elsewhere (Tétreault and al-Mughni 1995a) that women's autonomy and full citizenship rights also are threatening to the regime, dependent as it is on the family as a patriarchal paradigm to support its own legitimacy. Thus, it is even more ironic that women's political rights have become so prominent in Kuwaiti politics. In recent years women gained entry into "men's" political groups and came breathtakingly close to achieving equal political rights. The primary obstacle to the realization of women's rights is bitter opposition by Sunni Islamist groups, allies of the government in its campaign to maintain adherence to the traditional values it sees as the bulwark of the regime.

How Kuwaitis will maintain their traditions while acknowledging the political and moral significance of the modernization that already has taken place in their society is a story without a foregone conclusion. As Kuwaiti citizens are engaged in working out its plot, gender continues to be a focal point of the action. The political status of Kuwaiti women is a primary marker of Kuwait's continued status as a quasi state whose domestic politics formally excludes a majority of its population (Kazemi 1996). To accept women as full citizens, a status envisioned in Kuwait's Constitution, advocated by its ruler, and supported by nearly half of the parliament, would signify the achievement of a milestone in the ongoing transformation of Kuwait into a modern nation-state.

12

Passports and Passages

Tests of Yemeni Women's Citizenship Rights

SHEILA CARAPICO AND ANNA WUERTH

RIGHTS AND LEGAL STATUS are often tested at the margins. Questions are less likely to arise about how general principles apply under ordinary circumstances than about how specific articles of particular laws speak to unusual situations. The test of legal status comes through case law in the form of judgments about claims made in the context of specific, even peculiar, fact sequences. Rights are affirmed or asserted on behalf of social groups when courts or tribunals find that they have been violated in individual cases. So it is, too, with citizen rights for Yemeni women. Under ordinary circumstances the daughters of Yemeni parents, born and raised in Yemen, who marry Yemeni men and raise Yemeni children, are not conscious of limitations on their citizenship. Questions arise under unusual political or personal conditions where general principles are open to interpretation, where both the facts and the judgment are likely to be affected by race, class, regionalism, and partisanship. In this chapter we examine issues of gender and citizenship in Yemen through the prism of two asylum applications in which women claimed discrimination at least partly on the basis of gender. Both women had migrated across national boundaries during times of profound political changes. Their cases show how citizenship rights of women and their children can be affected directly by circumstances of national, regional, and global politics.

The Case Histories

The first case involves an Adeni woman we will call Ilham who went to Moscow to study in the 1980s when South Yemen, then formally known as the People's Democratic Republic of Yemen (PDRY), was ruled by the Yemeni Socialist Party (YSP). The PDRY was unique among Arab states in its propagation of state feminism, framed as equal rights and opportunities for women under the revolution.[1] Among thousands of men and women from Third World states of socialist orientation educated in the Soviet Union, Ilham met and married a Nicaraguan. Her father objected at the time, from afar, that Muslim women should not marry non-Muslims although it is not clear how progressive socialist legislation then in effect treated such marriages. Still in Moscow, Ilham gave birth to a girl who bore her father's surname. When she subsequently divorced the Nicaraguan (presumably under Soviet law), the child was registered at the South Yemeni embassy on Ilham's Aden-issued People's Democratic Republic of Yemen passport. In the meantime, in 1990, the PDRY united with the Yemen Arab Republic (YAR) to form the Republic of Yemen, and after four years of quarrelsome unity, the YSP was purged from the united government in a civil war.[2] Like many other PDRY students overseas, Ilham found herself without financial support from the Yemeni government after unification and made her way to a Scandinavian country. There she applied for asylum based on the argument that the Yemeni embassies abroad would not renew her passport nor issue a Republic of Yemen passport for her daughter because they would consider her child illegitimate under the 1992 personal status law forbidding and nullifying exogamous marriages between Muslim women and non-Muslim men.[3]

In the second case, a woman we will call Arwa was born in what was then part of Ethiopia of a Yemeni father and an Eritrean mother. She spent much of her life in her mother's homeland. Arwa and many others who were called "Arab" in Somalia, Kenya, Ethiopia, and Eritrea migrated—in some cases, fled—to what was then the YAR, that is, North Yemen. Thousands, if not

1. The work of Najib Shamiri (n.d.) and Maxine Molyneux (1985b, 1991, 1995) give the most comprehensive overview of legal development concerning women in the People's Democratic Republic of Yemen (PDRY).

2. For the political development in postunification Yemen, see Carapico 1998, 52–59 and 170–200; Glosemeyer 1995.

3. RoY, Personal Status Law 20/1992, article 29 (al-Jumhuriyya al-Yamaniyya, Wazara al-Shu'un al-Qanuniyya 1992). A child of a void union, however, is legitimate according to article 32 of the same law—a point that eluded Ilham and would probably also elude Yemeni passport officials, who would cling to a folk version of legitimate birth rather than to the intricate law.

hundreds of thousands, of repatriated so-called *muwallidin*—Muslim children of Yemeni men and foreign (usually African or Asian) wives—were among the first significant group to seek citizenship papers from the YAR government's fledgling passports and immigration service. North Yemen, at the time, had an open door policy toward refugees and promised citizenship to all sons and daughters of Yemenis. For instance, in the mid-seventies a Yemeni ambassador in Vietnam arranged repatriation of a large community of Yemeni-Vietnamese, their families, their in-laws, and some Vietnamese refugees, a significant proportion of whom later re-migrated to the West or, perhaps, the Gulf.

During the days of the "oil boom," many born-and-bred Yemenis migrated to Saudi Arabia in search of higher earnings. In the case of Afro-Yemenis, many hoped, and some, like Arwa, succeeded, to re-migrate to Saudi Arabia, which in those days allowed holders of Yemeni passports special privileges to travel and work in the kingdom. These privileges were suspended in the fall of 1990, soon after Yemeni unity and during the onset of the second Gulf war, prompting a precipitous return of roughly 750,000 to 800,000 Yemeni migrants. Unlike the majority of returnees who faced unemployment upon their return, as a result of her strong office and language skills, Arwa secured a transfer by her employer, Saudi Airlines. Although her passport is Yemeni and by law as the offspring of a Yemeni male she is Yemeni, in her asylum application Arwa told North American authorities that she faced probable treatment as an alien by virtue of her race, gender, and employment for a corporation owned by an unfriendly foreign government.

Some points about these two cases are immediately apparent. Both stories are based on asylum petitions where the burden of proof is to show a reasonable expectation of politically motivated persecution; they are not cases before Yemeni judges or even the Yemeni passports and immigration service. Both women are relatively highly educated and cosmopolitan, probably better prepared socially and psychologically for life in the West than for life in Yemen where neither has spent much time during adulthood. Their experiences reflect not only on Yemeni laws concerning citizenship and personal status but also on global forces such as wars, the market price of oil, regime changes, and migration flows. Both women have become world travelers whose fears of returning to the land of their official nationality are connected to Yemen's domestic politics, fraught with internal conflicts that bear directly on the definition of citizenship.

The Constitutional Context

Yemen's legal-constitutional system remains in a state of flux with the Constitution and most major legislation issued and, in many cases, also amended in the 1990s. Its legal and judicial history has been rich and varied, shaped by indigenous and exogenous influences: Zaydi and Shafi'i[4] precepts, highly localized tribal and customary law, Ottoman law in the north and Anglo-Indian law in the south, socialist legislation in the south and Egyptian-inspired legislation in the north, international conventions on matters such as human rights, and some laws drafted by foreign technical experts.[5] Citizenship laws as such, governing the issue and use of passports, came to Yemen from Europe via models from other Arab countries. Now-outmoded European concepts construing citizenship as a male attribute have been preserved in Yemeni legislation. The current penal and personal status codes reflect contemporary neofundamentalist interpretations of Islamic law partly influenced by practices in neighboring states such as Saudi Arabia. Discrimination against women is, thus, established in broad areas of Yemeni law, whatever the particular law's provenance. Gender discrimination rests on international, regional, and local precedent.

The public roles and civil rights of Yemeni women have been further conditioned by the vicissitudes of Yemini politics, with important differences between north and south.[6] In North Yemen, until the early nineteen sixties, very few laws were codified; passports were issued by order of the imam himself, and citizenship was not explicitly defined. When the Yemen Arab Republic was founded after a military coup d'etat in 1962, women were afforded legal rights of voting, public office, and special protection at the work place. For many reasons, these rights were not necessarily enjoyed in practice; moreover, the legal system of the YAR government was so rudimentary that it lacked a basic criminal code, administrative courts, or judges and lawyers trained on legislation enacted. A system for issuing passports and visas was introduced only in the nineteen seventies, with help from Sudanese and Egyptian advisors, and routinized in the eighties. In Aden, while it was a British Crown Colony, citizenship was limited to propertied males of established lineage. After South Yemeni revolutionaries established the Arab world's only Marxist regime in the early seventies, they gave

4. The Zaydi school of law, dominant in the northern parts of the former Yemen Arab Republic (YAR), is of Shi'i political allegiance, otherwise, however, closely connected to the Hanafi school. The western and southern parts of Yemen are mostly inhabited by followers of the Sunni Shafi'i school. Relations between followers of the schools have been peaceful at times, rocky at others, centering on political and economic issues rather than religious conflicts; see Vom Bruck 1999 and Haykel 1999.

5. Messick 1993, 38–70. Wuerth (forthcoming), 36–73, on legal and judicial traditions in North Yemen; Shamiry 1984 on South Yemen. On the recent activities of the World Bank in reforming the legal and judicial system, see Shamiry 1995, 237.

6. Boxberger 1998; Lackner 1995.

women rights unrivaled in the region, including parliamentary representation and appointments to judiciary positions. Equal opportunity was declared if not achieved. The PDRY's 1974 family law, always acknowledged as one of the Arab world's strongest legislative protection of women's rights, helped win women's political support for the revolution, mobilize their energies for economic development, and reform the conservative patriarchal family.[7] Polygamy was officially outlawed. Divorced women were granted custody of the children, and civil law entitled them to possession of the marital home. In the cities, this provision was given teeth by the fact that urban housing was public and could be disposed by the courts.

Under the transitional Constitution issued soon after unification and enacted by popular referendum in 1991, all preexisting legislation under either government remained in effect until specifically amended. For northern women, at least, unity seemed to usher in an era of greater public political participation.[8] Within the next few years, however, socialist-era legislation was explicitly repudiated in amendments to the Constitution, a new personal status law, and other legislation that curtailed many feminine rights.[9] The language of freedoms and social equality from the 1991 Constitution was retained in the amended version passed after the remnants of the PDRY army were defeated in the civil war of 1994. But new provisions, some of them taken from the YAR Constitution of 1970, were added: Women were called the "sisters of men" (art. 31), and discrimination on the basis of gender, class, race, language, or religion was not outlawed as it had been in the Constitution of 1991. Although "citizens are equal in general rights and obligations" (art. 40), the equality of rights is mitigated. Women were still constitutionally guaranteed full electoral suffrage, the right to serve in parliamentary and governmental offices, and equality in the workplace. Other legislation, however, barred women from enjoying equal rights in marriage, divorce, and inheritance and limited their legal competence to serve as witnesses in court. Even the penal law seems to favor men. Furthermore, de facto, wives require their husbands' permission to work, rent a house, obtain a passport, or travel abroad. Thus, the 1994 constitutional amendments legitimized gender discrimination existing de jure and de facto. Whereas electoral and labor laws are based on egalitarian models, the personal status and penal codes are deeply conservative. The nationality law combines a premise

7. See Molyneux 1985a. On citizenship laws in the PDRY, especially Law 10/1970 and Law 2/1981, see Shamiri n.d., 95ff. For an anthropological account of gender relations in postunification Aden, see Dahlgren 1998.

8. Carapico 1991.

9. Wuerth 1994; Ash-Sharqi et al. 1993.

of unfettered equality of citizenship with exceptions in the conferral/inheritance of citizenship.

The Citizenship Law

According to the letter of united Yemen's citizenship law, law 6 of 1990, Ilham and Arwa, both daughters of Yemeni fathers, are Yemeni citizens with the full rights thereof. But because the law distinguishes between male and female competence to pass their citizenship to their children or spouse, the nationality of Ilham's child is unclear. A Yemeni citizen is defined as a person who is born in Yemen or the child of a Yemeni father or one who has resided in Yemen for at least fifty years or whose parents or husband lived there for this amount of time; or the child of Yemeni parents who had citizenship when they migrated abroad. Regardless of paternity, any child born to a Yemeni woman in Yemen is automatically a Yemeni national. It seems that the state acknowledges offspring the father does not acknowledge, or children of Yemeni women who would otherwise be fatherless or stateless: that is, if the father is of unknown nationality, Yemeni soil can compensate for women's defective ability to transfer citizenship to their offspring.

This interpretation flows from the complicated language in article 4.1 of law 6/90. The child of a Yemeni mother and a father of unknown citizenship born abroad may be granted Yemeni citizenship by the interior ministry if the "child" lives in Yemen for ten consecutive years after reaching the age of eighteen (the age of legal majority defined by this law). These are similar to the criteria for conferral of naturalized citizenship on non-Yemeni Muslim Arabs, or children born and raised in Yemen of foreign parents. Broadly speaking, the spirit of the law seems to be that Yemenis are those born and raised in Yemen, or permanently settled there and living as Yemenis, and speaking Arabic; and all children, even re-settled descendants, of Yemeni men. In other words, citizenship flows from paternity or from the fatherland, and ideally from both.

The 1990 citizenship law deals with binational marriages very differently for men and women. The foreign wife of a Yemeni native may assume her husband's citizenship after four years of marriage, if she and the husband agree; if she stays married to him for another four years, the citizenship becomes permanent, and she retains citizenship even if she subsequently divorces. No guidelines whatsoever are given for foreign husbands. A Yemeni woman who legally marries a foreigner is given the option to change or keep her nationality. If, however, her marriage contract is "void under Yemeni law," meaning *inter alia* that, like Ilham, she has chosen to marry a non-Muslim, then she cannot renounce her citizenship: she remains a Yemeni national. If a Yemeni woman does take another nationality by virtue of marriage, she may reinstate Yemeni citizenship in the event of divorce. Wives and children of Yemeni citizens are not allowed to change nationality without permission, however.

In other words, on the positive side, women cannot be arbitrarily deprived of citizenship; once a citizen, always a citizen. Conversely, the law does condition foreign wives' and Yemeni daughters' freedom to change their citizenship on permission of Yemeni husbands or paternal relatives. This restriction makes it difficult or impossible for them to obtain passports without their men's approval. The terms, specific references, and underlying assumptions applying to the marriage of a foreign woman to a Yemeni man are quite different from those applying to the marriage of a Yemeni woman to a foreign man; in both cases, they assume that a wife lives in her husband's country. Women are equal citizens, but citizenship is patrilocal.

The case of a child born in Russia of a Yemeni mother and Nicaraguan father raises many legal ambiguities. Ilham's child's registration in her mother's passport seems to suggest recorded citizenship under PDRY law.[10] Whether or not PDRY law at that time explicitly recognized women's marriage to non-Muslims, or a Soviet civil ceremony, marriage of a Yemeni woman to a non-Muslim man is currently unlawful under the 1992 personal status law (and its amendment in 1999) that was specifically designed to revoke the PDRY's state feminism. By current standards, then, Ilham's marriage to the Nicaraguan may have been "void." It is conceivable, in a fiercely anti-socialist atmosphere, as Ilham contended in her asylum petition, that someone would retroactively challenge the legality of her marriage, thus her child's legitimacy. Yet ironically, under the citizenship law, if the child is illegitimate—the offspring of an "unknown," thus stateless, father—then it might be entitled to Yemeni citizenship in infancy, even if born abroad.[11] So the question of the child's citizenship is still unsolved. Can a void marriage confer citizenship rights on the child? Can a mother confer her Yemeni citizenship to her child who was born abroad? On the other hand, assuming the marriage is recognized as legal, then by deduction the child born abroad might be a Nicaraguan or, perhaps, a Russian citizen, or else eligible for Yemeni citizenship only at age twenty-eight, after extended residence. Either way, then, this child is in legal limbo, its national and cultural identity uncertain.

10. It is unlikely that such a registry still exists in Aden or, for that matter, Moscow. Many PDRY files and records were destroyed during the 1994 civil war.

11. Islamic jurisprudence is not unanimous on this question; some jurists think the child is legitimate, some think not; see Zahraa and Malek 1998, 165 n. 83.

There is other language in the citizenship law that does not apply directly to either Ilham or Arwa because under the law their nationality should be beyond question, but which, nonetheless, might affect their *de facto* status in the country. Children of non-Yemeni parents born in Yemen become citizens if they speak Arabic, reside permanently in the country, are of good moral character, and so forth. Foreigners may be naturalized if they are Muslim Arabs. Conferred citizenship may be withdrawn if people stay abroad for two consecutive years "without good reason," or if they work for another government against the orders or interests of the Yemeni government, or on other grounds. These clauses leave the impression that in case of doubt, language, propinquity, and political loyalty become relevant citizenship criteria.

Personal and Political Complications

Ilham's potential problems in Yemen, like Arwa's, are complicated by the tumultuous national and international politics of their still-young lives. Ilham must once have been a bright young Socialist, among not more than a few dozen in her class selected for graduate study in the Soviet Union. Many prurient tales of the PDRY's policy of sending young women and men unchaperoned to the coed dorms and free love of communist Europe have circulated in Yemen since the YSP's fall from power. Ilham's short-term marriage to a Latin American might well be read in terms of this salacious lore. On a more serious note, even a very earnest contemporary Yemeni judge might be hard-pressed to uncover relevant PDRY legislation and precedent, much less the relevant codes for Soviet civil marriages and Nicaraguan citizenship in the mid-eighties. In political terms, everything about Arwa's story brands her as a Socialist. Her extended absence from Yemen, her marriage to a non-Muslim, and finally her asylum application might all shed doubt on her patriotism or even be interpreted as the renunciation of Yemeni nationality claims.

For many Yemeni women the ability to press legal claims is facilitated or constrained by the presence or absence of male relatives with the standing and connections to represent them in a court of law. This is true in rural communities and in urban courts. Evidence from court cases in Sana'a shows that significant numbers of women do use the courts to defend their personal, family, and property rights, often challenging fathers, brothers, or husbands. If these women enjoy some support from their other menfolk, they are often more likely to succeed.[12]

12. For a detailed analysis in one village, see Mundy 1995; in one urban court, see Wuerth (forthcoming), 117–20.

This could well be the crux of the matter for both Ilham and Arwa. Ilham's disregard of her father's warning and her long stay abroad presumably speak to some distance from her family, who in any case as southern Socialists could well have experienced considerable downward mobility in the interim. If her male relatives will and can help her pursue a passport for her daughter through legal or informal channels, or by bribing the right officials, or even if she had neighbors or coworkers who might vouch for her, she might stand a good chance. Otherwise—in the absence of patrimonial support, relying only on her legal status as a citizen who is a woman— her chances of success are considerably reduced.

Arwa has a Yemeni name but does not "look" or "act" or "sound" like a *Yamaniyya*. She is taller and darker complected than the average Yemeni woman, and her carriage is identifiably African. Arabic is her third or fourth language, not that of a native Yemeni speaker. Even if she dressed in ultra-conservative Yemeni fashion, with a full veil, she could not really "pass"; just as Africans label her Arab, Yemenis call her *Habashiyya,* literally the feminine of Ethiopian, the term for East African women generally. She is among uncounted tens or hundreds of thousands of Afro-Yemeni *"Muwallidin"* who have migrated and remigrated across the Red Sea in the past twenty or thirty years or more. Men like Arwa's father traveled to Aden when it was a colonial hub, to Africa after the PDRY revolution, within the Horn during its various wars and revolutions, back to Yemen when things got intolerable, and into Saudi Arabia whenever they could get work permits. Neither she nor Yemeni officials know what Ethiopian laws of the Emperor Haille Selasse and Mengistu Miriam governed her own mother's nationality or hers when Eritrea was an irredentist province of Ethiopia.

Issues of race and gender are further complicated by politics and economics. Sex and ethnic discrimination are by no means trivial in Yemen. Yet compared with neighboring Saudi Arabia, even post–civil war Yemen is rather tolerant. Inside the Saudi kingdom, women are required to veil and forbidden to drive. Saudi citizenship evidently derives from patrilineal criteria, and naturalization is rare. Even if Saudi men voted, women would be prohibited. Moreover, it seems that in Saudi Arabia corporeal punishment, including amputations, floggings, and so forth, is carried out with greater frequency against non-Arab aliens. Given the many generations of Red Sea intercourse, there are black Saudis, just as there are black Yemenis, of full unquestioned parentage, nationality, and identity. There are also native Yemenis whose combination of intergenerational residence and financial success have gained them Saudi citizenship. Nonetheless, an Afro-Yemeni woman is even more vulnerable politically in Saudi Arabia than in Yemen.

In financial terms, if an Afro-Yemeni woman could obtain a visa and find a job, whatever her skill level, her earning power in Saudi Arabia would be greater than in Yemen or East Africa. For this reason she might well elect to live in Saudi Arabia. But like other women in the kingdom, Arwa faced there the world's most restrictive limitations on feminine mobility plus discrimination against Africans and, indeed, Yemenis. Presumably it was a combination of her race, her gender, her, Yemeni passport, and the lack of male intermediaries in Saudi Arabia that landed her back in Sana'a when Riyadh punished Yemeni citizens for their government's tilt toward Iraq. In Riyadh, as a noncitizen, and especially as a *Habashiyya*, Arwa had no rights of any kind. But she had air conditioning, as another woman in similar straits observed, and the streets were orderly. Arwa and others like her would have stayed, had politics not intervened.

In Yemen, Arwa's passport was not contested because she inherited her father's nationality. As the Yemeni government and the Saudi opposition are fond of pointing out, Yemeni women legally vote, work, drive, and dress as they wish. At issue was not her citizenship as such, but rather her loyalty, even her identity. She wore a Saudi Airlines uniform, and worked for the national airlines of an unfriendly foreign government. As Saudi-Yemeni relations worsened, this evidently drew mistrust from Yemen's Ministry of Interior, who, Arwa says, had her shadowed by security agents.

Furthermore, in Yemen, too, Arwa suffered social discrimination as a *Habashiyya*, primarily in the form of lewd comments from unemployed youth on the streets. Whatever distant kinfolk she has in Yemen are in some remote village she has never seen, scarcely people she could expect to intervene on her behalf with national security authorities. For a range of social, psychological, and cultural reasons, then, she interacted mainly with the *muwallidin* community, which is large enough to have its own class distinctions and sub-groups. Arwa's subgroup incorporated bourgeois tastes with African social styles, bemoaning the total absence of discotheques in Sana'a. Between her and the prim and proper Sana'ani society was a great deal of social distance and "otherness."

In an atmosphere where either socialist or Saudi sympathies were seen as potentially seditious, extralegal resort was sometimes made to loyalty-based tests of citizenship, among them residence in Yemen or registration with an embassy abroad. When, amidst a wave of political repression surrounding the 1994 civil war, Ilham remained abroad "without good reason," she demonstrated what in other cases has been interpreted as anti-Yemeni sentiment. Scores of Yemeni, Somali, and other men had been detained during the war.[13] Women still seemed relatively safe from arbitrary political arrest

13. Rone and Carapico 1994

and physical violence, but selected female regime critics, Africans, and others have been harassed and threatened, for instance, in near-collisions with military vehicles while driving. Ilham knows that in case of an accident or incident she will be powerless to defend the rights her passport supposedly confers.

These two cases are not representative of the experiences of ordinary Yemeni women but representational of the ways that changes in the international system affect national identities and their definition. Other Yemeni women who have lived their whole lives in Yemen might have known five or more distinct Yemeni governments each of which defined, or did not define, their subjects or citizens differently: the North Yemeni imamate, southern sultanates and autonomous tribes, Aden's colonial government, the PDRY, the YAR, and the Republic of Yemen. Any Yemeni past forty years of age remembers at least three distinct polities with very different views of citizenship. All Yemenis older than ten years of age have been citizens of more than one state and have seen major changes in legal, educational, political, and security systems. The current law is the current law, not an enduring foundation of national identity. Although the lives of women like Arwa and Ilham are exceptional for Yemeni women, they metaphorically embody the Red Sea, Middle Eastern, and global experience of creation and recreation of state entities, and with them of national identities. Changes in the relationship of states to nations and in fundamental legal philosophies have profound impact on the lives of individuals, how they define themselves, and how nationality is passed on to one's children. Issues of citizenship and nationality are a function of these global forces in interaction with internal political culture.

PART FIVE

THE NON-ARAB
MIDDLE EAST

13

Gender and Citizenship in Turkey

YEŞIM ARAT

IN THIS CHAPTER I examine the way citizenship is gendered in the Turkish context. I introduce the formal legal framework through which the state defines citizenship then discuss the marked differences between the legal framework and women's experiences of citizenship. Finally, I examine how different groups of women try to redefine the concept in theory and practice. Through women's own reactions to their experiences, I elucidate the gendered nature of citizenship in Turkey.

Historical Context of Citizenship in Turkey

Within a liberal framework, citizenship can be considered a contract that defines the rights and responsibilities between the state and its member individual. Michael Mann, in his historical anlaysis of citizenship, perceives the concept as a "ruling class strategy" whereby rights are given from above to promote social integration in the polity (Mann 1987, 339–54). Although his work has been criticized because it precludes the possibility of "citizenship from below as a consequence of social struggles over resources" (Turner 1992), Mann's observation sheds light on the historical basis of citizenship rights in the Turkish context.

Citizenship evolved in Turkey not as a result of a revolutionary social struggle from below wherein masses demanded their rights against those who withheld them but as a result of the choices enlightened ruling elites made to extend those rights to the masses to promote social integration and strengthen the state. In the pre-Republican Turkish context, the latter motive was predominant. The Ottoman society was organized into two groups:

those who ruled, *askeri,* and those who were subjects, *reaya* (İnalcik 1964). The subjects paid taxes but had no part in the executive responsibilities. The Muslim rulers entrusted the executive functions to those recruited from Christian families at a young age and trained in the court as the sultan's slaves. The political structure that denied citizenship was reinforced by an economic structure that increased state power. In theory, all land belonged to the state. The sultan granted land for specific periods of time to fief holders who cultivated the land and collected taxes. In the classical Ottoman system, there was no concept of citizenship but the concept of the absolute ruler and the subject. It was only in 1839 when the Ottoman state, which was declining in power, felt the need to strengthen the state and engaged in a series of reforms that the concept of the subject's rights as such surfaced. The 1839 Reform Edict declared that the life, honor, and property of all subjects would be secured, the particular fief holding system would be abolished, and each "citizen" would pay taxes in proportion to his means (İnalcik 1964, 56). In line with Mann's observation, in the Ottoman context the state had unilaterally granted these rights to its subjects under varying pressures to strengthen itself against potentially competing groups; these rights could begin to transform the subject into the citizen over time.

With the establishment of the Turkish Republic in 1923, the principles over which the polity was based in Ottoman times changed. The founding fathers conceived of a new republic where one could theoretically talk of the rights and responsibilities of citizens and the state. The 1921 Constitution had declared the principle of national sovereignty and had created a powerful national assembly. The republic stood for the rule of the people, even though in practice some time would have to pass for the people's will to reign. Over time the religious legal structure of the polity was completely abandoned and a secular legal framework was established. In 1926 the founding fathers discarded the Qur'an-based personal status code and adopted the Swiss Civil Code, which extended critical rights to women. In 1934 the same men extended suffrage to women and made women formally just as eligible for election to the national assembly with the same requirements as men.

The responsibilities of the state toward the citizens were extended in 1961 by a new constitution that elaborated the civil liberties and social rights of the citizens. Although some of these rights were retracted with the 1982 Constitution, the 1961 Constitution guaranteed the protection of civil liberties and prohibited the making of laws that could restrict the "essence" of these rights (Soysal 1986, 100–101). The concept of a social state was introduced. Accordingly, citizenship rights were extended to cover the right to strike for workers, the provision of social security, health and housing needs, and the protection of the family, the mother, and the child. Just as the basic legal framework of the republic was shaped by the founding fathers during the early decades of the polity, the new Constitution was shaped after a military coup by a group of bureaucrats and intellectuals who were ideologically close to the military leaders. In Turkey extension of citizenship rights was once again the result of the decisions of enlightened elites rather than the historical struggles of the people for those rights. As Mann put it, citizenship, once again, had been used as the strategic device of the ruling elites.

Women and Formal Citizenship

Although the citizenship rights of both men and women were shaped from above, there were differences both at the formal and the substantive level regarding these rights. According to the Constitution, men and women are equal before law (*Türkiye Cumhuriyeti Anayasasi 1982*, art. 10). Although gender discrimination is unconstitutional, some articles in laws still discriminate between men and women.

Turkish citizenship devolves from membership in the secular political community of the Turkish state. The Turkish Citizenship Law allows both men and women to pass their citizenship to their children, independent of the citizenship of their spouses (Arin 1997). Both men and women can retain their citizenship if they marry a noncitizen. The law, however, does not accept a Turkish man taking the nationality of a foreign woman he marries. The situation is different for women. A Turkish woman can obtain the nationality of a foreign man she marries if she declares her intention to do so according to lawfully established procedure (Nomer 1982, 56). Along the same lines, a foreign woman married to a Turkish man is automatically granted Turkish citizenship. The same right is denied to a foreign man married to a Turkish woman (*The Status of Women in Turkey* 1994, 17). In other words, women cannot pass citizenship to their foreign spouses, whereas men can.

Similar biases exist in the civil law that was adopted in 1926. In Turkey a marriage is legalized only by an authorized civil servant. The option of a religious marriage is possible only after the civil marriage has been registered. Once married, according to the civil code, the husband is declared to be the head of the family and responsible for providing for his wife and children (art. 152). It follows that he represents the marriage union (art. 154) and establishes the place of residence for the family (art. 21).

Equality and Women's Citizenship

The secular legal framework that had been promoted from above, in principle, upheld gender equality and has not been critically challenged by the populace. In the last decade women acted to have the remaining vestiges of unegalitarian laws, especially those in the civil code, amended. Article 159, which declared that wives had to have their husbands' permission to work outside the home, was repealed. Article 153, which required wives to assume their husbands' last name, has been changed so that now married women can choose to use their own last names before their husbands'. In the criminal code, article 438, which granted a rapist a reduction in punishment if his victim was a prostitute, has been annulled. Again, in the criminal code, articles that defined adultery differently for men and for women have been replaced by the relevant commission working on the issue (arts. 440 and 441). Before the change, a married woman was considered to have committed adultery if she had sexual intercourse even once with a man other than her husband, whereas a man could be charged of the same crime only if he could be shown to have had a continual relationship with a woman other than his wife. According to the amendment, both men and women can be charged with adultery if it can be proved they have had intercourse with someone other than their spouses. (Many women's groups are very disappointed in the amendment because they would like to see adultery left outside the scope of the criminal code and be, instead, a cause for divorce, *Yeni Yüzyil* 1997, 17 Dec.).

The civil code is also being reviewed. Since the late 1980s women have campaigned to have the code amended. They signed petitions (one with one hundred thousand signatures was presented to the president of the Grand National Assembly) and lobbied to have the amendment passed even though there are some dissenting voices among women regarding the nature of the changes desired. One such controversy surrounds the issue of the property regime. Within marriage, the civil code maintains the separation of goods between the spouses in apparent conformity with the principle of equality. Because, however, most wives are housewives who do not earn income, property bought during marriage is bought with the money the husbands earn and is registered in their names. Wives who have subsidized their husbands' work outside the family are uncompensated. Under these circumstances, women's groups proposed that the amendment in the civil code allow women to select the option of sharing assets acquired during the marriage.

Others reacted to this proposal on the grounds that it would violate the principle of equality and encourage the division of labor along gender lines.

The columnist Gülay Göktürk waged a war on women's groups who were against the separation of goods regime because she believed that by protecting housewives, women would continue to see becoming a housewife as an attractive prospect (*Yeni Yüzyil* 1997, 11, 15, 18 Nov.). Women would be discouraged from working outside the house for income and aspiring to have careers that could sustain them on their own. In a series of acrimonious columns, she decried the feminist consciousness that upheld women's difference under the prevailing Turkish circumstances and wrote in support of a basic egalitarian stance. Feminists responded in defense of the proposed amendment (*Pazartesi* 1998, 15 Jan., 1–5).

Formal Versus Substantive Equality in Citizenship

Since the foundation of the republic, formal equality between men and women in citizenship has been a high priority for both the founding fathers and Turkish women. Since the 1980s, women have acted to redress the remaining unegalitarian articles of the legal framework. Formal legal equality, however, is different from substantive equality. In Turkey, as in the West or in other countries in the Middle East, women experience citizenship very differently from what the formal legal framework maintains. To the extent that Turkey aspires to be a liberal, secular democracy, it is assumed that its citizens, male and female, signed their social contract with the state to become equal bearers of rights and responsibilities, irrespective of their gender roles.

What feminist critiques have taught about the male-biased, exclusionary concept of liberal citizenship is also relevant in Turkey. The allegedly neutral, seemingly universal concept of liberal citizenship endorses the ubiquity of male norms and male experiences (Pateman 1988; Jones 1990). If the rights and responsibilities of citizenship allow one the protection of one's "life, liberty, and property" and expect one to vote and be voted into office, pay taxes and defend the country militarily when need be, then one is implicitly expected to assume gender roles associated with men. It is men who earn more money than women, have the money or the property to pay taxes, are voted into political office, and go into military service when needed. Similarly, it is men's property that is protected because women simply own much less property than do men, whereas women have difficulty finding protection against physical violence. Because women are less educated than men, freedom of speech and thought have also been male privileges in practice if not in theory. The list could be elaborated and extended with examples drawn from Turkey.

In Turkey, although suffrage was extended to women in 1934, and women did not have any special requirements for voting or election to political office different from those for men, the percentage of women in the national assembly has never been more than 4.5 percent. Only in the most recent 1999 elections could 24 women in the 550 member parliament (4.4 percent of the whole) be elected. In the cabinet that was formed in May 1999, there were no women ministers. According to statistics gathered in the 1990s, in urban areas, only 4.66 percent of property that has been registered is in women's names, whereas 77.96 percent is in men's names (*The Status of Women in Turkey* 1994, 61). Thirty-one percent of women and 10 percent of men are illiterate (*The Status of Women in Turkey,* 1994, 62). Only 1.85 percent of women and 4.22 percent of men are university graduates. In urban areas, labor force participation of women and men is 16.1 percent and 69.2 percent, respectively. Of those who work as unpaid family workers, 65 percent are women and 14 percent are men (*The Status of Women in Turkey* 1994, 68). Beyond these statistics, the violence that women are exposed to reaches frightening proportions; a study carried out in the villages of South East Anatolia in 1995 found that 76 percent of women were beaten from "time to time"(CEDAW report 1996, 31).

Beneath these statistics is the patriarchal tradition that has been deeply absorbed by the populace. In Turkey, although there is no legal grounding, high school principals and dormitory superintendents have been known to send girls who are suspected of having intercourse to virginity exams. In 1992 there were two suicide cases of high school girls who had been ordered by school authorities to have virginity exams (*International Women's Rights Action Watch, 1997* 1996, 34). Women in police custody and political detainees have also been exposed to forced virginity exams, although it is difficult to gather information on the subject. An interview conducted in 1997 with Işilay Saygin, the female minister of state responsible for women and the family at the time, showed again how far patriarchal prejudices were internalized by women themselves, including those who were positioned to protect women against those traditions (*Yeni Yüzyil* 1997, 29 Dec.). When asked if forced virginity exams were not degrading to girls, Işilay Saygin responded that this was the problem of the girl concerned and elaborated how hard it would be to relate to the girl after she was six months pregnant. She emphasized that traditions, customs, and norms should not be forgotten. When the reporter reminded the minister that girls had committed suicide because they had been taken to virginity exams, Saygin commented, "if they did they did." She elaborated that until the age of eighteen, deterrent rules that threatened to shame girls had to be enforced so that girls would behave as they should. Teaching children the good, the right, and educating them was the responsibility of the mother, the father, and the state. When asked how the state figured in, she replied that the state was the father. Under these conditions, the state explicitly advocated its right to control the bodies of its female citizens and privilege its male citizens. Although there were immediate reactions to the minister's interview from women's organizations protesting her views and asking her to resign (*Yeni Yüzyil* 1997, 30, 31 Dec.; *Yeni Yüzyil* 1998, 1 Jan.) and an interview with her feminist advisor who was completely against forced virginity examinations followed (*Yeni Yüzyil* 1998, 5, 29 Jan.), the minister did represent a common perception and did so from a position of authority. According to this view, the state had the right to define norms and to control women's bodies in the name of those norms although this attitude was difficult to reconcile with a liberal concept of citizenship that prioritized the integrity of the individual.

Another lethal manifestation of patriarchal norms, irreconcilable with the liberal concept of citizenship, that the state allegedly upholds is the occurrence of "honor killings." Women who are accused of disobedience or disgracing the family name because of their lax relationships with men are publicly murdered to clean the family name. Although honor killings might not be very common, and the cases that have taken place in eastern and southeastern Turkey where feudal family relations still prevail have been widely publicized (*Pazartesi* 1996, Apr.), the state has not taken any effective action to prevent them or to provide effective punishments that could be deterrent.

In Search of Substantive Equality

Since the mid-1980s women have contested their citizenship status. They have worked, as mentioned above, to have the legal framework amended to make it more egalitarian. In the process, they tried to reformulate the principle of equality that shapes the prevailing concept of citizenship so that it could promote more substantive equality in practice. They upheld the principle of difference as opposed to sameness in defining the criteria for equality. As such, they advocated positive discrimination to make women substantively more equal to men.

Feminists, among a larger group of women who lobbied to redefine the rights and responsibilities pertaining to women's citizenship, contested not merely the content of their citizenship rights but also the way that they were given. They criticized the Republican framework where the founding fathers used women's citizenship as a "ruling class strategy" to promote Westernization, arguing, instead, that time had come for them to define their rights as they deemed necessary, in their own name, for their individual benefits

(Tekeli 1991; Sirman 1989; Arat 1997). Feminists declared themselves ready to struggle for their rights so that the contract of citizenship between the state and its women members could be redefined and better realized. In the Turkish context, where communal priorities had traditionally stifled individual prerogatives, feminists upheld the secular liberal contract the state formally adhered to rather than contest it in principle, working instead to realize its full potential.

The fight against domestic violence, a critical feminist initiative, had implications for women's citizenship. Various women's groups and feminists prioritized domestic violence as a critical issue around which they mobilized societal support. Feminist groups demonstrated their most significant public presence on this issue. When the feminists organized their first public demonstration against domestic violence on May 1987, they knew from common experience and observation that beating of women within families was prevalent. Research on domestic violence followed to document its threatening prevalence across class lines. Meanwhile, feminists, first in Istanbul (1990), then in Ankara (1991), established foundations to open shelters and to help women who were exposed to domestic violence. Their initiatives trickled down as the state and various municipalities opened shelters in towns and provinces (*CEDAW Report* 1996, 33–35). Attempts to amend legislation and policy suggestions to alleviate the problem heralded the expansion of women's citizenship rights.

Present legislation remains ineffective to protect women from domestic violence. Domestic violence within the family is considered as a crime only if the victim files a formal complaint. Accordingly, the woman has to show witnesses, who are very difficult to find in cases of domestic violence because violence takes place in private and because culturally, family is deemed sacred, and potential witnesses would not want to threaten this sanctity by reporting violence. The woman who does try to file a complaint is confronted with the police, who usually urge women, if not ridicule them, to go back to their husbands rather than file a complaint. It has been argued that reports about victimized women prepared by the doctors and by the police do not always reveal the truth (*The Status of Women in Turkey* 1994, 39).

For those cases of domestic violence that make it to the courts, problems remain. Judges consider regional traditions and customs that have accommodated, for example, beating of women as extenuating circumstances and, thus, legitimize the prevailing patriarchal violence toward women. The terms of punishment remain far from deterrent. Most prison sentences are for seven days even though the law does suggest up to thirty months imprisonment in cases of domestic violence.

Under these conditions women lobbied to have the criminal code reviewed. A new "law to protect the family" was prepared by a commission convened by the Ministry of Justice. The new law, supported by a wide spectrum of radical women's groups, aims to ameliorate the prevailing situation (*Pazartesi* 1997, 11 Nov.). According to the law, the public prosecutor can file a suit against the spouse who has committed violence, prohibit that spouse from coming home for up to six months, and prevent him or her from persecuting and bothering the victim at the workplace. Although this proposal aims to punish whichever spouse has been a victim of domestic violence, in effect, it will work to protect women, who are the usual victims.

Beyond this law, feminists advocate other means to ensure protection to those exposed to domestic violence. They argue that civil servants, such as the police, doctors, health and legal administrators with whom the victims of violence come in contact, be given special training and collaborate on how to deal with the victims. They propose that special "family courts" with specially trained judges be set up to adjudicate issues concerning domestic violence, victimized women receive free legal consultation, crisis centers offering immediate protection for victims of violence be established, and the number of women's shelters be increased and made available in every district (Arin 1996, 138). These women also seek to expand the concept of domestic violence and to include rape within the family as domestic violence (Yüksel 1996).

The agenda that the feminists in Turkey offer might seem only too familiar to those that have existed in the West. Turkish feminists do not deny the influence of Western feminism. To those leftists who attack them for imitating the West, they have been known to retort that socialism did not blossom in the plateaus of Konya (in Central Anatolia) either. In their more reflective modes, as was the case when the monthly feminist magazine *Pazartesi* prepared its cover story on the prospect of an indigenous Turkish feminism, they argue that the possibility still needs to be worked out (*Pazartesi* 1997, Sept.). Although the feminists in Turkey might share the goals of feminists in the West, the context in which these goals are worked out is different. A critical difference defining the parameters of the domestic violence debate in Turkey is that Turkish feminists must have the proposal of a new law concerning domestic violence ratified in a parliamentary committee by traditional Muslim Turks who grew up in a patriarchal culture that legitimizes domestic violence and accommodates honor killings. In the Turkish context, communal values, rather than liberal individualism, are emphasized, which continues to undermine women's citizenship rights. In a polity where the state defines the rights and responsibilities of citizenship and where the patriarchal culture legitimizes violence toward women so that even women are made to endorse it (revealed by empirical research), a liberal rhetoric that prioritizes the individual rights of women as human beings is more radical than is the case in the West.

Islamist Women and Substantive Equality

It is not merely secular feminists but also Islamist women who contest their citizenship rights. Since the mid-1980s, Islamist women, including those who called themselves Islamist feminists, have intensely criticized the parameters within which women's citizenship was defined. They demanded a new framework that could better accommodate their religious convictions.

Criticism of Islamist women mainly targeted the republican project of modernity and its implications for women. Accordingly, the process of Westernization made Turkish women imitate their Western counterparts and endorse their problems, including their feminism. Cihan Aktaş, a leading Islamist woman advocate, argues that "some privileges that were granted to some women as rights could mean injustice to others" (Aktaş 1986, 211). She elaborates with sarcasm that the process of Westernization gave women the right to go to Europe to follow fashion closely, to snuggle in their furs in winter, and wear their bikinis during summer. For others, it was the right to become prostitutes and dancers to exhibit their bodies without control to fulfill a "social" duty. Still others had gained the right to work double shifts with meager wages as secretaries, cleaners, nurses, and so on, to come home late at night to do their housework and forego their right to educate their children (Aktaş 1986, 212). Feminists who articulated these concerns had problems themselves. Liberation and difference could not make women happy and satisfy their hunger. Feminists included "psychologically sick, those in search of adventure who ran after fantasies, dumb socialites who aspired to give color to their lives, and finally those who equated being a feminist with being enlightened, elite, progressive, and Westernist" (Aktaş 1986, 221). In turn, the feminist movement could not go beyond a limited narrow circle, could not reach large masses, and, as a reaction to its imitative culture, could not find a base for itself. Islam could redefine rights that the republican state had so narrowly defined in imitation of the West.

First, however, the parameters within which Islam was circumscribed had to be enlarged. Islamist women, those who used Islam as an explicit political ideology to define themselves, had to wage a fight to have themselves accepted publicly rather than merely privately. The most visible and politically critical battle was given in defense of women's right to cover their heads as they claimed Islam dictated. The republican state that defined secular citizenship rights did not merely seek separation of religion and the state but also effectively exercised control over religion through various institutions of the state. Within this framework, the goal was to confine religion to the private realm and monopolize religious authority in the public realm through the state. Covering the hair was prohibited in public office or educational institutions because it was deemed to stand for and propogate a religious ideology perceived to be inimical to the secular foundations of the republic. Until the mid-1980s, this particular definition of religious rights remained uncontested. When women began attending universities with covered heads during the mid-1980s, it was duly interpreted as an act of protest that triggered a tug of war between the secular state and Islamist women concerning their alternative definitions of citizenship rights. These women, supported by Islamist men, waged an ongoing fight, engaging in demonstrations and boycotts.

The religious Welfare Party, which came to power in 1996 as the dominant partner of a coalition government (and which was consequently closed by a Constitutional Court decision in 1998 and superseded by the Virtue Party), made the promise to allow women to cover their heads in public institutions, especially universities, a critical building block of its campaign. In turn, women supported the Welfare Party in large numbers. They worked as party activists to mobilize other women. Before the local elections in March 1994, eighteen thousand women worked in the Welfare Party campaign in Istanbul (*Pazartesi* 1995, Sept., 2). After the 1995 elections, the Ankara Women's Commission of the party registered sixty-five thousand women members in February 1996 only (*Yeni Yüzyil* 1996, 6 Mar.). During its term in office the Welfare Party repeatedly raised the issue as a bargaining chip toward its coalition partner who was reluctant to lift the ban on headcovering. To this day, although the Welfare Party has been closed by the Constitutional Court, the formal prohibition of headcovering in public offices and universities remains. It has, however, increasingly become more difficult to enforce the rule in universities as the number of women who cover their heads increased and the liberal proclivities of many instructors restrain them from mustering the political will to enforce the rule.

Islamist criticism of the secular republican concept of women's citizenship and the attempts to extend religious rights in the public domain are not unproblematic. To the extent that Islamist women are promoting a religious worldview through their demands to wear the religious headscarves in public offices and by supporting Refah, they are promoting their contract with God at the same time as they attempt to change their contract with the state. Whereas the contract of citizenship with the state might have its formal and substantive limitations, the contract with God might leave women defenseless to shape their predicament. The secular contract allows women to contest its terms, while in the sacred contract it is God who dictates the terms. Women who refer to their secular citizenship rights to extend their religious rights paradoxically might be promoting a worldview in which their capacity to shape their lives might be irrelevant (Arat 1996, 30).

◆   ◆   ◆

In the Turkish context, citizenship has been defined by the ruling elites as a "ruling class strategy" to Westernize and modernize the polity. The concept has been gendered both through the formal legal framework and through women's experiences of citizenship. The secular republic that promised men and women allegedly equal rights and responsibilities of citizenship based on a liberal contract failed to deliver them in practice. The biases and differences that existed in the legal framework were exacerbated by the patriarchal context of the country.

Since the mid-1980s, women have contested the marked differences that exist between themselves and men. They challenged the way their citizenship rights and responsibilities were defined in their name by the ruling elites. Although masses might not have been actively involved in this challenge, at the discourse level, there was a radical demand to define citizenship from below as a result of struggle and bargaining with the ruling elites. Both secular feminists and Islamist women were involved in revising citizenship as a "ruling class strategy" whereby rights were given from above for purposes defined by the ruling elite.

Substantively, women's protest expanded the confines of citizenship. Secular feminists who rallied to have the legal codes amended to make them more egalitarian and others who pushed for legislation to protect women from domestic violence all demanded that women's rights be extended and the responsibilities of the state toward women be more inclusive. Radical feminists brought in the concept of positive discrimination in order to protect women from physical violence. They demanded that women be treated differently, specially and "unequally" so that substantive equality in citizenship between men and women could be sought. Islamist feminists challenged the fairness of republican secularism that excluded them from the public domain and struggled to extend their rights to practice and propogate Islam in the public realm. Although the extent to which a liberal contract of citizenship could be compatible with Islam was problematic, Islamist women used the benefits of the secular legal framework to elaborate their rights. Islam remained to maintain a contract between an almighty God and the believer where the sacred terms were set by God rather than by the contracting individual. Women's attempt to redefine their contract with the state exhibited the gendered nature of citizenship in Turkey and the directions in which it could be regendered.

14

Iranian Women at the Intersection of Citizenship and the Family Code

The Perils of "Islamic Criteria"

HOMA HOODFAR

FOR WOMEN, the worldwide struggle to become full citizens has been long and is still ongoing. In the course of changing all subjects of a state into full-fledged citizens, women have been relegated to a subordinate status (Pateman 1988), including exclusion from political processes. An important aspect of women's struggle against this subordination has been the analysis and refutation of the rationales and grounds used to justify the discriminatory treatment. In Europe and North America discriminatory laws and ideological positions were rationalized through the deployment of science, biology, and conceptualizations of what is "natural," in addition to philosophy and sociology. The introduction of matrimonial laws effectively transformed women into silenced legal subjects of their husbands (Clark 1987; Pateman 1988; Smart 1982, 1989).

This situation meant that women had to challenge the ideologies of male supremacy on several fronts. Some focused on dispelling scientifically the theory that women are naturally inferior to men and of lesser intellectual ability.[1] Others reexamined the odd philosophical idea that although no man

The data presented here is based on comprehensive research on the impact of codification of "Islamic" law on women in Iran, which I carried out under the auspices of Women Living under Muslim Laws Network, Women and Law Program 1993–97.

1. See Maccoby and Jacklin 1974 for an early and classic review of literature in this area. See also Gould 1981 for a brief and wry account of how "science" relegated women and

was good enough to be the master of other men, all men were deemed good enough to be the master of women, predominantly through marriage and family laws (Pateman 1988, 219). Not surprisingly, a substantial body of feminist writing addresses the politicization of "male sex-rights" in the context of marriage contracts (Thompson 1970; Shoulter 1874; Weitzman 1981). More recently, as the welfare state came to play a much more substantial role in regulating the lives of its citizens, the urgency of removing discrimination against women has meant that feminists had to develop diverse political strategies besides effective collective and formal political organizations to push for legal equality, nationally and internationally. Although, by the 1990s, legal discrimination against Western European and North American women has been rectified to a large extent, social and economic discrimination have proved more difficult to challenge. Furthermore, success in removing legal discrimination against women in societies outside North America and Western Europe has been limited.

In Iran, as in the Middle East generally, women continue to face legal and social discrimination and continue to struggle for recognition of their rights as full-fledged citizens.[2] As with their European counterparts in the past, the single most important area of Iranian women's concern is the family code, which, as it stands, effectively renders any legal gains women may have made in other areas futile (Kar and Hoodfar 1996). What makes the situation startling is that the discriminatory attitude has persisted despite women's visible roles in, and considerable contributions to, the success of the last two major political revolutions in 1906 and 1979. Ironically, each of these revolutions has rendered women worse off than in the past in some important legal sense. The primary vehicles through which the discriminatory attitudes and laws have been introduced and sustained have been theology and the notion of cultural authenticity, the latter rephrased as "resistance to Western Cultural Imperialism."

Yet women are determined to occupy the limited political space that has been left for them and to agitate for change and improvement of their lot as bona fide citizens of Iran. Because the political and social context determines what strategies activists adopt, it is not surprising that a considerable sector of women's activism in Iran employs not secular debates on women's rights but women-centered interpretations of Islam and of the political con-

---

nonwhites to inferior levels. See Ridley 1993 for more recent discussions of sex differences in particular abilities.

2. Turkey is exceptional in that many of the legal (although not social and economic) barriers have been removed. With the revival of political Islam, however, and the male-centered worldview of its increasing proponents, feminists are wary of potential legal developments.

cept of "Islamic justice." Through this strategy women not only derail the claim that feminism and issues of legal equity are Western paradigms that aim to undermine the authenticity of Iranian society but they also break the male monopoly on interpreting Islamic texts. As one woman activist whom I interviewed summed up her comparison of Iranian versus European strategies: "Europeans advanced feminist thought in the area of science and secular philosophy. Now we, of course, use their experience, but, to achieve our goals here and in the Islamic world generally, we have to advance feminist Islamic theology and feminist Islamic jurisprudence as they [male-dominated institutions] are holding us hostage to their male-centric understanding of Islam and not science per se."

In this chapter I first examine briefly the Iranian debate on women's rights and the emergence of "Islam" as a political obstacle to women acquiring full citizenship during the process of establishing Iran's first constitution in 1906. The persistence of these obstacles is then followed through the formation of the Constitution of the Islamic Republic in 1979. My intent here is twofold. First, I present the Iranian women's strategy of applying their women-centered understanding of Islamic justice to the Islamic Republic's family code—the code intended to ensure the "Islamization" of Iranian society but which rendered women lesser citizens.[3]

My second purpose is to draw attention to the way in which "Islamic" laws and logic, used to justify discriminatory attitudes, have taken different twists and turns to accommodate the interests of male politicians since the Iranian constitutional movement in 1906. Using Iran as a case study, I reiterate what other Islamic scholars such as An-Na'im (1992, 1993a, 1993b), Rifat Hassan (1996), and Vakili (1996) have argued, namely, that Islamic *shari'a* (jurisprudence) has been a masculine/males only discipline and should not be permitted as justification for discrimination against women at national and international levels. In much the same way, it is unacceptable for the constitution and laws of a Muslim country to defend the slave trade because Islam, along with other major religions, once condoned it. Moreover, a brief overview of these discussions indicates that Islamic justifications are frequently reinterpreted and changed even during the life of a single government, or, even more strikingly, the same ayatollah, depending on political expediency. These overlooked realities make a mockery of the cultural relativists' position that has come to be part of the United Nation's institutional culture, particularly as it pertains to women (Clark 1991; Mayer

---

3. Thus, they have managed not only to turn their issues into some of the most hotly debated political issues but they have, to a considerable extent, pushed the Iranian legislative bodies and the Islamic ideologues into defensive positions.

1995a; Mayer 1991).[4] I argue that this state of affairs effectively silences the voices of women, especially Muslim women who object to being relegated to second-class citizens in the name of Islam.

The Emergence of "Islam" as an Impediment to Women's Rights: The Constitutional Movement, 1906–1911

Although it was the 1979 revolution that drew world attention to Iranian women as political actors, Iranian women played a considerable role during earlier revolutions and social movements. Reflecting, however, the centuries-old Iranian saying that "women should be seen and not heard," history has largely overlooked women's vital contributions. Exceptions have been rare, and only in recent years have many accounts slowly emerged (Afary 1996; Bamdad 1977; Bayat-Philipp 1978; Paidar 1995; Shuster 1912).

During the Tobacco Movement, for instance, women not only participated in the meetings, they also marched in the front with the protesters who walked to the palace (Keddie 1966). In 1905 women formed a human shield for the *ulama* who had taken sanctuary in a shrine near Tehran.[5] Women had formed many secret and semisecret associations that supported the nationalist and constitutionalist movement (Afary 1996; Paidar 1995). They helped to organize strikes and boycotts, to spread news, and to encourage the public to protest against the influence of foreigners and the despotic rule of the shah (Afary 1996; Bamdad 1977; Bayat-Philipp 1978; Paidar 1995; Shuster 1912). Women also organized to raise funds for a national bank, which had become the concern of the first parliament after the success of the constitutionalists. Once the general concerns of nationalists were met and the political crisis had passed, however, women's participation was overlooked and their rewards, if any, were meager. The history of their struggles, except for a few publications and references here and there, was hidden from the world and from their children.

The new Constitution, signed in 1906, forbid women from participating in parliamentary political processes on the grounds that it was against the text of the Qur'an! Thus, while the political leaders were concerned with transforming men from subjects of the shah into citizens of Iran, a totally

---

4. The relativist position was originally popularized by anthropologists in the face of much racism and cultural chauvinism in white and Western cultures. For a brief discussion of the topic, see Donoho 1991 and Howard 1993.

5. Given the community's ethics, protestors assumed that it would be much more difficult for the armed guards to open fire if they had to kill women. This tactic, however, has not always worked.

unprecedented and untraditional event, it was not deemed necessary for women to become citizens instead of subjects. Rather, women were viewed as subjects of their fathers and husbands, and their political participation was supposed to be in support of male kin. In contrast to the process of exclusion that Pateman (1989) describes as having taken place during the development of male citizenship in the West, Iranians seemed in no need of philosophers like Hobbes, Kant, and Locke to advance and justify the male prerogative of citizenry or the exclusion of women. They merely put a new twist on the Qur'anic interpretation, even though there is not a single reference to citizenship, in its modern sense, in the Qur'an. The wheel of exclusion, which ensured the legal and political alienation of women from formal processes, was already turning in 1906.

Ayatollah Mudress, the representative of the grand mufti in the Majlis, claimed that God had not given women the capacity to engage in politics. God, he claimed, had said in the Qur'an that women are in the custody of men and may not have the right to vote.[6] Supported by other clergies, he claimed that it is the responsibility of male relatives to ensure that women's rights are not overlooked,[7] just as James Mill said "that women did not need to have the vote because their interests were subsumed in the interest of their fathers or husbands" (Pateman 1989, 157). What is significant about the Iranian case is that the exclusion of women took place in the name of "Islam" and was alleged to be the word of God.

Another significant blow was the failure of the government to support women's demands for girls schooling. Ayatollah Sheikh Fazlullah Nuri issued a *fatwa* (a religious decree), saying that girls schools were against *shari'a* (Bayat-Philipp 1978, 300). Ayatollah Shushtari organized protests (which included women from the least-privileged classes) and distributed a leaflet entitled "Shame on a Country in Which Girls Schools Are Founded" (Paidar 1995, 70).[8] Women had hoped to avoid hostility from the conservative clergies and to preempt the use of Islam as an obstacle by pointing out the extent to which women's education in Iran lagged behind that in other

6. See minutes of *Majlis* (the Iranian Parliament) 1911, 4 Aug., as quoted in Afary 1996, 202–4; Sansarian 1982, 23–4.

7. It is, however, important to note that later in 1911 some of the more enlightened deputies, when there were opportunities to debate amendments to the Constitution, called for women's suffrage. They pointed out there are no religious justifications for denying women such political rights, a position that shocked not only the conservative *ulama* but also many of the other deputies. The debates were reported both nationally and internationally.

8. Ayatolah Nuri and other conservative clergy were collaborating with the constitutionalists against the shah, but what he had in mind was a form of clericalism in which *ulama* had the highest influence (Afary 1996, 89–115).

Muslim countries in the region and in Japan, which represented for Iranians, as it does today, an example of development without Westernization. Indeed, the first girls school in Istanbul was established in 1858, and women's teacher training began in 1863 (Najmabadi 1991, 55). Similarly, in Egypt girls schools had existed since 1832, and many women's magazines had begun operation before the turn of the century (Jayawardena 1985; Bayat-Philipp 1978). In fact, *One Leg Crossed Over the Other,* a book in support of women's education, had been published in Egypt in 1855, while a guide for boys' and girls' education was published in 1872. Qasim Amin, in his book of 1899, *The Emancipation of Women,* had created a heated discussion among conservative sheikhs in Egypt which influenced other Arab countries (Bayat-Philipp 1978). In a sense, the Iranian intellectual debates in 1906 around gender issues, particularly from Islamic points of view, were rudimentary. This worked against women' concerns during the development of the first Constitution.

Nonetheless, the earlier political motives for the exclusion of women (as opposed to a genuine concern to avoid deviating from Islamic doctrine) become more obvious when one considers that one of the main goals of the contemporaneous Islamic Republic of Iran is to improve literacy among women. A commonly heard saying is "In a truly Islamic society, there would not be even one illiterate person." In the same light, whether in mosques or other buildings, rooms where adult education classes are held are decorated with the Islamic saying that a Muslim should go as far as China (then the farthest civilization) in search of knowledge. The primary constituents of these classes are women (Mehran 1991). The obvious question, then, is why the early opposition to women's education and why in the name of Islam?[9]

Women's disappointment with the outcome of the Constitution motivated activists to focus on women's issues. They formed semisecret associations to discuss women's concerns and tried to change the situation, primarily through opening schools for girls but also by writing and publishing. Until then, the political mobilization of women had occurred not around gender issues but around national matters. Women began to raise funds and establish schools for girls. At the incitement of the conservative clergy, however, female teachers and students were frequently harassed, physically and verbally (Bamdad 1977).

As women's voices and demands found more support among more

---

9. This is particularly important because at the time girls' schools were not coeducational and employed only female teachers. Moreover, there seemed to be no opposition to women going to traditional *maktabs* where they, along with boys, would learn to read the Qur'an and other major Persian texts from, very often, male mullahs.

moderate groups and intellectuals, the clergy began to target women's associations, claiming that they were against *shari' a*. More liberal-minded members of parliament pointed out that Muslim women had always had their gatherings. Not only was there no religious obstacle to these gatherings, they argued, but why should women not get together and learn from each other? (Afary 1996; Paidar 1995) Women's counterstrategy was to demand that women's associations be legally recognized along with others. The legality and legitimacy of women's associations continued to be hotly debated for some time. Although many conservatives remained opposed to the associations, the grand ayatollah came short of calling them against *shari' a*. The parliament then recognized their legal status but provided no financial support for them.

Despite such disappointment, women remained on the political scene, particularly throughout 1911 when both the British and Russians were lobbying the shah to close the parliament so that they might maintain their political and economic stranglehold over the country. Although today an overlooked (if not totally forgotten) chapter of Iranian history, the presence of women and their large meetings were a major force in maintaining the momentum of the struggle (Afary 1996, 203–5; Shuster 1912). As Paidar (1995, 70–76) has pointed out, the experience provided women with an opportunity to develop their own political language. Women wrote demanding citizenship for everyone in the nation, including women, whereas men wrote about protecting the country and women of the nation (Najmabadi 1993).

Thus, women's early manifestations of gender consciousness were concurrent with their objections to the *ulama*'s use of Islam. The *ulama*, while carving an untraditional role for themselves in parliamentary politics, were determined to prevent women from breaking out of their traditional and customarily subordinate position in the family and society. While women wrote to refute the clergy's claims that women's demands were contrary to Islam, the clergy and conservative members of parliament turned women's customary subordination into a legal subordination. The reverberations are still being felt each day by every Iranian woman. Now, not only did women have to combat customary prejudices, they also had (and continue to have) the state to deal with.

Women in the Pahlavi Era

The success of the constitutionalist movement further weakened the rule of the Qajar dynasty and, finally, despite heated political debates about republicanism versus monarchy, led to the establishment of a new monarchy, the Pahlavi dynasty (1921–79). The Constitution was duly amended to allow the transition. The amendment made no immediate material change in women's status.

Yet by making the position of the monarch heritable among sons, women were constitutionally excluded from the nation's highest political position. During his rule, Reza Shah Pahlavi built a powerful state that pursued social reform and modernization. At the same time, however, this regime also sought to depoliticize civil society and exercised considerable repression of critical views. Women's associations, which by then had proliferated in all major cities and had established many girls schools, were similarly repressed, even though their demands and activities were in line with the goals of the regime. The verdict was against independent political and social initiatives.

Women's education was strongly encouraged as an integral part of the modernization policies. Apart from the civil legislation act, which required the registration of all marriages and divorces and required that girls must reach the age of fifteen before marrying, no other major reforms in the area of family code were put forth. The most controversial change for women, however, was the antiveiling policy of 1936. To many intellectuals, the veil, or *chador,* had come to represent women's oppression, but, more importantly, the backwardness of the country. It has also became a battleground, a show of force, for both conservative clergy and modernists. Thus, demonstrating his triumph, Reza Shah imitated the Turkish model and made it illegal for women to wear veils in the street. The ban was enforced by the police. The law was initially well received by many upper-class women and activists, but it pushed many less-privileged traditional women back to their homes (see Hoodfar 1997). Women's right to choose was denied by the modernist regime. There were, however, some attempts to encourage women's education and their entry into the labor market.

The advent of the Second World War and the removal of Reza Shah by the Allied forces in favor his young son (1941) meant a new opportunity for political space. Once again, there was a considerable flurry of activity among women in favor of their civil and political rights. Besides informal and independent activities, many women's magazines and women's organizations (including a women's political party) came into existence (Paidar 1995; Sansarian 1982). The attainment by women of full citizenship in their own country was their explicit goal. Thus, they concentrated their political demands on universal suffrage. They were also the first organized group to link women's full citizenship with the reform of the family code, viewing the democratization of home and marriage as a major step toward the democratization of the country.

As the state became more stable, it imposed censorship and adopted tactics to co-opt women's groups gradually and to bring them under state control by imposing Princess Ashraf, the shah's twin sister, as head of the Iranian Women's Organization. This move had mixed consequences. Many activist groups became depoliticized. Yet increased influence over the shah and the government led to the belated approval of Iranian women's enfranchisement in a national referendum as part of a package of reforms introduced by the shah. Women's enfranchisement, however, took place amid objections from conservative clergy, including Ayatollah Khomeini, who viewed such an act as un-Islamic and a corruption of Muslim mores. As the country moved rapidly toward dictatorship, however, the value of such a right was more symbolic than actual.

Women's enfranchisement was followed by the right to become judges, and, at last, a modest package of family code reforms, influenced by the Iranian Women's Organization, was introduced. Under the reformed law, all divorces except those by mutual consent had to be heard before the family court. Furthermore, women could also file for divorce. Custody, although not guardianship, would be decided in the best interest of the child, which meant that women often stood improved chances of being awarded custody.

Polygamy was not banned, although it was restricted because it required the permission of the first wife or of the court. This modest reform was called un-Islamic and drew a wave of opposition from the clergy despite the government's efforts to justify each section on the basis of some interpretation of shari'a or of a precedent established in other Muslim countries where similar or even more radical reforms had been introduced. Ayatollah Khomeini, then in exile, announced that women whose divorces had been decreed by the court against their husbands' will would be committing adultery if they remarried (Mir-Hosseini 1996). The age of marriage in 1975 was increased for women from sixteen to eighteen; during the uprising of 1978, however, as a concession to the conservative clergy, it was again reduced to sixteen. On the one hand, these limited reforms, despite their top-down character and the fact that they had been introduced at the cost of depoliticizing the women's movement, managed, nonetheless, to bring about a sense of entitlement among women. On the other hand, the depoliticization of the women's movement meant that gender issues were once again removed from the political agenda, from the concerns of the regime's critics, and from intellectual debates that tended to concentrate solely on democratizating the political structure.

Women and the Constitution of the Islamic Republic

The constitutional debates and documents of the Islamic Republic, in contrast to the first Constitution, are full of images of women, as political actors, Islamic warriors, agents of construction of Islamic society, mothers, and creators. This is the reflection of women's massive participation in the revolution. Moreover, because women and their black *chadors* had become an icon of the revolution, it was impossible to ignore them. On the contrary, the leaders of the revolution viewed the Islamization of women and gender relations as the cornerstone of an Islamic nation, and clearly the Constitution was the first vehicle in which to express their views. After taking control of the state machinery and realizing that women could form a strong political constituency, particularly in their favor, the *ulama* and religious leaders no longer wished to see women outside public politics.

The change of heart about women's role in politics, of course, preceded the constitutional debates. The caretaker government under the leadership of Ayatollah Khomeini had already announced that women's voting right was not under question, even though in 1963, Ayatollah Khomeini himself was the most vocal opponent to women's political rights on the grounds that this was against shari'a (Algar 1983). Although in opposition, many *ulama* had argued that a woman who does not have freedom of choice in her own home and is under control of her husband should scarcely be trusted with the power to decide the policies and laws of the country and, hence, to have a say in the responsibilities of Muslim men. These arguments, advanced in the 1960s, amply explain why many Iranian women intellectuals, writers, and activists (along with members of the Women's Party of the 1940s and 1950s) had produced critiques that linked family code reform and democratization of the home with women's full citizenship rights (Golban 1975). Nonetheless, once the government was dominated by religious leaders, these contradictions ceased to appear problematic to *ulama* and "Islamic" ideologues, as though *shari'a* had undergone a total transformation in just twenty-five years. In striking contrast, religious leaders began to call participation in the political process a religious duty and encouraged women not to take this responsibility lightly. Despite women's large-scale participation in the first election, however, only one woman was among the seventy-four elected representatives.

The Constitution mandates the Islamic state to ensure the participation of all citizens, men and women, in shaping their country's economic, social, and political destiny, in eradicating all forms of illegitimate discrimination, and in providing for justice for all. All citizens of the nation, both men and women equally, enjoy protection of the law and enjoy all human, political, economic, social, and cultural rights in conformity with Islamic criteria (art. 20). Women are also more or less explicitly given the most responsibility for building the Islamic nation through their role in the family, identified as the basic unit of the Islamic society. Thus, the Constitution seems to view women primarily as mothers, and states that all laws, regulations, and programs must facilitate the foundation and strengthening of families according to Islamic principles.

What has been the most unsettling aspect of the Constitution, as far as women are concerned, is the stricture, "in accordance of the Islamic principles or criteria," particularly in articles 20, 21, 151, and 163. Because the Constitution does not specify what is intended by this catch phrase, its interpretation is, in effect, left to the Council of Guardians, the administrative government, and other legislative bodies. This situation could theoretically provide a channel for introducing reforms and change through reinterpretation, for example, by privileging more liberal interpretations over more orthodox ones without reopening constitutional debate. And in practice, since the mid-1990s, such reinterpretation has taken place (see below). The political and legal developments immediately after the revolution, however, clearly indicate that the ambiguity of the "Islamic criteria" phrase reflected a tension between the conservative agenda on gender relations and the views held by sizable politicized and vocal sections of the nation during this period. Because the regime and the conservatives leading the caretaker government were not yet well established or confident of their political position, they were reluctant to alienate important sectors of the population. They were conscious that their views on women and gender relations were not acceptable to many groups as was apparent from the number of speeches given by Ayatollah Khomeini reminding Iranians that Islam has given more rights to women than to men.

Conservative religious leaders were appointed to the Council of Guardians, which presides over the country's election processes besides the elected Islamic parliament. The council's prime task, according to article 98 of the Constitution, is to interpret the Constitution and to make sure the laws of the country are in accordance with their interpretation of *shari'a*. Appointment is for life, and only the council can elect new members and spiritual leaders. Nor is the council responsible to any elected or even nonelected body. This in itself is an indication that the stage was set for the Republic's Islamic model of gender relation to emerge as a very conservative one.

Nonetheless, as Kar (1997) and other legal and religious scholars have pointed out, the most important aspect of the Constitution for women from a religious or Islamic vantage point is that it resolved the problematic of women's presence along with men in the formal political arena (Saeid Zadeh 1998). Even if the rights accorded to women are fewer than those accorded to men, the legitimacy of women's presence can no longer come under scrutiny in the framework of Iranian religion/politics.

"Islamic Criteria" as Applied to Women's
Civil and Political Rights

It is important to examine how Islamic criteria have been used as a vehicle to relegate women to lesser citizens by denying them the same
opportunities granted to men. Technically, as Kar's legal review (1997)
demonstrates, there appears to be no barrier to women's appointment to
the Council of Guardians, criteria for appointment being mastery of Islamic
legal debates and jurisprudence, not sex. This theoretical assumption is possible because in Shi'i tradition there is no religious barrier against women
becoming *mujtahids*, (an authority in religious matters whom others may
follow) although historically very few women have reached that status.

The application of "Islamic criteria" however, has meant that women
have been deprived of becoming judges because, according to conservative
ulama, "judgment" was considered the prerogative of Muslim males only.
Accordingly, women judges were removed from their posts despite much
criticism and resistance from diverse quarters. The subject, therefore,
has remained one of the most hotly debated, both nationally and internationally, because it is one of the few areas of glaring discrimination against
women. Many women and men both from secular and Islamist camps have
campaigned to overturn this law. The government has made some concessions by adding a clause in 1374/1995 permitting women to serve as advisors to family court judges. Furthermore, in December 1997 the head of the
Ministry of Justice announced that a group of religious leaders and Islamic
law specialists were studying the possibility of allowing women to serve as
judges. Resistance to the proposal is strong on the part of conservative *ulama*. The significance of eliminating this discrimination against women
stems from the fact that any serious participation of women in formal politics is jeopardized by this law whose principal logic is that women are inher-
ently deficient in "judgment," an assumption that questions their
intellectual ability, integrity, or perhaps their courage in taking tough stands
(analogous to the brutal acts assumed to be necessary in warfare).

Another aspect of the constitutional debates that met with some resistance was the attempt to make presidential candidacy an exclusively male
role. Because there were no immediate religious grounds for such outright
discrimination and because public objection was considerable, a compromise was made when writing the Constitution and the word *male* in the
phrase "the president would be elected from among the male politicians"
was replaced with *rajal*. Although this Arabic word is grammatically masculine (Persian words have no gender), it refers to both men and women of
significant standing in the community. This usage has left the question of

whether women could be persidential candidates subject to, one may sur-
mise, the interpretation of the Council of Guardians. The question, however, was never officially discussed after the ratification of the Constitution.
Many women activists and some religio-political leaders had expressed the
view that there were no theoretical or legal obstacles to women's election.
The elections in recent years of female leaders, such as Benezir Bhutto in
Pakistan, Tansu Çiller in Turkey, and Begum Khaleda Zia in Bangladesh,
has given this issue particular salience. In an attempt to resolve the constitutional ambiguity, some eight women presented their candidacy in 1997. The
most prominent was Azam Talaghani, daughter of the late, much respected,
Ayatollah Talaghani, who had been an active opponent of the shah's regime,
later an elected member of the first Islamic parliament, and had remained
actively involved in issues concerning women. Despite their credentials, the
candidacies of the women, and of many men, were rejected by the council,
which thus far has refused to explain its reasons. Although some council
members and other *ulama* have publicly announced that they see no obstacle preventing women from becoming president, so far women's only
achievement in this respect has been to force considerable public discussion
on the topic.

The other major vehicle through which women have been relegated to
lesser citizenship is the introduction of "Islamic criteria" into the criminal
code. Under these criteria, for instance, the testimony of two women is
equal to that of one man. Furthermore, the law clearly states that because
women's lives are worth only half as much as men's, a man who has killed a
woman can only be taken to justice if her family pays the difference in value
in "blood money." Although women have to take full responsibility for their
actions from the time they reach "maturity" (marriageable age) at age nine,
males take responsibility for their actions only from the age of fifteen. Yet
although women's punishment is no different from men's, they are told
their lives are valued only half as much. These instances of glaring discrimination replaced sections of a criminal code introduced in 1304/1925 in
which, at least theoretically, men and women were treated as equals. This
earlier law had been drawn up on the basis of the spirit of Islam, common
practice, and an ethos of social development and had been passed by parliament at a time when there were a considerable number of clergy in parliament. Moreover, Ayatollah Mudress, the conservative representative of the
grand *mufiti* (the supreme religious leader) in the first parliament approved
and signed the law, affirming that it was compatible with the spirit of *shari' a*
in the early twentieth century. Thus, after some sixty years, the use of
"*shari' a*" and "Islamic" criteria have symbolically, ideologically, and mate-
rially relegated women to second-class citizenship in ways that leave little

room for alternative interpretation. Working to repeal these laws has become a major preoccupation of many women and men activists of diverse political tendencies in Iran.

Of course, most women get on with their lives and only in unusual situations are forced to deal with criminal laws and their differential treatment of men and women. In contrast, it is in the area of family code (which regulates marriage, divorce, custody, and inheritance) that every woman experiences on a daily basis her relegation, in the name of "Islam" and religious dictate, to lesser citizenship and personal status. Thus, it is not surprising that Iranian women activists of diverse tendencies have focused their energy on demonstrating the contradictions between the revolution's promises of social justice and fairness and the deterioration of women's status under the Islamic regime. In fact, many observers have pointed out that the family code has become one of the most salient political issues for Iranian society.

Family Code

Within two weeks of the revolution, the family protection law, which was deemed contrary to shari'a, was nearly annulled. Thus, under the Islamic regime, men could now unilaterally divorce with no justification and could marry up to four permanent wives and as many temporary wives as they wished. Custody of boys after the age of two and of girls after the age of seven was automatically granted to the father, whereas the mother's visiting rights were not legally guaranteed. The legal age of marriage and legal adulthood under criminal law for women was reduced from sixteen to nine lunar calender years, although sixteen remained the age at which both men and women were allowed to vote. The irony is, as the attorney Abadi and others have pointed out, that a girl of nine is deemed capable of choosing a husband whom she has to live with and obey all her life yet not able to choose a president for four years.[10] Actually, because even infant girls can be given in marriage by their fathers or grandfathers, not even the right to choose one's spouse necessarily applies to women.[11] And whereas men can marry without their father's permission at the age of fifteen, women, regardless of their age or education, cannot enter into their first marriage without

10. For more recent discussion on these issues, see Attorney Abadi's comments on the most important concerns of women in Iran printed in *Zanan* 1997, 12–20.

11. Iranian women can legally marry at nine, work at fifteen, vote at sixteen, and travel at eighteen. One consequence of this situation is that a teenaged girl may be raising several children and taking care of a husband and household at an age at which she could not be employed as a housekeeper to do the same work because of laws against child labor.

their father's or other male guardian's permission.[12] Thus, although women are treated as minors as far as their marriage choice is concerned, they are deemed competent to face criminal charges by the age of nine.

There is a glaring contradiction between the eloquent praise for motherhood and women as mothers in the text of the Constitution, and the lack of legal rights and state protection for mothers. Women have no rights over the very children they mother whether in respect to the children's education and training, their marriage, or their financial affairs, which, at the death of the father, are left to the grandfather (father's father) and the agnate kin. In a context in which many social and commercial affairs suffer from the absence of regulation, the legislature has painstakingly outlined the disempowerment of mothers in areas as trivial as their lack of right to withdraw money from a minor child's bank account even if it was the mother who opened the account and deposited the money in the first place. Such prerogatives, until the child reaches the age of eighteen, belong to the father or grandfather. The question arises, why does the Iranian state now view the disempowerment of mothers so essential for its vision of Islamic society?

It is not only in relation to their children that women are disempowered. Once married, not only does a woman have to live wherever her husband chooses to live, but she also needs his permission to leave the residence. Even after the recent reform (see below), a woman who does not observe this rule may be branded *nashiza* and divorced with no compensation. Under the Constitution a woman has the right to "work" outside the home provided her job does not detract from the dignity of the family. But this right loses some of its meaning as soon as she needs her husband's permission to go out or if the husband chooses to live in a geographical location that makes it impossible for the woman to attend her job while residing in her husband's domicile. Here the husband's property/control rights take priority over his wife's right to mobility. For married women, obtaining a passport (itself a recent invention of modern states, and even more recent for Iran and other Muslim nations) has become, on analogous ideological/religious grounds, subject to the husband's permission. One woman explained with sarcasm that the logic of these laws was lost on her.

It would make more sense if the law had made it necessary for husbands to have the permission of their wives when obtaining a passport or leaving the country because women are assumed to be financially dependent on their husbands. What if a husband had not left enough money for his wife or *wives* (emphasis was given in the original statement) and the children?

---

12. If the male guardian is absent or if his denial of permission is judged unreasonable, girls can apply to the court for permission to marry.

Moreover, if he goes and does not come back or doesn't write to her, it will take years and much cost for a woman to get a divorce. Who is supposed to pay for her during that time? Who worries about her lonely marriage? But if a wife leaves the country, her husband can divorce her or just go and marry one, two, or three other wives. He will not suffer. One cannot assume that the lawmakers did not understand what they were doing. The only acceptable explanation is that Iranian laws assume that, at marriage, a wife becomes a slave and property of her husband but not vice versa. And the law is for protecting men, the first-class citizens, just as it is in South Africa where all the whites had rights but blacks had duties. Here, we women have duties and men have privileges.

It is under these conditions that many women in Iran find the debate over the expansion of women's "political" rights—which rose in volume, particularly after the parliamentary elections in the spring of 1995 and more recently with the presidential election in May 1997—to be a pointless exercise as long as the family code deprives them of the basic rights that all citizens should enjoy. To illustrate this point, I quote from several interviews on women's legal rights in 1996 and 1997.[13] One women interviewee eloquently and sadly said,

> What does it mean for the Iranian women to have the right to choose the president and members of parliament if they find themselves divorced without compensation for having gone to the polling stations to exercise those rights? . . . What does it mean for a woman to become a president or an ambassador if she has to ask for permission of her husband to leave her house to attend the presidential office and rule the country? Or beg his permission to allow her to get a passport, and then ask him to issue her permission to leave the country to attend her job as the ambassador to this or that country?

Several other women dwelt upon exactly the same point, some asking rather sarcastically whether Fatemeh, the Prophet's daughter, had had to beg her husband for the right to have a passport. Or what would Khadija, the Prophet's beloved and much respected wife whose advice and wisdom the Prophet sought frequently as long as she was alive, would say about the state of affairs of Muslim women in Iran? How would she feel if she were subject to these ridiculous laws simply because she was a married woman?

In a group interview a few other women talked about different personal

---

13. The data presented here are based on comprehensive research on the impact of codification of "Islamic" law on women in Iran, which I carried out under the auspices of the Women Living under Muslim Laws Network, Women and Law Program 1993–97.

experiences, sometimes with great anger. They argued that it was pointless for women to become president or members of parliament if every time they needed to travel within their own country without a male relative they needed certificates of virtue to confirm that they were not prostitutes and, thus, should be permitted to stay in hotels. Women are assumed by the state to be prostitutes, a priori, unless proven otherwise. One women reported having read that in other parts of the world, "people are struggling for the human rights of prostitutes, but when you live in Iran that sounds so unbelievable. It is a luxury that is hard to believe exists. Here we stone women to death for having had sexual relations with the person they loved but had not, for whatever reason, been able to marry."

Images of the daughters of the Prophet or famous *imams* are frequently presented by Islamic ideologues as models for Iranian women. Women, in turn, by applying their legal situation to these exemplary women, have turned them into important political vehicles for criticizing the regime and ridiculing the treatment of women under the Islamic laws. One angry woman in her forties, whose husband and two brothers had been martyrs of the war, had been asked to go to her city of birth, Isfehan, to correct an inconsistency in her birth document before she could receive her deceased husband's salary. When she arrived in Isfehan, still in her black mourning outfit, she was obliged to go to the morality police to explain why she had traveled alone and then had to obtain a certificate stating that she was a virtuous woman and could be allowed to stay in the hotel. Although this had occurred several years earlier, she was still outraged at the treatment she received and asked rhetorically,

Can you imagine that Hazrat Zaynab, having fought along with her brother, Imam Hossein, arrives at a town after Karbala where all her brothers and male kin have given their lives to establish justice in Islam. When she needs to stay in a guesthouse, they ask her first to go and obtain a certificate of virtue from some strange men she has never met in some strange office in order to be able to sleep in a private room away from the gaze of *namahram* [men who are not close kin], like a Muslim woman is supposed to. Otherwise she has to sleep in the street. Can you imagine how scandalized she would feel? Would she still be proud to be a Muslim woman? We do not need Americans to let us down! Our government and laws are doing it in the name of Islam!

Sitting in a government clinic waiting to see a nurse, a woman holding a child explained that she had had problems giving birth to her son when she was only sixteen and too young for pregnancy. The doctors at the hospital where she was finally taken, at the insistence of the local birth attendant,

had explained that she needed to have a Cesarean immediately to save the
child and, perhaps, her own life as well. Her husband, a Pasdar [member of
the Revolutionary Guard] with his gun over his shoulder, refused permission, and her pleas to the doctors went unheard because "it was he who
could decide about my body and the child I was giving birth to. He refused
permission, saying if God were willing, I and the child would survive. If not,
he would bury us personally." She sadly explained,

> In the end, the child was born brain damaged, and I barely survived. My
> husband is now married to another wife and has other children because he says
> he does not want any more brain-damaged children. Though he has not di-
> vorced me, I have to look after this child. I cry and ask God daily in my
> prayers why is it that my husband can decide about my life and child while I
> have no say in his life—even though it is much harder for a woman to replace
> a husband than it is for men to marry again. What is the justice of him making
> decisions about my life when my own pleas go unheard? Why do I want politi-
> cal rights when I cannot decide how and where I can give birth? First, I have
> to be recognized as a person and not a worthless slave; then I will worry about
> what political rights I should have. First things first.

What these interviews indicate is that women are highly concerned about
their legal and social status within marriage. They feel that equity and democracy in marriage, divorce, and parenthood is the cornerstone of full citizenship for women, and, thus, they see that as their first demand from the
legislative bodies, the government, and society. Whereas in the past it was
the activists and intellectuals who articulated this position (Golban 1975),
today the demands are widely vocalized among Iranian women regardless of
where they are located culturally, geographically, or in terms of social class.[14]

It is important to note that women's expressed lack of concern for their
political rights is only a means of demonstrating their priorities rather than a
reflection of disinterest in that domain. In fact, women turned out heavily
for the last two elections, as did the whole nation, particularly in 1997 when
88 percent of those eligible voted for the presidency. Even by conservative
estimates, some 40 percent of voters were women, a considerable achievement for any country, but particularly for Iran where women's literacy rate
leaves much to be desired and many women continue to live in small and
scattered villages. More importantly, women, and men, used their electoral

14. This postion was specially articulated by the Hazab Zanan (Women's Party) in the
1940s and 1950s.

right to elect the candidate least favored by the clergy establishment and with the most liberal views on the situation of women.

Citizenship

Equal nationality rights would acknowledge women's relation to the state as full citizens. It is not possible for women to enjoy many basic rights without having full citizenship and nationality (Freeman 1995; Stratton 1992). Discriminatory laws with respect to citizenship and nationality have imposed much misfortune on Iranian women and their families, particularly their children (Kar 1997). Even though stories about hardships caused by women's legal incapacity to pass on citizenship to their children or to obtain residence permits for their spouses appear frequently in the newspapers, equality in citizenship rights has failed to attract the attention of the government and legislative bodies. In part, this is because those who suffer most from these laws are women from the least-privileged classes.

It is estimated that three million Afghani and thousands of Kurdish and Shi'i Iraqi refugees live in Iran. Moreover, in addition to Iranians who travel abroad for educational and business purposes, an estimated two million Iranians have taken up residence outside Iran as a result of the Iranian Islamic Revolution and the eight-year Iran-Iraq war. This situation has meant that many Iranians have married nationals of other countries, making the question of legal capacity to transmit citizenship to children and obtain residence permits for spouses a national concern.[15]

Evidently citizenship, per se, is yet another area in which men and women face very different situations. According to the civil status law, the offspring of an Iranian man is recognized as Iranian regardless of the child's birthplace or the nationality and religion of the man's wife. Moreover, even if the marriage is not a formal arrangement, as long as the father admits that he has fathered the child, the child is entitled to citizenship. In contrast, only in rare situations can a woman analogously transmit citizenship to her child: specifically, only if she had obtained official permission to marry a nonnational before the marriage, the marriage was legally registered with Iranian authorities, and the child was born in Iran and lived there at least one year after reaching the age of eighteen. It is noteworthy that all Iranian women are legally required to obtain official permission to marry a nonnational; men, however, require permission only if they are in certain key gov-

---

15. The stories of many women married to Afghani refugees and their children who are left in limbo and without nationality are frequently reported in the national newspaper. See Kar 1997, 79–110.

ernmental positions or if they are foreign students receiving government scholarships. A major restriction applying to women but not men is that the spouse must be Muslim: marriages between Iranian Muslim women and non-Muslims are forbidden.

Given the fact that the Iranian Constitution expressly views women/ mothers as agents for the transmission of Islamic culture, it seems doubly ironic that women cannot pass their citizenship to their children, whereas men married to nonnationals of a different religion can (evidently, the transmission of genes is of little relevance in all this). In practice it also means that women as mothers have no voice in issues related to custody of these children because the Iranian legal system considers the children of international/interstate marriages subject to the laws of the father/husband's country, regardless of the child's birth in Iran.

Furthermore, Iranian women lose their citizenship if the law of their husband's country, as in Afghanistan, imposes the husband's citizenship on them.[16] This blatant discrimination against Iranian women, which in practice again limits women's right to choose their marriage partner, clearly contradicts article 41 of the Constitution of the Islamic Republic as Kar (1997, 107) has pointed out. According to article 41, Iranian citizenship is the absolute right of all Iranians, and the government cannot deny citizenship to any Iranian except if the latter so desires or has accepted another nationality.

Obtaining residence permits for nonnational husbands and children is a forbidding task, imposing even more hardships on the women concerned and their children. At times, these women are forced to leave the country or to accept separation from their children. Not being able to obtain an Iranian birth certificate affects the welfare of the children as much as the mother: they cannot register in the state school system nor can they use public health services. Here, for example, is a grandmother whose son and daughter were both married to Afghani nationals and who was disappointed at not being able to obtain a birth certificate for her daughter's child. Bewildered, she asked,

How come one of my grandchildren is not Iranian and the other is? They both were born in Iran, live in the same building, play together. What kind of law is this? They tell me, send your daughter to Afghanistan, her husband's country. She does not want to go. It was not part of her marriage arrangement. She

16. They may regain their citizenship and birth certificates only at the termination of their marriages. Only after they refute their non-Iranian citizenship can they reobtain their Iranian birth certificates.

married on the understanding that she would live here and her husband agreed although his life is not so easy here. He has to spend half his time in different offices trying to get his papers straight even though he is a highly skilled technician.

There are other contradictions and bureaucratic practices that harm women because of their gender. For instance, many women have oral religious marriages, which, although legitimate, leave couples without a certificate and disadvantages women disproportionately. First, many women who marry refugees, particularly Afghanis, cannot register their marriages because the men lack valid passports and birth certificates without which the registry office cannot register the marriage. Consequently, out of necessity, many women and their families opt for religious marriage ceremonies only. Thus, even if their children are born in Iran, in the absence of a proper marriage certificate they will not receive residency papers. Men in a similar situation face no problem because, once they admit to fathering the child, the child is granted citizenship.

This state of affairs has forced many Iranian women and their Afghani husbands to go to Afghanistan where, again, because they lack documents, they face a whole other range of problems. Because the wife automatically loses her Iranian citizenship because of the Afghani law that requires her to take her husband's citizenship, the couple cannot expect help from the Iranian government. Over the last decade this situation has created such hardship that the United Nations has precipitated a series of formal and informal negotiations with the Iranian and Afghani governments to find ways of easing the situation of those women subject to dual discrimination from both countries. Even though citizenship problems can no longer be pushed aside as an "upper-class" problem, the self-proclaimed government of the oppressed shows no indication that citizenship laws will be revised to eliminate this form of discrimination against women.

Women's Strategies for Change

The appalling legal situation of women in Iran has increasingly become the subject of critical writing, occasional films and radio programs, and both public and private discussion. Many women activists have devoted their energy to research and writing, particularly in the legal domain, and have pointed out the contradiction of making a supposedly just Islamic society through extremely unjust laws subjugating women in the name of Islam.

Broadly speaking, one can distinguish two opposing perspectives in present-day Iran, Islamist and secularist, with many often overlapping views between. The secularists base their arguments on modern science, international conventions on human rights issues, and on philosophical ideas of social justice. The overall position of this perspective is that laws should ensure equity and the same rights for individuals regardless of gender. In their scenario, if a woman believes that as a Muslim she should obtain the permission of her husband to leave her home or to find employment, no one should prevent her. In fact, one can argue that if she does this of her own free will, she can then claim much more spiritual and public recognition for her beliefs. Thus, adopting a secular perspective does not mean being against Muslim beliefs. A problem is seen only if a state intended to impose one particular form of religious interpretation.

Not surprisingly, the secularist voices are frequently dismissed by the officials. Nevertheless, as attorney Mehranguiz Kar puts it:

> That is not a problem. The fact is that many Islamist activist women read these writings, and while they may disagree with our perspective and framework, it is rare to meet a woman who disagrees with the essence of the message. What woman, regardless of her ideological orientation would defend the free hand that men have in polygamy, divorce, or custody issues not to say criminal law? No woman really accepts that the value of her life is half as much as that of a man. So they (the Islamists) try to find ways and means of fighting these discriminations from their perspective and are often more successful than we are since many are trained in religious matters and language.[17]

The 1979 revolution also gave birth to an Islamist feminist movement(s) incorporating several groups and individuals (Hoodfar 1997; Paidar 1995; Ramazani 1993; Tabari and Yeganeh 1982).[18] Although they are critical of the way West and East have treated women, they also strongly object to the way Islam has been distorted and manipulated by a male-centric view that has tended to oppress women for centuries. Far from romanticizing a "glorious past," the Islamist women target many of the unfair aspects of traditional and conventional religious beliefs and practices as they relate to women. They dismiss the idea of a once just Islamic society. They then present alternative visions of Muslim women in an "ideal Islamic society" yet to be created.

The Islamist women have managed to politicize gender dimensions of

17. Personal communication, 1996.

18. The term "Islamist feminist" is mine, and rarely do the Islamist women activists present themselves as feminist. Because, however, their demands and activism are meant to improve women's legal and social position, I do consider them feminist although others prefer the term "gender activist."

Islam and to distinguish Islam and Muslim tradition from man-made interpretation. This position has afforded them a political space in which to challenge the law, and they have managed to bring about some major changes (Hoodfar 1995, 1996; Mir-Hosseini 1996; Kian 1997; Paidar 1995). Post-revolution events, particularly the fact that the much belated and modest reform of the family code was abrogated by the stroke of a pen and the realization that the revolutionary leaders had little time or patience to consult with women even on issues and concerns of women such as the family code and dress code, quickly brought a certain political maturity to the women's movement, for the most part made up of informal and decentralized small groups and individuals. They realized that to bring real and long-lasting change they would have to lobby not the government, as they did before the revolution, but the public.

Thus, they began a campaign to publicize terrible cases of "legal injustice" done to women in the areas of divorce and custody in the Islamic family court. Others concentrated on stories of polygyny, or of men neither fair nor wealthy enough to afford two households ruining, without any legal obstacle, the lives of all the women and children involved. All the men had to worry about was being punished on Judgment Day. If, however, a woman's scarf were pushed slightly too far back or if it were deemed the wrong color, there was a whole army of moral police, laws, and courts to punish them. Was it because the Islamic regime was worried about the heavy load God has to deal with on Judgment Day? Where was the wisdom and justice in this system except for the men who made the laws for their own convenience?[19]

The language and writing style of Islamist activist women is particularly simple and accessible, full of everyday or religious expressions and concepts. Because the discourse appears "personal," usually in the context of real life stories and with little overt political commentary, it has largely escaped censorship. Because they are well versed in Qur'anic and religious issues, these activists frequently back their discussions with religious and Qur'anic texts and sometimes even with a new interpretation. This process made many more women with religious tendencies interested in women's issues because no longer did they see a contradiction between their religiosity and the desire to improve their social and legal position in society. Moreover, many Islamist women have used their influence to gain access to national radio and television or to invite more liberal male religious leaders to give inter-

19. More recently, domestic violence and physical violence against women and children also are receiving so much attention that parliament has felt obliged to address the issues (Hoodfar forthcoming).

views on gender issues. Similarly filmmakers are encouraged to weave some of these contradictions into their films. Through these strategies the issues surrounding the legal treatment of women have become so much a part of public discourse that officials are forced not only to address the subject publicly but also to adopt a much more conciliatory tone on gender issues.

Major Achievements

The first manifestation of the success of the campaign was Ayatollah Khomeini's introduction of a new national marriage contract and family law in 1987 (Kar and Hoodfar 1996). Although this law did not go as far as many Muslim women activists had hoped, it was, nevertheless, one of most advanced marriage laws in the Middle East (perhaps right behind Tunisia and Turkey). Yet it did not deviate from conventional assumptions about "Islamic" law. Under this new law an official marriage contract stipulates conditions that put women in a stronger legal position within the marriage.

Because Muslim marriage is a contractual relationship, Muslim women and men had always had the opportunity to insert conditions in the marriage agreement although people rarely did. The new and standard contract removed much of the burden on individual brides (and their families) trying to secure a fairer marriage deal for themselves. Instead, the burden is shifted to the groom, who now must negotiate to remove the clauses he disagrees with, giving the bride's party leverage to request additional conditions of their own. This official format also provides some protection for those given in marriage too young to be able to negotiate effectively more equitable marriage conditions for themselves.

This success was followed by a decree from Ayatollah Khomeini granting martyrs' widows custody of their children even after remarriage.[20] Although this law does not extend to all women, its significance stems from breaking with the Shi'i belief that custody laws are Qur'anic and not subject to challenge. Thus, it opens the door for further change, especially because the stature of Ayatollah Khomeini prevents accusations that the law conflicts with Islamic jurisprudence. Similarly, in the area of divorce rights, several amendments have improved women's legal rights (Kar and Hoodfar 1996; Mir-Hosseini 1993, 1996).

Women continue to agitate for more fundamental changes by asserting that Islamic texts and traditions may be reinterpreted and then enacted into law. For instance, Iranian women campaigned for the *ojrat ol-mesal* (wages

20. For more discussion see Kar and Hoodfar 1996.

for housework) law, which was passed in December 1992. Islamist women activists argued that women, like all other Muslims, are entitled to the fruit of their labor on the grounds that Islam is against exploitation; that for centuries women had been denied this basic right; that in Islamic tradition wives have no duties to their husbands beyond being faithful and are not required to work in their husbands' homes, to the extent that women are not even obliged to breast-feed their children without payment from their husbands. Therefore, because all women do, in fact, work in their husbands' homes, they are entitled to the fruit of their labor! The argument, although novel and unconventional, was based on Islamic texts supported by Qur'anic verses.

The bill was initially resisted by the Islamic parliament and conservative religious leaders because it was an unconventional interpretation of "Islamic law." Because, however, the conservatives could not prove that it was un-Islamic, it gathered considerable popular support, and the law was eventually passed. Presently, a man who intends to divorce his wife without proving fault on her part must first pay housework wages for the duration of the marriage. Many women feel that, despite its problematic application, this law has provided a better bargaining position than ever before (Mir-Hosseini 1996; Kar and Hoodfar 1996). Nonetheless, to most women it is the symbolic and ideological value of this law that is significant. It stresses to society and to women, themselves, that their labor should not be taken for granted. More importantly, it demonstrates that there are many possible and unconventional interpretations of Islamic texts that have not yet been explored.

Criticism of government performance from women activists also resulted in the establishment of the Bureau of Women's Affairs, which reports directly to the president. This office coordinates the development of government policies and programs and is charged with improving the status of women. Thus, the bureau has established offices in many of the critical ministries such as justice and labor, to examine women's issues. Although members of these governmental organizations are appointed by the government, they have emerged, nonetheless, as a forum for women's complaints and for successful lobbying groups. In the past, the council has used its visibility to draw attention to women's concerns and gender discrimination.

◆   ◆   ◆

Both nationally and internationally, Islam is frequently used by the governments of Muslim societies to justify their discriminatory laws against women and their subordination as lesser citizens. In this chapter by examining the evolution of several debates, such as schooling for girls, the vicissitudes of women's political rights among religious authorities in Iran since the constitutional revolution in 1906, I demonstrate that "Islam" and *shari' a* have been adopted as convenient political excuses to deny women their social, legal, and political rights. Thus, acceptance of Islam and *shari' a* as justifications by national and international bodies such as the United Nations and other human rights organizations will inevitably compromise women in the name of religious tolerance.[21] Acquiescence amounts to silencing the voices of women and slowing down their legitimate right to be full-fledged citizens in their own country on the grounds that they are Muslims, which precludes equality with their male counterparts before the law.[22]

Faced with exclusion and discrimination, women worldwide have adopted appropriate strategies to improve their social and legal stand. In Iran, as in many other Muslim societies, the harsh legal treatment of women in the name of Islam has brought about, besides the secular feminist movement, a strong Islamist women's movement that has managed to mobilize women and to politicize women's issues and play a prominent role in the national political arena. The proponents of Islamist activism have taken issue with the male-centered interpretation of "sacred text" and the tradition of the Prophet, which they claim has been selectively used to deprive women of their rights. They distinguish "Islamic" from traditional practice, much of which is patriarchal. They present a women-centered interpretation of women's "Islamic rights" and have managed to popularize their version of Islamic interpretation to a considerable degree. In this manner they placed pressure on government to bring about some reforms, including in unconventional areas such as wages for housework. Given, however, that *shari' a* has been the single most weighty impediment to women's full citizenship, the significance of their achievements rests in their contesting the monopoly of male theological interpretation and producing a women-centered view of what are to be understood as Muslim women's rights and legal status.

An important element of their success stems from their realization that the current family code has prevented many of women's achievements to be translated to their empowerment. Therefore, they have made its reform their top priority. This has proved to be a strategic choice for the movement because all women regardless of their class, geographical, and cultural back-

21. Scarcely needing mention are the dubious grounds on which governments that frequently demonstrate religious intolerance are permitted to hide behind the principle of religious tolerance.

22. Moreover, because Islam, like all other religions, is understood and practiced differently in different cultures, the question arises as to which Islam should be given legitimacy by governments and extragovernmental bodies.

ground do experience daily their relegation to second-class citizens through imposition of family code. Thus, they have been much more receptive to the women-centered interpretation of women's Islamic rights, and relieved from accusations that they have turned their backs against Islam, they raise their voices and demand change. Without much formal organization, women make full use of their limited political space, not just by participating in political elections and making women's issues a prominent subject but also by the use of other spaces available to them such as radio and television, women's magazines, and traditional women's religious and semi-religious gatherings.

It is also important to point out that whereas Islamist women activists' conceptualization of women's position may appear to be diametrically opposed to that of secular feminists, in practice, they are close allies. Their demands are generally parallel as both groups strive to improve women's social and legal situation.

Their effectiveness in the political context of Iran, however, depends on them occupying seemingly opposing camps. Moreover, in the process of articulating their perspectives on women's rights, each side is educating the other side and the general public about the complex ways that ideology, culture, religion, and science may come together in justifying or denying women's rights and pushing for the empowerment and achievement of full personhood and citizenship for women.

15

The Citizenship of Jewish and Palestinian Arab Women in Israel

BARBARA SWIRSKI

IN 1998 JEWS IN ISRAEL celebrated the fiftieth anniversary of the transformation of the Jewish community in Palestine into a sovereign state. At the same time, the Palestinians in Israel bemoaned the fiftieth anniversary of the *nakba* (disaster)—the defeat of the Palestinian forces and their allies and the flight and expulsion of most of the Palestinian majority from the boundaries of the Jewish state. In the following pages I analyze the construction of citizenship in Israel and its impact on Jewish and Palestinian female citizens. Despite their different positions—as Jews and as non-Jews—in the Jewish state and despite their belonging to different religious communities, Jewish and Arab women have a number of meeting grounds. Foremost is the patriarchal family. Despite a prevailing myth that the "Israeli woman" is Western (Fogiel-Bijaouie 1997), neither Jewish nor Arab women fit the liberal model (itself a reification, as Joseph [1996a] has pointed out) of free, autonomous individuals whose relations with other, free autonomous individuals are based on contract. Rather, women's rights and obligations as citizens and their behavior as citizens depend not only on their "personhood" but also on their "familyhood"—their roles as daughters, wives, mothers, aunts, and so on, and the presence or absence of other family members—or the assumption of the same. This family is not a free association of individuals but an institution characterized by unequal power relations and governed by rules invented, interpreted, and administered by male communal authorities.

I thank Shlomo Swirski, Frances Raday, and Yoav Peled for their constructive comments.

Indeed, Berkovitch contends that the citizenship of Jewish women is constructed primarily through their family roles as bearers of children and as mothers. These roles are not seen as confined to the private sphere, but as transcending into the public one where women's childbearing roles are valorized: they become "mothers of soldiers" and "mothers of the nation." Berkovitch argues that the very presence of a Palestinian Arab minority in Israel contributes to this construction: Jewish women are assigned the duty of preserving the Jewishness of the Jewish state through reproduction (Berkovitch 1997). Although the point is, perhaps, overstated—the reproductive citizenship roles of Jewish women in Israel are certainly not unique—the emphasis on women's participation in the collective through the mediation of religious communities (in this case, the Jewish one), the basic unit of which is the family, is relevant to the present line of argument.

The second common ground for all female citizens in Israel is the construction of civil rights, which, failing to take women's gender disadvantage into account in their very conception (Rhode 1989), are much less relevant to the citizenship of women—Jewish or Arab—than they are to the citizenship of men, for whom they were designed. The third is the political right to serve in public office where both Jewish and Arab women are conspicuous by their absence. Presence may not constitute power, but absence surely presages powerlessness. The fourth is feminist political activity, the "civic behavior" that has shown the greatest potential for enhancing women's citizenship in Israel. As should already be clear, the following analysis combines rights and participatory approaches to citizenship (Lister 1996, 2).

Citizenship Mediated by Religious Communities

In contrast to the states of Western Europe and North America, there is no heritage of a republican construction of citizenship in Israel. Neither was there ever a separation between religion and state amongst the two major religious ethnic communities in Palestine: both Jews and Muslims were citizens of the British Mandatory state (1918–48), which preceded the establishment of the state of Israel, through their respective religious communities. This followed the practice of the Ottoman empire, in which each religious community, or *millah*, had been granted autonomy.

Shortly before Britain obtained the area of Palestine as part of the spoils of war, it had declared its intention of allowing the Jews to create a national homeland on that soil. Accordingly, in 1920, Palestine was opened to Zionist immigration. The British Mandate government made efforts to create an integrated political community in Palestine composed of both Arabs and Jews. The failure of those efforts increased the separateness of the Arab and

Jewish institutions and enhanced the powers of each (Wasserstein 1991). During the reign of the British Mandate government, Jews were allowed not only to maintain control over their own religious institutions and their own schools but also to create new institutions of self-rule, like the Zionist Executive, a quasi government; the Assafat Hanivharim, a representative political assembly; the Histadrut, a federation of Jewish labor unions; and the Haganah, a military organization. In contrast, the main quasi-governmental institution in the Arab community was the Supreme Muslim Council established by the government of Palestine in 1921 "with the conscious intention of conciliating Muslim Arabs and providing them with a form of representation and a certain autonomy that would compensate to some extent for the autonomous representative institutions granted to the Zionists. It involved the creation of, as it were, a Muslim *millet* in Palestine" (Wasserstein 1991, 132), to which the religious trusts and *shari'a* courts were transferred. During the British Mandate government, in both the Jewish and the Muslim communities, personal status matters remained under the jurisdiction of the respective religious communities.

In 1948, one *millah*—the Jewish one—the state of Israel, and a unitary regime were constituted. The situation is different from that in Lebanon where with the creation of the Lebanese state, each of the seventeen religious sects became subcommunities in their own right and with their own rights (Joseph 1991). In Israel one subcommunity became identical with the state; the other subcommunities did not maintain their autonomy but became residual categories, "non-Jews." All came under the jurisdiction and control of the Israeli state, but the "state" was defined as a Jewish state whose concerns were particularistic, that is, Jewish.

The Basis of Israeli Citizenship

The citizenship law of 1952 and its subsequent amendments set the rules for Israeli citizenship. Basically, there are two kinds of rules, those that apply to Jews and those that apply to non-Jews. Jews are granted citizenship on the basis of their Jewishness, that is, primarily on the basis of *birth to Jews* (jus sanguis), whereas Arabs are granted citizenship on the basis of *birth to parents who are citizens of Israel* (jus sanguis). While the citizenship law and its 1980 amendment accorded Arabs who remained within the borders of Israel after the 1948 war Israeli citizenship on the basis of residence, this was a one-time arrangement. Subsequently, Arabs have been granted citizenship only on the basis of birth to citizens (regardless of whether the birth takes place in Israel or abroad).

Neither Jewish nor Arab women are disadvantaged by Israeli citizenship regulations on the basis of their gender. Jewish women were formerly privileged because Jewishness was conceived of as passed on only by mothers: according to Jewish *halakha* (religious law), a Jew is a person born to a Jewish mother or a person who has converted to Judaism. Thus, Jewish religious law views women, not men, as the repositories of ethnic ascription, which in Israel translates into national affiliation. A 1971 amendment to the *Law of Return* expanded the criteria of eligibility for the benefits granted by the law to include persons not considered Jews under Jewish religious law: it accorded Israeli citizenship based on Jewishness also to children of Jewish fathers and to children with at least one Jewish grandparent. Since then, citizenship has been automatically conferred on almost all Jews and on the children and grandchildren of Jews (regardless of gender), on the spouses of Jews (regardless of gender), and on the spouses of the children and grandchildren of Jews who come to live in Israel. Exceptions are persons born abroad who have criminal records.

It is also possible to become a citizen of Israel through naturalization, but in practice this avenue is closed to Arabs (Adalah 1998, 38). The law states that the conditions for naturalization are residence in Israel for three of the five years preceding the naturalization request, the intention to settle in Israel, renouncement of previous citizenship or at least ceasing to act as citizen of another state, and "some" knowledge of the Hebrew language. The best an Arab woman or man who marries an Arab citizen of Israel can hope for is permanent residency. The procedure for family reunification is designed to discourage naturalization and permanent residency requests for Arab and other non-Jewish spouses of Israeli citizens: the alien spouse can only enter Israel on a tourist visa, and the visa has to be renewed every few months by leaving and re-entering the country. In the meantime, the spouse who is a citizen applies for family unification. During the waiting period, the alien does not enjoy social rights such as health care or social security insurance. In contrast, permanent residents are eligible for social rights, and although they cannot vote in national elections or run for national office, they can participate in local elections (Adalah 1998, 40). To become an Israeli citizen, non-Jews are required to denounce their foreign citizenship; in contrast, Jewish citizens can hold dual citizenship (Davis 1997, 48).

In 1998, the Israel Ministry of the Interior, which has always discouraged family unification requests by Arab citizens, took new measures to discourage the same requests by Jewish citizens marrying non-Jewish aliens—a not uncommon phenomenon among 1990s immigrants from the former Soviet Union (Dayan 1998). Among those measures were reexamination of the "Jewishness" of the Jewish applicant for family unification and, in some cases, nullification of the applicant's Jewish status—and citizenship. Thus, although the law accords Israeli citizenship to spouses and blood relations of Jews, in an attempt to prevent fictitious marriages, the Israel Ministry of the Interior is attempting to implement the law in a way that renders it void.

Among the conditions precluding permanent residence in Israel for both Jews and non-Jews is a criminal record, and for non-Jews, prior citizenship in one of the following countries: Lebanon, Syria, Saudi Arabia, Jordan, Iraq, or Yemen. Thus, Jordanian citizens marrying Palestinian citizens of Israel, including those residing in East Jerusalem, cannot become Israeli citizens, but their progeny are Israeli citizens by virtue of birth to an Israeli citizen. Consistent with a security interest, citizenship is also conferred on the parents of persons killed in the line of duty while serving in the Israeli Defense Forces, on the condition that they wish to make Israel their permanent home and also know some Hebrew.

Two Kinds of Citizenship

Analyzing citizenship in Israel, Peled distinguishes between two different bases. One, first-class citizenship, he calls "ethno-republican citizenship. "Only the holders of this type of citizenship, reserved, by definition, for Jews, can demonstrate true civic virtue, reflected, first and foremost, in military service. Three years of military service are compulsory for Jewish males and two for Jewish females; Arab males and females are in practice (but not by law) exempt (Shafir and Peled 1998). Jewish married and pregnant women and mothers have always been exempt, and the consensus on the matter has never been challenged because the soldiering role is perceived as adversely affecting the more important citizenship roles of childbearing and mothering (Berkovitch 1997). Feminist scholars have argued that the fact that Jewish women are obliged to do military service is not a reflection of basic equality between the sexes; rather, for most women, it arrests their development and later disadvantages them in the labor market vis-à-vis Jewish men (Bloom 1993; Izraeli 1993, 1997). Druze and Bedouin men—but not women—can volunteer for military service under an arrangement between Jewish state officials (males) and Arab heads of extended families (males), in which the former allow the latter to retain control of their own women.

Peled describes the second basis for citizenship as a "quasi-liberal" second-class citizenship that is reserved for those who are not Jewish, that is, Palestinian Arabs. Arab citizens are entitled to lower-level civil and political rights. Another difference is that their exemption from the military has served as a basis for discrimination regarding social rights. But the real difference between Jewish and Arab citizens is inherent in the definition of Israel as "the state of the Jewish people." On the one hand, it is not necessary for a Jew to be a believer or a religiously observant person to be included in "the Jewish people"; for most, this is an ascriptive, not an acquired status. On the other hand, there is no way—short of conversion—that Arab citizens can accept and identify with Israel as "the state of the Jewish people"; obviously, such identification would involve the negation of their own identity as Arabs and as Palestinians. As Sarsour notes: "Due to his [*sic*] very ascription, the Israeli Arab citizen cannot accept the ideology of the Zionist movement. . . . Israeli Arabs have low social status, because in Israel the social status of the citizen is determined not only by education and professional achievements, but by the degree of identification with the central goals of Israel as a Jewish Zionist state" (Sarsour 1985, 479).

Because Arabs cannot, by definition, be Zionists, they cannot partake in the common good of society (Shafir and Peled 1998). The problem is not just one of identity, of course; those Arabs who do openly identify with the Jewish state, like some of the Druze and Bedouins who volunteer for military service, remain second-class citizens, for national origin is more important than support of Zionism in the exercise of political and social rights.

Davis (1997) conceptualizes the two tiers of citizenship in Israel as *jinsiyya*, "passport citizenship," and *muwatana*, "democratic citizenship": the former, which characterizes both Arabs and Jews, bestows equal access to civil and political rights, whereas the latter, which characterizes Jews only, bestows equal access to social and economic rights (7–9).

The Implications of the Nonseparation of Religion and State for Jewish and Palestinian Arab Female Citizens of Israel

It has already been noted that there is no separation between state and religion in Israel, and that citizenship is mediated by membership in religious communities. This is a critical distinction, for the separation of religion and state makes it possible for women to become emancipated from religious law, which is patriarchal under Jewish, Christian, and Islamic traditions, and to come under the jurisdiction of civil law, which, in contrast to religious law, is assumed to be gender neutral (but not equally beneficial to women and men). Although Jewish women are privileged in comparison with Arab women, their ability to act in matters of faith and personal status is circumscribed by Jewish law, which defines them as inferior to Jewish men.

In Israel gender equality does not have the status of a fundamental right;

it was defined as "a fundamental principle" by the Supreme Court in 1987 but was not accorded constitutional priority (Raday 1993, 19). Lacking constitutional status, the principle of gender equality can be overriden by religious considerations. It is symptomatic of this situation that in 1992, when the Basic Law of Human Dignity and Freedom was legislated, it came short of removing the main legal obstacle to the attainment of gender equality in Israel—the jurisdiction of religious courts in personal status matters. As Raday points out, "The significance of [the] priority of religious values over egalitarian values is that it incorporates and endorses a patriarchal concept of women's role in the family" (1993, 19). The subordination of the principle of equality to precepts of patriarchal religious law cannot be understood without the political context: since the establishment of the state of Israel, governments have been formed by coalitions that have nearly always included Jewish religious political parties. These have been able to impose a certain degree of adherence to Jewish law on all Jews living in Israel, regardless of whether they consider themselves secular or observant. The most damaging stipulations of an arrangement in force since 1948, referred to as the "status quo," allow rabbinic (Jewish religious) courts to maintain jurisdiction over person-status matters. This means that, in domestic litigation, women's status continues to be inferior at the very outset, women cannot be judged by other females (only men can sit as judges in religious courts), and they have no choice but to plead their causes in a framework of laws prejudicial to their gender. The arrangement was a political compromise made between socialist and fundamentalist Jewish male leaders (Friedman 1988) at the expense of Jewish women, and it has been kept for fifty years.

There are those who argue that this is too narrow an interpretation, and that even without the Jewish religious parties' participation in coalition governments, Jewish religious law (and, by implication, Muslim, Druze, and Christian religious law) would retain its jurisdiction over personal status matters because there is general consensus among Jews in Israel that one expression of the Jewishness of the state should continue to be reflected in the autonomy of the Jewish religious courts in personal status matters. Such an arrangement represents a continuity with that in effect in Poland, the largest Jewish community in the Diaspora before World War I where assimilationist elements represented the Jewish community vis-à-vis the Polish authorities while the Orthodox retained control of the rabbinate, the cemeteries, the religious schools, and the ritual baths (Frost 1998, 57).

The nonseparation of religion and state and the jurisdiction of religious law in personal status matters means, in the words of Joseph, that "membership in a religious sect is not voluntary but a requirement of citizenship"

(Joseph 1996a). Certain acts—foremost among them marriage and divorce—cannot be performed without the mediation of religious institutions. There is no civil marriage and no civil divorce in Israel. This principle, however, impacts differently on Jewish and Muslim women.

Jewish Women

Halakha (Jewish law) defines women as precious commodities (under the oft-quoted Talmudic phrase, marriages are consummated by contract, by money, or by sexual relations). A Jewish woman cannot divorce without the consent of her husband even if she is battered or her husband is missing or insane. Although contemporary Jewish law does not permit a Jewish man to divorce without consent either, there are special conditions under which he may take a second wife. The Jewish religious courts privilege men in other ways as well: a man can commit adultery and eventually marry his lover, whereas a married woman is forbidden to marry hers, and any children born from such a union are considered bastards. A bastard cannot marry another Jew unless he or she is also a bastard; neither can a bastard marry outside the faith (unless the ceremony takes place abroad) because there is no provision for intermarriage in Israel.

Another vestige of women's subjection to men in the framework of the family, written into Jewish religious law and still enforced in rabbinic courts in Israel, is the levirate marriage. A woman whose husband dies, leaving her childless, must be released from her deceased husband's brother (who otherwise is obligated to marry and impregnate her to perpetuate the family line) in a humiliating ceremony carried out in rabbinic court. Often extortion payments are involved before the "anchored" woman gets her release. Jewish women's organizations—Na'amat, the Women's International Zionist Organization, the shelters for battered women, the Israel Women's Network, and the Agunot (anchored women) Association—have expended considerable energy in attempts to find religious or civil solutions to these problems, but without much success.

Wife Battering and Rape. In Israel, as elsewhere, violence against women, especially marital violence, is common. Whereas Jewish religious law generally puts women at a disadvantage, the case of marital rape is an exception. In 1981 an Israel Supreme Court judgment defined marital rape as a criminal offense. The basis for that decision was *halakha* (Jewish religious law), which instructs men to woo their wives, not force themselves upon them (Maimonides). The majority of the justices indicated that the ruling would not be applicable to Muslims if Muslim law differed on the issue; the solo woman justice on the case dissented, stating that in her opinion, the decision could apply equally to women of different religions (Raday 1996). In 1989 an amendment to the penal code was passed prohibiting marital rape for all Israeli women, regardless of their religious community.

In 1977, when the first shelter for battered women was founded, there was no law against wife battering. Moreover, the founders of the shelter (the writer among them) were warned that Jewish women, not to mention Arab ones, would never leave their families to seek refuge in a shelter. Within two months of opening, the facility was overcrowded and has remained so ever since. In 1998 there were twelve shelters for battered women in Israel. The first rape crisis center was also set up in 1977.

In the wake of lobbying by feminist organizations, new civil legislation enacted in 1991 made wife battering a crime and enabled women to obtain six-month restraining orders to keep abusive husbands out of the house. The literature is replete with reasons why women do not often have recourse to this remedy; most focus on the nature of the family and the control it exerts over women or on the nature of the relations between spouses (Swirski 1993b).

Muslim Women

Because 76 percent of Palestinian Arab citizens are Muslims, I focus here on Islamic religious law as practiced in Israel. Under *shari'a* women's subordination to their husbands and families is evinced in the fact that they are not considered the natural custodians of their own children, in contradiction to Israeli civil law; *shari'a* (Muslim religious) courts in Israel generally grant divorced women custody of young children (they are viewed as in need of a woman's care), but when males reach age seven and females age nine, custody reverts to the father or his family. In such a situation women may relinquish custody in the present so as to avoid a painful separation in the future. Moreover, pressure is often brought to bear on a woman by her husband's family to give up the children altogether in return for a divorce, and the *shari'a* courts in Israel accept extortion of this kind. Under Muslim law the man is the master of the house; when a couple divorce, the woman leaves and the home and furniture remain with the man unless the marriage contract states otherwise.

In practice, the Israeli legal system gives Jewish, Druze, and Christian women more autonomy than Muslim women: Jewish and Druze women have the option of taking child custody, child support, alimony, and property rights litigation to either the religious or the civil courts; in the latter, their status is equal to that of their husbands and their appeals have more chance of success. Moreover, the judgment may be handed down by a member of their own sex, but not by a member of their own religious community because to date no Arab women have served as judges in Israeli civil courts. Christian women can go to civil courts for child custody and child support. Muslim women, however, have no choice in any of these matters (Working Group on the Status of Palestinian Women in Israel 1997, 57): in all matters of personal status, religion—in the form of religious courts—determines who they will live with, where they will live, and how well they will live. The state—in the form of officialdom or legislature—has failed to intervene. This policy of nonintervention is not a case of cultural autonomy; for example, state officials do not hesitate to interfere with community practices in other matters. "Communal control" is maintained primarily in one area of life—gender relations. This arrangement is an example of the alliance between men—Jewish officials and Muslim heads of extended families—at the expense of Muslim women over whom Jewish men have permitted Muslim men to maintain tight control.

Early Marriage and Forced Marriage. Women who marry at an early age are usually more amenable to the control of the husband and his family. The minimum legal marriage age in Israel for girls is seventeen, unless special permission is obtained to marry younger, and underage marriage is rare for women of all religions. Marriage under the age of twenty is another matter: in 1995 nearly half of Muslim and Druze brides were under the age of twenty, compared with 19 percent of Christian and 12 percent of Jewish brides (Israel Central Bureau of Statistics 1998b, table 3.5).

According to the report of the Working Group on the Status of Palestinian Women in Israel (1997, 59–60), forced marriage is widespread in Israel, particularly among Muslims and especially among Bedouins. Fathers and other male relatives may sell young women to older men. Women cannot marry without the consent of their parents and "even the consent of brothers or other relatives" (Haj Yahia 1995, 438). Thus, the life chances of Palestinian females in Israel are determined by the practices of their religious community and of the male members of their families. The state—the police and the courts—does not intervene: there is no law against forced marriages, probably because the phenomenon is scarcely known among Jews in contemporary Israel. The Working Group describes another practice that evinces the lack of autonomy of some Palestinian women: fathers or other male relatives may sign the marriage contract in lieu of the bride. Thus, she has no say either about whom she marries or what the conditions of that union are. The legality of this practice is questionable, but it has not been challenged (Working Group on the Status of Palestinian Women in Israel 1997, 60).

Another type of forced marriage is the exchange marriage (*badal*), under which a man avoids paying the bride price by giving his sister or daughter to the father or brother of his bride. Henceforth, the futures of the two women depend not on their own actions or even on their own relations within the family. If one marriage breaks up, the other does as well, regardless of the sentiments of the persons involved. The one who has the least to say is the woman who has been traded away (Swirski and Hasan 1998).

Just as the Muslim law permits the marriage of women against their wills, it also permits "tyrannical divorce" in which all a man need do to divorce his wife is to say, "You are divorced." *Shari'a* courts in Israel uphold these summary divorces in violation of the Equal Rights for Women Law of 1951, which expressly forbids divorcing a woman against her will. In addition to the consequences of divorce mentioned above—the loss of home, property, and the custody of older children—a divorced woman cannot register even younger children in her passport without the signature of her former husband. Here again Jewish men (in the Israel Ministry of the Interior) appear to have conspired with Muslim men against Muslim women because there is no equivalent requirement for Jewish women (Working Group on the Status of Palestinian Women in Israel 1997, 60).

Polygamy. Although *shari'a* law allows a man to marry as many as four wives, the Equal Rights for Women Law outlawed polygamy in 1951. According to the Working Group on the Status of Palestinian Women, the civil law has not been enforced among Muslims (1997, 59), and polygamous marriages involving Muslim citizens of Israel are still being performed in Israel, in the Palestinian Authority, and in Egypt. Some are registered and reported and others are not. Like tyrannical divorce, granting child custody to fathers, and awarding all the marital property to divorcing husbands, the case of polygamy illustrates the differential enforcement of civil laws intended to be universal. It also highlights the importance of the religious community in determining the life chances of Palestinian Arab women in Israel.

Wife Battering and Marital Rape. For Muslim, Druze, and Christian women in Israel, marital rape is an oxymoron; a woman has no rights over her own body and is supposed to be sexually available to her husband at all times (Working Group on the Status of Palestinian Women in Israel 1997, 15–16). Women's subjugation to their husbands may also involve physical abuse (Shalhoub-Kevorkian 1997). The *Prevention of Domestic Violence Act* of 1991 does not provide an effective remedy, as many young couples live in the same building as the husband's parents, and a woman who has the courage to request a restraining order is likely to be threatened by her inlaws and other members of her husband's family. Moreover, her husband will most likely take up residence downstairs.

Thus, although Israeli civil law—in the form of the Equal Rights for Women Law and the Prevention of Domestic Violence Act—appears to alter the boundary between the public and the private spheres, enlarging the area of the public one, the Muslim family, by means of the religious autonomy of the Muslim community, moves the border right back to where it was before. And the public defenders—the police and the courts—lack both the will and the wherewithal to reclaim the territory. The winner is the Palestinian Arab family, that is, Arab men, and the losers are Arab women. Recognizing this reality, in the 1990s Palestinian Arab women have begun organizing advocacy groups, shelters for battered women, and rape crisis centers.

Family Honor Murders. The most extreme example of the absence of women's right to the integrity of their own bodies is evinced in so-called "family honor" murders. Between 1990 and 1997, *Albadeel* (The Alternative), a coalition of Palestinian organizations monitoring such killings, documented fifty-two cases of Israeli Palestinian women murdered for breaking sexual codes (Working Group on the Status of Palestinian Women in Israel 1997, 63). These murders are carried out by members of the woman's family, who view the murder as the only way to "cleanse" the family name. Women sometimes cooperate with male family members in dealing out the ultimate punishment to sisters who have gone astray and, thus, contribute to their own subjugation. Israeli courts treat the perpetrators of "family honor" crimes with leniency; prosecutors often charge the accused with manslaughter rather than with premeditated murder, which carries a mandatory sentence of life imprisonment (64).

This brief examination of how family and religion construct citizenship for Jewish and Palestinian Arab women in Israel belies the liberal notion of the private sphere as a refuge from the tyranny of the state. On the contrary, it is often the state that is called upon to liberate women from the tyranny of religion as reflected in the institution of the family. Both Jewish and Palestinian Arab feminists have expressed their citizenship through political activity that involves demanding that the state protect women from both family and religious dictates and by creating alternative frameworks—shelters, rape-crisis centers, and advocacy groups. It should be noted, however, that this strategy has been more effective for Jewish than for Arab women. Firstly, as second-class citizens who often belong to a lower social class, Arab women feel less able to challenge the family norms of their community than do Jewish women. Secondly, as Mar'i and Mar'i point out, after 1948, the only domain that remained under the control of Palestinian Arab men was the domestic one. In this situation, the concept of family honor took on greater importance than it had before the establishment of the state (Mar'i and Mar'i 1993). A third factor in the equation is the Israeli state, whose officials allowed the traditional leadership of Palestinian Arab localities—male clan heads—to maintain control over their own women in exchange for compliance with other policies. Thus, state institutions—the law, the police and the courts—provide in practice more protection to Jewish than to Arab women.

The Civil Rights of Jewish and Palestinian Arab Women Citizens of Israel

Adopting Marshall's distinction between the civil, political and social rights of citizenship (1964), the following sections will attempt to illustrate the meaning of these rights for Jewish and Arab women in Israel.

Civil rights were drawn up by men of a particular class in an era in which the public sphere was their exclusive domain. The fact that since that time women have been entering the public domain in greater numbers is not generally reflected in civil rights laws and their interpretations (Rhode 1989; Weisberg 1993). The point can be illustrated by examining the Basic Law: Human Dignity and Freedom, legislated by the Israeli Knesset in 1992, a law that enjoys constitutional status. The Basic Law protects six basic rights: (1) the right to life, body integrity, and human dignity, (2) the right to property, (3) the right to the protection of life, body, and dignity, (4) the right to individual liberty, (5) the right to leave and enter Israel, and (6) the right to privacy. The law states, "There shall be no violation of the life, body or dignity of any person as such." The lawmakers saw no necessity of providing explanations because the meaning of the phrase was deemed obvious. But is it? A number of questions immediately come to mind: Is the law valid in the public sphere only, or does it apply to the private one as well? Is it meant to deter violations of human dignity on the part of public institutions—the police, the courts, the prisons, and the schools—or is it intended to prevent such violations also within the framework of the private sphere, the family? Is it meant to prevent "impersonal" violations on the part of persons who are strangers to one another, or does it refer to damage to life, person, and human dignity perpetrated by family members or lovers? The question is relevant because women's basic human rights are violated mostly in the private sphere, not in the public one, and the perpetrators are mainly spouses and other family members. Although the question has not been tested in the courts, I venture to say that the answer to all of the above is negative. And if this is the case, the progress made by ensconcing this right in constitutional law is much less relevant for Israeli women than for Israeli men.

The same could be said of the fifth article of the Basic Law: "There shall be no deprivation or restriction of the liberty of a person by imprisonment, arrest, extradition or by any other manner." Here the law provides examples of specific ways in which individual liberty can be infringed upon, and these examples belie the intention: the law refers primarily to institutions of the state—police departments, detention halls, prisons—against whose abuses the law aims to protect the individual. Although theoretically it applies equally to women and men, the fact is that male citizens of Israel are far more likely to be detained than female ones because they are more active in the public sphere. In contrast, women are in need of protection in the private sphere because that is the locus of most of the infringements on their rights to individual dignity and freedom. It is not enough for the law to add "by any other manner"; obviously, it was not intended to give women protection from husbands and partners who lock them in the house or infringe on their liberty in more subtle ways.

The sixth right protected by the Basic Law may even conflict with women's right to individual liberty: "There shall be no entry into the private premises of a person who has not consented thereto." The premises in question are, of course, the home. Most homes are occupied jointly by men and women, so to provide protection for the woman it is necessary to violate the privacy of the man. Although the law expressly refers to the person's private premises or home (a man's home is his castle), it does not expressly refer to the most frequent site of violations of women's bodies, women's human dignity, and women's individual freedom—the home (a woman's home is her prison). Had the law been formulated with women besides men in mind, it would have expressly stated that in case of conflict, the right to privacy is to be subordinated to the right to life, body integrity, and individual liberty.

The second right protected by the Basic Law is the right to property. There should be no doubt that this right was designed for men, who in Israel—as elsewhere—own most of the private property. Although a 1972 civil law stipulates that all the property accumulated during a marriage belongs to both spouses in equal measure and is to be equally divided between them in the event of divorce, Jewish men usually control the so-called family assets, and, in the case of divorce, walk away with the lion's share. This is the best scenario. The worst is reserved for Muslim women, who have to adjudicate in the *shari'a* courts where in case of divorce home and hearth belong to the man.

Thus, civil rights, as illustrated in a Basic Law that has been hailed as a great step forward for the Israeli democracy, are more relevant for male property owners operating in the public sphere than for women without private assets and in need of protection in the private sphere. Raday argues (personal communication 1998) that the concept of civil rights does not preclude its application to relations between private citizens, pointing to the U.S. *Roe v Wade* decision in which a majority of Supreme Court justices concluded that the Fourteenth Amendment guarantee of personal liberty implies a right of privacy "broad enough to encompass a woman's decision whether or not to terminate her pregnancy" unless there was a more compelling state interest such as protecting maternal health or fetal life (Rhode 1989, 208–9).

She admits, however, that in Israel the application of the concept of civil rights to relations between citizens has been less dramatic than in the United States and less "liberating" because the decisions handed down by the courts "have ignored the history of women's deprivation and their inferior socio-economic power" (Raday 1994, 39). Moreover, Raday further contends that "the doctrine of privatization of civil rights [their application to relations between private citizens] may paradoxically weaken the principle of group equality . . . without directives relating to the prevention of the abuse of socio-economic power, it may reinforce the formalistic-individualistic approaches to application of the principle" (40).

Catherine MacKinnon clinches the point: "[The privacy doctrine, one of the basic civil rights, is] defined by everything that feminism reveals women have not been allowed to be or to have. . . . Women have no privacy to lose or to guarantee. . . . The ultimate meaning of privacy in Roe: women are guaranteed by the public no more than what we can get in private—that is, what we can extract through our intimate association with men. Women with privileges get rights" (MacKinnon 1996, 990–91).

The present discussion would be incomplete without reference to the peculiar Israeli aspects of the Basic Law: Human Dignity and Freedom of 1992. The first is the wording of article 1: "The purpose of this Basic Law is to protect human dignity and liberty in order to anchor in a Basic Law the values of the State of Israel as a Jewish and democratic state." As has been pointed out, the law emphasizes the ethnic nature of the Israeli state; at the same time, it fails to relate to the Arab minority (Adalah 1998, 17–18). Moreover, the law fails to supersede earlier laws that are prejudicial both to women (all women) and to Arab citizens, as "This Basic Law should not affect the validity of any law in force prior to the commencement of the Basic Law." The laws prejudicial to women that the Israeli equivalent of a Bill of Rights fails to supersede are those giving religious courts exclusive jurisdiction in matters of marriage and divorce (and, as noted, for Muslim women—all personal status matters). Criticizing the failure to supersede the prerogative of the religious courts, Raday warns, "New generations of children, legislatures and judges, brought up on the proposed Basic Law, would be socialized into accepting the idea that marriage is beyond the boundaries of justice and that inequality for women is constitutionally tolerable" (Raday 1998, 16).

The laws prejudicial to Arab citizens are the Emergency Regulations of 1945 enacted by the British Mandate government and still in force in Israel. These provide the mechanism by which the Israeli government can confiscate lands belonging to Arab citizens and impose censorship, illegalize organizations considered hostile, and restrict the use of telecommunications (Bardenstein 1998, 60).

Another aspect of the concept of civil rights relevant to this discussion is the fact that the institutions of the state most closely connected with civil rights are the courts: whether civil rights are not only recognized in principle but also enjoyed in practice depends on a person being aware of her rights and being able to afford the costs of litigation if those rights are violated (Marshall 1964). But how many women who suffer from "domestic" violence know that not only their bodies but also their *rights* are being violated? How many go to the police? How many go to a lawyer? How many will be able to afford a good defense?

The courts may be the venue for the realization of civil rights, but they are also the home turf of the dominant groups in society. This means that even if a woman does get "her day in court," it is likely to end unfavorably. This tendency is evinced in a study conducted in the early 1990s on gender bias in Israeli courts. Although the cases analyzed were criminal ones, the findings are relevant to the present discussion. Firstly, judges appeared to attribute greater credibility to men than to women. Secondly, when the accused was a stranger to a woman victim, the prison term he received was nearly double that received when the accused was a family member. Thirdly, the conviction rate in crimes against life was found to be lower when the victim was a woman and the sentence shorter (Bogosh and Don Yechiya 1997). Thus, the study supports the above contention that men are the primary subjects of civil rights and that these rights are designed to be realized in the public, not the private sphere.

The Social Rights of Jewish
and Palestinian Arab Women

Social rights are conceived of as claims citizens have on the state for conditions that are the sine qua non of the active exercise of citizenship: the right to work, the right to economic security, the right to education, health care, and housing. A brief look at some of these reveals a dual system with different standards for Jewish and Palestinian Arab citizens and different standards for women and men as well. It also demonstrates that despite the trend of increasing universalization and individualization of social rights, changes in eligibility criteria do not have the power to erase the Jew/Arab dichotomy or to neutralize the mediating effects of family and social class on the actual enjoyment of social rights. I examine the right to work, the right to economic security, and the right to education.

The Right to Work

The right to work was the issue around which Jewish feminists in the pre-state Jewish community in Palestine rallied at their first meeting in 1911. They won the right to do the kind of work most valued at the time—farming, and, somewhat later, road and house building. Although the Jewish women who fought the men in their community for this right were never more than a small minority, they set the tone (see Bernstein 1987; Izraeli 1981; Swirski 1993a). The fact that they were young women unfettered either by religious tradition or marriage and buttressed by socialist ideals is also extremely relevant.

The state of Israel has no basic law guaranteeing the right to work (or any other social right, for that matter), but there are a number of laws forbidding gender discrimination at the workplace (Raday 1993). Women's employment is characterized by (1) large differences between Jewish and Arab women and (2) a gendered labor market: most women work in occupations in which they constitute the majority of employees, and women constitute 75 percent of employees in education, health, and social services (Israel Central Bureau of Statistics 1998a), and (3) among Jews, class differences in accordance with ethnic origin, and (4) lower pay for women, especially at the upper rungs of the occupational ladder.

The most salient trend is increased workforce participation for Jewish women, which began with the expansion of public services in the 1970s and continued with the growth of the business and financial sectors of the economy in the 1980s and 1990s. Another factor that encouraged women's entry into the labor market was the rising standard of living, which the average family could not maintain without two salaries. Between 1976 and 1996 the labor force participation of Jewish women increased from 36 percent to 51 percent.

Antidiscrimination laws, notwithstanding, women receive lower remuneration than men for the same or equivalent work. The gap is 25 percent in the public services (Commission on Women's Salaries in the Public Sector 1998) and 50 percent in the financial sector (Atzmon and Izraeli 1993).

The former gap appears to be narrowing, the latter widening. Since 1992 women's unemployment has been higher than men's.

Among Jewish women the employment patterns of Mizrahi women (whose origins are in the Middle East and North Africa) differ from those of Ashkenazi women (whose origins are in Europe or the Americas) owing to differences in education: Ashkenazi women are concentrated at the upper end of the occupational scale, with 46 percent working in the academic and free professions and 4 percent in management, whereas Mizrahi women are concentrated in the middle, with 62 percent working in clerical, sales, or service jobs (Israel Central Bureau of Statistics 1996, table 12.15).

Among Palestinian Arab women the average labor force participation (1996) of Christian women is 33 percent, Druze women, 29 percent, and Muslim women, 13 percent (Israel Central Bureau of Statistics 1998a). The differences reflect differential openness of the respective religious communities to women's employment outside the home besides differences in education. Whereas Jewish women won the right to work in productive labor before the establishment of the state, Arab women ceased to engage in productive labor with the establishment of the state. Formerly, rural Arab women had worked in the fields owned by their own families; the expulsions during and immediately following the 1948 war, in which many Arab families were uprooted from their villages and became internal refugees, and the subsequent state confiscation of additional Arab lands left Arab peasant women confined to their households while their husbands sought employment outside the village or town. The military government, in force until 1966, and the state's neglect of Arab localities in its development plans from 1948 to the present (1999) meant that employment opportunities for both men and women were and still are extremely limited, more so for women than for men because "family honor" norms often prevent Muslim and Druze women from traveling any distance by themselves or from working side by side with men. The present obstacles to Arab women's realization of the right to work include the norms of their religious communities, the shortage of local employment opportunities, limited education, and discrimination; many public service positions have been closed to Arab citizens. Moreover, the limitation of employment opportunities has been and is still used by the state as a method of social control: Arab candidates for teaching and other public service positions need to pass a "security test" before they are hired. This knowledge may cause male family members to discourage female ones from engaging in political activities that may be frowned upon by state authorities.

The higher their education, the higher the workforce participation of Palestinian Arab women in Israel, whose families and communities expect them to cease working after marriage, unless they are highly educated and work in socially acceptable fields such as teaching or social work. In 1996 Arab women were found mostly near the top and at the bottom of the occupational ladder: 28 percent worked in the academic or free professions, and 36 percent were employed as skilled or unskilled laborers, mostly in the textile, clothing, and food-processing industries (Israel Central Bureau of Statistics 1998c, table 12.15). Palestinian Arab women employed in industry are mostly unmarried, and their jobs are becoming redundant as Israeli and multinational firms move their factories and workshops to the new JET set—Jordan, Egypt, and Turkey—where wages are 80 percent lower. Arab women earn less, on the average, than Jewish women, especially in small localities (Bendelac 1996).

The Right to Economic Security

Israel has a highly developed welfare state that can be examined using the criteria suggested by Esping-Andersen (1990), Orloff (1993), and O'Connor (1996), who look at the extent of commodification (workforce participation) and decommodification (ability to maintain a socially acceptable standard of living without working) of citizens, in general, and of women citizens, in particular. Esping-Andersen makes a distinction between the right to social benefits based on (1) need, (2) workforce participation, and (3) citizenship (1990); Orloff (1993) finds this paradigm inadequate, because it fails to take into account the extent to which legislation and praxis are based on patriarchal values, evinced in whether the recipient of the benefit is the family or the individual, and the inclusion or exclusion from the welfare state of issues of particular relevance to women, such as maternity benefits, childcare, violence against women, and care for the elderly. She suggests that the welfare state be examined for its capacity to enable a person to form and maintain an autonomous household (Orloff 1996, 39).

To illustrate, I examine old-age pensions, children's allowances, and special benefits for solo mothers and how these benefits impact on different female citizens of Israel.

State Old-Age Pensions (Social Security). Examining the development of old-age pensions in Israel, I find the same trend that characterizes most of Israel's social transfers—a gradual change from family-based benefits to individual-based ones.

First instituted in 1954, state old-age pensions were conceived as a social insurance program for minimum income security. At inception, they were flat rate, but later increments were added for longer years of work contribution and for retirement postponement. In 1999 employers and employees paid a certain percentage of wage to the National Insurance Institute, and, at the age of retirement, employees receive a minimum pension: 16 percent of the average wage for a single person (man) and 24 percent for a person (man) with a dependent (wife). Following the European example, the retirement age for men was set at five years later than that for women: seventy compared with sixty-five (early retirement: sixty-five compared with sixty)— the rationale being that women were more frail than men and should be decommodified earlier.

Before January 1996, women who did not work outside the home did not receive old-age pensions; rather, their husbands received a 50 percent increment for them as dependents. Thus, homemakers' claims—or rather their husbands' claims—were based on women's marital roles and not on their own caretaking contributions to family and society or on their citizenship. As such, they were "worth" 50 percent of what men were worth. Moreover, their "worth" at retirement age was determined by their husbands' employment record: if he received the maximum state pension, he was entitled to an additional 50 percent of the maximum for a dependent spouse, but if he received no more than the minimum, the increment for his spouse was 50 percent of the minimum (minimum monthly state pension was U.S.$240, maximum, $420 in January 1999). This changed in January 1996 when women who did not work outside the home could claim, for the first time, a minimum old-age pension for themselves at the age of sixty-five as a result of a new law drawn up by feminist legislators.

The limitations of the new law are, first, that it does not apply to women who reached retirement age before January 1996. Homemakers are not entitled to increments for additional years of service to the family or for postponing "retirement"; there is no "caretaker parity" that compensates women for their service to the family the way men are compensated for their service to the economy (Orloff 1996, 40). Although the arrangement for men and women working outside the home is technically gender neutral, it favors men because it is modeled on male patterns of labor participation. It disadvantages women because women work fewer years, on the average, and because care work is not taken into account. It also disadvantages Palestinian Arab women and, to a lesser degree, Mizrahi Jewish women for the same reason. Were the pension law to take women's care work into account, it would give women an additional benefit for each year spent in care work just as it gives wage earners an additional benefit for each year spent in the labor force.

The maximum state old-age pension (including increments for additional years of work and for postponing retirement) for a sole individual and for an individual plus dependent spouse is 28 percent and 42 percent, respectively, of the national average wage. This is only slightly above poverty level. Those whose incomes fall below that level can apply for income supplements, which operate on the same principle as the old-age pensions before 1996 under which the basic unit is the family and a dependent wife is worth one-half the pension of a working man. Income supplements bring the individual or couple up to the poverty line. No figures are available on differences between the actual benefits received by Palestinian Arab and Jewish women of retirement age, and there are no figures on differences between Jewish women of different ethnic origin.

Child Allowances. Together with old-age pensions, child allowances make up the lion's share of transfer payments in Israel. Like old-age pensions, they are what raises many low-income families above the poverty line. Because they form part of a system that includes income tax deductions, they also constitute a significant contribution to the income of middle-class families. First instituted in 1959, the original purpose of the child allowance was to raise the family income of recent Jewish (male) immigrants from the Middle East and North Africa, who, owing to a limited labor market, discrimination, and family size, did not earn enough to support their families. The allowances were first given only to heads of families with four or more children; they were tax exempt and not very high. In 1965 wage earners became eligible for additional allowances for their first three children paid together with their monthly salaries and taxed. In 1970, following economic expansion, the widening of the socioeconomic gaps between Ashkenazi and Mizrahi Jews and social unrest, a third allowance, called the "special increment for army veterans," was introduced for the fourth and subsequent children to parents whose immediate family members had served in the Israel Defense Forces. Most Arab families, who were, on the average, much poorer than Jewish families, were excluded from this benefit while ways were found to award it to Jews who did not conform to the criterion (Rosenhek 1995, 190). For families eligible for all three benefits, the additional income was very significant.

In 1975 a new reform was instituted that combined the child allowance with the income tax system, under which every family received both an income tax deduction and an allowance for every child up to the age of eighteen, and allowances were transferred monthly to the bank account of the children's mothers. "Special increments for army veterans" continued to be paid for the third and subsequent children, which meant that most Arab mothers, who had, on the average, more children than Jewish ones, were excluded. Between 1994 and 1997, the "special increment for army veterans" was gradually extended to all families. Thus, in 1997 child allowances became truly universal, paid to every mother who was a citizen or permanent resident of Israel for every child under the age of eighteen. As a result, about 220,000 Arab families were able to improve their standards of living (Israel National Insurance Institute 1998).

Since 1975, child allowances have been transferred directly to the bank accounts of their mothers. Although the intention was not necessarily to provide a benefit to women but a benefit to the family through the agency of the women, for many low-income women child allowances are the only monies they control.

Special Benefits for Women. The Israeli welfare state has "feminine programs" that form part of national pronatal policies for Jewish women and support of their roles as mothers. Although these benefits were not designed with Palestinian Arab women in mind, they are eligible for them. The benefits include alimony and child support payments, maternity benefits, long-term home care benefits and special benefits for solo mothers.

Under the alimony law the National Insurance Institute pays minimum (poverty-level) alimony and child support to women who have court judgments but whose husbands refuse to pay. The law releases the women from the burden of enforcement procedures and entrusts the institute with collecting from the delinquent husbands.

Maternity benefits in Israel include a hospitalization grant for the birth and a grant to all mothers for the purchase of supplies and equipment for the newborn, three months of leave at full pay for women in the labor force, special birth allowances for a period of nine months for women bearing triplets or more (a not uncommon phenomenon after fertility treatments, which are state subsidized), and a special pension for women who for medical reasons need to stop working during pregnancy. Jewish women benefit more from these provisions because of their larger workforce participation.

Long-term care benefits for elderly persons limited in their daily functioning are gender neutral, but 70 percent of the recipients are women because they live longer than men, on the average, and are more likely to be without a caregiver. Under the long-term care law of 1988, elderly persons with disabilities can receive up to sixteen hours of home care per week financed by the National Insurance Institute. About 10 percent of persons over sixty-five receive such care, and there are indications that the percentage is higher among Arab citizens than among Jewish ones (Weihl 1995). On the other hand, the national health insurance law that came into effect in 1995 does not include long-term care in nursing homes, 70 percent of whose residents are also women.

Finally, the Israeli welfare state recognizes the difficult straits of solo mothers—who in 1997 constituted 9 percent of heads of families with children—by providing special support payments, book allowances for children, rent participation grants, and special increments to housing loans. These benefits were introduced because of the convergence of two factors: the large proportion of solo mothers among 1990s immigrants from the former Soviet Union—a social group that received high priority among policy-makers—and the efforts made on their behalf by feminist legislators. These benefits, however, do not bring solo mothers up to the average income level of men, whose welfare is secured through the labor force.

The Right to Education

The right to education, as defined by Marshall (1964) is not the right of the child to attend school, but the right of the adult to have been educated. This right is not accompanied by any legal obligation—on the part of the state—to provide a quality education for all its citizens. While the education system may provide most children with whatever level of education is considered minimal for citizenship, it also serves as an instrument of social stratification (Marshall 1964).

In Israel there are basically three education systems, one for Jews (who study in two separate subsystems, one for the religiously observant and another for the secular), another for Palestinian Arab citizens (who also attend two different subsystems, one for "Arabs" and the other for Druze), and a third for ultra-Orthodox Jews. The latter consists of private, state-supported schools outside the reach of curricular guidelines or standards set by the state. The first two systems are state supervised and consist of mainly public schools but also contain some private ones. Because these are a legacy of the Ottoman *millet* and, in the case of Arab schools, of the British Mandate system, Jewish and Arab schools are entirely separate. Both are under the direct control and supervision of the state. This is not a case of multi-culturalism or cultural autonomy but of control and exclusion that has the effect of maintaining the Arab population "in marginal spaces" (Davis 1997, 86).

The system of separate school systems for Jews and Palestinian Arabs and for secular and observant Jews received state sanction with enactment of the State Education Law of 1953. As Swirski points out, "Instead of introducing a new, republican universalistic conceptualization of education, the law merely dressed the historic 1920 compromise between religious and secular Jews [under which ultra-Orthodox Jews living in Palestine retained control over their own schools] in the new apparel of state, while failing to deal with the separation between Jews and Arabs and with the growing segregation between Ashkenazi and Mizrahi Jews" (Swirski 1999).

The state has applied different standards to Jews and Arabs in the framework of its educational systems, investing considerably less in Arab schools, teachers, auxiliary personnel, curriculums, and special programs for students with special needs. Eliminating these differences has become a major goal for Palestinian Arab NGOs active in the 1980s and 1990s. Enforcement of the Compulsory Education Law of 1949, which mandates class attendance up to age thirteen, later (1968) extended to fifteen, has always been lax in Arab localities: the latest figures show that about one-fourth of school-children drop out before they reach the ninth grade, and another fourth drop out before the twelfth (Israel Ministry of Education 1997, table 3.9). The unequal quality of the different educational systems is also evidenced in the success rates in the national matriculation examinations administered at the end of the twelfth grade: in 1997 some 44 percent of Jewish seventeen year olds succeeded, compared with 23 percent of Muslims and 10 percent of Negev Bedouins (Israel Ministry of Education 1998, 8), whose results are listed separately because of the large gap between their achievements and those of other Arab students. Among Jews there are significant differences between Mizrahim and Ashkenazim: the latest available breakdown (for 1994–95) shows that the success rate was 50 percent for Ashkenazi seven-teen year olds, compared with 34 percent for Mizrahim seventeen year olds (Israel Ministry of Education 1997, table 3.13). Breakdowns between males and females for the same year (1994–95) show that the Israel educational system of the 1990s provided more opportunities for girls than for boys of the same social group: among Jewish youth, 51 percent of girls, compared with 38 percent of boys in the seventeen-year-old cohort successfully passed the matriculation examinations; among Arab youth, 21 percent of girls suc-ceeded, compared with 16 percent of boys (Israel Ministry of Education 1997, table 3.13).

The trend is increasing educational achievements for women of all ethnic and religious groups in Israel. In 1995–96, 56 percent of degree candidates at Israeli universities were women, including nearly 48 percent of doctoral candidates. Looking at the proportion of women among the different reli-gious and ethnic groups, women constituted 33 percent of Druze students, 40 percent of Muslim students, 54 percent of Christian students, 59.3 per-cent of Mizrahi Jewish students and 52 percent of Ashkenazi Jewish stu-dents (Swirski and Swirski 1998).

The Political Rights and Political Participation of Jewish and Palestinian Arab Women

The Right to Vote and Be Elected

Although both Arab and Jewish women citizens of Israel have the right to vote and be elected to public office, the actual enjoyment of these rights is different for Jewish and Arab women. Both are relatively powerless in comparison with the men in their own communities.

Jewish women fought for and won the right to vote and be elected to the Constitutive Assembly, the national self-governing body of Jewish settlers in Palestine, as early as 1920. After that, the suffrage movement continued to struggle for the right to vote in local elections, winning over one locality after another until the last Jewish municipality granted women the vote in 1940. The principle having been established long before the state, Jewish women voted in the first national elections (1949), as did Arab women (and men). This right was ensconced in law the following year: The Basic Law: The Knesset 1950 stipulated that every citizen eighteen years of age or older has the right to vote and every citizen twenty-one years of age or older the right to run for public office.

A high proportion, about 80 percent of Jewish women and men, generally vote in national elections, and an even higher proportion of Arab women and men, 89 percent and 81 percent, respectively (Kaddari 1997, 68). Voting involves identifying the letter of the alphabet representing the political party of one's choice; the Working Group on the Status of Palestinian Women Citizens of Israel points out that 15 percent of Arab women in Israel, mostly elderly women, are illiterate (Working Group on the Status of Palestinian Women in Israel 1997, 19) and, therefore, unable to read the letter identifying the party of their choice in either Arabic or Hebrew. The family often mediates between Palestinian individuals and the political institutions of the Israeli state: extended families often vote en bloc for a specific party list in return for after-election favors. Thus, although Arab women citizens vote, their "choices" may well be those of the elder males in their extended families. It could be said that for some Palestinian women citizens of Israel, voting is an obligation rather than a right: in a sense, the "right to vote" belongs to the family, not to the individual.

The right to run for public office has not resulted in a high proportion of either Jewish or Arab women actually taking office. Since 1948 women have constituted only between 6.6 percent and 9 percent of the 120 Members of Knesset (parliament). In the 1996 elections only nine Jewish women were placed high enough on their parties' lists to make it into the Knesset. In the May 1999 elections, women received their largest representation ever—fourteen members of Knesset (12.5 percent), including one Arab woman—the first ever. There has been one female prime minister, Golda Meir (1969–74), and six women cabinet members. In 1998 there was one woman minister in the eighteen-member cabinet. The heads of two government ministries—Environmental Protection and Justice—were women.

The record in local elections has not been much better although it has undergone some improvement. In 1950 women constituted 4.2 percent of local councilpersons, whereas in 1993 they constituted 7.3 percent (10.9 percent of Jewish councilpersons), still a very low rate of participation (Israel Women's Network 1997). Of these women, only four have been Arab women (in 1998, two Arab women were serving as local councilwomen). According to the Working Group on the Status of Palestinian Women in Israel, male heads of families often decide who will serve as local council members, and this practice limits women's opportunities in view of "the prevailing attitude that representative roles [public roles] are male roles rather than female roles" (1997, 19). A total of ten women have served as mayors of local governments. At the time of writing (1999), there are two (Jewish) women mayors in all of Israel. One of the ten women who have served as mayors was an Arab woman (Violet Khoury, 1972–73), the wife of the outgoing mayor. This is in keeping with the paradox described by Davis (1997, 81), whereby in societies where familial relations are important for politics, women related to former political leaders have the best chances of becoming political leaders themselves.

Why do so few women attain public office? The Working Group on the Status of Palestinian Women Citizens of Israel contends that "Palestinian women are educated to concentrate on domestic issues rather than public issues and to conform rather than oppose. Also, women also often internalize a sense of their own inferiority, which limits their options and choices. Due to this education, women's perception of themselves and their abilities is an obstacle to their participation in politics and public life." The Working Group also mentions the double burden of work inside and outside the home, the lack of support systems, and the limited political opportunities for all Palestinian citizens of Israel.

These factors are certainly crucial, but they do not tell the whole story. Jewish society in Israel, too, is patriarchal, but much less so than Palestinian society; Jewish women's participation in the labor force is much higher (51 percent, compared to an average of 18 percent for Arab women), but they, too, shoulder the major responsibility for children and household (Katz and Peres 1986). They have more opportunities than Arab women, and they have better support systems. Still, their record remains unimpressive. Among the additional explanations offered for Jewish women's poor performance are lack of the "excess capital" (Blumberg quoted in Buber-Agassi 1993) needed to conduct political campaigns. A successful woman candidate interviewed by Herzog for a study of Israeli women in local office summed up the sine qua non for entering politics, "In order to 'have time for' political involvement a woman needs a strong economic base, a stable family base, and a broad education" (Herzog 1994, 72). Family support is crucial. For both Arab and Jewish women in Israel, there is no question of choosing between family and political career; family comes first, and the vast majority of women marry and bear children. Those who "go into politics" also work both inside and outside the home. By the time most women are able to become politically active, their male cohorts are way ahead. Thus, Golda Meir—and Shulamit Aloni, who founded and led the Civil Rights Party for twenty years (1973–93)—are exceptions who prove the rule.

Women in the Civil Service and the Judiciary

Israeli women's opportunities to participate in the formulation of public policy are limited not only by the fact that they constitute a small minority of elected officials but also because they constitute no more than a minority of senior civil service officials. Although women account for 60 percent of civil service employees, they are concentrated in the lower echelons and occupy only 14 percent of the three highest ranks. Very few women present their candidacy in the tenders for top public service positions (Kaddari 1997, 73). No Arab women have held top civil service positions.

The judiciary is the only branch of government in which women's partici-pation approaches men's. Women constitute 40 percent of Israel's judges although the higher the court, the fewer the women: women account for 15 percent of Supreme Court justices—2 of 13 (Raday 1996, 526). In 1998 the state attorney was a woman (her predecessor was the first woman to occupy this high position). No Arab women have ever served as judges.

Women's relatively high representation in the judiciary may be because it is a common career choice for female law school graduates, who generally opt for government service rather than private practice, in view of the rela-tive security and shorter working hours involved in the former, along with—for most women—lower income levels.

Women's Political Activity in
the Framework of NGOs

Herzog views activity in the framework of women's organizations as no less political than what is conventionally referred to as "politics." She describes it, however, as a double-edged sword. On the one hand, the women's organization shields a woman from public and self-criticism for crossing the boundary into what is perceived as men's territory. On the other, the very construction of activity in the framework of women's organi-zations as "not political" and "for women" negates the relevance of that activity for "real politics" and neutralizes its potential (Herzog 1994).

Moreover, the hierarchical nature of the conventional Israeli women's organizations means that only a privileged few attain positions of power and influence that can be translated into political power, turning the feminist insight "the personal is political" upside down—that is, the political is personal. Cohen and Arato contend that the success of social movements should be judged not only by the achievement of certain substantive goals "but rather in terms of the democratization of values, norms and institutions that are rooted in a political culture" (Cohen and Arato 1995, 562). If one views citizenship as an action or practice (Oldfield 1990) rather than as a status, and if one accepts the above premise, the citizenship record of Israeli women, both Jewish and Palestinian Arab, is much more impressive than that indicated by their activity in more traditional political frameworks. To illustrate, I review their major actions in the framework of feminist NGOs, looking at Jewish and Palestinian Arab women separately because most of their actions have been carried out in separate frameworks.

Jewish Women. Like the feminist movements in the United States and Europe, Jewish women in Israel mobilized around issues in the private, nonpolitical sphere, namely abortion and violence against women. When it began in 1970 with consciousness-raising groups in the three largest cities—Haifa, Tel Aviv, and Jerusalem—this new type of political activity was an expression of civil society par excellence: a social group previously unrecognized as having common interests or legitimate claims on society—as a group—created new frameworks in which members developed a new identity and formulated new demands on the political institutions of the state. In the 1970s Jewish women created a number of alternative institutions, including women's cultural centers, a Woman's Party that ran in the national elections of 1977, two shelters for battered women, and a service for rape victims. In most, the mode of action was more egalitarian and less bureaucratic than that in conventional women's organizations. Demands were addressed primarily to state institutions—the police, the courts, the Knesset, the Ministry of Social Affairs.

In the 1980s peace was the foremost feminist issue as new organizations were created to protest the Israel's invasion of Lebanon (Women Against the Occupation) and, after the Palestinian *intifadah,* the uprising against the Israeli occupation in 1987, to demand that the Israeli government recognize the Palestine Liberation Organization, make peace, and end its occupation of the West Bank and Gaza Strip (Women in Black, Women for Women Political Prisoners, Women Against the Occupation). This activity was in addition to women's participation in protest activities within the framework of the political parties and within the framework of extraparliamentary organizations dominated by men, such as Peace Now. Thousands of women became active on behalf of peace in a large number of different frameworks, more than were mobilized by any other cause addressed by Israeli feminism. Chazen gives a sense of the different reasons for action:

> Some women are drawn into peace work because they are mothers and wives, while others reject these stereotypes. Activists include women frustrated by their incapacity to affect decision-making in other frameworks, and those who have shifted their attention to women's actions on tactical grounds, viewing the women's constituency as fluid and hence more malleable and recep-tive. . . . Finally, some women have joined women's peace movements because they feel a need to do something and are more comfortable in the non-hierarchical and less threatening setting of all-women's groups. (Chazen 1993, 156)

If peace was the issue that succeeded in mobilizing the largest number of women, the next most compelling issue—perhaps the most compelling over time—has been violence against women. Throughout the 1980s and 1990s, women worked to aid victims of violence by setting up shelters, hotlines, and centers for rape victims, by demanding better laws and better police protection, and by conducting media campaigns to raise public awareness. It is a measure of their success that the shelter movement gave traditional women's organizations—Na'amat and the Women's International Zionist Organization—a new agenda, as they hastened to set up their own hotlines and shelters for battered women and to expand their legal services to victims of violence. As a result of these actions, legal changes were instituted.

Arab Women. Palestinian Arab women in Israel created the first politi-cally oriented women's organization in Israel in the 1970s. The founders were secular women students and graduates from the city of Acre. They, too, had an "outside influence": the process of re-Palestinianization that developed as a result of contact with Palestinians living in the West Bank and Gaza Strip in the wake of the 1967 war and subsequent Israeli occupa-tion of those areas and the discovery that the issue of women's emancipation was an issue of concern not only to Western nations but to Palestinians as well (Mar'i and Mar'i 1993, 217). The other background factor was the increased university attendance of Arab women in Israel. Women students' first political actions were taken in the framework of Arab student unions. They formed their own associations and ad hoc groups. In 1974 a local body, the Acre Arab University Student Association, was formed under the leadership of women students and graduates. Its aim was to improve hous-ing conditions and education in Acre, to revive Palestinian folklore, and to raise the sociopolitical awareness of Arab youth. Mar'i and Mar'i view this action as a landmark: "The role of women had changed from that of culture preserver to that of culture tranformer" (1993, 217). Despite the untraditional political behavior of the women, the Arab community of Acre supported the organization until the Israeli authorities intervened by applying two tried and true methods of control: preventing activists from receiving teaching positions and spreading the rumor that a crackdown was imminent: sensitive to the possible imprisonment and disgrace of their women, male family members withdrew their support of the women's political activity.

The Acre Student Association was the beginning, not the end, of Palestinian Arab women's political activity in frameworks of their own making. The leaders of the defunct association formed the Acre Arab Women's Association. Although their activities were no longer overtly "political"—the women engaged in consciousness raising and in training preschool teachers in Acre and the surrounding villages—they activated women and provided them with both inspiration and experience. Women who worked at the Acre Arab Women's Association later founded similar organizations in other towns and cities.

The Palestinian uprising in the occupied territories further mobilized Arab women in Israel; they were especially active in solidarity and protest activities (Espanioli 1993). Although the context was not one of their own creation, it served to politicize Palestinian women in Israel. Some worked together with Jewish women in the framework of organizations such as Women in Black, Women and Peace, and Women for Political Prisoners. Although their focus was on national issues and not gender ones, the "click" would not be long in coming. In the words of the Working Group, "Contact with Palestinian activists from the Occupied Territories, with Israeli feminists, and with repressive Israeli political tactics has awakened among Palestinian women in Israel a consciousness of the gender inequities in their own society" (1997, 16). Thus, during the 1990s secular Palestinian women have increasingly worked on gender issues and especially violence against women by male family members. This is entirely of their own creation and their own choosing. Their efforts have involved monitoring "family honor" crimes and demonstrating publicly against them, and setting up shelters and intervention centers for rape victims. The number of NGOs is growing; in 1998 these included such organizations as Al-Fanar (The Lighthouse—a group that links women's rights with the struggle for Palestinian national liberation—the first to raise the issue of "family-honor" murders of Israeli Palestinian females), Women Against Violence, and Al-Siwar—Arab Feminist Movement in Support of Victims of Sexual Abuse. This political activity by Palestinian Arab women represents a sharp break with the past because it involves opposing the very institutions that formerly mediated women's relations in the public sphere—the family and religion. Rather than placing all the blame on the central government of the Jewish state, Palestinian Arab women have also begun to criticize the major institutions of Palestinian society in Israel.

The distinction made by Mohanty (1991) between Western feminists, whose activities are described as singularly focused on gender, and Third World feminists, whose concern with gender is viewed as part of a wider struggle for liberation, is relevant to the present discussion–although, as pointed out at the outset, Israeli Jewish women do not fit the "Western" stereotype; neither do Palestinian Arab women citizens of Israel conform to the "Third World" one. The tone of Jewish feminist activity in Israel was first set by Ashkenazi women (immigrants or descendants of immigrants from Europe or the Americas), who, indeed, concentrated on gender and assumed that their major concerns were common to all women in Israel. In contrast, Arab feminists in Israel focused on issues relevant to national liberation for Palestinians. In the 1980s Jewish feminists shifted their focus to peace issues, and the movement diversified as Mizrahi women (whose origins are in Arab countries) began to examine the position of their own social group vis-à-vis the dominant Ashkenazic Jews. And in the 1990s Arab feminists shifted their focus to gender issues although these have rarely been divorced from issues of Palestinian national liberation and equality for Arab citizens of Israel. In other words, there has been a certain convergence, although the two major groups of women in Israel, Jewish women and Arab women, like their respective societies and religious communities, remain apart.

Works Cited
Index

Works Cited

Abdeen, Sa'di. 1991. Musoat al-jaib lil-tashira' wa-al-qada wal-fiqh. The Residency Law and Foreigners' Affairs no. 24 for 1973. Dar. Al-jib lilnashir wal-tawzea, Amman.

———. 1993. Musoat al-jaib lil-tashira' wa-al-qada wal-fiqh. The Jordanian Nationality Law no. 5 for 1954, as amended in Law no. 22 for 1987. Dar. Al-jib lilnashir wal-tawzea, Amman, Jordan.

———. 1993. Musoat al-jaib lil-tashira' wa-al-qada wal-fiqh. The Jordanian Citizenship Law no. 6 for 1954. Dar. Al-jib lilnashir wal-tawzea, Amman, no. 10.

Abdul Qader, Hatem. 1998. *The Palestinian Legislative Council and Civil Society.* Jerusalem: PASSIA.

Abu Amr, Ziad. 1997. "The Palestinian Legislative Council: A Critical Assessment." *Journal of Palestine Studies* (summer): 90–97.

Abu Jaber, Kamal S. 1967. "The Millet System in the Nineteenth-Century Ottoman Empire." *Muslim World* 57, no. 3: 212–23.

Adalah, the Legal Center for Arab Minority Rights in Israel. 1998. *Legal Violations of Arab Minority Rights in Israel, A Report on Israel's Implementation of the International Convention on the Elimination of All Forms of Racial Discrimination.* Shefaram: Adalah.

Afary, Janet. 1996. *The Iranian Constitutional Revolution 1906–1911: Grassroots Democracy and the Origins of Feminism.* New York: Columbia Univ. Press.

Afkhami, Mahnaz, ed. 1995. *Faith and Freedom: Women's Human Rights in the Muslim World.* Syracuse, N.Y.: Syracuse Univ. Press.

Afkhami, Mahnaz, and Erika Friedl, eds. 1997. *Muslim Women and the Politics of Participation. Implementing the Beijing Platform.* Syracuse, N.Y.: Syracuse Univ. Press.

AfricaWatch. 1991. "Sudan," 3, 9. 9 Apr., 1–15.

Ahmed, Leila. 1992. *Women and Gender in Islam.* New Haven, Conn.: Yale Univ. Press.

Aktaş, Cihan. 1986. *Kadýnýn Serüveni* (Adventure of woman). Istanbul, Turkey: Giriþim Yayýncýlýk.

Alexander, Esther. 1997. "The Image of Discrimination: Women at Work." In *Women: The Rising Force,* edited by Anat Maor, 37–44. Tel Aviv: Sifriat Hapoalim (Hebrew).

Algar, Hamid. 1983. *The Roots of Islamic Revolution.* London: Open Univ. Press.

Algérie: Naissance d'une Société Nouvelle. 1976. Le Texte Integral de la Charte National Adoptée par le Peuple Algerien. Paris: Edition Sociale.

AlMunajjed, Mona. 1997. *Women in Saudi Arabia Today.* London: Macmillan.

Altorki, Soraya. 1986. *Women in Saudi Arabia.* New York: Columbia Univ. Press.

Altorki, Soraya, and Donald Cole. 1989. *'Unayza: An Arabian Oasis Town.* Austin: Univ. of Texas Press.

an-Na'im, Abdullahi Ahmed. 1990. *Toward an Islamic Reformation: Civil Liberties, Human Rights, and International Law.* Syracuse, N.Y.: Syracuse Univ. Press.

———. 1993a. "Toward an Islamic Reformation: Responses and Reflections." In *Islamic Law Reform and Human Rights: Challenges and Rejoinders,* edited by Tore Lindhom and Kari Vogt, 97–116. Copenhagen, Denmark: Nordic Human Rights Publication.

———. 1993b. "The Application of Shari'a (Islamic law) and Human Rights in the Sudan." In *Islamic Law Reform and Human Rights: Challenges and Rejoinders,* edited by Tore Lindhom and Kari Vogt, 136–309. Copenhagen, Denmark: Nordic Human Rights Publication.

Anderson, Benedict. 1983. *Imagined Communities.* London: Verso.

Annual Report by His Britannic Majesty's Government on the Palestine Administration, submitted to the Council of the League of Nations, 1923. Public Records Office, United Kingdom.

"'Ar fi al-Bayt al-Sa'udi" (Scandal in the House of Sa'udi). 1992. Pt. 4. *Al-Jazira al-'Arabiyya* (The Arabian peninsula) 2, no. 22 (Nov.): 39–47.

Arab Times (Kuwait). 1995. 26 Aug., 3; 3 Sept., 6.

———. 1997. 2 Jan.; 21 Oct., 3; 25 Oct.

Arabia Monitor. 1992. Vol. 1, no. 8, Sept., 1–8.

Arat, Yeşim. 1996. "On Gender and Citizenship in Turkey." *Middle East Report* (Jan.–Mar.): 28–31.

———. 1997. "The Project of Modernity and Women in Turkey." In *Rethinking Modernity and National Identity in Turkey,* edited by S. Bozdoğan and R. Kasaba, 95–112. Seattle: Univ. of Washington Press.

Arin, Canan. 1996. "Kadina yönelik şiddet açisindan Türk hukuku'nun kadina yaklaşimi" (Turkish law on violence toward women). In *Evdeki Te*r*ör,* 130–39. Istanbul, Turkey: Mor Çatí Yayinlari.

———. 1997. *The Legal Status of Women in Turkey.* Istanbul: Women for Women's Human Rights Reports, 1.

Ash-Sharqi, Ra'ufa, et al. 1993. "Woman [sic] Status in the Legislation of the Republic of Yemen Sana'a: Proposal for a Conference, 12–16 November." Sana'a, Yemen.

Atzmon, Yael, and Dafna Izraeli. 1993. "Introduction: Women in Israel: A Sociological Review." In *Women in Israel,* edited by Yael Atzmon and Dafna Izraeli, 1–13. New Brunswick: Transaction.

al-Awadhi, Badria. 1996. Interview with Mary Ann Tétreault.

———. 1998. Interview with Haya al-Mughni.

al-Ayyam. 1998. "The Final Session of the Model Parliament in Gaza: A Call for New Forms of Social Actions to Ensure the Rights of Women?" (in Arabic), 28 Apr. Ramallah: Al-Haq.

al-Badawi, Suad al-Fatih. 1986. Al-Sahafa, 3 May, 10. Khartoum, Sudan.

Badran, Margot. 1995. Feminists, Islam and Nation: Gender and the Making of Modern Egypt. Princeton, N.J.: Princeton Univ. Press.

———. 1996a. "Gendering the Islamic Globalization Offensive." People's Rights, Women's Rights—Quarterly Women's Human Rights Journal 3: 12.

———. 1996b. "Khartoum's Answer to Beijing." Al-Ahram Weekly, 5–11 Sept.

Balibar, Etienne, and Immanuel Wallerstein. 1991. Race, Nation, Class: Ambiguous Identities. London: Verso.

Bamdad, Badrol-Molouk. 1977. From Darkness into Light: Women's Emancipation in Iran. Translated from Farsi and edited by F. R. C. Bagley. Smithtown, N.Y.: Exposition Press.

Barakat, Halim. 1985. "The Arab Family and the Challenge of Social Transformation." In Women and the Family in the Middle East, edited by Elizabeth Warnock Fernea, 27–48. Austin: Univ. of Texas Press.

———. 1993. The Arab World: Society, Culture and State. Berkeley and Los Angeles: Univ. of California Press.

Barbalet, J. M. 1988. Citizenship: Rights, Struggle, and Class Inequality. Minneapolis: Univ. of Minnesota Press.

Bardenstein, Richard. 1998. Implementation of the International Covenant on Civil and Political Rights (ICCPR). Jerusalem: Israel Ministry of Justice and Israel Ministry of Foreign Affairs.

Bayat-Philipp, Mangol. 1978. "Women and the Revolution." In Women in the Muslim World, edited by Lois Beck and Nikki R. Keddie, 295–309. Cambridge, Mass.: Harvard Univ. Press.

Bellah, Robert, Richard Madsen, William M. Sullivan, Ann Swidler, and Steven M. Tipton. 1985. Habits of the Heart: Individualism and Commitment in American Life. Berkeley and Los Angeles: Univ. of California Press.

Bendelac, Jacques. 1996. Average Wages, Employment, Membership in Sick Funds and Employment Status, by Locality, 1993–1995. Jerusalem: National Insurance Institute (Hebrew).

Bendix, Reinhardt. 1964. Nation-Building and Citizenship. New York: J. Wiley.

Benziman, Uzi, and Atallah Mansour. 1992. Subtenants. Jerusalem: Keter (Hebrew).

Berkovitch, Nitza. 1996. "Women and the Women's Equal Rights Law in Israel." Middle East Report, no. 198. Vol. 26, no. 1: 19–21.

———. 1997. "Motherhood as a National Mission: The Construction Womanhood in the Legal Discourse in Israel." Women's Studies International Forum 45, no. 5/6: 605–19.

Bernstein, Deborah. 1987. The Struggle for Equality: Urban Women Workers in Pre-state Israeli Society. New York: Praeger.

Al-Bilad (Baghdad). 1930. 30 Nov.

Binder, Leonard, ed. 1966. *Politics in Lebanon.* New York: J. Wiley.

Bint al-Nil. 1954. Apr., no. 102.

Bishara, Azmi. 1993. "On the Question of the Palestinian Minority in Israel" (in Hebrew). *Theory and Criticism,* no. 3: 7–20.

———. 1998. "Reflections on the Reality of the Oslo Process." In *After Oslo, New Realities, Old Problems,* edited by George Giacaman and Dag Jorund Lonning, 212–26. London: Pluto Press.

Bizri, Dalal. 1997. "Authority and Society in Family Law: The President's Independence Day Initiative and the Reaction to It." Paper presented at the conference, "Gender and Citizenship in Lebanon," Mar., American Univ. in Beirut.

Bloom, Anne. 1993. "Women in the Defense Forces," In *Calling the Equality Bluff: Women in Israel.* Edited by Barbara Swirski and Marilyn Safir, 128–38. New York: Teachers College Press.

Blumberg, Rae L. 1984. "A General Theory of Gender Stratification." *Sociological Theory.* Quoted in Judith Buber-Agassi. 1993. "How Much Political Power Do Israeli Women Have?" In *Calling the Equality Bluff: Women in Israel,* edited by B. Swirski and M. Safir, 203–12. New York: Teachers College Press.

Bogosh, Bryna, and Rochelle Don-Yechiya. 1997. *Gender and the Administration of Justice in the Israeli Courts, Summary of Findings.* Jerusalem: Jerusalem Institute for Israel Studies (Hebrew).

Botman, Selman. 1999. *Engendering Citizenship in Egypt.* New York: Columbia Univ. Press.

Boulatta, Terry. 1998. *The Role and Achievements of Women's NGOs in Palestinian Civil Society: Lobbying and Actions.* Jerusalem: PASSIA.

Boxberger, Linda. 1998. "From Two States to One: Women's Lives in the Transformation of Yemen." In *Women in Muslim Societies: Diversity Within Unity,* edited by Herbert Bodman and Nayereh Tohidi, 119–33. Boulder, Colo.: Lynne Rienner.

Brand, Laurie A. 1998. *Women, the State, and Political Liberalization. Middle Eastern and North African Experiences.* New York: Columbia Univ. Press.

Briceno, Rosa. 1998. "Reclaiming Women's Human Rights." In *Women in the Third World: An Encyclopedia of Contemporary Issues,* edited by Nelly Stromquist; assistant editor, Karen Monkman, 49–58. New York: Garland.

Buber-Agassi, Judith. 1993. "How Much Political Power Do Israeli Women Have?" In *Calling the Equality Bluff: Women in Israel,* edited by Barbara Swirski and Marilyn Safir, 203–12. New York: Teachers College Press.

Butenschon, Nils, A., Uri Davis, and Manuel Hassassian, eds. 2000. *Citizenship and the State in the Middle East: Approaches and Application.* Syracuse, N.Y.: Syracuse Univ. Press.

Butros, Gabriel M., trans. 1973. *The Lebanese Constitution.* Beirut: Bureau of Lebanese and Arab Documentation.

Cainkar, L. 1993. "The Gulf War, Sanctions and the Lives of Iraqi Women." *Arab Studies Quarterly* 15, no. 2 (spring): 15–51.

Carapico, Sheila. 1991. "Women and Participation in Yemen." *Middle East Report* 21, no. 173: 15.

———. 1998. *Civil Society in Yemen: The Political Economy of Activism in Modern Arabia.* New York and Cambridge, Eng.: Cambridge Univ. Press.

CEDAW. 1997. Workshop. The U.N. Interagency Gender Taskforce, Royal Cultural Center, Amman, Jordan, 4 Aug.

CEDAW Report; Second and Third Periodic Reports of State Parties: Turkey. 1996.

Chafi, Mohamed. 1996. *Code du statut personnel annoté: Textes législatifs, doctrine et jurisprudence* (Codes of personal status annotated: Legal texts, doctrine and jurisprudence). Marrakech, Morocco: Walili.

Chamari, Alya Cherif. 1991. *La Femme et la loi en Tunisie* (Women and law in Tunisia). Casablanca: United Nations Univ. and Editions le Fennec.

Charrad, M. M. 1990. "State and Gender in the Maghrib." *Middle East Report* 20, no. 2: 19–24. Updated and reprinted in *Gendering Political Culture in the Middle East,* edited by Suad Joseph and Susan Slyomovics. In press. Philadelphia: Univ. of Pennsylvania Press.

———. 1994. "Repudiation Versus Divorce: Responses to State Policy in Tunisia." In *Women, the Family and Policy: A Global Perspective,* edited by Esther N. Chow and Catherine W. Berheide, 51–69. Albany: State Univ. of New York Press.

———. 1996. "Formation de l'état et statut personnel au Maghreb: Esquisse d'une étude comparative et théorique" (State formation and personal status in the Maghrib: Toward a comparative and theoretical approach). In Vol. 2, *Femmes, Culture et société au Maghreb* (Women, culture and society in the Maghrib), edited by R. Bourquia, M. M. Charrad, and N. Gallagher, 15–32. Rabat, Morocco: Afrique Orient.

———. 1997. "Policy Shifts: State, Islam and Gender in Tunisia, 1930s–1990s." *Social Politics* 4, no. 2: 284–319.

———. 1998. "Cultural Diversity Within Islam: Veils and Laws in Tunisia." In *Women in Muslim Societies: Diversity Within Unity,* edited by Herbert L. Bodman and Nayereh Tohidi. Boulder, Colo.: Lynne Rienner.

———. In press. *Origins of Women's Rights: State and Tribe in Tunisia, Algeria and Morocco.* Berkeley and Los Angeles: Univ. of California Press.

La Charte d'Alger. 1964. Alger: FLN Commission Centrale d'Orientation.

Chater, Souad. 1992. *Les Emancipées du harem: Regard sur la femme Tunisienne* (Emancipated from the Harem: Perspectives on Tunisian Women). Tunis: Editions la Presse.

Chatterjee, Partha. 1993. *The Nation and Its Fragments. Colonial and Postcolonial Histories.* Princeton, N.J.: Princeton Univ. Press.

Chazen, Naomi. 1993. "Israeli Women and Peace Activism." In *Calling the Equality Bluff: Women in Israel,* edited by Barbara Swirski and Marilyn Safir, 152–64. New York: Teachers College Press.

Cheriat, Boutheina. 1996. "Gender, Civil Society and Citizenship in Algeria." *Middle East Report,* no. 198. Vol. 26, no. 1: 22–26.

Chodorow, Nancy. 1974. "Family Structure and Feminine Personality." In *Women, Culture, and Society,* edited by Michelle Z. Rosaldo and Louise Lamphere, 43–66. Stanford, Calif.: Stanford Univ. Press.

Clark, A. 1987. *Men's Violence: Women's Silence.* London: Pandora.

Clark, Belinda. 1991. "The Vienna Convention Reservations Regime and the Convention on Discrimination Against Women." *American Journal of International Law* 85: 282.

Cobbett, D. 1989. "Women in Iraq." In *Saddam's Iraq: Revolution or Reaction?* edited by Committee Against Repression and for Democratic Right in Iraq, 120–37. London: Zed Books.

Code de la Nationalité. 1970. Quoted in Zouhir Bhusbhaba, *Être Algérien: Hier, Aujord'hui, Demain* (Algiers: Edition Mimouni, 1977), 177–81.

Cohen, Jean L., and Andrew Arato. 1995. *Civil Society and Political Theory.* Cambridge, Mass.: MIT Press.

Collier, Jane F., Bill Maurer, and Laura Suarez-Navaz. 1995. "Sanctioned Identities: Legal Constructions of Modern Personhood." *Identities* 2, nos. 1–2: 1–27.

Collins, Randall. 1986. *Weberian Sociological Theory.* Cambridge, England: Cambridge Univ. Press.

Commission on Human Rights. 1994. *Report on the Situation of Human Rights in Iraq,* by Max van der Stoel, special rapporteur, 25 Feb. E/CN.4/1994/58. New York: UNESCO.

Commission on Women's Salaries in the Public Sector. 1998. *Report of the Commission on Women's Salaries in the Public Sector.* Jerusalem (Hebrew).

Courbage, Yusef. 1997. "Palestinian Fertility in the Aftermath of the Intifada" (in French). *Population* 52e: 222–33.

Crystal, Jill. 1990. *Oil and Politics in the Gulf: Rulers and Merchants in Kuwait and Qatar.* New York and Cambridge, Eng.: Cambridge Univ. Press.

Culpitt, Ian. 1992. *Welfare and Citizenship. Beyond the Crisis of the Welfare State.* London: Sage.

Dahlgren, Susanne. 1998. "Islam, the Custom, and Revolution in Aden: Reconsidering the Background to the Changes of the Early 1990s." Paper presented at the conference "Yemen: The Challenge of Social, Economic, and Democratic Development," 1–4 Apr., at the Centre for Arab Gulf Studies, Univ. of Exeter, U.K.

Daud, Sabiha al-Shaikh. 1958. *Awal al-tariq ila al-nahdha al-nasawiah fi al-Iraq* (The first road to women's awakening in Iraq). Baghdad, Iraq: Al-Rabitah Press.

Davis, Uri. 1995. "Jinsiyya Versus Muwatana: The Question of Citizenship and the State in the Middle East–The Case of Israel, Jordan and Palestine." *Arab Studies Quarterly* 17, nos. 1–2: 12–50.

———. 1996. "Citizenship Legislation in the Syrian Arab Republic." *Arab Studies Quarterly* 18, no. 1: 29–47.

———. 1997. *Citizenship and the State: A Comparative Study of Citizenship Legislation in Israel, Jordan, Palestine, Syria and Lebanon.* Reading, UK: Ithaca Press.

Dayan, Arieh. 1998. "I Have Decided to Nullify Your Citizenship." *Haaretz Magazine,* 26 June: 18–24.

Delaney, Carol. 1995. "Father State, Motherland, and the Birth of Modern Turkey." In *Naturalizing Power. Essays in Feminist Cultural Analysis,* edited by Sylvia Yanagisako and Carol Delaney, 177–200. New York: Routledge.

Deleuze, Gilles. 1997. "The Rise of the Social." Foreward to *The Policing of Families* by Jacques Donzelot. Baltimore, Md.: Johns Hopkins Univ. Press.

Dib, George M. 1975. "Law and Population in Lebanon." Law and Population Monograph Series, no. 29. Medford, Mass.: Fletcher School of Law and Diplomacy, Tufts Univ.

Dietz, Mary G. 1985. "Citizenship with A Feminist Face: The Problem with Maternal Thinking." *Political Theory* 13, no. 1 (Feb.): 19–37.

———. 1987. "Context Is All: Feminism and Theories of Citizenship." *Daedalus* 116, no. 4 (fall): 1–24.

di Leonardo, Micaela. 1987. "The Female World of Cards and Holidays: Women, Families and the Work of Kinship." *Signs* 12, no. 3: 440–53.

Donoho, Douglas. 1991. "Relativism Versus Universalism in Human Rights: The Search for Meaning Full Standards." *Stanford Journal of International Laws* 27, no. 3: 54–91.

Donzelot, Jacques. 1997. *The Policing of Families.* Baltimore, Md.: Johns Hopkins Univ. Press.

Doornbos, Paul. 1988. "On Becoming Sudanese." In *Sudan: State, Capital and Transformation,* edited by Tony Bennet and Abbas Abdel Karim. London: Croom Helm.

al-Duaij, Abd al-Latif. 1995. "In Defense of Liberalism and Women." *Al-Qabas.* 19 Aug.: 31.

Durkheim, Emile. 1964. *The Division of Labor in Society.* 1893. Reprint. Glencoe, Ill.: Free Press.

Economist Intelligence Unit. 1979. "Annual Supplement: Kuwait." London: EIU.

Ehrenreich, Barbara. 1983. *The Hearts of Men: American Dreams and the Flight from Commitment.* Garden City, N.Y.: Anchor Press, Doubleday.

Eilberg-Schwartz, Howard. 1996. "The Father, the Phallus, and the Seminal Word: Dilemmas of Patrilineality in Ancient Judaism." In *Gender, Kinship Power. A Comparative and Interdisciplinary History,* edited by Mary Jo Maynes, Ann Waltner, Birgitte Soland, and Ulrike Strasser, 27–42. New York: Routledge.

Eisenstein, Zillah. 1994. *The Color of Gender. Reimaging Democracy.* Berkeley and Los Angeles: Univ. of California Press.

Elshtain, Jean Bethke. 1992. "The Power and Powerlessness of Women." In *Beyond Equality and Difference: Citizenship, Feminist Politics, Female Subjectivity,* edited by Gisela Bock and Susan James, 110–25. London: Routledge.

EqualityNow. 1997. "Report in Response to the Sudan Government Report on Human Rights before the Human Rights Committee in Geneva, October. 1997."

Espanioli, Nabila. 1993. "Palestinian Women in Israel Respond to the *Intifada.*" In *Calling the Equality Bluff: Women in Israel,* edited by Barbara Swirski and Marilyn Safir, 147–51. New York: Teachers College Press.

Esping-Andersen, Gosta. 1990. *The Three Worlds of Welfare Capitalism*. Cambridge, England: Polity Press.

Esposito, John L. 1982. *Women in Muslim Family Law*. Syracuse, N.Y.: Syracuse Univ. Press.

al-Essa, Shamlan Y. 1992. "The Political Consequences of the Crisis for Kuwait." In *The Gulf Crisis: Background and Consequences,* edited by Ibrahim Ibrahim, 169–85. Washington, D.C.: Center for Contemporary Arab Studies.

Falk, R. 1994a. "Democracy Died at the Gulf." In *The Gulf War and the New World Order,* edited by T. Y. Ismael and J. S. Ismael, 536–48. Gainesville: Univ. Press of Florida.

———. 1994b. "Reflections on the Gulf War Experience." In *The Gulf War and the New World Order,* edited by T. Y. Ismael and J. S. Ismael, 25–39. Gainesville: Univ. Press of Florida.

Fanon, Frantz. 1963. *The Wretched of the Earth*. New York: Grove Press.

al-Fauri, Nawal. 1995. *Ad-Dustour Daily*. 25 Sept.

The Final Communiqué and Recommendations for "Woman and the Criminal Legislation." 1996. Dec. Al-Tawfiq Printing Press, Jordanian Women's Union, Amman, Jordan. Presented at the "Woman and the Criminal Legislation" seminar, Royal Cultural Center, Dec.

al-Fiqi, Mustafa. 1991. *Al-'Aqbat fi al-Siyasa al-Misriya*. Cairo: Dar al-Hilal.

Fluehr-Lobban, Carolyn. 1994. *Islamic Society in Practice*. Gainesville: Univ. Press of Florida.

Fogiel-Bijaouie, Sylvia. 1997. "Women in Israel: The Social Construction of Citizenship as a Non-Issue." *Israel Social Science Research* 12, no. 2: 1–30.

Foucault, Michel. 1983. "Afterword: The Subject and Power." In *Michel Foucault: Beyond Structralism and Hermeneutics,* edited by H. Dreyfus and P. Rabinow. Chicago: Univ. of Chicago Press.

Fox-Genovese, Elizabeth. 1991. *Feminism Without Illusions: A Critique of Individualism*. Chapel Hill: Univ. of North Carolina Press.

Freeman, Marsha A. 1995. "The Human Rights of Women in the Family: Issues and Recommendations for Implementation of the Women's Convention." In *Women's Rights Human Rights: International Feminist Perspectives,* edited by Julie Peters and Andrea Wolper, 149–66. New York: Routledge.

French Criminal Law. Arts. 96, 97.

Friedman, Menachem. 1988. "The History of the Status Quo" (in Hebrew). In *The Passage from Pre-State Settlement to State 1947–49,* edited by Varda Pilovsky, 47–79. Haifa, Israel: Herzl Foundation for the Humanities, Haifa Univ. Press.

Frisch, Hillel. 1997. "Modern Absolutist or Neo-Patriarchal State Building? Customary Law, Extended Families and the Palestinian Authority." *International Journal of Middle East Studies* 29: 341–57.

Frost, Shimon. 1998. *Schooling as a Socio-Political Expression*. Jerusalem: Magnes.

Gasiorowski, Mark J. 1991. *U.S. Foreign Policy and the Shah: Building a Client State in Iran*. Ithaca, N.Y.: Cornell Univ. Press.

Gavrielides, Nicolas. 1987. "Tribal Democracy: The Anatomy of Parliamentary Elections in Kuwait." In *Elections in the Middle East: Implications of Recent Trends*, edited by Linda Layne, 153–223. Boulder, Colo.: Westview Press.

General Union of Palestinian Women. 1994. "Draft Document of Principles of Women's Rights." Jerusalem: GUPW.

Ghabra, Shafeeq. 1991. "Voluntary Associations in Kuwait: The Foundation of a New System?" *Middle East Journal* 45, no. 2: 199–215.

———. 1997. "Kuwait and the Dynamics of Socio-Economic Change. *Middle East Journal* 51, no. 3: 358–72.

Giacaman, George. 1998. "In the Throes of Oslo: Palestinian Society, Civil Society and the Future." In *After Oslo, New Realities, Old Problems*, edited by George Giacaman and Dag Jorund Lonning, 1–15. London: Pluto Press.

Giacaman, Rita 1997. "Population and Fertility: Population Policies, Women's Rights and Sustainable Development." In *Palestinian Women: A Status Report, no. 2,* Bir Zeit: Women's Studies Program.

Giacaman, Rita, Islah Jad, and Penny Johnson. 1996. "For the Public Good? Gender and Social Citizenship in Palestine." *Middle East Report*, no. 198. Vol. 26, no. 1: 11–17.

Glosemeyer, Iris. 1995. *Liberalization and Democratization in the Republic of Yemen, 1990–1994* (in German). Hamburg, Germany: Deutsches Orient Institut.

Golban, Mohammad. 1975. *Naghd va Siahat: Majmueh Maghalat va Toghrirat Fatemeh Sayyah.* Tehran: Entesharat Tus, 1354.

Goldberg, Ellis. 1992. "Smashing Idols and the State: The Protestant Ethic and Egyptian Sunni Radicalism." In *Comparing Muslim Societies: Knowledge and the State in a World Civilization*, edited by Juan R. I. Cole, 195–236. Ann Arbor: Univ. of Michigan Press.

Goody, Jack. 1983. *The Development of the Family and Marriage in Europe.* New York and Cambridge, Eng.: Cambridge Univ. Press.

Gould, Steven J. 1981. *Mismeasure of Man.* New York: Norton.

Gran, Peter. 1996. "Organization of Culture and the Construction of the Family in the Modern Middle East." In *Women, the Family and Divorce Laws in Islamic History*, edited by Amira El Azhary Sonbol, 64–78. Syracuse, N. Y.: Syracuse Univ. Press.

Grewal, Inderpal. 1996. *Home and Harem. Nation, Gender, Empire, and the Cultures of Travel.* Durham, N.C.: Duke Univ. Press.

Guy, Donna J. 1992. "'White Slavery': Citizenship and Nationality in Argentina." In *Nationalities and Sexualities,* edited by Andrew Parker et al., 201–17. New York: Routledge.

Haeri, Shahla. 1987. *Law of Desire: Temporary Marriage in Shi'i Iran.* Syracuse, N.Y.: Syracuse Univ. Press.

Haj Yahia, Muhammed. 1995. "Towards a Culturally Sensitive Intervention with Arab Families in Israel." *Contemporary Family Therapy* 17, no. 14 (Dec.): 429–47.

Hale, Sondra. 1991. "Feminist Method, Process, and Self-Criticism: Interviewing Sudanese Women." In *Women's Words: The Feminist Practice of Oral History*, edited by Sherna Gluck and Daphne Patai, 121–36. New York: Routledge.

———. 1993. "Transforming Culture or Fostering Second-Hand Consciousness? Women's Front Organizations and Revolutionary Parties—The Sudan Case." In *Arab Women: Old Boundaries, New Frontiers,* edited by Judith Tucker, 149–74. Bloomington: Indiana Univ. Press.

———. 1996a. *Gendering Politics in Sudan: Islamism, Socialism, and the State.* Boulder, Colo.: Westview Press.

———. 1996b. "'The New Muslim Woman': Sudan's National Islamic Front and the Invention of Identity." *Muslim World* 86, no. 2: 177–200.

Hamadeh, Najla, Jean Said Makdisi, and Suad Joseph, eds. 1999. *Gender and Citizenship in Lebanon.* Beirut: Dar al-Jadid Press.

Hamrouch, Ahmed. 1974. *Qisat Thawrat 23 Yulyu.* Cairo: Al-Muassast al-'Arabiya lil Dirasat wa al-Nashr.

Hann, Chris. 1996. Introduction to *Civil Society: Challenging Western Models,* edited by Chris Hann and Elizabeth Dunn. New York: Routledge.

Al-Haq. 1995. *Women, Justice and the Law* (in Arabic). Ramallah: Al-Haq.

Harik, Iliya. 1968. *Politics and Change in a Traditional Society.* Princeton, N.J.: Princeton Univ. Press.

Hartsock, Nancy. 1983. *Money, Sex and Power: Toward a Feminist Historical Materialism.* New York: Longmans.

Hashim, Hisham, trans. 1990. *The Jordanian Civil Code of Moslem Jurisprudence.* Amman, Jordan: Al-Tawfiq Printing Press.

al-Hassan, Hani. 1972. "Fateh: Between Theory and Implementation" (in Arabic). *Palestine Affairs* (summer): 22–30. Beirut.

Hassan, Rifat. 1994. *Selected Articles.* Montpellier, France: Women Living under Muslim Laws.

———. 1996. "Rights of Women Within Islamic Communities." In *Religious Human Rights in Global Perspective,* edited by John Witte, Jr. and Johan D. van der Vyver. The Hague and Boston, Mass.: M. Nijhoff.

Hassouna, 'Issam. 1990. *Shahadati.* Cairo: Markaz al-Ahram lil Tarjama wa al-Nashr.

Hatem, Mervat F. 1986. "The Enduring Alliance of Nationalism and Patriarchy in Muslim Personal Status Laws: The Case of Modern Egypt." *Feminist Issues* 6, no. 1: 19–43.

———. 1994a. "Egyptian Discourses on Gender and Political Liberalization: Do Secularist and Islamist Views Really Differ?" *Middle East Journal* 48, no. 4: 661–76.

———. 1994b. "The Paradoxes of State Feminism." In *Women and Politics Worldwide,* edited by Barbara Nelson and Najma Chaudhury. New Haven, Conn.: Yale Univ. Press.

———. 1994c. "Privatization and the Demise of State Feminism." In *Mortgaging Women's Lives: Feminist Critiques of Structural Adjustment,* edited by Pamela Sparr. London: Zed Press.

———. 1995. "Political Liberalization, Gender and the State." In *Political Liberalization and Democratization in the Arab World,* edited by Rex Brynen, Bahgat Korany, and Paul Noble, 187–210. Boulder, Colo.: Lynne Rienner.

Haykel, Bernard. 1999. "Rebellion, Migration or Consultative Democracy? The Zaydis and Their Detractors in Yemen." In *Le Yémen contemporain,* edited by Rémy Leveau, Franck Mermier, and Udo Steinbach, 193–202. Paris: Karthala.

Haykel, Muhammed Hassanin. 1983. *Kharif al-Ghadab.* Beirut: Shrikat al-Matbu'at lil Tawzi'a wa al-Nashr.

Heller, Thomas C. 1986. Introduction to *Reconstructing Individualism,* edited by Thomas C. Heller et al., 1–15. Stanford, Calif.: Stanford Univ. Press.

Herald Tribune (London). 1991. 4 June.

Hernes, Helga Maria. 1987. *Welfare State and Woman Power: Essays in State Feminism.* Oslo: Norwegian Univ. Press.

Herzog, Hannah. 1994. *Realistic Women—Women in Local Politics.* Jerusalem: The Jerusalem Institute for Israel Studies (Hebrew).

Hess, S. 1966. *America's Political Dynasties from Adams to Kennedy.* Garden City, N.Y.: Doubleday.

al-Hibri, Aziza. 1994. "A Critical Research Project for Personal Status Codes in Selected Arab Countries, ESCWA, Expert Group Meeting on the Arab Family in a Changing Society: A New Concept for Partnership." 10–14 Dec., Abu-Dhabi. E/ESCWA/SD/1994/WG.4–WOM/5.

Al-Hoda Society. 1998. "The Palestinian Woman and the Conspiracy of Secularist Women" (in Arabic). Birzeit Univ.: Student Committee of the Islamic Bloc.

Hoodfar, Homa. 1995. "State Policy and Gender Equity in Post-Revolutionary Iran." In *Family, Gender and Population Policy in the Middle East,* edited by Carla Makhlouf Obermeyer. Cairo: American Univ. Press.

———. 1996. "Bargaining with Fundamentalism: Women and the Politics of Population Control in Iran." *Reproductive Health Matters,* no. 8 (Nov.): 30–40.

———. 1997. "The Veil in Their Minds and on Our Heads: The Persistence of Colonial Images of Muslim Women." In *The Politics of Culture in the Shadow of the Capital,* edited by David Lloyd and Lisa Lowe, 248–79. Durham, N.C.: Duke Univ. Press.

———. 1999. *The Women's Movement in Iran: Women at the Crossroads of Secularization and Islamization.* Montpellier, France: Women Living under Muslim Laws.

———. In press. "Domestic Violence: A Public Debate." In *Domestic Violence Debates in the Muslim World.* Women and Law Publication Series. Montpelier, France: Women Living under Muslim Laws.

Hooks, B. 1984. *Feminist Theory: From Margin to Center.* Boston: South End Press.

Howard, Rhoda. 1993. "Cultural Absolutism and the Nostalgia for Community." *Human Rights Quarterly* 15: 315–38.

Hudson, Michael. 1968. *The Precarious Republic: Political Modernization in Lebanon.* New York: Random House.

———. 1977. *Arab Politics: The Search for Legitimacy.* New Haven, Conn.: Yale Univ. Press.

Hunt, Lynn. 1992. *The Family Romance of the French Revolution.* Berkeley and Los Angeles: Univ. of California Press.

Huqayl, Sulayman Bin 'Abd al-Rahman. 1996. *Fi afaq al-tarbiya fi al-Mamlaka al-'Arabiyya al-Sa'udiyya* (On the dimensions of education in the Kingdom of Saudi Arabia). 3d ed. Riyad, Saudi Arabia: Matabi' al-Taqniya li al-Ufsit.

Husseini, Rana. 1996. *Jordan Times.* 22 Apr.

Huxley, Fred. 1975. "Wasita Revisited: Social Exchange in a Lebanese Village," Ph.D. diss., Yale Univ.

Immigration and Refugee Board, Canada. 1996. Human Rights in Iraq: Transcript of a meeting held on 2 July 1996. Interview with Dr. Hussein al-Shahristani, an internationally prominent Iraqi scientist and, since 1991, a human rights activist working with the International Refugee Aid Council.

International Committee for Human Rights in the Gulf and Arabian Peninsula. 1992. "The Consultative Council: The Old and the New." *Arabia Monitor* 1, no. 8 (Sept.): 1–8.

International Women's Rights Action Watch (IWRAW). 1996. In *1997 IWRAW to CEDAW Country Reports on Saint Vincent and the Grenadines, Slovenia, Morocco, Turkey, Philippines.* H. Humphrey Institute of Public Affairs, Univ. of Minnesota, Minneapolis.

"Intihakat al-hukuma al-Sa'udiya li huquq al-insan" (Abuses of the Saudi government against human rights). 1993. Pt. 2. *Al-Jazira al-'Arabiyya* 3, no. 28 (May): 31–33.

Ismael, J. S. 1980. "Social Policy and Social Change: The Case of Iraq." *Arab Studies Quarterly* 2, no. 3: 235–48.

Ismael, T. Y., and J. S. Ismael, eds. 1994. *The Gulf War and the New World Order: International Relations of the Middle East.* Gainesville: Univ. Press of Florida.

Israel Central Bureau of Statistics. 1996. *Labor Forces Surveys,* Table 16. Jerusalem.

———. 1998a. *Women in the Mirror of the Figures.* Jerusalem (Hebrew).

———. 1998b. *Statistical Abstract of Israel 1997,* Jerusalem.

———. 1998c. *Labor Force Surveys 1996.* Jerusalem.

Israel Ministry of Education. 1997. *The Education System as Reflected in the Figures.* Jerusalem (Hebrew).

———. 1998. *Matriculation Examination Figures 1997.* Jerusalem (Hebrew).

Israel National Insurance Institute. 1998. *Summary of Developments and Trends in Social Security 1997.* Jerusalem.

Israel Women's Network. 1997. *Women in Israel. Information and Figures.* Jerusalem (Hebrew).

Issa, Salah. 1982. *Al-Thawrat al-'Urabiya.* Cairo: Dar al-Mustaqbal al-'Arabi.

Itihad al-Shaab. 1959. 16 June. Baghdad, Iraq.

Izraeli, Dafna. 1981. "The Zionist Women's Movement in Palestine, 1911–1927: A Sociological Analysis." *Signs* 7, no. 1 (autumn): 87–114.

———. 1993. "Outsiders in the Promised Land." In *Competitive Frontiers.* Cambridge, Eng.: Blackwell.

———. 1997. "Gendering Military Service in the Israeli Defense Forces." *Israel Social Science Research* 12, no. 1: 129–66.

Jackson, Robert H. 1990. *Quasi-states: Sovereignty, International Relations and the Third World.* Cambridge, Eng.: Cambridge Univ. Press.

Jad, Islah. 1990. "From Salons to the Popular Committees: Palestinian Women 1919–1989." In *Intifada: Palestine at the Crossroads,* edited by Jamal Nassar and Roger Heacock, 125–42. New York: Praeger Press.

Jagger, Alison M. 1983. *Feminist Politics and Human Nature.* Totowa, N.J.: Rowman and Allanheld.

Jayawardena, Kumari. 1986. *Feminism and Nationalism in the Third World.* London: Zed Books.

al-Jaza'iri, Z. 1994. "Baathist Ideology and Practice." In *Iraq since the Gulf War: Prospects for Democracy,* edited by Fran Hazelton for CARDI, 32–51. London: Zed Books.

Johnson, Penny. 1997. "Social Support: Gender and Social Policy in Palestine," *Palestinian Women: A Status Report,* no. 5. Bir Zeit: Women's Studies Program.

Jones, Kathleen B. 1990. "Citizenship in a Woman-Friendly Polity." *Signs* 15: 711–812.

———. 1993. *Compassionate Authority. Democracy and the Representation of Women.* New York: Routledge.

Jordan Times. 1997. 30 Nov., 7.

Jordanian Civil Code. 1976. Law no. 43. *Official Gazette,* no. 2645, 1 Aug. Amman, Jordan.

———. 1996. Arts. 34, 35, 37, 154, 155, 156, 158, 161, 162, 166. *The Jordanian Civil Code of Moslem Jurisprudence,* translated and annotated by Hisham Hashem. Amman, Jordan: al-Tawfiq Printing Press.

Jordanian Civil Service Health Insurance Law. Arts. 3, 8; 1993 amendments.

Jordanian Civil Service Law. Art. 24.

Jordanian Constitution. Khair, Hani. The Constitution of the Hashemite Kingdom of Jordan, Jordan's National Assembly, Amman, Jordan. Arts. 6, 7, 105, 108, 109; sec. 44.

Jordanian Family Rights Law no. 92. 1951.

Jordanian National Assistance Fund Eligibility Criteria. 1997. Amawi, Abla, Musa Shtewi, Fayiz Suygh. Jordan Social Productivity Program: National Aid Task Force, End-of-Mission Report for NAF Component. Unpublished report for Ministry of Planning and UNDP, Amman. Jordan.

Jordanian Nationality Law no. 6 for 1954. *Official Gazette,* no. 1171, p. 105, 16 Feb.

Jordanian Nationality Law no. 22 for 1987. *Official Gazette,* no. 3496, 1 Sept., p. 1623. Amman, Jordan.

Jordanian Passport Law no. 2 for 1969.

Jordanian Penal Code no. 16 for 1960, and its amendment no. 9 for 1988, Art. 98.

Jordanian Temporary Personal Status Law. 1976. Arts. 21, 22; art. 39, no. 61; art. 132; chap. 4, no. 61.

Joseph, Suad. 1978. "Muslim-Christian Conflict in Lebanon: A Perspective on the

Evolution of Sectarianism." In *Muslim-Christian Conflicts: Economic, Political and Social Origins,* edited by Suad Joseph and B. L. K. Pillsbury, 63–90. Boulder, Colo.: Westview Press.

———. 1982a. "The Family as Security and Bondage: A Political Strategy of the Lebanese Urban Working Class." In *Towards a Political Economy of Urbanization in Third World Countries,* edited by Helen Safa, 151–71. New Delhi: Oxford Univ. Press.

———. 1982b. "The Mobilization of Iraq Women into the Wage Labor Force." *Studies in Third World Societies,* no. 16: 69–90.

———. 1983. "Working Class Women's Networks in a Sectarian State: A Political Paradox." *American Ethnologist* 10, no. 1: 1–22.

———. 1988. "Family, Religion and State: Middle Eastern Models." In *Dialectics and Gender: Anthropological Approaches,* edited by Richard R. Randolph, David M. Schneider, and May N. Diaz. Boulder, Colo.: Westview Press.

———. 1990. "Working the Law: A Lebanese Working Class Case." In *The Politics of Law in the Middle East,* edited by Daisy Dwyer, 143–60. South Hadley, Mass.: J.F. Bergin Publishers.

———. 1991."Elite Strategies for State Building: Women, Family, Religion and State in Iraq and Lebanon." In *Women, Islam and the State,* edited by Deniz Kandiyoti, 176–200. London: MacMillan.

———. 1993a. "Connectivity and Patriarchy among Urban Working Class Arab Families in Lebanon." *Ethos* 21, no. 4: 465–84.

———. 1993b. "Gender and Civil Society: An Interview with Suad Joseph." *Middle East Report* (July–Aug.): 22–26.

———. 1994a. "Brother/Sister Relationships: Connectivity, Love and Power in the Reproduction of Arab Patriarchy." *American Ethnologist* 21, no. 1: 50–73.

———. 1994b. "Problematizing Gender and Relational Rights: Experiences from Lebanon." *Social Politics* 1, no. 3: 271–85.

———. 1996a. "(En)Gendering Citizenship in the Middle East," 1–37. Paper presented at the conference "Citizenship in the Middle East," Univ. of Norway, Oslo.

———. 1996b. "Gender and Citizenship in Middle Eastern States." *Middle East Report,* no. 198 (Jan.–Mar.): 4–10.

———. 1997. "The Public/Private—The Imagined Boundary in the Imagined Nation/State/Community: The Lebanese Case." *Feminist Review* 57: 73–92.

———. 1999a. "Descent of the Nation: Kinship and Citizenship in Lebanon." *Citizenship Studies* 3, no. 3: 295–318.

———. 1999b. "Women Between Nation and State in Lebanon." In *Between Women and Nation: Nationalisms, Transnational Feminisms, and the State,* edited by Caren Kaplan, Norma Alarcon, Minoo Moallem, 162–181. Durham, N.C.: Duke Univ. Press.

———, ed. 1999c. *Intimate Selving: Self, Gender, and Identity in Arab Families.* Syracuse, N.Y.: Syracuse Univ. Press.

———. 1999d. "My Son/Myself, My Mother/Myself: Paradoxical Relationalities of Patriarchal Connectivity." In *Intimate Selving: Self, Gender, and Identity in Arab Families,* edited by Suad Joseph. Syracuse, N.Y.: Syracuse Univ. Press.

———. In press. "Civil Society, The Public/Private, and Gender in Lebanon." In *Social Constructions of Nationalism,* edited by Fatma Muge Gocek. Albany: State Univ. of New York Press.

Jreisati, A. 1997. "Gender in Lebanon's Criminal Code." Conference on Gender and Citizenship in Lebanon, Mar., American Univ. in Beirut.

Al-Jumhuriya al-'Arabiya al-Mutahida. 1964. *Al-Dustur.* Cairo: Maslahat al-'Istilamat.

Jumhuriyat Misr, Wizarat al-'Adl. 1956a. *Al-Dustur.* Cairo: Al-Matb'at al-Amiriya.

———. 1956b. *Majmut Qawanin al-Mutaliqa bi Qadha' al-'Ahwal al-Shakhsiya.* Cairo: Al-Matb'at al-Amiriya.

al-Jumhuriyya al-Yamaniyya, Wazara al-Shu'un al-Qanuniyya. 1992. *al-Qirar al-Jumhuri b' al-Qanun Raqim 20m. 1992 bi-Shan al-Ahwal al-Shakhsiyya.* Sana'a: 14 Uktubir Press.

Kaddari, Ruth Halperin. 1997. *Implementation of the United Nations Convention on the Elimination of All Forms of Discrimination Against Women (CEDAW).* Jerusalem: Israel Ministry of Foreign Affairs and Israel Ministry of Justice.

Kaddoumi, Rehab. 1997. "Women in Jordanian Legislation." Background paper presented at the CEDAW Workshop, U.N. Interagency Gender Taskforce, 4 Aug., Royal Culture Center, Amman, Jordan.

Kahhaleh, May. 1997. "Concerns of the State as It Addresses Women." Paper presented at the conference, "Gender and Citizenship in Lebanon," Mar., American Univ. in Beirut.

Kandiyoti, Deniz. 1988. "Bargaining with Patriarchy." *Gender and Society* 2 , no. 3: 274–90.

———, ed. 1991. *Women, Islam and the State.* London: Macmillan.

———. 1998. "Some Awkward Questions on Women and Modernity in Turkey." In *Remaking Women. Feminism and Modernity in the Middle East,* edited by Lila Abu-Lughod, 270–88. Princeton, N.J.: Princeton Univ. Press.

Kaplan, Caren, Norma Alarcon, and Minoo Moallem, eds. 1999. In *Between Women and Nation. Nationalisms, Transnational Feminisms and the State.* Durham, N.C.: Duke Univ. Press.

Kar, Mahranguiz. 1997. *The Political Rights of Women.* Tehran: Roshangaran and Women Studies Publication.

———. 1996. "Women on Their Way: A Report on the Presence of Women in the Election." *Zanan* 28: 20–24.

Kar, Mehranguiz, and Homa Hoodfar. 1996. "Personal Status Law as Defined by the Islamic Republic of Iran: An Appraisal." *Special Dossier* (WLUML) 1:7–35.

Karaja, Sa'd. 1996. "The Constitutionality of Article 340 of the Criminal Law." Unpublished paper, Jordanian Women's Union, Dec., Amman, Jordan.

Katz, Ruth, and Yochanan Peres. 1986. "The Sociology of the Family in Israel: An Outline of Its Development from the 1950s to the 1980s." *European Sociological Review* 2, no. 2: 148–59.

Katz, Sheila Hannah. 1996. "Adam and Adama and Ard: En-gendering Political Conflict and Identity in Early Jewish and Palestinian Nationalisms." In *Gendering the Middle East,* edited by Deniz Kandiyoti, 85–105. Syracuse, N.Y.: Syracuse Univ. Press.

Kazemi, Farhad. 1996. "The Inclusion Imperative." Presidential address, Middle East Studies Association. Published in *MESA Bulletin* 30, no. 2: 147–53.

Keane, John, ed. 1988a. *Democracy and Civil Society.* London: Verso.

———. 1988b. "Despotism and Democracy: The Origins and Development of the Distinction Between Civil Society and the State." In *Civil Society and the State,* edited by John Keane, 35–72. London: Verso.

Keddie, Nikki R. 1966. *Religion and Rebellion in Iran: The Tobacco Protest of 1891–1982.* London: Frank Cass.

———. 1999. "The New Religious Politics and Women Worldwide: A Comparative Study." *Journal of Women's History* 10, no. 4 (winter): 11–34.

Keller, Catherine. 1986. *From a Broken Web. Separation, Sexism, and Self.* Boston: Beacon Press.

Khader, Asma. 1994. Equality and Participation Within the Family, a Legal Perspective. Paper presented at "Peace for the Advancement of Arab Women," Arab Regional Preparatory Meeting for the Fourth World Conference on Women (Beijing, 1995), 6–10 Nov. 1994, Amman, Jordan. E/ESCWA/SD/1994/WG.3–WOM/9 (in Arabic).

———. 1995. "Editorial." *Ad-Dustour Daily.* 25 Sept.

———. 1996. The Jordanian National Charter and Women. Unpublished paper, Jordanian Women's Union, Amman, Jordan.

———. 1998. *The Law and Women's Future* (in Arabic). Jerusalem: Women's Center for Legal Aid and Counseling.

al-Khafaji, I. 1989. "The Parasitic Base of the Baathist Regime." In *Saddam's Iraq: Revolution or Reaction?* edited by the Committee Against Repression and for Democratic Right in Iraq, 73–88. London: Zed Books.

———. 1994. "State Terror and the Degradation of Politics." In *Iraq since the Gulf War,* edited by Fran Hazelton, 20–31. London: Zed Books.

Khairy, S. 1981. *Thawrat 14 Tamuz* (The July 14 revolution). Beirut: Dar Ibn Khaldun.

Khairy, Z., and S. Khairy. 1984. *Dirasat fi Tarikh al-Hizb al-Shiouee.* Prague: Center for Socialist Studies.

Khalidi, Ramla, and Judith Tucker. 1992. "Women's Rights in the Arab World." *Middle East Research and Information Project Reports* (Feb.). Washington, D.C.: MERIP.

al-Kharsan, S. 1993. *Safahat min tarikh al-harakah al-shiou'yah fi al-Iraq* (Pages from the history of the communist movement in Iraq). Beirut: Dar al-Furat.

Khayat, J. 1950. *Al-Qariyah al-Iraqiyah* (The Iraqi village). Beirut: Dar al-Kashaf.

Khayyat, Abdul Aziz. 1992. "Women in Society: In Islam and Christianity." Paper presented at the Third Symposium in Cooperation with the Pontifical Council for Interreligious Dialogue, p. 8 (the Vatican), 24–26 June, Rome, Italy.

"Khitab al-malik yakshif 'ajz al-umara' 'an muwajaha al-tayyar al-salafi" (The king's address reveals the weakness of rulers confronting the current of salafism). 1993. *Al-Jazira al-'Arabiyya* 3, no. 24 (Jan.): 12–14.

Khuri, Fuad. 1970. "Parallel Cousin Marriage Reconsidered: A Middle Eastern Practice that Nullifies the Effects of Marriage on the Intensity of Family Relationships." *Man* 5: 597–618.

Kian, Azadeh. 1997. "Women and Politcs in Post-Islamist Iran: The Gender Conscious Drive to Change." *British Journal of Middle Eastern Studies* 24, no. 1: 75–96.

Kim, A. L. 1998. "Name-Brand Politicians." *Los Angeles Times,* 24 Nov., A5.

Kondo, Dorinne. 1990. *Crafting Selves: Power, Gender, and Discourses of Identity in a Japanese Workplace.* Chicago: Univ. of Chicago Press.

Kuttab, Eileen, et al. 1995. "Investing in Half the Population: The World Bank and Economic Policy." In *Gender and Public Policy,* working paper no. 2, 19–35. Bir Zeit: Women's Studies Program.

Kuwait, State of. 1992. Ministry of Planning. *Annual Statistical Abstract, 1992.* Kuwait.

———. N.d. (c. 1963). Ministry of Guidance and Information. *Kuwait Today: A Welfare State.* Nairobi: Quality Publications.

———. 1997a. Ministry of Justice, Department of Legal Documentation. *Statistical Report on Marriage and Divorce.* Kuwait.

———. 1997b. Ministry of Social Affairs and Labor, Oct. Personal communication with Haya al-Mughni.

Kymlicka, Will. 1995. *Multicultural Citizenship.* Oxford: Clarendon Press.

Lackner, Helen. 1995. "Women and Development in the Republic of Yemen." In *Gender and Development in the Arab World,* edited by Nabil F. Khoury and Valentine M. Moghadam, 71–96. London: Zed Books.

Lavie, Smadar, and Ted Swedenburg. 1996. *Displacement, Diaspora, and Geographies of Identity.* Durham, N.C.: Duke Univ. Press.

Layoun, Mary. 1992. "Telling Spaces: Palestinian Women and the Engendering of National Narratives." In *Nationalisms and Sexualties,* edited by Andrew Parker, Mary Russo, Doris Sommer, and Patricia Yaeger, 407–23. New York: Routledge.

Lazreg, Marnia. 1994. "Algerian Women in Question." In *The Eloquence of Silence: Algerian Women in Question,* edited by M. Lazreg, 216–17. New York: Routledge.

Le Monde. 1993. "Les Femmes accueillent avec prudence la réforme de leur statut." 22 Oct.

Lebanese Criminal Law. Art. 562. Beirut.

Lipset, S. M. 1960. *Political Man: The Social Bases of Politics,* 8. Garden City, N.Y.: Doubleday. Quoted in Tilly, Charles. 1995. "Citizenship, Identity, and Social History. *International Review of Social History,* supplement 3, 40: 1–17.

———. 1963. *The First New Nation.* New York: Basic Books.

"Legal Aid, New Laws and Violence Against Women in Sudan." 1997. *Women Living under Muslim Laws* 18: 81–90.

Lister, Ruth. 1996. "Citizenship: Towards a Feminist Synthesis." Paper presented at the conference, "Women and Citizenship," July, Univ. of Greenwich.

———. 1997a. *Citizenship. Feminist Perspectives.* New York: New York Univ. Press.

———. 1997b. "Citizenship: Towards a Feminist Synthesis." *Feminist Review*, no. 57 (fall): 19–38.

Longva, Anh Nga. 1996a. *Walls Built on Sand: Migration, Exclusion, and Society in Kuwait.* Boulder, Colo.: Westview Press.

———. 1996b. "Citizenship in the Gulf States: Conceptualisation and Practice." Paper presented at the Conference on Citizenship and the State in the Middle East, 22–24 Nov., Oslo, Norway.

Lowrie, Arthur L., ed. 1993. *Islam, Democracy, the State and the West: A Round Table with Dr. Hasan Turabi.* Monograph no. 1, 10 May, 1992. Tampa, Fla.: World and Islam Studies Enterprise.

Maccoby Eleanor, E., and C. J. Jaklin. 1974. *The Psychology of Sex Differences.* Stanford, Calif.: Stanford Univ. Press.

Macpherson, C. B. 1962. *The Political Theory of Possessive Individualism.* London: Oxford Univ. Press.

MacKinnon, Catharine A. 1989. *Toward a Feminist Theory of the State.* Cambridge, Mass.: Harvard Univ. Press.

———. 1996. "Privacy v. Equality: Beyond Roe v. Wade." In *Applications of Feminist Legal Theory to Women's Lives: Sex, Violence, Work and Reproduction,* edited by D. Kelly Weisberg, 985–94. Philadelphia: Temple Univ. Press.

Majmu'at al-Muhtamat bi Shu'un al-Mar'at al-Misriya. 1988. *Al-Huquq al-qanuniya lil mar'at al-misriya.* Cairo, Egypt: N.p.

Makdisi, Ussama. 1997. "Gender, Citizenship and the Nation." Paper presented at the conference, "Gender and Citizenship in Lebanon," Mar., American Univ. in Beirut.

al-Makhawi, Buthaina. 1994. "The Situation of Kuwaiti Women Married to non-Kuwaiti and to Stateless Individuals." Paper presented at the first "Post-Liberation Conference on Women's Role in Cultural, Social, and Economic Development at Kuwait," Kuwait, Apr.

Makiya, K. 1993. "State Rape: Violation of Iraqi Women." *New Stateman and Society,* 7 May, 16–17.

Al-Mamlaka al-'Arabiyya al-Sa'udiyya (The Kingdom of Saudi Arabia). N.d. *Madda al-tarbiya al-wataniyya: Al-siff al-thalith al-mutawassit* (The national educational curriculum: The third intermediate grade). Jidda, Saudi Arabia.

Mann, Michael. 1987. "Ruling Class Strategies and Citizenship." *Sociology* 21: 339–54.

Manzo, Kathryn A. 1996. *Creating Boundaries: The Politics of Race and Nation.* Boulder, Colo.: Lynne Rienner.

Mar'i, Mariam, and Sami Kh. Mar'i. 1993. "The Role of Women as Change Agents in Arab Society in Israel." In *Calling the Equality Bluff: Women in Israel,* edited by Barbara Swirski and Marilyn Safir, 213–21. New York: Teachers College Press.

Mariscotti, Cathlyn. 1994. "Consent and Resistance: The History of Upper and Middle Class Egyptian Women Reflected Through Their Published Journals (1925–39), Ph.D. diss., Temple Univ.

Markaz al-Abhath wa al-Dirasat al-Sukaniyya. 1972. *Al-Mar' at al-misriya fi 'Ashrin 'Amm: 1952–1972*. Cairo, Egypt: Markaz Abhath wa al-Dirasat al-Sukaniyya.

Marshall, T. H. 1950. "Citizenship and Social Class." In *Citizenship and Social Class and Other Essays*, 1–85. Cambridge, Eng.: Cambridge Univ. Press.

———. 1964. *Class, Citizenship and Social Development*. Garden City, N.Y.: Doubleday.

Massad, Joseph. 1995. "Conceiving the Masculine: Gender and Palestinian Nationalism." *Middle East Journal* 49, no. 3 (summer): 467–83.

Mayer, Ann Elizabeth. 1991. *Islam and Human Rights*. Boulder, Colo.: Westview Press.

———. 1995a. "Cultural Particularism as a Bar to Women's Rights: Reflection on the Middle Eastern Experience." In *Women's Rights Human Rights: International Feminist Perspectives*, edited by Julie Peters and Andrea Wolper, 176–88. New York: Routledge.

———. 1995b. "Reform of Personal Status Laws in North Africa: A Problem of Islamic or Mediterranean Laws?" *Middle East Journal* 49, no. 3 (summer): 432–46.

———. 1995c. "Rhetorical Strategies and Official Policies on Women's Rights: The Merits and Drawbacks of the New World Hypocrisy." In *Faith and Freedom: Women's Human Rights in the Muslim World*, edited by Mahnaz Afkhami, 104–32. Syracuse, N.Y.: Syracuse Univ. Press.

Mazrui, A. 1994. "Race and Religion in the New World Order." In *The Gulf War and the New World Order: International Relations of the Middle East*, edited by T. Y. Ismael and J. S. Ismael, 521–35. Gainesville: Univ. Press of Florida.

McElroy, Wendy, ed. 1991. *Freedom, Feminism, and the State*. New York: Holmes and Meier.

Medimegh, Aziza Darghouth. 1992. *Droits et vécu de la femme en Tunisie* (Law and women's conditions in Tunisia). Lyon, France: Hermes-Edilis.

Meeker, Michael E. 1976. "Meaning and Society in the Near East: Examples from the Black Sea Turks and the Levantine Arabs." *International Journal of Middle Eastern Studies* 7: 383–422.

Mehran, Golnar. 1991. "The Creation of the New Muslim Woman: Female Education in the Islamic Republic of Iran." *Convergence* 23, no. 4:42–52.

Meillasoux, Claude. 1983. "The Economic Bases of Demographic Reproduction: From the Domestic Mode of Production to Wage Earnings." *Journal of Peasant Studies* 11, no. 1: 50–61.

Meriwether, Margaret L. 1993. "Women and Economic Change in Nineteenth Century Syria: The Case of Aleppo." In *Women in Arab Society*, edited by Judith Tucker, 65–83. Bloomington: Indiana Univ. Press.

Mernissi, Fatima. 1992. *Islam and Democracy*. New York: Addison Wesley.

———. 1996. *Women's Rebellion & Islamic Memory.* London: Zed Books.

Messick, Brinkley. 1993. *The Calligraphic State, Textual Domination and History in a Muslim State.* Berkeley and Los Angeles: Univ. of California Press.

———. 1998. "Written Identities: Legal Subjects in an Islamic State." *History of Religions* 3, no. 1. (Aug.): 25–51.

Metcalf, Barbara Daly. 1990. *Perfecting Women. Maulana Ashraf 'Ali Thanawi's Bihishti Zewar.* Berkeley and Los Angeles: Univ. of California Press.

Middle East Report. Special issue, *Gender and Citizenship in the Middle East,* no. 198 (Jan.–Mar.).

Middle East Watch. 1990. *Human Rights in Iraq.* New Haven, Conn.: Yale Univ. Press.

———. 1992. *Needless Deaths in the Gulf War: Civilian Casualties During the Air Campaign and Violations of the Laws of War.* New York: Human Rights Watch.

———. 1993. *Genocide in Iraq: The Anfal Campaign Against the Kurds.* New York: Human Rights Watch.

Minh-ha, Trinh. 1989. *Woman, Native Other: Writing, Postcoloniality, and Feminism.* Bloomington: Indiana Univ. Press.

Mir-Hosseini, Ziba. 1993. *Marriage on Trial: A Study of Islamic Family Law, Iran and Morocco Compared.* London and New York: IB Tauris & Co.

———. 1996. "Women and Politics in Post-Khomeini Iran: Divorce, Veiling, and Emerging Feminist Voices." In *Women and Politics in the Third World,* edited by Haleh Afshar, 142–70. London: Routledge.

Mitchell, Timothy. 1988. *Colonising Egypt.* New York: Cambridge Univ. Press.

Moawad, Nayla. 1997. "Gendered Participation in Civil Society." Paper presented at the conference, "Gender and Citizenship in Lebanon," Mar., American Univ. in Beirut.

Moghadam, Valentine M. 1993. *Modernizing Women: Gender and Social Change in the Middle East.* Boulder, Colo.: Lynne Rienner.

———. 1998. *Women, Work and Economic Reform in the Middle East and North Africa.* Boulder, Colo.: Lynne Rienner.

Mogheizel, Laur. 1985. *Al-Mara fi al-Tashri al-Lubnani: Fi daou al-itifiaqiyat ad-dualia maa mukarana bi-al-tashriaat al-Arabiah* (Woman in the Lebanese Constitution: In light of the international agreements and a comparison with other Arabic constitutions). Beirut: Mahad ad-Dirassat al-Nisaiyah fi al-Alam al-Arabi, Kuliyat Beirut al-Jamiyah (Institute for the Study of Women in the Arab World, Beirut Univ. College).

———. 1994. Personal communication, Nov.

———. 1997. "Gender and the Transmission of Citizenship in Lebanese Law." Paper presented at the conference, "Gender and Citizenship in Lebanon," Mar., American Univ. in Beirut.

Mohanty, Chandra. 1991. "Introduction." In *Third World Women and the Politics of Feminism,* edited by C. Mohanty, A. Russo, and L. Torres, 1–47. Bloomington and Indianapolis: Indiana Univ. Press.

Molyneux, Maxine. 1985a. "Legal Reform and Socialist Revolution in Democratic

Yemen: Women and the Family." *International Journal of the Sociology of Law* 13: 147–72.

———. 1985b. "Mobilization Without Emancipation? Women's Interests, the State, and Revolution in Nicaragua." *Feminist Studies* 11, no. 2: 227–54.

———. 1991. "The Law, the State and Socialist Policies with Regard to Women: The Case of the People's Democratic Republic of Yemen, 1967–1990." In *Women, Islam, and the State,* edited by Deniz Kandiyoti, 237–71, Philadelphia: Temple Univ. Press.

———. 1995. "Women's Rights and Political Contingency: The Case of Yemen, 1990–1994." *Middle East Journal* 49, no 3: 418–32.

Morocco, Kingdom of. 1996. *The Constitution.* Ministry of Communication, Rabat, Morocco.

———. 1958. *Bulletin Officiel* no. 2394, du 12 Septembre, Dahir no. 1-58-250 du 21 Safar 1373 (6 Sept. 1958) portant *Code de la nationalité Marocaine.*

Moulay Rchid, Abderrazak. 1991. *La Femme et la loi au Maroc* (Women and law in Morocco). Casablanca: United Nations Univ. and Editions le Fennec.

al-Mughni, Haya. 1993. *Women in Kuwait: The Politics of Gender.* London: Saqi Books.

———. 1996. "Women's Organizations in Kuwait." *Middle East Report* no. 198. Vol. 26, no. 1: 32–35.

———. 1997. "From Gender Equality to Female Subjugation: The Changing Agendas of Women's Groups in Kuwait." In *Organizing Women: Formal and Informal Groups in the Middle East,* edited by Dawn Chatty and Annika Rabo, 195–209. Oxford: Berg Publishers.

Muhammed, Ahmed Taha. 1979. *Al-Mar' at al-Misirya.* Cairo: al-Matba't al-Ta'lif.

Al-Munazzama al-'Arabiyya li Huquq al-Insan (The Arab Organization on Human Rights). 1993. "Al-Islahat al-mu'lina lam tuhaqiq al-hadd al-adna min huquq al-afrad" (The announced reforms have not achieved the minimum rights of individuals). *Al-Jazira al-'Arabiyya* 3, no. 33 (Aug.): 22–26.

Al-Munazzama al-Huququiyya al-Amirkiyya (Middle East Watch). 1992. "Wa Taqrir 'an Awda' Huquq al-Insan fi al-Sa 'Udiyya Li 'am 1991." *Al-Jazirah al-'Arabiyya* 2, no. 14 (Mar.): 30–33.

Mundy, Martha. 1995. *Domestic Government: Kinship, Community, and Polity in North Yemen.* London: I. B. Tauris.

Murphy, Robert F., and Leonard Kasdan. 1959. "The Structure of Parallel Cousin Marriage." *American Anthropologist* 6: 17–29.

Musa, 'Abd al-Amir. 1992. "Mudhakkira al-nasiha (Memorandum of advice)," pt. 1. *Al-Jazira al-'Arabiyya* 2, no. 21 (Oct.): 35–47.

Najjab, Selwa. 1994. *Policy Statement of the Women's Health Programme at the Union of Palestinian Medical Relief Committees in the West Bank and Gaza Strip.* Jerusalem: Union of Palestinian Medical Relief Committees.

al-Najjar, Ghanim. 1999. "Kuwaiti Parliament Fails Women's Rights." *Gulf 2000.* 30 Nov.

Najmabadi, Afsaneh. 1991. "Hazards of Modernity and Morality: Women. State and

Ideology in Contemporary Iran." In *Women, Islam and the State,* edited by Deniz Kandiyoti, 48–76. London: Macmillan.

———. 1993. "Zanha-yi Millat: Women or Wives of the Nation?" *Iranian Studies* 26, nos. 1–2: 51–72.

———. 1998. "Crafting an Educated Housewife in Iran." In *Remaking Women: Feminism and Modernity in the Middle East,* edited by Lila Abu-Lughod, 91–125. Princeton, N.J.: Princeton Univ. Press.

Naqeeb, Khaldoun Hasan. 1990. *Society and State in the Gulf and Arab Peninsula: A Different Perspective.* Translated by L. M. Kenny. London: Routledge.

Nasir, Jamal. 1990. *The Islamic Law of Personal Status.* 2d ed. London: Graham and Trotman.

———. 1994. *The Status of Women under Islamic Law.* 2d ed. London: Graham and Trotman.

Nasser, Lamis. 1997. "Important Policy Measures and Other Initiatives to Promote the Implementaion of CEDAW in Jordan." Paper presented at a UNDP and UNICEF workshop on CEDAW, Amman, Jordan, Aug.

National Bank of Kuwait. 1997. "Special Topic: The Labor Force in Kuwait." *Economic and Financial Quarterly iii.* (Kuwait: NBK): 33–41.

National Democratic Alliance (Sudan), Secretariat for Organization and Administration. 1996. *Documents of the Conference on Fundamental Issues, Asmara, 15–23 June, 1995.* Asmara, Eritrea: National Democratic Alliance.

Nedelsky, Jennifer. 1989. "Reconceiving Autonomy: Sources, Thoughts and Possibilities." *Yale Journal of Law and Feminism* 1, no. 7: 7–36.

———. 1990. "Law, Boundaries, and the Bounded Self." *Representations,* no. 30 : 162–89.

———. 1993. "Reconceiving Rights as Relationship." *Review of Constitutional Studies* 1, no 1 :1–26.

Nelson, Cynthia. 1996. *Doriya Shafiq, Egyptian Feminist.* Cairo: American Univ. Press.

Newton, Sarah. N.d. Senior honors thesis, Anthropology Department, Univ. of California, Davis.

Nicholson, Linda. 1997. "The Myth of the Traditional Family." In *Feminism and Families,* edited by Hilde Lindeman Nelson, 27–42. New York: Routledge.

Nidhal al-baath (The struggle of the bath). 1963. Vol. 6. Beirut: Dar al-Talia.

Nomer, Ergin. 1982. *Vatandaplýk hukuku dersleri.* Istanbul, Turkey: Fakülteler Matbaasý.

O'Conner, Julia. 1996. "From Women in the Welfare State to Gendering Welfare State Regimes." *Current Sociology* 44, no. 2: 1–47.

Ofeish, Sami Adeeb. 1996. "Sectarianism and Change in Lebanon: 1843–1975," Ph.D. diss., Univ. of Southern California.

Official Gazette. 1954. No. 1171, 16 Feb., p. 105. Amman, Jordan.

———. 1963. No. 1675, p. 290. Amman, Jordan.

———. 1972. No. 998, 1003, 3829, 1 June. Amman, Jordan.

———. 1973. No. 2426, 16 June, p. 1112. Amman, Jordan.

————. 1987. No. 3496, 1623. Amman, Jordan.

————. 1991. No. 3740, 16 Jan., p. 73. Amman, Jordan.

————. 1992. No. 3829, 1 June, pp. 998, 1003. Amman, Jordan.

Okin, Susan Moller. 1979. *Women in Western Political Thought.* Princeton, N.J.: Princeton Univ. Press.

————. 1989. *Justice, Gender and the Family.* New York: Basic Books.

Oldfield, Adrian. 1990. *Citizenship and Community: Civic Republicanism and the Modern World.* London: Routledge.

Olsen, Frances E. 1985. "The Myth of State Intervention in the Family." *Journal of Law Reform* 18, no. 4 (summer): 835–64.

Omar, S. 1994. "Women: Honour, Shame and Dictatorship." In *Iraq since the Gulf War: Prospects for Democracy,* edited by Fran Hazelton, 60–71. London, England: Zed Books.

Ong, Aihwa. 1996. "Cultural Citizenship as Subject-Making: Immigrants Negotiate Racial and Cultural Boundaries in the United States." *Current Anthropology* 37, no. 5: 737–62.

————. 1999. "Muslim Feminism: Citizenship in the Shelter of Corporatist Islam." *Citizenship Studies* 3, no. 2.

Orbinski, J. 1996. "New Frontiers in Health in a Changing Global Context." In *International Social Welfare in a Changing World,* edited by J. S. Ismael, 137–50. Calgary, Canada: Detselig Enterprises.

Orloff, Ann Shola. 1993. "Gender and the Social Rights of Citizenship: The Comparative Analysis of Gender Relations and Welfare States." *American Sociological Review* 58: 303–28.

————. 1996. *Gender and the Welfare State.* Discussion Paper no. 1082–96. Institute for Research on Poverty, Univ. of Wisconsin-Madison.

Ortner, Sherry. 1974. "Is Female to Male as Nature Is to Culture?" In *Women, Culture and Society,* edited by Michelle Z. Rosaldo and Louise Lamphere, 67–88. Stanford, Calif.: Stanford Univ. Press.

Osman, Dina Sheikh el-Din. 1985. "The Legal Status of Muslim Women in the Sudan." *Journal of Eastern African Research and Development* 15: 124–42.

Paidar, Parvin. 1995. *Women and the Political Process in Twentieth-Century Iran.* Cambridge, Eng.: Cambridge Univ. Press.

Palestinian Central Bureau of Statistics (PCBS). 1996. *The Demographic Survey in the West Bank and Gaza: Preliminary Report.* Ramallah: PCBS.

Papanek, Hanna. 1994. "The Ideal Woman and the Ideal Society: Control and Autonomy in the Construction of Identity." In *Identity Politics and Women. Cultural Reassertions and Feminisms in Interntional Perspective,* edited by Valentine M. Moghadam. Boulder, Colo.: Westview Press.

Parker, Andrew, Mary Russo, Doris Sommer, and Patricia Yaeger, eds. 1992. *Nationalisms and Sexualities.* New York: Routledge.

Parsons, Talcott. 1971. *The System of Modern Societies.* Englewood Cliffs, N.J.: Prentice-Hall.

Pateman, Carole. 1988. *The Sexual Contract.* Stanford, Calif.: Stanford Univ. Press.

Pazartesi. 1995. Sept.

———. 1996. Apr.

———. 1997. Nov.

———. 1998. Jan.

Pederson, Jon, and Rick Hooper. 1998. *Development Assistance in the West Bank and Gaza.* Oslo: FAFO.

Personal Status Law (Provisional Law No. 61 for 1976). Quoted in Sa'di Abdeen, *Musoat al-jaib lil-tashira' wa-al-qada' wal-fiqh* (the Pocket Encyclopedia for Legislation and Judiciary and Jurisprudence) (Amman, Jordan: Dar al-Jaib lil-nashir wa-al Tawzea', 1994).

Peteet, Julie. 1991. *Gender in Crisis: Women and the Palestinian Resistance Movement.* New York: Columbia Univ. Press.

Phillips, Anne. 1991. *Engendering Democracy.* Cambridge, Eng.: Polity Press.

———. 1993. *Democracy and Difference.* Cambridge, Eng.: Polity Press.

Phythian, M. 1997. *Arming Iraq: How the U.S. and Britain Secretly Built Saddam's War Machine.* Boston: Northeastern Univ. Press.

Pocock, J. G. A. 1998. "The Ideal of Citizenship since Classical Times." In *The Citizenship Debates,* edited by Gershon Shafir. Minneapolis: Univ. of Minnesota Press.

Al-Qaidah (Baghdad). 1955. May.

al-Qassem, Anis. 1996. "Introduction to the Palestinian Authority Basic Law." *Palestine Report,* 16 (9 Feb.). Jerusalem: Jerusalem Media and Communication Center.

Raday, Frances. 1993. "The Concept of Gender Equality in a Jewish State." In *Calling the Equality Bluff: Women in Israel,* edited by Barbara Swirski and Marilyn Safir, 18–28. New York: Teachers College Press.

———. 1994. "The Privatization of Civil Rights and the Abuse of Power." *Law* 23: 21–53 (Hebrew).

———. 1995. "On Equality" (in Hebrew). In *Women's Status in Israeli Law and Society,* 19–63. Tel Aviv: Schoken.

———. 1996. "Women in Law in Israel: A Study of the Relationship Between Professional Integration and Feminism." Symposium: The Comparative International Role of Women Attorneys in Law and Society. *Georgia State University Law Review* 12, no. 525: 525–52.

———. 1998. "Constitutional Evolution in Israel and Equality Between Men and Women. Paper presented at Canada-Israel Law Conference, "Chartering Human Rights," 20–23 Dec., Hebrew Univ. in Jerusalem.

Rahal, Ghsoon. 1996. "Al-Azar al-Muhila, wal Azar al-Mukhafifa in the Jordanian Criminal Law." Presented at seminar, "Women and Criminal Law," Jordanian Women's Union, Amman, Jordan, Dec.

al-Rahmani, Eqbal. 1996. "The Impact of Traditional Domestic Sexual Division of Labor on Women's Status: The Case of Kuwait." *Research in Human Capital and Development* 9: 79–101.

Ramadan, Abdel 'Azim Muhammed Ibrahim. N.d. *Tatawur al-harakah al-wataniya fi misr (1918–1936).* Cairo: Dar al-Katib al-'Arabi lil Tiba'a wa al-Nashr.

Ramazani, Nesta. 1993. "Women in Iran: The Revolutionary Ebb and Flow." *Middle East Journal* 47, no. 3: 409–28.

Ramirez, Francisco O., Yasemin Soysal, and Suzanne Shanahan. 1997. "The Changing Logic of Political Citizenship: Cross-National Acquisition of Women's Suffrage Rights, 1890–1990." *American Sociological Review* 62, no. 5: 735–45.

al-Rasheed, Madawi. 1996a. "God, The King and the Nation: Political Rhetoric in Saudi Arabia in the 1990s." *Middle East Journal* 50, no. 3 (summer): 359–71.

———. 1996b. "Saudi Arabia's Islamic Opposition." *Current History* 95, no. 597 (Jan.): 16–21.

Rawls, John. 1971. *A Theory of Justice.* Cambridge, Mass.: Belknap.

Razack, Sherene H. 1998. *Looking White People in the Eye. Gender, Race, and Culture in Courtrooms and Classrooms.* Toronto: Univ. of Toronto Press.

Regional Command, Baath Party of Iraq. 1974. *Al-Taqarir al-siyasi al-sadir an al-Mutamar al-Qutri al-Thamin* (The political report issued by the Eighth Regional Congress). Baghdad, Iraq: Dar al-Thawra Press.

Report by His Britannic Majesty's Government on the Palestine Administration, submitted to the Council of the League of Nations, 1929. Treaty of Lausanne, Arts. 30–33.

Republic of Iraq. 1978. *Annual Abstract of Statistics, 1977.* Baghdad: Ministry of Planning.

République Tunisienne (Republic of Tunisia). 1997. *Code du statut personnel* (Code of personal status). Tunis: Imprimerie Officielle. First promulgated on 13 Aug. 1956, periodically updated.

———. 1998a. *Code de la nationalité Tunisienne* (Code of Tunisian citizenship). Tunis: Imprimerie Officielle.

———. 1998b. *Constitution de la République Tunisienne* (Constitution of the Republic of Tunisia). Tunis: Imprimerie Officielle.

Republic of Yemen (RoY). 1990a. Constitution of the Republic of Yemen (in Arabic). *Official Gazette* 1.

———. 1990b. Law 6/1990 on Yemeni Citizenship (in Arabic). *Official Gazette* 7.

———. 1992. Republican Decree of Law 20/1992 on Personal Status (in Arabic). *Official Gazette* 3, no. 3 (amended by Law 27/1998 issued on 23 Nov. 1998. *Al-Qistas.* 1999. Jan.)

———. 1994. Constitution of the Republic of Yemen (in Arabic). *Official Gazette* 19, no. 2.

Rhode, Deborah L. 1989. *Justice and Gender.* Cambridge, Mass.: Harvard Univ. Press.

Ridley, Matt. 1993. *The Red Queen: Sex and the Evolution of Human Nature.* New York: Penguin Books.

Rishmawi, Mona. 1992. "An Introduction to the Family Law Applied in the Palestinian West Bank." *International Review of Comparative Public Policy* 4: 245–61. JAI Press.

Roche, Maurice. 1995. "Citizenship and Modernity." *British Journal of Sociology* 46, no. 4 (Dec.): 715–33.

Rone, Jemera, and Sheila Carapico. 1994. *Yemen: Human Rights in Yemen During and after the 1994 War* 6, no. 1 (Oct.). New York: Human Rights Watch.

Rosaldo, Michelle Z. 1974. "Women, Culture, and Society: A Theoretical Overview." In *Women, Culture and Society,* edited by Michelle Z. Rosaldo and Louise Lamphere, 17–42. Stanford, Calif.: Stanford Univ. Press.

Rosenhek, Zeev. 1995. *The Origins and Development of a Dualistic Welfare State: The Arab Population in the Israeli Welfare State.* Ph.D. diss., The Hebrew University, Department of Political Science (Hebrew).

Roy, Olivier. 1994. *The Failure of Political Islam.* London: I. B. Tauris.

Ruddick, Sara. 1997. "The Idea of Fatherhood." In *Feminism and Families,* edited by Hilde Lindemann Nelson, 205–20. New York: Routledge.

Rush, Alan. 1987. *Al-Sabah: History and Genealogy of Kuwait's Ruling Family.* London: Ithaca Press.

Sacks, Karen. 1975. "Engels Revisited: Women, the Organization of Production, and Private Property." In *Towards an Anthropology of Women,* edited by Rayna Reiter, 211–34. New York: Monthly Review Press.

Sadowski, Yahya. 1993. "The New Orientalism and the Democracy Debate." *Middle East Report,* no. 183. Vol. 23, no. 4: 14–26.

Saeid Zadeh, Mohsen. 1998. *Women in Civil Society: What Is Their Share?* Tehran, Iraq: Ghatreh Publishing House.

Sainsbury, Diane. 1994. *Gendering Welfare States.* London: Sage.

Saleh, Ibrahim. 1988. "The Writing of the 1971 Egyptian Constitution." In *Constitution Makers on Constitution Making: The Experiences of Eight Nations,* edited by Robert Goldwin and Art Kaufman. Washington, D.C.: The American Enterprise Institute.

Salem, Paul, K. Shehade, M. Young, and Z. Majed. 1996. Preliminary Draft of Report on Associational Life and Public Space in Beirut: Dialects of Unity and Diversity. Beirut: Lebanese Center for Policy Studies.

el-Sanousi, Magda M., and Nafisa Ahmed El-Amin. 1994. "The Women's Movement, Displaced Women, and Rural Women in Sudan." In *Women and Politics Worldwide,* edited by Barbara Nelson and Najma Chowdhury, 674–89. New Haven, Conn.: Yale Univ. Press.

Sansarian, Eliz. 1982. *The Women's Rights Movement in Iran: Mutiny, Appeasement, and Repression from 1900 to Khomeini.* New York: Praeger.

Sapiro, Virginia. 1993. "Engendering Cultural Differences." In *The Rising Tide of Cultural Pluralism,* edited by Crawford Young. Madison: Univ. of Wisconsin.

Sarsour, Sa'ad. 1985. "The Problem of the Education of a Minority Who Are Foreigners in Their Own Country." In *Education in an Evolving Society,* edited by Walter Ackerman, Arik Carmon, and David Zucker, 473–526. Tel Aviv: Hakibbutz Hameuchad and Van Leer Institute (Hebrew).

Sayigh, Rosemary. 1993. "Palestinian Women and Politics in Lebanon." In *Arab Women: Old Boundaries New Frontiers,* edited by Judith E. Tucker, 175–92. Bloomington: Indiana Univ. Press.

al-Sayyid Marsot, Afaf Lutfi. 1984. *Egypt in the Reign of Muhammad 'Ali.* Cambridge, Eng.: Cambridge Univ. Press.

Schneider, David M. 1984. *A Critique of the Study of Kinship.* Ann Arbor: Univ. of Michigan Press.

Schneider, Jane. 1984. "Review of Jack Goody, The Development of the Family and Marriage in Europe." *Man* 19, no. 4: 686–88.

Scribner, S. 1995. *Policies Affecting Fertility and Contraceptive Use: An Assessment of Twelve Sub-Saharan Countries.* World Bank Discussion Papers, African Technical Series no. 259. Washington, D.C.: World Bank.

Shaban, A. 1994. *Asafa ala Bilad al-Shams* (A Storm on the Country of the Sun). Beirut: Dar al-Kunouz al-Adadiya.

Shafir, Gershon, ed. 1998. *The Citizenship Debates.* Minneapolis: Univ. of Minnesota Press.

Shafir, Gershon, and Yoav Peled. 1998. "The Dynamics of Citizenship in Israel and the Israeli-Palestinian Peace Process." In *The Citizenship Debates,* edited by Gershon Shafir, 251–61. Minneapolis: Univ. of Minnesota Press.

Shah, Nasra. 1994. "Changing Roles of Kuwaiti Women in Kuwait: Implications for Fertility." Paper presented at the First Post-Liberation Conference on Women's Role in Cultural, Social, and Economic Development, 11–13 Apr., Kuwait.

Shah, Nasra, and Sulayman S. al-Qudsi. 1990. "Female Work Roles in a Traditional Oil Economy." *Research in Human and Capital Development* 6: 213–46.

Shakry, Omnia. 1998. "Schooled Mothers and Structured Play: Child Rearing in Turn-of-the-Century Egypt." In *Remaking Women. Feminism and Modernity in the Middle East,* edited by Lila Abu-Lughod, 125–70. Princeton, N.J.: Princeton Univ. Press.

Shalhoub-Kevorkian, Nadera. 1997. "Wife Abuse: A Method of Social Control." *Israel Social Science Research* 12, no. 1: 59–72.

Al-Shall Economic Consulting Group. 1997. *Weekly Economic Report.* 24 Oct.

Shamiry, Naguib. 1984. "The Judicial System in Democratic Yemen." In *Contemporary Yemen: Politics and Historical Background,* edited by Brian R. Pridham, 175–94. London: Croom Helm.

———. 1995. "Yemen (Country Survey)." *Yearbook of Middle Eastern and Islamic Law* 2: 236–45.

———. N.d. *Rights of Women in PDRY Legislation* (in Arabic). Aden, Yemen: Dar al-Hamdani.

Sharabi, Hisham. 1988. *Neo-patriarchy: A Theory of Distorted Change in Arab Society.* New York: Oxford Univ. Press.

Sharafeddine, Fahmiyyi. 1997. "The Constitution and Gendered Punishment: Discussion." Paper presented at the conference, "Gender and Citizenship in Lebanon," Mar., American Univ. in Beirut.

Sharara, Yolla Polity. 1978. "Women and Politics in Lebanon." *Khamsin* 6: 6–32.

Sha'rawi, Hoda. 1981. *Muthakarat hoda sha'rawi: Ra'idat al-mar'at al-'Arabiya.* Cairo: Dar al-Hilal.

Sharoni, Simona. 1995. *Gender and the Israeli-Palestinian Conflict.* Syracuse, N.Y.: Syracuse Univ. Press.

Shehadeh, Raja. 1997. *From Occupation to Interim Accords: Israel and the Palesti-*

nian Territories. The Hague, Netherlands: Kluwer Law International.

Sh'ira, Wafa'. 1995. "Min ajl al-talaq: Nisa' al-'aqbat yutalibna bil shari'a al-Islamiya." *Rose al-Youssef.* 23 Oct.

Shoulter, J. 1874. *A Treatise on the Laws of Domestic Relations.* Boston: Little Brown.

Showstack Sassoon, Anne, ed. 1987. *Women and the State: The Shifting Boundaries of Public and Private.* London: Hutchinson.

Shukri, Ghali. 1991. *Al-'Aqbat fi watan mutaghiir.* Cairo: Dar al Shuruq.

Shuqeir, Masoon. 1996. "The Legal and *Shari'a* Ruling for Domestic Violence by the Husband to His Wife in Jordan." Committee for Women's Conditions, Arab Lawyer Federation, Jordanian Syndicate.

Shuster, William Morgan. 1912. *The Strangling of Persia.* New York: Century.

Sirman, Nükhet. 1989. "Feminism in Turkey: A Short History." *New Perspectives on Turkey* 3:1.

Smart, Carol. 1982. "Regulating Families or Legitimating Patriarchy Family Law in Britian," *International Journal of Sociology of Law* 10, no. 2: 129–47.

———. 1989. *Feminism and the Power of Law.* London: Routledge.

Smith, Patricia, ed. 1993. *Feminist Jurisprudence.* New York: Oxford Univ. Press.

Smith, Rogers M. 1997. *Civic Ideals. Conflicting Visions of Citizenship in U.S. History.* New Haven, Conn.: Yale Univ. Press.

al-Sobki, Amal Kamil Bayumi. 1986. *Al-Harakah al-nisa'iya fi misr mabayn al-thwratayn.* Cairo: Al- Hay'al al-Misriya al-Amma lil Kitab.

Sommers, Margaret R. 1993. "Citizenship and the Place of the Public Sphere: Law, Community and Political Culture in the Transition to Democracy." *American Sociological Review* 58 (Oct.): 587–620.

Sonbol, Amira. 1998. "Women's Witness and Other Fallacies." Paper presented to the Faculty Workshop, Islamic Law and Gender: Interdisciplinary Approaches, Georgetown University, Washington, D.C., 3 Apr.

Soysal, Mümtaz. 1986. *100 Soruda Anayasanýn anlamý* (Meaning of the Constitution in 100 Questions). Istanbul, Turkey: Gerçek Yayýnevi.

Soysal, Yasemin. 1994. *Limits of Citizenship: Migrants and Postnational Membership in Europe.* Chicago: Univ. of Chicago Press.

Spelman, Elizabeth. 1988. *Inessential Woman. Problems of Exclusion in Feminist Thought.* Boston: Beacon.

Stack, Carol. 1974. *All Our Kin: Strategies for Survival in a Black Community.* New York: Harper and Row.

The Star. 1991. 31 Aug.

The Status of Women in Turkey. 1994. The Turkish National Report to the Fourth World Conference on Women. Ankara, Turkey: Bizim Büro Basýmevi.

Stevens, Jacqueline. 1999. *Reproducing the State.* Princeton, N.J.: Princeton Univ. Press.

Stowasser, Barbara Freyer. 1996. "Women and Citizenship in the Qur'an." In *Women, the Family, and Divorce Laws in Islamic History,* edited by Amira El Azhary Sonbol, 23–38. Syracuse: Syracuse Univ. Press.

Stratton Lisa. 1992. "The Rights to have Rights: Gender Discrimination in Nationality Laws." *Minnesota Law Review* 77, no. 1: 66–78.

Stromquist, Nelly, ed. 1998. *Women in the Third World: An Encyclopedia of Contemporary Issues.* New York: Garland Books.

Suleiman, Michael. 1967. *Political Parties in Lebanon: The Challenge of a Fragmented Political Culture.* New York: Cornell Univ. Press.

Suleiman, Sweiss. 1995. *Jordan Times.* 27 Aug.

Swirski, Barbara. 1993a. "Israeli Feminism Old and New." In *Calling the Equality Bluff: Women in Israel,* edited by Barbara Swirski and Marilyn Safir, 285–302. New York: Teachers College Press.

———. 1993b. "Jews Don't Batter Their Wives: Another Myth Bites the Dust," In *Calling the Equality Bluff: Women in Israel,* edited by Barbara Swirski and Marilyn Safir, 319–27. New York: Teachers College Press.

Swirski, Barbara, and Manar Hasan. 1998. "Jewish and Palestinian Women in Israeli Society." In *Women in the Third World: An Encyclopedia of Contemporary Issues,* edited by Nelly Stromquist, 524–32. New York: Garland Books.

Swirski, Barbara, and Marilyn Safir. 1993. "Living in a Jewish State: National, Ethnic and Religious Implications." In *Calling the Equality Bluff: Women in Israel,* edited by Barbara Swirski and Marilyn Safir, 7–17. New York: Teachers College Press.

Swirski, Shlomo. 1999. *Politics and Education in Israel.* New York: Falmer.

Swirski, Shlomo, and Barbara Swirski. 1998. "Higher Education in Israel." *Israel Equality Monitor,* no. 8. Tel Aviv: Adva Center.

Tabari, Azar, and Nahid Yeganeh, eds. 1982. *In the Shadow of Islam: The Women's Movement in Iran.* London: Zed Books.

Taha, Batoul Mukhtar Muhammed. 1988. "The Women Deputies/Delegates of the Muslim Brethren and Women's Representation." *Al-Sahafa,* 16 May, 8. Khartoum, Sudan.

Tamari, Salim, and Anne Scott. 1991. "Fertility of Palestinian Women: Between the National Perspective and Social Reality" (in Arabic). *Sh'un al-Mara,* no. 1: 151–86. Nablus, Jordan: Women's Affairs.

"Taqrir Wizarat al-Kharijiyya al-Amirkiyya li 'Am 1992." 1993. Pt. 2. *Al-Jazira al-'Arabiyya* 3, no. 28 (May): 31–33.

Taraki, Lisa. 1995. "Society and Gender in Palestine: International Agencies." In *Gender and Public Policy,* working paper no. 2, 37–66. Bir Zeit: Women's Studies Program.

Tekeli, Şirin. 1981. "Women in Turkish Politics." In *Women in Turkish Society,* edited by Nermin Abadan-Unat, 293–310. Leiden: Brill.

———. 1991. "Tek parti döneminde kadin hareketi de bastirildi" (Women's movement too was repressed during the single party rule). In *Sol kemalizme bakiyor,* edited by L. Cinemre and R. Çakir, 93–107. Istanbul, Turkey: Metis Yayinlari.

Tétreault, Mary Ann. 1990. "Kuwait's Democratic Reform Movement." *Middle East Executive Reports* 9 (Oct.): 16–19.

———. 1991. "Autonomy, Necessity, and the Small State: Ruling Kuwait in the Twentieth Century." *International Organization* 45, no. 4: 565–91.

———. 1993. "Civil Society in Kuwait: Protected Spaces and Women's Rights." *Middle East Report* 47, no. 2: 275–91.

———. 1994. "Whose Honor? Whose Liberation? Women and the Reconstruction of Politics in Kuwait." In *Women and Revolution in Africa, Asia, and the New World,* edited by Mary Ann Tétreault, 297–315. Columbia: Univ. of South Carolina Press.

———. 1997. "Designer Democracy in Kuwait." *Current History* 96, no. 606: 36–39.

———. 2000. *Stories of Democracy: Politics and Society in Contemporary Kuwait.* New York: Columbia Univ. Press, forthcoming.

Tétreault, Mary Ann, and Haya al-Mughni. 1995a. "Gender, Citizenship, and Nationalism in Kuwait." *British Journal of Middle Eastern Studies* 22, nos. 1–2 : 64–80.

———. 1995b. "Modernization and Its Discontents: State and Gender in Kuwait." *Middle East Journal* 49, no. 3 (summer): 403–17.

al-Thaher, Ratib. 1996. "The Position of the Islamic and Christian Religion Towards Crimes of Honor Against Women." Jordanian Women's Union, Dec.

al-Thakeb, Fahed, and Joseph E. Scott. 1982. "Islamic Fundamentalism: A Profile of Its Supporters." *International Review of Modern Sociology* 12: 175–95.

Al-Thawra. 1976. 28 Jan. Baghdad, Iraq.

Thompson, W. 1970. *Appeal of One Half the Human Race, Women, Against the Pretension of the Other Half, Men to Retain Them in Political and Civil and Domestic Slavery.* New York: Source Book Press.

Thorne, Barrie, and Marilyn Yaom, eds. 1992. *Rethinking the Family: Some Feminist Questions.* Boston: Northeastern Univ. Press.

Tilly, Charles, ed. 1975. *The Formation of National States in Western Europe.* Princeton, N.J.: Princeton Univ. Press.

Tilly, Charles. 1995. "Citizenship, Identity, and Social History. *International Review of Social History,* suppl. 3, 40 : 1–17.

———, ed. 1996. *Citizenship, Identity and Social History.* New York: Cambridge Univ. Press.

Tiltnes, Aage Arild. 1996. "Jordanian Women's Participation in Formal Politics." Paper presented at al-Urdun al-Jadid Research Center on "The Jordan Living Conditions Survey."

Toennies, Ferdinand. 1957. *Community and Society.* Edited and translated by C. P. Loomis. 1897. Reprint. New York: Harper and Row.

Touati, Amine. 1995. *Algérie: Les Islamistes a l'Assaut du Pouvoir.* Paris: Editions L'Harmattan.

"Towards Crimes of Honor Against Women." 1996. Unpublished paper, Jordanian Women's Union, Dec. Presented to the Women's Studies Program, Amman, Jordan.

Tucker, Judith. 1985. *Women in Nineteenth Century Egypt.* New York: Cambridge Univ. Press.

———. 1991. "The Ties that Bound." In *Women in Middle East History: Shifting*

Boundaries in Sex and Gender, edited by Nikki Keddie and Beth Baron, 233–53. New Haven, Conn.: Yale Univ. Press.

———. 1998. *In the House of the Law. Gender and Islamic Law in Ottoman Syria and Palestine.* Berkeley and Los Angeles: Univ. of California Press.

Türkiye Cumhuriyeti Anayasasi 1982 (Constitution of the Republic of Turkey). 1984. Istanbul, Turkey: Yasa Yayinlari.

Turner, Bryan S. 1990. "Outline of a Theory of Citizenship." *Sociology* 24, no. 2 (May): 189–217.

———. 1992. "Outline of a Theory of Citizenship." In *Dimensions of Radical Democracy,* edited by C. Mouffe, 33–62. London: Verso.

———, ed. 1993a. *Citizenship and Social Theory.* London: Sage.

———, ed. 1993b. "Contemporary Problems in the Theory of Citizenship." In *Citizenship and Social Theory,"* 1–18. London: Sage.

———, ed. 1993c. Preface to *Citizenship and Social Theory,* vii–xiv. London: Sage.

Twine, Fred. 1994. *Citizenship and Social Rights. The Interdependence of Self and Society.* London: Sage.

United Nations. 1991. *Women: Challenges to the Year 2000.* New York: United Nations Department of Public Information.

———. 1995. *The World's Women 1995: Trends and Statistics.* New York: United Nations.

———. 1996. *Statistical Yearbook 1994.* New York: United Nations.

———. International Labor Conventions. Agreements 3, 100, 103, 111, 118, 122, 156.

United Nations Development Programme (UNDP). 1996. Human Development Report 1996. Oxford: Oxford Univ. Press.

United Nations Economic and Social Council. 1992. *Report on the Situation of Human Rights in Iraq,* 18 Feb. E/CN.4/1992/31. New York: United Nations.

———. 1994. *Report on the Situation of Human Rights in Iraq,* 25 Feb. E/CN.4/1994/58. New York: United Nations.

———. 1995. *Report on the Situation of Human Rights in Iraq,* 15 Feb. E/CN.4/1995/56. New York: United Nations.

United Nations, General Assembly of. 1967. "Equality of Men and Women in Rights." Nov. Arts. 1, 2; Decision no. 2263, D22.

U.S. Department of State. 1997. *Sudan Country Report on Human Rights Practices for 1997.* In Discussion Group for Sudan Concerns, 3 pts. [cited 31 Jan. 1998]. Available from SUDANESE@msu.edu; INTERNET.

Vakili, Valla. 1996. *Debating Religion and Politics in Iran: The Political Thought of Abdolkarim Soroush.* Occasional paper series no. 2. New York: Council of Foreign Relations.

Voet, Rian. 1998. *Feminism and Citizenship.* London: Sage.

Vogel, Ursula. 1991. "Is Citizenship Gender-Specific?" In *The Frontiers of Citizenship,* edited by Ursula Vogel and Michael Moran, 58–85. New York: St. Martin's Press.

———. 1994. "Marriage and the Boundaries of Citizenship." In *The Condition of Citizenship,* edited by Bart van Steenbergen, 76–89. London: Sage.

Vom Bruck, Gabriele. 1999. "Being a Zaydi in the Absence of an Imam: Doctrinal Revisions, Religious Instruction and the (Re-)Invention of Ritual." In *Le Yémen contemporain,* edited by Rémy Leveau, Franck Mermier, and Udo Steinbach, 169–92. Paris: Karthala.

Walby, Sylvia. 1989. "Theorizing Patriarchy." *Sociology* 23, no. 2 (May): 213–34.

———. 1994. "Is Citizenship Gendered?" *Sociology* 28: 379–95.

Walker, Susan. 1983. "Women and Housing in Classical Greece: The Archaeological Evidence." In *Images of Women in Antiquity,* edited by Averil Cameron and Amélie Kuhrt. London: Croom Helm: 81–91.

Walzer, Michael. 1965. *The Revolution of the Saints: A Study in the Origins of Radical Politics.* Cambridge, Mass.: Harvard Univ. Press.

Wasserstein, Bernard. 1991. *The British in Palestine. The Mandatory Government and the Arab-Jewish Conflict 1917–1929.* 2d ed. Oxford: Blackwell.

Weber, Cynthia. 1995. *Simulating Sovereignty: Intervention, the State and Symbolic Exchange.* New York: Cambridge Univ. Press.

Weber, Max. 1978. *Economy and Society: An Outline of Interpretive Sociology.* Edited by Guenther Roth and Claus Wittich. Berkeley: Univ. of California Press.

Weihl, Hanna. 1995. *The Implementation of the Long-Term Care Law in the Arab Sector.* Jerusalem: Israel National Insurance Institute (Hebrew).

Weisberg, D. Kelly, ed. 1993. *Foundations: Feminist Legal Theory.* Philadelphia: Temple Univ. Press.

———. 1996. *Applications of Feminist Legal Theory to Women's Lives: Sex, Violence, Work, and Reproduction.* Philadelphia: Temple Univ. Press.

Weitzman, L. J. 1981. *The Marriage Contract: Spouses Lovers and the Law.* New York: Free Press.

Welchman, Lynn. Forthcoming. *Statistical Study of Six Shari'a Courts in the West Bank and Gaza.* Jerusalem: Women's Center for Legal Aid and Counseling.

Williams, Patricia. 1991. *The Alchemy of Race and Rights. Diary of a Law Professor.* Cambridge, Mass.: Harvard Univ. Press.

Williams, Patrick, and Laura Chrisman. 1994. *Colonial Discourse and Post-Colonial Theory: A Reader.* New York: Columbia Univ. Press.

Wizarat al-Ta'lim al-'Ali. 1975. *Al-Mar'at fi Misr.* Cairo: Al-Matb'at al-'Amiriya.

Wizarat al-Tarbiya wa al-Ta'lim. 1968. *Al-Mithaq wa Taqriruhu.* Cairo: Dar wa Matab'a al-Sha'b.

"Women and the Personal Status Law." 1996. Unpublished paper, Jordanian Women's Union, Amman, Jordan, 2 June.

Women's Center for Legal Aid and Counseling. 1997. *Towards Equality: The Law and Palestinian Women* (in Arabic). Jerusalem: Women's Center for Legal Aid and Counseling.

Women's Studies Center. 1996. *Palestinian Women in Decision-Making.* Jerusalem: Women's Studies Center.

Working Group on the Status of Palestinian Women in Israel. 1997. *NGO Report: The Status of Palestinian Women Citizens of Israel.* Shefaram.

World Health Organization. Press Release. Cited 27 Apr. 1998. Available from WHO/23.http://www.who.org/press/l996/pr96~23.html; INTERNET.

Wuerth, Anna. 1994. *The Legal Status of Women in Yemen.* Report submitted to CID/WID Project, Bureau of Applied Research in Anthropology, Univ. of Arizona, Tucson.

———. 1995. "A Sana'a Court: The Family and the Ability to Negotiate." *Islamic Law and Society* 2, no. 3: 320–40.

———. Forthcoming. *Ash-Shari'a fi Bab al-Yaman: Law, Judges and the Application of Law. The Family Chamber of the South Sanaa Court (Republic of Yemen), 1983–1995* (in German). Berlin, Germany: Dunker and Humblot.

Yakan, Mona. 1997. "Islam and International Law." Conference on Gender and Citizenship in Lebanon, Mar., American Univ. in Beirut.

Yanagisako, Sylvia J., and Carol Delaney, eds. 1995. *Naturalizing Power, Essays in Feminist Cultural Analysis.* New York: Routledge.

Yanagisako, Sylvia J., and Jane Fishburne Collier, eds. 1987. *Gender and Kinship: Essays Toward a Unified Analysis.* Stanford, Calif.: Stanford Univ. Press.

Yeatman, Anna. 1994. *Postmodern Revisionings of the Political.* New York: Routledge.

Yeganeh, Nahid. 1982. "Women's Struggle in Islamic Republic of Iran." In *In the Shadow of Islam: The Women's Movement in Iran,* edited by Azar Tabari and Nahid Yeganeh, 26–75. London: Zed Books.

Yeni Yüzyil. 1996. 6 Mar.

———. 1997. 11, 15, 18 Nov.; 17, 19, 30, 31 Dec.

———. 1998. 1, 29 Jan.

İnalcik, Halil. 1964. "The Nature of Traditional Society: Turkey." In *Political Modernization in Japan and Turkey,* edited by R. Ward and D. Rustow, 42–63. Princeton, N.J.: Princeton Univ. Press.

Young, Iris M. 1989. "Polity and Group Difference: A Critique of the Ideal of Universal Citizenship." *Ethics* 99, no. 2: 250–74.

———. 1990. *Justice and the Politics of Difference.* Princeton, N.J.: Princeton Univ. Press.

———. 1993. "Gender and Nation." *Ethnic and Racial Studies* 16, no. 4: 621–32.

———. 1997. "Women, Citizenship and Difference." *Feminist Review,* no. 57 (autumn): 4–27.

Yüksel, Şahika. 1996. "Özyuvadaki Tecavüz" (Rape at home). In *Evdeki Terör,* 117–21. Istanbul, Turkey: Mor Çati Yayinlari.

Yuval-Davis, Nira. 1991. "The Citizenship Debate: Women, Ethnic Processes and the State." *Feminist Review,* no. 39 (autumn): 58–69.

———. 1993. "Gender and Nation." *Ethnic and Racial Studies* 16, no. 4: 621–32.

———. 1997. "Citizenship and Difference." In *Gender and Nation,* 68–92. London: Sage.

Zaher, U. 1986. "Political Developments in Iraq, 1963–1980." In *Saddam's Iraq: Revolution or Reaction?* edited by Committee Against Repression and for Democratic Right in Iraq. London: Zed Books.

Zahraa, Mahdi, and Normi A. Malek. 1998. "The Concept of Custody in Islamic Law." *Arab Law Quarterly* 13, no. 2: 155–77.

Zalzal, Marie Rose. 1997. "Personal Status and Sectarian Laws." Conference on Gender and Citizenship, Mar., American Univ. in Beirut.

Zidani, Farida. 1992. *L'Enfant né hors mariage en Algérie.* Alger: Edition En A. P.

Zubaida, Sami. 1988. *Islam, the People, and the State.* London: Routledge.

Zulficar, Mona. n.d. *Al-Mar'at al-Misriyat fi 'Alam Mutaghiir.* Cairo: Rasa'il al-Nid'a al-Jadid.

Index

Palestinian Central Bureau of Statistics
(PCBS), 152–53
Palestinian Declaration of Independence,
142–43, 146, 148
Palestinian Election Law, 143
Palestinian Legislative Council, 141, 148,
150–51
Palestinian National Charter of 1964, 143,
144
"Palestinian Women and the Conspiracy of
Secular Feminism, The" (Al-Hoda
Women's Society), 150
Palestinian Women's Charter, 146–47
Papaneck, Hanna, 7
passports: for Algerian women, 64; for Iranian women, 301; Jordanian Passport
Law of 1969, 164–65; for Palestinian
women, 143, 150; for Yemeni women,
262, 263, 264, 265, 269, 270
Pateman, Carole: on civil society and patriarchy, 26; on contract and patriarchy,
22, 127; on the individual and
women's rights, 29; on marriage as sexual contract, 109, 115; on paternal and
fraternal patriarchy, 17; on political
right as paternal right in Middle East,
21; on public/private binary, 132; on
women's political rights subsumed by
men's, 291
patriarchal connectivity, 24
patriarchy: of Baathists, 196; civil society
theorists neglecting, 26; and extended
kinship, 109; fraternal versus kin-based,
17; Iraqi women attempting to overcome, 185–91; in Jews and Palestinian
Arabs, 314, 339; in Jordan, 169, 171,
184; and kinship, 16, 17–18; and
Lebanese kin contract, 116, 125, 133;
and legal pluralism, 21; masculine legal
subject privileged in, 22; modern versus
traditional, 191; as negotiated and renegotiated, 221–22; neopatriarchy,
191, 238, 239, 258; and public/private
binary, 28; religion supporting, 13;
sanctification of the family supporting,
22; sanctions as disciplinary tool of
globalized, 211; and state sovereignty,
196; structures of, 227–28; suprana-

tional nature of modern, 202, 206–7;
in Turkey, 280, 281, 283; women/
nation and men/state linkage in, 7
patrilineality: Christianity supporting, 13;
Islam supporting, 13; in Lebanon, 116,
117, 120, 125, 128, 129, 131, 135,
136; limitations on women's rights associated with, 86; matrimonial guardian
as voice of, 82; in Morocco, 71, 72,
73, 74–76; and nation-building, 7, 18;
privileging of blood and hyper-
valorization of, 8; in Saudi Arabia, 224;
in Tunisia, 71, 72, 73, 74–76
patrilocality, 118, 267
patronage, 27–28; in Lebanon, 120, 121–
22; in Palestinian Authority, 151
Pazartesi (magazine), 283
PDRY (People's Democratic Republic of
Yemen), 262, 265, 268
peace, 341–42
Peace Now (Israel), 341
Peled, Yoav, 318
People's Democratic Republic of Yemen
(PDRY), 262, 265, 268
personal rights: defined, 73; in Tunisia and
Morocco, 79–84. *See also* personal status law
personal status law: Egyptian Coptic law of
1938, 41; and Egyptian law no. 462,
51–52; Egyptian Muslim law of 1920,
39–41; in Egypt under Sadat and
Mubarak, 55; in Iraq, 193, 195; in Israel, 320, 328; in Jordan, 168–71; in
Kuwait, 247; in Lebanon, 20, 129–32;
Palestinian Women's Charter on, 147;
personal rights in, 73; in religious
courts, 19; in Saudi Arabia, 224; in Tunisia and Morocco, 79–84; in Turkey,
276; West Bank and Gaza differing on,
150; in Yemen, 262, 267. *See also* family law
Personal Status Law of 1976 (Jordan),
148
Personal Status of Muslims Act of 1991
(Sudan), 95
PLO (Palestine Liberation Organization),
139, 142, 144, 147, 341
Pocock, J. G. A., 72